The United States
and World War II

The United States and World War II

Robert James Maddox

PENNSYLVANIA STATE UNIVERSITY

Westview Press

BOULDER • SAN FRANCISCO • OXFORD

Acknowledgment is due to Martin Gilbert and George Weidenfeld & Nicolson Ltd. for permission to reproduce the maps, all of which were taken from Martin Gilbert, *Recent History Atlas: 1870 to the Present Day* (London: Weidenfeld & Nicolson, 1966).

Copyright © 1992 by Westview Press, Inc.

Published in 1992 in the United States of America by Westview Press, Inc., 5500 Central Avenue, Boulder, Colorado 80301-2847, and in the United Kingdom by Westview Press, 36 Lonsdale Road, Summertown, Oxford OX2 7EW

Library of Congress Cataloging-in-Publication Data
Maddox, Robert James.
  The United States and World War II / Robert James Maddox.
    p. cm.
  Includes bibliographical references and index.
  ISBN 0-8133-0436-9 — ISBN 0-8133-0437-7 (pbk.)
  1. World War, 1939–1945—United States. 2. United States—
History—1933–1945. 3. World War, 1939–1945. I. Title.
D769.M3 1992
940.53′73—dc20   91-24321
                                                                           CIP

Printed and bound in the United States of America

The paper used in this publication meets the requirements
of the American National Standard for Permanence of Paper
for Printed Library Materials Z39.48-1984.

10   9   8   7   6   5   4   3   2

Contents

Maps

Author's Note

There is a staggering number of books about World War II, and more appear every year. They range from multivolume accounts of the entire war to personal reminiscences written by people who served at the lowest ranks. The works cited in the selected bibliographies at the end of each chapter are the ones I found most helpful—hundreds more might have been included. Books covering extended periods are listed where they first become appropriate. To avoid repetition, they are not cited in subsequent chapters.

In recent years, the Pinyin system has been used to render Chinese names and places into the Roman alphabet. Chiang Kai-Shek, for instance, has become Jiang Jieshi. I have used the spellings employed during the World War II period.

Robert James Maddox

1
The War to End All Wars (1914–1921)

The guns at last fell silent on November 11, 1918. What had begun as a war of movement that both sides hoped to win in weeks or months had lasted through more than four years of appalling slaughter and physical destruction. Estimates of military casualties alone ran as high as 30 million, and an unprecedented number of civilians were killed, wounded, or left homeless. The psychic effects lasted for decades. What had happened could not be undone, but what of the future? If the armistice brought merely a pause until exhausted nations could recover sufficiently to resume fighting, the terrible sacrifices would have been in vain. But if a lasting peace could be created, the war would have served some purpose.

THE GREAT WAR

Although almost thirty nations took part in the conflict, with campaigns in Italy, Asia, Africa, and the Middle East, most of the fighting took place on two fronts. In the west, France and Great Britain, later joined by the United States, opposed Germany and the Austro-Hungarian Empire. The war had begun with Germany's invasion of Belgium and its penetration of France to the outskirts of Paris. Stalemate had followed as the opposing armies kept extending their flanks until a line was established from the English Channel to Switzerland. Weapons such as the machine gun and rapid-firing artillery made bloodbaths of offensive operations, although they continued to be mounted throughout the war. The struggle became one of attrition, with each side battering away in hopes of exhausting the other.

On the eastern front, Imperial Russia and its lesser allies confronted the Germans and Austro-Hungarians, who had initially permitted the

Russians to advance west in order to envelop them in devastating pincer movements. Russia proved to be a major disappointment to its allies—sheer manpower counted for little in modern warfare. Although individual units often fought courageously, Russian forces were demoralized by ineffective leadership, inadequate training, and obsolete equipment. Their soldiers took hideous casualties, were captured by the tens of thousands, and deserted in droves. In fact, military disasters were instrumental in the collapse of the czarist government in March 1917 and in Russia's departure from the war a year later.

The European alliances that fought the war were forged during the first decade of the century. Germany's unification in 1870 and its rapid emergence as the most powerful continental power had caused former rivals Great Britain, France, and Russia to create an alliance known as the Entente (or Allies). Meanwhile, Germany joined with Austro-Hungary to form the Central Powers. Both coalitions sought to strengthen themselves through agreements with smaller nations, but what appeared to promote the national interests of each participant had the unfortunate aspect of ensuring that a conflict between two members of the rival groups might engulf them all.

The triggering event of what became known as the Great War was the July 1914 assassination of Archduke Ferdinand, heir to the Austro-Hungarian crown, by Serbian terrorists. In retaliation, the Austro-Hungarian government made demands on tiny Serbia that would have reduced it to a vassal state. Russia, posing as the protector of the Slavic peoples in the Balkans, supported Serbia's rejection of the terms. Germany backed its ally, and France stood by Russia. The Germans, believing that time ran against them because they feared Russia would mobilize its vast reserves, were unwilling to have the crisis drag on. Their strategy was to eliminate the French threat in the west as quickly as possible, thereby permitting them to move against Russia before its mobilization was complete. When they launched an invasion of Belgium to get at France, Great Britain adhered to its guarantee of Belgium's neutrality. By early August, almost all of Europe was at war.

Assessing responsibility for the conflict has engaged historians ever since. American writers during and immediately after the war portrayed a militaristic Germany as the chief culprit. Then, during the late 1920s and early 1930s, "revisionists" challenged this view and emphasized Allied culpability. Owing largely to the work of a German scholar, Fritz Fisher, the prevailing interpretation now is that Germany should, indeed, bear the onus. Documents in German archives reveal that military and civilian leaders sought German domination of Europe, as well as other parts of the world.

AMERICA GOES TO WAR

President Woodrow Wilson responded to the outbreak of war by calling on the public to remain neutral "in thought and deed." His appeal coincided with America's long-standing suspicion of European affairs and a desire to avoid entanglement. Because of its enormous productive capacity, however, the United States could not remain aloof. If it invoked traditional neutral rights and traded with belligerents, its foodstuffs, raw materials, and manufactured products would primarily benefit Great Britain and France. A U.S. embargo against the combatants, on the other hand, would help the Central Powers because of Britain's dependence on imports. Wilson chose the former course and, within a few months, violated his own stricture about neutrality by permitting the extension of credits to the Allies, thereby financing their purchases in the United States.

When war broke out, the British navy, aided by the French, mounted a naval blockade against Germany and Austro-Hungary. Germany retaliated—but with a difference. Britain's command of the sea enabled its vessels to follow traditional rules of naval warfare. British ships could signal merchant vessels to stop so they could be commandeered if they belonged to the enemy and boarded and searched for contraband if they were neutral. Should the signal be ignored, a shot would be fired across the bow, and only if that failed would attack be called for. Because Germany's surface fleet was bottled up during most of the war, it had to rely on the submarine, or U-boat. Submarines of the day were slow, carried only light deck cannon, and could be outgunned by armed merchantmen and rammed by others. The submarine's only advantage was its ability to submerge and fire torpedoes. Although U-boat commanders at first tried to follow conventional rules, losses sustained by British ships under orders to shoot or ram on sight led them to attack without warning. Mistakes were made, and American vessels were sunk.

President Wilson not only invoked the broadest definition of neutral rights, he also insisted that the American flag protected its citizens even when they traveled on commercial vessels operated by belligerents. When the British passenger liner *Lusitania* was torpedoed off the coast of Ireland on May 17, 1915, with the loss of 128 American lives, Wilson sent such stiff notes to the German government that Secretary of State William Jennings Bryan resigned in protest against what he reached as dangerous provocation. The Germans, who had taken out newspaper advertisements warning U.S. citizens against sailing on the vessel, tried to placate the American government by issuing periodic pledges to limit submarine activity. But they insisted on reciprocal concessions by Great Britain, which the latter refused to make. The British also infringed on

Wilson's version of neutral rights, by means such as blacklisting firms that traded with Germany, but their conduct cost no lives.

The final chapter began late in 1916 when German military leaders prevailed upon their government to resort to unrestricted submarine warfare. Advocates of the policy wished to deny Great Britain vitally needed imports from anywhere in the world. They understood it probably would bring the United States into the war, but they were prepared to take the risk. The U.S. already was aiding the Allies economically, they argued, so nothing would be lost on that score. They also believed that, because the United States did not maintain a large standing army, it would take many months before American forces could be mobilized, trained, and sent to the battlefield. During that period, submarine depredations would so weaken the Allies as to cause them to seek peace on terms favorable to the Central Powers. This estimate of the situation proved incorrect—but not by much.

Meanwhile, Woodrow Wilson narrowly won reelection in November 1916. Although he did not use the phrase himself, he undoubtedly profited from the Democratic slogan of the day, "He kept us out of war." But even before his second inauguration, the Germans proclaimed their new policy on submarine use on January 31, 1917. Wilson reacted by severing relations with Germany and asking Congress for legislation to arm merchant vessels. When Senate opponents successfully filibustered the bill, Wilson refused to be stymied by what he referred to as "a little group of willful men" and began arming these vessels anyway on the basis of existing statutes.

A bizarre revelation made the situation even more explosive. On January 16, the German foreign office had cabled its ambassador in Mexico, instructing him that if the United States entered the war, he should seek a Mexican-German alliance. As an enticement, he was to offer German assistance to Mexico in recovering territories it was forced to cede to the United States in 1850! The British had intercepted and decoded this message earlier, but they waited until an appropriate time in late February to reveal its contents to the United States. The proposal was ridiculous, but its publication in the American press on March 1 aroused great public indignation against Germany. When U-boats sank four American ships over the next few weeks, Wilson concluded he had no choice but to ask Congress for a declaration of war. He made his request before a joint session on April 2. The Senate overwhelmingly approved the declaration on April 4, and two days later, the House concurred.

Although there is no dispute about the sequence of events that led to war, scholars have continued to question Wilson's motives in acting as he did. Why, for instance, did he insist so rigidly on traditional neutral rights when he knew they were incompatible with the use of

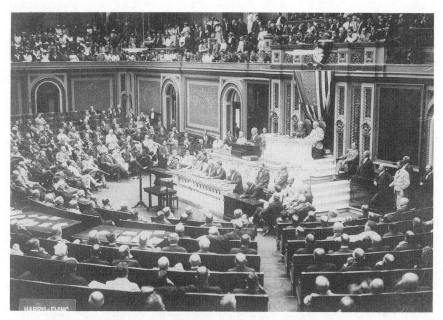

President Woodrow Wilson before Congress, announcing the break in official relations with Germany, February 3, 1917. (National Archives photo no. W&C 428)

U-boats as blockaders? Would he have done so if Germany had possessed the powerful surface fleet and Great Britain had had to rely on submarines? Theories about Wilson's conduct include those stressing common bonds on language, law, and culture between the United States and Great Britain; the effectiveness of British propaganda; and America's economic stake in an Allied victory. There is truth in all these views, but Wilson had a larger consideration, as well. His grave doubts about Allied goals notwithstanding, he feared American national interests would be compromised by a Europe dominated by Germany and its partners.

OVER THERE

The United States had embarked upon a limited "preparedness" campaign before entering the war, but it was unable to provide immediate military help to the Allies beyond "show the flag" detachments. When American troops finally landed in France in large numbers, a dispute arose over how to use them. British armies were exhausted, and the French were in even worse shape. There had also been mutinies in French divisions, some of which were deemed unreliable and had to be withdrawn from combat. The Allies wanted to integrate U.S. forces within the existing structure, both to augment the numbers and because they believed their officers had the experience that Americans lacked. The commander of the American Expeditionary Force (AEF), General John J. Pershing, backed by his superiors in Washington, fought to establish an independent army manning its own sector of the line. Pershing argued that his soldiers would fight better under their own flag, and he privately discounted the value of experience. Years of trench warfare, he believed, had rendered the Allied military leadership poorly suited for the kind of bold, offensive operations he thought necessary to defeat the Germans.

A compromise was reached. American units were fed into Allied positions where the need was greatest, while preparations were made for U.S. occupation of its own part of the fighting line. American divisions helped stop the last great German offensive in the spring of 1918, and a few months later, they spearheaded the Allied push that resulted in Germany's decision to sue for peace.

Opposing views about the contribution made by the United States complicated its relations with the French and British after the armistice. The latter had borne the brunt of a war that President Wilson had called a crusade to "make the world safe for democracy." In addition to human losses and physical destruction, their economies verged on bankruptcy, with huge debts owed the United States. In contrast, the U.S. had enjoyed unprecedented prosperity during the same period, due in part to Allied orders from abroad. It had taken relatively light casualties in its few months of military operations against an enemy that was already weakened by years of fighting and by the blockade. Small wonder that the British and French considered their sacrifices largely responsible for the victory and that they were not disposed to behave as junior partners.

Americans perceived the outcome differently. Not only had the AEF arrived just in time to pull Allied "chestnuts out of the fire," as a popular saying went, but U.S. loans had kept France and Britain afloat through most of the war. Their disagreement with American policies after the armistice, from this standpoint, appeared as rank ingratitude. How much President Wilson counted on gratefulness to achieve his aims is not clear, but he did intend to exploit the economic situation. He knew the Allies did not share his peace aims, but as early as July 1917, he wrote that "when the war is over, we can force them to our way of thinking because by that time they will among other things be financially in our hands."

A VISION OF PEACE

Woodrow Wilson was a man of great vision who possessed an equally large ego. He saw himself as an instrument through which the elusive quest for world peace finally might be realized. He had offered to mediate between the combatants several times before the American entry into World War I, only to be rebuffed. At war's end, however, the United States could not be denied a dominant position at the negotiating table. This nation was uniquely suited to guide the way to a lasting settlement, he believed, because it alone among the major powers sought no territory or other selfish goals.

The president was a scholar as well as a politician, and his reading of history had convinced him that several prerequisites were necessary for enduring peace. First, he shared with many Americans the belief that democracies were inherently peace loving, whereas authoritarian governments of any kind were prone to violence. He also believed that, despite setbacks and false starts, all societies eventually would evolve into something resembling democracies and that the United States should do what it could to help the process. When a quasi-republican form of government had replaced the czar in March 1917, for instance, he welcomed Russia as "a fit partner in a league of honor" in his message asking for a declaration of war. And when Imperial Germany asked for an armistice in October 1918, he refused to deal with the government "as then constituted."

Wilson's second assumption was that past wars usually planted the seeds for subsequent ones. Victorious nations almost always extracted from the vanquished penalties such as the cession of territory or money payments. He also believed that such behavior, however understandable, instilled in the loser a desire for revenge. And peace, in such cases, was merely a pause during which the defeated nation bided its time until it could take back what had been seized. The only way out of this cycle, Wilson maintained, was to negotiate a settlement equitable to all or, as he put it in January 1917, a "peace without victory."

Finally, Wilson realized that under the best of circumstances, there would be friction among nations. He therefore wanted to establish a world organization within which differences could be resolved without the use of force. He did not originate the idea; a number of private groups in the United States had advocated such a body after the Great War began. But debates stimulated by these groups revealed deep differences. Most Americans, it seemed, approved of an international organization, provided it served only as a forum for an aggrieved nation to state its case in hopes of gaining the support of others. This apparent consensus broke down, however, over the issue of whether a league should be endowed with powers to enforce its decisions. When Wilson made clear his adherence to the concept of an organization with "teeth," as the saying went, he placed himself in opposition to a long-standing American tradition of complete independence in foreign affairs.

The league Wilson envisaged would serve many functions, but its most important would be to hear and vote on disputes among nations. Ideally, parties to a quarrel would abide by its verdict without further recourse, but should one or more nations refuse to comply, especially those charged with aggression, the league could call on its other members to provide whatever was necessary to compel adherence, including military contingents. Wilson contended that such drastic measures rarely would be necessary, if the organization functioned properly, because it would be folly for offenders to stand alone against the rest of the world. His task was to convince the American public and his European counterparts that a league of nations was the best way to banish war.

In January 1918, Wilson had issued his famous Fourteen Points, which constituted his prescription for durable peace. In this, he called for "open covenants openly arrived at," as opposed to the web of secret treaties he believed had helped cause the Great War; for freedom of the seas; for the lowering of trade barriers; for arms reductions; and for a series of territorial adjustments, most of which were based on what became known as the principle of self-determination. This principle held that national groups should be freed from governments imposed upon them in the past and be permitted to follow autonomous development. Two of the most important points in this category provided for the resurrection of an independent Poland (partitioned centuries earlier) and the breakup of the Austro-Hungarian Empire. The capstone of Wilson's program called for the creation of a league of nations, which would become the vehicle for an orderly transition into the new era.

Once he embraced an idea, the president tended to cling to it tenaciously. The league was no exception. He became so fervent in its behalf that it clouded his otherwise astute political judgment. Shortly before the congressional elections of 1918, he told voters that if they wished to support him in obtaining a constructive peace, as they had supported him in waging war, they should elect Democrats. When his party lost seats in both houses, critics claimed that the American people had repudiated Wilson himself. This was untrue—the opposition party almost always gains strength in by-elections—but it gave league opponents a useful weapon. Wilson also made a tactical error in failing to appoint any prominent Republicans to the American peace delegation sent to the Versailles peace conference, thereby inviting charges that he was playing partisan politics with an issue of national importance. Finally, his decision to attend the conference probably was a mistake. As some around him pointed out, he enjoyed unparalleled prestige at war's end that could only be sullied by the inevitable compromises that negotiations would entail. He would better retain his stature and influence by staying home and sending a trusted subordinate to represent him. Nonetheless, he spurned this advice on the grounds that he alone possessed the vision and the prominence to achieve his goals.

MEETING AT VERSAILLES

Wilson arrived at the French port of Brest on December 13, 1918, and the following day received a tumultuous welcome in Paris. When he learned that the conference would be delayed because Allied officials had not completed preparations, he made state visits to England and Italy. Although his appearance in England occasioned less fervor, Italy received him with wild acclaim. Banners proclaimed him the "savior of humanity" and "God of peace." Such enthusiasm probably confirmed his belief that he represented the aspirations of peoples all over the world, whereas Allied statesmen sought only to further narrowly defined national interests.

The conference finally began on January 18, 1919, at the Palace of Versailles in Paris. As plenary sessions of all the Allies and Associated powers proved too cumbersome, the most important questions were taken up by a council referred to as the Big Five. It consisted of Woodrow Wilson, British Prime Minister David Lloyd George, French Premier Georges Clemenceau, Italian Premier Vittorio Orlando, their foreign ministers, and two Japanese representatives. (Later, some decisions about European affairs were made without Japanese participation.) Despite the reduced number of participants, there was such a bewildering assortment of issues, many requiring detailed technical knowledge, that much of the work was referred to commissions of experts.

Wilson's most pressing concern was to get agreement on a league of nations. He insisted that the subject be taken up first and that the league charter be part of the final peace treaty. Anticipating a struggle over the issue at home, he wanted the charter and the peace terms to be combined in hopes that the league might ride through on the wave of the sentiment for peace. He secured acceptance, with minor variations, of a league conforming to the U.S. draft that he had helped to write.

The treatment of Germany was of more consequence to British and French statesmen. Whatever their thoughts about the proposed league, Lloyd George and especially Clemenceau were not prepared to rely on it to maintain peace. Instead, they intended to prevent defeated Germany from emerging to threaten their security in the future. Many of the terms they sought to impose ran counter to a peace without victory, an idea by which they set no great store anyway. Wilson was able to ameliorate the more severe of their demands in some cases, but he acquiesced in others. His earlier belief that European leaders would be "in our hands" proved unfounded. In fact, the reverse was more nearly

Council of Four of the Peace Conference, Hotel Crillon, Paris, France, May 27, 1919: *left to right*, David Lloyd George, Vittorio Orlando, Georges Clemenceau, and President Woodrow Wilson. (National Archives photo no. W&C 722)

true. His commitment to a league was so strong that others were able to use it as a bargaining tool—for example, they could indicate that if a particular demand were denied, they would have to reconsider their support for a league. Wilson consoled himself with the thought that "war psychosis" was responsible for much of what was being done, which could be rectified through the league when passions abated.

Terms for Germany were agreed on after months of grueling negotiation. France, which had suffered most in the war, favored the harshest territorial and military penalties. It obtained from Germany the regions of Alsace and Lorraine, lost in a previous war, and the coalfields of the predominantly Germanic Saar Valley. Clemenceau tried but failed to have a buffer state created in the Rhineland, a strategic area that lay between the major industrial centers of France and Germany. At Anglo-American insistence, a compromise was reached whereby the Rhineland would remain under German political control but be occupied by Allied forces for a period of fifteen years. German colonies in Africa and the Far East were to be turned over to the League of Nations when it began functioning and administered as "mandates" by various Allies, principally Great Britain and Japan. Severe limitations were placed on the military forces Germany would be permitted to retain: an army of 100,000 men without tanks or aircraft and a small navy with ships of limited size.

Although the British acted as a restraint against France on issues of territorial disposition, they showed no such moderation on economic matters. It should be pointed out that both delegations were influenced by strong domestic pressure to take revenge upon Germany. Postwar boundaries were of little interest to the British public, but making the Germans "pay" for the costs of war was a popular theme. Afraid of public outrage if he did not appear sufficiently vindictive, David Lloyd George consistently argued for large financial indemnities. These indemnities, or "reparations," were to be paid by Germany in the form of goods and money sent to the respective Allies. In the end, it was agreed that the determination of sums would be left to a reparations commission, which would arrive at figures by 1921. Meanwhile, Germany would be required to pay $5 billion to help in the reconstruction of the Allied economies. To justify such penalties, a clause was inserted in the treaty referring to Germany's "aggression" in causing the war.

Scholars still argue about whether the treaty was unduly harsh and whether the amount of reparations that was finally set exceeded Germany's capacity to pay. The perception of most Germans at the time was unequivocal. Territorial losses, financial extractions (with the uncertainty of how large they would be), military limitations, and what became known as the "guilt clause" constituted terms almost all Germans found humiliating. They regarded the treaty as a betrayal of the equitable settlement Wilson promised in his "peace without victory" statement and in the Fourteen Points. And because German representatives were not permitted to take part in negotiations, there was the additional insult of having the peace terms dictated to them.

The treaty and the manner in which it was drawn up had an unanticipated consequence. Wilson's refusal to deal with the German government in October 1918 had helped spark revolts that forced the kaiser to abdicate and led to the creation of a more representative government. Officials of the new regime were now forced to sign the enormously unpopular treaty. This gave rise to the "stab in the back" thesis, according to which Germany's armies were undefeated and its borders intact by autumn 1918. Furthermore, Jewish- and Communist-led uprisings, not military realities, were said to have undermined the nation, and disloyal people from these groups were also regarded as responsible for the punitive peace settlement. Although this version of events was false—Germany's military leaders had advised the kaiser that the war was lost—Adolf Hitler and others used it to weaken support for what became known as the Weimar Republic.

A number of separate treaties redrew the map of central and eastern Europe. The Austro-Hungarian Empire was broken up into Austria, Hungary, and the new nation of Czechoslovakia. An independent Poland was reconstituted, and Serbia, focus of the crisis that led to war in 1914, absorbed several other small Balkan states and became Yugoslavia. All this was done amidst the squabbling of new and existing states over boundaries, port cities, and other points of contention. The resolution of such quarrels often violated the principle of self-determination, as did the fact that populations were not settled in tidy ethnic groups. In consequence, every nation involved wound up with minorities, some of whom would prove troublesome in the future.

One subject left unresolved by the peace conference was the issue of what to do about Russia. The provisional government that had succeeded the czar in March 1917 had, in turn, been overthrown by the Bolsheviks (Communists) in November, in part because it had continued to wage an increasingly unpopular war against Germany. Upon seizing power, the Bolsheviks issued appeals to end the fighting and urged populations to overthrow governments that failed to cooperate. Such inflammatory rhetoric, along with Communist social and economic doctrines, alienated the Allies and the United States. When the Bolsheviks signed a peace treaty with Germany in March 1918, violating Russia's earlier pledges not to make a separate peace, they came to be regarded as enemies by the Allied nations. Some people even claimed that their leaders were agents of the German government.

In June 1918, President Wilson had agreed to a joint American-Japanese intervention in Siberia. Scholars have debated his motives ever since. Some believe he acted to forestall unilateral Japanese occupation of the region. Others claim he wished to support regimes engaged in civil war against the Bolsheviks. Certainly, the Bolsheviks took the latter view for the main function of the occupying troops was to guard the trans-Siberian railway, across which food, clothing, and arms were shipped from the Pacific port of Vladivostok to anti-Bolshevik forces in the interior.

The troops were still in Siberia when the peace conference opened. Lloyd George and Clemenceau urged that the intervention be enlarged in order to overthrow the Bolsheviks. They were afraid radical contagion might spread west, perhaps even to their own societies. Wilson, aware that even the limited operation he had authorized was causing mounting criticism at home, refused. But he did hold out the promise that he might be willing to commit more resources after the peace treaty was passed in the Senate. Without the United States, Great Britain and

France could do nothing because their war-weary publics would have thrown out of office anyone who dared suggest another military campaign. Ultimately, a delegation was sent from Paris to talk with Bolshevik leaders, but its recommendation that accommodation be tried was rejected. Meanwhile, the Russian civil war ground on.

The inability to agree on action toward Russia must be counted as one of the conference's greatest failures. Strengthening the intervention, aside from being politically unfeasible, probably would not have been decisive because the anti-Bolshevik forces were divided and poorly led. However, had Wilson, Clemenceau, and Lloyd George been able to overcome their detestation of communism and negotiated with the Bolsheviks, the course of history might have been changed. As it was, Russia remained a pariah for many years, and its leaders' hostility toward capitalist powers was reinforced.

In hindsight, it is easy to criticize the Versailles Peace Conference and to see that it planted the seeds of World War II. Wilson himself was frustrated by the defeats he had suffered and the compromises he had had to make. He believed the League of Nations provided an opportunity to mitigate or undo the inequities. To get the organization functioning as quickly as possible, his task after the conference was to secure passage of the Versailles treaty containing the league covenant.

THE UNITED STATES AND THE LEAGUE OF NATIONS

American opposition to Wilson's plans had grown while he was in Paris. As reports of the proceedings were made public, it became clear that few of his Fourteen Points had emerged intact. Some publications even printed box scores of points won, lost, and compromised, and many of Wilson's ardent supporters were dismayed at what the conference had produced. Most ominous was the fact that thirty-seven senators, more than enough to block passage of the treaty, had signed a round-robin proclaiming that they found the league covenant unacceptable as drawn.

Wilson arrived in Hoboken, New Jersey, on July 8, 1919, and two days later presented the treaty to the Senate. Contrary to popular myth, which holds that the American public and Senate rejected his bold departure in favor of retreat into traditional isolationism, most observers agreed that the treaty would have passed had it been voted on during the summer. But any such early consideration was made impossible by Republican Senator Henry Cabot Lodge, chairman of the Senate Committee on Foreign Relations. The committee's responsibility was to consider the treaty before submitting it with recommendations to the Senate. Lodge sought and received cooperation from committee members who either opposed the league or wanted the covenant amended, to follow a strategy of delay. Lodge's own position on a world organization is unclear, but he opposed having the one drawn up in Paris hurried through because of public fervor.

The struggle over the League of Nations has been written about at great length and was incredibly complicated. Many participants acted out of conviction. Others were motivated by political considerations: There were Republicans, for instance, who did not wish to have a Democratic president take credit for what was being heralded as a major step toward world peace. Some senators resented Wilson's domination of American foreign policy during and after the war, and some simply detested him for what they perceived as his arrogance.

The league's most controversial aspect was Article 10 of the covenant, which provided that members would "respect and preserve" each other's territorial integrity and independence from aggression. The wording lacked precision. If it meant that members were obligated to provide military forces to carry out a league decision, critics pointed out, it violated the United States Constitution, which reserved warmaking power solely for Congress. Some of the more imaginative opponents predicted a future in which American boys would be sent to die in far-off corners of the earth at the direction of foreigners sitting in Geneva. In this matter, Wilson did not help his own cause. Denying that Article 10 constituted a "legal" obligation, he added to the confusion by pronouncing it a "moral" and therefore a "higher" one.

Lodge prevented Senate consideration of the treaty throughout the summer of 1919 by such tactics as reading the ponderous volume aloud to an almost empty room and by holding interminable public hearings. Finally, in September his committee reported the treaty to the Senate with fourteen amendments, or "reservations." The Lodge reservations, as they became known, purportedly safeguarded American interests that were jeopardized by the league covenant. The senator had been correct in predicting that public enthusiasm would diminish with the passage of time.

Meanwhile, determined to rekindle support, President Wilson embarked on an arduous speaking tour. The strains caused by travel, tight schedules, and speeches made without voice amplification to huge crowds proved too much for him. He collapsed in Pueblo, Colorado, on September 26, and, after returning to Washington, he suffered a near-fatal stroke. At a time when he should have been using all his personal and political powers to build a proleague coalition in the Senate, Wilson lay paralyzed in the White House, all but isolated by his wife and personal physician.

The Versailles treaty containing the league covenant was voted on late in November, once as written and once with the Lodge reservations attached. It failed both times to gain even a simple majority. The figures are misleading because everyone assumed this was a preliminary vote and that the treaty would be considered again. A vigorous attempt to reach accommodation was made early in 1920 by senators of both parties who wished to salvage something. But their effort was sabotaged by a small but powerful group of sixteen senators who opposed a league of any kind. When the treaty was voted on again in March 1920, it failed by seven votes to gain the two-thirds majority necessary for passage. This was the final vote, although no one knew it at the time.

Several factors determined the outcome. Antileaguers were able to wield influence out of proportion to their numbers because those who differed over the need for strong or mild reservations could not reach consensus. But Woodrow Wilson himself bore major responsibility. His unwillingness to compromise and his contemptuous treatment of the Senate alienated those who might otherwise have supported a modified league. He defended his stand by claiming that reservations would weaken the organization and amount to a breach of faith with other nations; such nations might, in turn, be emboldened to attach qualifications to their own participation. Still believing that the public stood behind him, he preferred defeat to compromise because he hoped the election of 1920 would be a "solemn referendum" on the league, the results of which would force eventual passage.

The election was nothing of the sort. Voters rarely cast their ballots on a single issue, and the nation was beset by problems such as a postwar recession, labor unrest, and an anti-Communist hysteria known as the "red scare." Even those who wished to vote solely on the league would have been hopelessly confused. Democratic candidate James M. Cox began his campaign as a staunch Wilsonian regarding the organization but later announced he would accept "responsible" reservations. His opponent, Warren G. Harding, also straddled the issue. He denounced what he referred to as "Wilson's league" but said he favored a world organization, though he never made clear whether he meant the league with reservations or an entirely new structure. The only message voters delivered in electing Harding by a landslide was that they wanted to return to what he called "normalcy."

The significance of the U.S. failure to join the league can only be guessed. Some contend that the organization was crippled at birth because the United States abandoned its responsibilities as a world power. Others doubt U.S. membership would have altered the course of events appreciably. They point out that every nation put its own perceived interests above collective security when aggression occurred, and they express doubt that the United States would have behaved differently. Whatever the truth, it is ironic that the man most responsible for creating the organization spent the few years remaining to him as an invalid cursing those who had destroyed his dream.

SELECTED BIBLIOGRAPHY

Cooper, John M. (ed.). *World War I: Causes and Consequences* (New York: Quadrangle, 1972).

_____. *The Warrior and the Priest: Woodrow Wilson and Theodore Roosevelt* (Cambridge, Mass.: Harvard University Press, 1983).

Ferrell, Robert H. *Woodrow Wilson and World War I* (New York: Harper & Row, 1985).

Ferro, Mark. *The Great War, 1914–1918* (London: Routledge and Kegan Paul, 1973).

Fisher, Fritz. *Germany's Aims in the First World War* (New York: Norton, 1967).

_____. *War of Illusions: German Policies from 1911 to 1914* (New York: Norton, 1975).

Geiss, Immanuel. *German Foreign Policy, 1871–1914* (London: Routledge and Kegan Paul, 1976).

Hale, Oron J. *The Great Illusion: 1900–1914* (New York: Harper & Row, 1971).

Joll, James. *The Origins of the First World War* (London: Longman, 1984).

Kennan, George F. *Russia Leaves the War* (Princeton, N.J.: Princeton University Press, 1956).

_____. *The Decision to Intervene* (Princeton, N.J.: Princeton University Press, 1958).

Kennedy, David M. *Over Here: The First World War and American Society* (New York: Oxford University Press, 1980).

Lee, Dwight E. (ed.). *The Outbreak of the First World War* (Lexington, Mass.: D. C. Heath, 1975).

Levin, N. Gordon, Jr. *Woodrow Wilson and World Politics: America's Response to War and Revolution* (New York: Oxford University Press, 1968).

Link, Arthur S. *Wilson the Diplomatist* (Baltimore, Md.: Johns Hopkins University Press, 1957).

Maddox, Robert James. *The Unknown War with Russia: Wilson's Siberian Intervention* (Presidio, Calif.: Presidio Press, 1977).

May, Ernest R. *The World War and American Isolation* (Cambridge, Mass.: Harvard University Press, 1959).

Remak, Joachim. *The Origins of World War I, 1871–1914* (New York: Holt, Rinehart and Winston, 1967).

Roth, Jack J. *World War I: A Turning Point in History* (New York: Knopf, 1967).

Smith, Daniel M. *The Great Departure: The United States and World War I, 1914–1920* (New York: J. Wiley, 1965).

Stokesbury, James L. *A Short History of World War I* (New York: Morrow, 1981).

Stone, Ralph A. *The Irreconcilables* (Lexington: University Press of Kentucky, 1970).

Tuchman, Barbara W. *The Guns of August* (New York: Macmillan, 1962).

_____. *The Zimmerman Telegram* (New York: Macmillan, 1966).

Walworth, Arthur. *Wilson and His Peacemakers* (New York: W. W. Norton, 1986).

2
The Illusion of Stability
(1921–1930)

The war and its aftermath brought profound changes around the globe. Some, such as the Bolshevik Revolution in Russia and the destruction of the Austro-Hungarian Empire, were obvious. Others were less so. The psychic trauma the war inflicted on societies, nationalist sentiments stirred up among colonial peoples, and altered balances of power are easier to see in retrospect. The U.S. failure to join the League of Nations did not signify a return to "normalcy" in international relations, as many people assumed. The United States emerged from the war as the world's largest creditor, and its economic interests alone required greater participation. Hesitantly and often inconsistently, it assumed responsibilities and initiatives that would have been unthinkable a few years earlier.

THE FAR EAST

The enlarged role of the United States in world affairs can be seen in its response to conditions in the Far East during the first year of Warren Harding's administration. A weak and divided China had been despoiled by European imperialism since the nineteenth century. The United States had profited from economic concessions wrested from the Chinese, but, unlike other nations, it demanded no "spheres of influence." In times of crisis, it usually followed the lead of Great Britain, with whom its interests generally coincided. At the turn of the century, the U.S. had proclaimed officially what had been its actual policy for years— the Open Door. This was little more than an appeal to other nations involved in China to refrain from setting up barriers to trade and investment within their spheres.

The emergence of Japan as a major power added a new ingredient. Japan had easily defeated China in 1895 and would have exacted large concessions had it not been for the intercession of Great Britain and France. Victory over ineffectual China was no great achievement, but a subsequent war against Russia in 1904–1905, during which Japan won every major battle, was more impressive. The treaty ending the war recognized Japan's influence over Korea and southern Manchuria. Japan annexed Korea in 1910, and whatever restraints the European powers had imposed vanished with the onset of the Great War. Japan, allied with the Triple Entente, seized Germany's island possessions in the Pacific and its sphere of influence in China's Shantung Peninsula. More ominous, Tokyo issued what became known as the Twenty-One Demands in 1915, which would have made China a vassal state.

American policymakers had viewed these developments with dismay, fearing they would jeopardize U.S. economic opportunities in the Far East. Lacking the means to stop Japanese expansion—no one in a position of authority even suggested using threats of force—the United States had tried to come to terms with it. In the agreements of 1905 and 1908, the United States recognized Japan's newly acquired position in return for assurances that American interests would be respected. President Wilson had protested against the Twenty-One Demands but to little effect. Japan modified its more extreme demands for internal reasons, and in 1917, Secretary of State Robert Lansing negotiated yet another agreement acknowledging Japan's "paramount" influence over China. Throughout these years, racial issues poisoned the atmosphere: Japan's pride was injured by U.S. immigration policies and by open discrimination against the Japanese living on the American West Coast.

Relations deteriorated during and after the Versailles Peace Conference. Japan insisted that its status in Shantung be recognized and that it retain islands seized from Germany. This violated self-determination, of course, and President Wilson reluctantly acquiesced only after the Japanese threatened to walk out and to boycott the league. Later in the conference, the United States refused to support a Japanese proposal to adopt a statement on racial equality in the league covenant. Japan kept its troops in Siberia even after the United States and others pulled out in 1920, increasing suspicions that it meant to annex that region. Finally, the continuation of shipbuilding programs undertaken during the war threatened to turn into a naval race between the two powers. The possibility of war was widely discussed in both nations.

In December 1920, Senator William E. Borah of Idaho introduced a resolution calling for a naval disarmament conference between the United States, Great Britain, and Japan. His motives are unclear. An outspoken opponent of the League of Nations, he may have been trying to draw attention away from the organization, which had begun functioning in Geneva. In any event, the proposal aroused so much popular support in the following months that President Harding felt compelled to act upon it soon after his inauguration.

Harding left management of the Washington Conference to his able secretary of state, Charles Evans Hughes. Hughes went beyond the Borah resolution for two reasons. He believed naval disarmament was feasible only after underlying friction was eliminated, and he was under pressure from the British, who wanted to end what had become an embarrassing alliance with the Japanese. He invited France, Italy, and several smaller powers with Asian interests, as well as Great Britain and Japan, and broadened the agenda to include consideration of "all outstanding issues" in the Far East.

Hughes consciously avoided the mistakes Woodrow Wilson had committed with the league. He made the conference a bipartisan endeavor by naming prominent Democrats to the U.S. delegation. And he forestalled charges of negotiating behind closed doors by publicly offering a detailed program for naval limitation at the conference's first plenary session on November 12, 1921, which most people had expected would be confined to expressions of goodwill. His dramatic action also was intended to demonstrate U.S. leadership, rendering ineffective any complaints about "foreign" influence on the Harding administration.

Substantive negotiations during the conference *were* conducted behind closed doors. The most popular agreement that emerged was the Five Power Pact, pertaining to naval strength. Deviating only slightly from Hughes's public proposal, it established ratios in battleships and aircraft carriers among the United States, Great Britain, Japan, France, and Italy. These ratios were, respectively: 5; 5; 3; 1.67; and 1.67. The idea was that the United States and Great Britain required larger numbers of ships because they were two-ocean powers, but assuming they divided their navies more or less evenly, Japan would have the strongest fleet in the far Pacific. The ratios assigned to France and Italy were arbitrary. Not incidentally, the French were so angered at being bracketed with Italy that they prevented efforts to extend limitations to other categories of ships. The pact also prohibited construction of fortifications on specified islands.

Other treaties were drawn up, as well. The Four Power Pact abrogated the Anglo-Japanese alliance and provided that the signatories (the United States, Great Britain, Japan, and France) would respect each other's Far Eastern possessions. Furthermore, conferences would be held to consider disputes unresolved by bilateral negotiations. The Nine Power Pact elevated the American Open Door policy to the status of an international agreement. And in separate negotiations, Japan promised to remove its troops from Siberia in the near future and to return Shantung to Chinese control while retaining economic concessions there.

The Washington Conference produced some benefits for the United States, although nothing like what the administration hailed as a "new era of peace." For example, ship ratios, which approximated existing strengths, avoided for a decade an expensive and potentially dangerous naval race in accumulating battleships and carriers. The Four Power Pact appeared to have enhanced the security of the Philippines and other islands, although it contained no provisions for enforcement, and the adoption of the Open Door policy and Japan's pledges to withdraw military forces from Siberia and Shantung vindicated traditional American principles. These treaties would remain in effect only as long as the signatories found it in their interests to cooperate, but that is true of most international agreements. All the documents save one passed in the Senate easily. The Four Power Pact, which some senators professed to see as a "baby League of Nations," passed by only four votes, even after a reservation had been attached denying any commitment to the use of force.

The conference and its aftermath had less-fortunate consequences over the long run. An isolated Japan had to make concessions on practically every issue. Even the naval agreement, which removed a burden from Japan's strained economy, stirred resentment among extreme nationalists because it assigned Japan to an inferior position. Secretary Hughes, like Wilson before him, had refused to agree to any statements on racial matters, and the United States added insult to injury three years later when it barred all immigration from Japan. The net effect of these developments is difficult to measure, but they no doubt strengthened the belief held by many Japanese that the United States was their enemy.

INVOLVEMENT IN EUROPE

American participation in European affairs had to be less conspicuous in the aftermath of the league struggle. The issue was considered so explosive that the Harding administration at first refused even to acknowledge communications from Geneva. But as emotions waned, the United States gradually began taking part in league activities. Americans served on commissions dealing with matters such as world health and suppression of the drug traffic, and "unofficial observers" attended meetings of political and economic significance. Harding's successor, Calvin Coolidge, even tried to obtain American membership on the league-related World Court in 1925, but he was stymied when the Senate insisted upon reservations that the league was unwilling to accept.

The most obvious U.S. stake in European matters lay in the tangled business of reparations and debts. In 1921, the Allied reparations commission set the amount to be collected from Germany at $33 billion, with half going to France. U.S. policymakers regarded the figure as excessive: They feared the burden of payments would retard Germany's economic recovery, which they believed was essential to European stability and which, in turn, would stimulate American trade and investment. A prosperous Germany, furthermore, might be less inclined to challenge the peace settlement.

The United States showed no such forbearance toward the debts it sought to collect. Great Britain, France, and the other Allies had borrowed a total of more than $10 billion from the U.S. government, raised through the sale of Liberty Bonds to American citizens. Throughout the 1920s, the United States insisted that these loans were purely financial transactions unrelated to other issues. It renegotiated interest rates downward but insisted on payment of principals in full.

The debtor nations viewed the situation differently. Europeans argued that the loans ought to be canceled outright or vastly scaled down. The war had been a common effort, they said, during which they had suffered hideous casualties, as well as a depletion of resources; the American contribution had consisted primarily of financial aid until the last few months of fighting. The loans, moreover, had been spent in the United States, thereby contributing to the booming American economy. Nothing could bring back the young men who had died in battle, Europeans complained, and now the United States wanted its dollars returned. Uncle Sam came to be seen as Uncle Shylock, demanding his pound of flesh.

Led by France, the Allies sought to tie their debts to reparations. In view of their financial difficulties, they claimed, their ability to pay what they owed depended upon their ability to collect reparations. And if the United States wanted the latter modified, it would have to adjust the former. At one point, Great Britain offered to reduce its reparations claims dollar for dollar with a reduction by the United States of the British debt. The offer was spurned, and successive American presidents refused to acknowledge any connection between the issues. The United States compounded the problem by raising tariff rates, thereby making it more difficult for other nations to earn money by selling in the American market. Both sides felt wronged.

In retrospect, it can be argued that the United States and the Allies acted shortsightedly in not canceling or greatly reducing both debts and reparations. Domestic considerations precluded such action. Debt reduction in any form was widely denounced in the United States because it would have required American taxpayers to assume the burden of paying those who held Liberty Bonds. The situation was similar with regard to reparations in France and Great Britain, where the people had been assured by their governments that Germany would be made to pay for the war. Few politicians were willing to renege on that promise and thereby invite charges that they were more sympathetic to the detested "Boche" than to their own countrymen.

Germans across the political spectrum denounced the reparations figure as excessive—a Franco-British plot to keep them impoverished. Whether they would have accepted any amount as just is unclear for they resented all the penalties imposed upon them by the peace settlement. Then, in 1923, the German government precipitated a crisis by failing to meet its financial obligations. Franco-Belgian forces quickly occupied the Ruhr industrial complex to compel payment. The Germans responded by refusing to work under occupation, and the situation approached chaos when an unchecked inflation made German currency virtually worthless. People with fixed incomes became paupers as their life savings were wiped out. Further resentment was stirred and would remain long after the crisis ended.

The United States played an important though unofficial part in coping with the emergency. At Secretary Hughes's suggestion, several commissions were established, with American financial experts placed in key positions. The most important of these, headed by banker Charles G. Dawes, worked out a program in the spring of 1924 whereby Germany would make reduced reparations installments that would escalate as its economy improved. Loans from U.S. banking houses would help finance these transfers. The French stood to lose the most from lower reparations payments, but they acquiesced because they also needed American loans. Dawes and other participants, technically private citizens, for all practical purposes had acted as representatives of the U.S. government.

The European nations began to prosper after the crisis of 1923–1924, and the American economy already was booming. U.S. bankers, attracted by high interest rates, loaned huge amounts of money to Germany. The Germans devoted portions of these loans to reparations payments, which France and Great Britain used to meet their debt obligations. Economic progress soon smoothed the way for diplomatic accommodation. At a conference held in Locarno, Switzerland, in late 1925, France, Belgium, and Germany negotiated agreements pledging to respect their mutual boundaries and providing for evacuation of the Rhineland. Great Britain and Italy joined as guarantors. The atmosphere of accommodation gave rise to the notion of a "spirit" of Locarno, which appeared to herald a new era of cooperation, rather than rivalry, in Europe. The following year, Germany was admitted into the League of Nations.

The combination of economic well-being and Germany's reintegration into the European community cooled passions over reparations. In 1929, another committee was formed to deal with the issue, this one headed by Owen D. Young, chairman of the board of directors of the General Electric Company. The resulting Young Plan lowered reparations from $33 to $9 billion. France and Great Britain accepted it as a means of assuring Germany's continued good behavior. Some American officials had reservations about aspects of the plan, but on the whole, it accomplished what the United States had advocated for years.

Without formal participation, therefore, the United States had an enormous impact on European affairs. U.S. loans helped finance economic recovery, and the need for these exerted pressure on governments to accept American principles and goals. Through unofficial observers at league discussions and through men like Dawes and Young, Washington exercised influence merely by making its wishes known. As events would make clear, this influence rested upon little more than the willingness of American investors to continue supplying capital.

BOLSHEVIK RUSSIA

The Great War had catastrophic effects on Russia. The nation suffered enormous casualties and physical devastation, which helped destroy the czarist regime and the provisional government that replaced it. Russia left the war under the punitive Brest-Litovsk Treaty of March 1918, but it suffered further bloodshed in civil conflict and in fighting with newly independent Poland. Large amounts of territory were lost during this period: Part of Poland had been Russian; former Russian possessions such as Finland, Latvia, Lithuania, and Estonia gained independence; and neighboring countries seized chunks of land that the Bolsheviks were unable to defend.

Led by V. I. Lenin, the Bolsheviks attempted to impose a revolutionary social and economic system on traditional Russia while spreading their doctrines worldwide through propaganda and subversion orchestrated by the Comintern. Their assumptions about the hostility of capitalist powers had been fortified by foreign participation in efforts directed against them during the civil war. Moreover, they were not invited to the Versailles Peace Conference, where French and British officials had urged President Wilson to enlarge military operations against them. Consequently, the Bolsheviks denounced the conference as a meeting of imperialist plunderers and the League of Nations as a conspiracy to protect the division of spoils.

Leaders of Western nations feared the spread of Bolshevik contamination. Throughout the 1920s, Republican presidents followed Wilson's policy of refusing to recognize the government in Moscow, known as the Russian Socialist Federated Soviet Republic (RSFSR). The Bolsheviks were condemned for repudiating foreign debts, for persecuting churches, and for trying to overthrow the governments of other nations. This nonrecognition was more than just a gesture of disapproval. Men such as Herbert Hoover, the powerful secretary of commerce under Harding and Coolidge who later became president, hoped to undermine the Bolsheviks by impeding much-needed American trade and investment.

France also treated the RSFSR as an outlaw during the immediate postwar years. The French government and private bankers had lost heavily through debt repudiation and nationalization, conservatives feared radical doctrines, and Bolshevik Russia no longer could be counted on as an ally against Germany, should the need arise. Beyond that, French alliances with central and eastern European nations created a buffer zone against communism, as well as a counterweight to a resurgent Germany. Great Britain concluded a trade agreement with Russia in 1921, but it was scarcely an indication of friendship. Prime Minister David Lloyd George defended the treaty with the remark, "After all, we deal with cannibals too." And though most of the former Allies had extended recognition by the mid-1920s, they remained apprehensive. In 1926, Britain broke off relations because of Comintern interference in British politics.

Isolated or at least kept at arm's length by the other major powers, Russia and Germany sought advantage in collaboration. Beginning in the winter of 1920–1921, the former enemies entered a number of secret arrangements permitting Germany to manufacture in Russia weapons of all kinds, including aircraft, that were prohibited by the Versailles treaty and to train German soldiers and pilots on Russian soil. Relations were formalized, though the military aspects were kept hidden, by the Treaty of Rapallo in April 1922. It provided for diplomatic and economic cooperation and renunciation of all the claims each had against the other. The alignment of these temporarily crippled giants, both committed to revision of the peace settlement, had ominous implications. Whether different policies on the part of the United States and the former Allies could have prevented this development will never be known.

OUTLAWING WAR

On April 6, 1927, the tenth anniversary of America's entry into the Great War, French Minister for Foreign Affairs Aristide Briand publicly called on the United States to sign a treaty with France that would "outlaw war" between the "two great democracies." Briand's proposal went largely unnoticed in this country until the president of Columbia

University called attention to it in a letter published in the *New York Times*. The ensuing discussion caused a problem for President Calvin Coolidge and Secretary of State Frank B. Kellogg. They knew the Senate would never accept what amounted to a passive alliance, yet to spurn the offer would invite charges that they lacked interest in promoting peace. Kellogg privately denounced supporters of the proposal as "God-damned fools" and stalled for time in hopes that interest would wane. How this inauspicious beginning culminated in the Kellogg-Briand Pact of 1928 sheds light on attitudes within the United States and other nations at the time.

The revulsion to war had spawned numerous peace organizations in the United States during the 1920s. One of the most prominent of these, the "outlawry of war" movement, was headed by a Chicago lawyer, Salmon O. Levinson. He considered the League of Nations inadequate because it did not address what he believed to be the real causes of war. All nations professed to want peace, he argued, but they glorified war in their legends, songs, and history books; it would continue to be considered a rational means of resolving conflict as long as such conditions existed.

Levinson envisioned a global crusade by individuals, groups, and, ideally, governments to teach people that war was an abomination. If the masses were educated to regard it with horror and loathing, they would reject those leaders who advocated it. His program provided for an international court before which such officials, handed over by irate publics, would be tried. Levinson was hazy about how this would work in practice, but he regarded details as secondary to the need to convert attitudes. He often responded to criticism that his plan was unrealistic by citing the practice of dueling, which had disappeared from civilized societies because opinion had changed. War, he said, could be banished, as well.

A tireless worker, Levinson had enlisted public figures in his cause, among them Senator Borah and educator-philosopher John Dewey. Still, the movement had little prospect of attaining wide influence until Briand issued his proposal to bilaterally "outlaw" war. Now the outlawrists, joined by other peace groups, women's organizations, and prominent individuals, prodded the administration into action. Briand added pressure in June by submitting a draft treaty for U.S. consideration. What had begun as a nuisance for Coolidge and Kellogg now threatened to become a major source of embarrassment.

After months of hesitation, Kellogg made a dramatic counterproposal in December: He asked the French government to cosponsor a pact renouncing war that *all* nations would be invited to sign. Stunningly simple and breathtaking in scope, Kellogg's offer received enormously favorable publicity in the United States and abroad. With one stroke, he had made himself and Coolidge appear to be men of bold vision, and he had placed the responsibility on France to demonstrate its commitment to peace. Evidence indicates that he was motivated more by his desire to get the administration out of a tight spot than by a belief in such a treaty or any expectation that France would accept his offer.

Sometime during the following weeks, Kellogg became a true believer, to the astonishment of subordinates who had heard him disparage what he called the "moonmen" who believed war could be outlawed. Although Kellogg had at first responded without enthusiasm to the expected complaints from the French that a multilateral pact would compromise their existing security arrangements, he now began courting their approval. In February 1928, relying on an article Senator Borah had published in the *New York Times* (drafted by Levinson), he earnestly defended his proposal to the French ambassador. Because the treaty would provide no machinery or definition of aggression, he argued, resort to war by any signatory automatically would release the rest from the pact and permit them to carry out other commitments. The ambassador said he thought an agreement "might readily be reached" along such lines. Whether Kellogg had experienced a conversion or whether he scented a Nobel Prize, which he later courted shamelessly and won, can only be guessed.

Although much diplomatic jockeying followed, only one obstacle of substance remained. The "release" clause, strictly interpreted, might mean that it could be invoked only when a nation's territorial possessions were attacked. Those nations with large empires found this inadequate and sought to list all the special interests they wished to have included as a basis for release. Kellogg, by now enamored of his project, pronounced such reservations unnecessary. Every nation had a right to defend its interests, he said, "whatever that degree of interest is." In effect, each signatory would promise not to go to war over any issue that would not have prompted war if no agreement existed. Kellogg also denied that the treaty implied any obligations, legal or moral.

On August 27, representatives of fifteen nations assembled in Paris to sign a treaty renouncing war as "an instrument of national policy." Other nations approved it later. Supporters greeted the Kellogg-Briand Pact, or Paris Peace Pact, as a major contribution to world peace. Detractors, who were in the minority, derided it as "an international kiss" or "a letter to Santa Claus." It was so popular in the United States that the Senate passed it in January 1929 by a vote of 85 to 1, though not without attaching informal reservations in the form of an "interpretation." After ratification by other nations, the Kellogg-Briand Pact was officially promulgated in July 1929.

Those who had hoped the treaty would be the first of a series of steps to banish war were disappointed. Neither the United States nor any other government mounted the educational campaigns the outlawrists had called for. Furthermore, the extravagant praise heaped upon the agreement actually helped to make it impossible to arouse interest in going further. Public opinion had been pandered to and reputations were enhanced, but nothing had changed. The only discernible effect the Kellogg-Briand Pact had was purely cosmetic: In deference to it, governments began using euphemisms instead of the word "war" when they fought one another.

PROSPECTS

U.S. foreign policy during the 1920s was deceptive. It operated most vigorously in the economic realm, where informal partnership between government and financial institutions helped stabilize the European nations that the war had nearly bankrupted. Yet few were aware of the active part Washington played. The two most publicized diplomatic achievements, the Washington Conference at the beginning of the decade and the Kellogg-Briand Pact at its end, contributed to an illusion that many Americans shared: that world peace could be furthered by signing properly worded agreements, requiring no commitment beyond good faith.

The prospects for continued international stability seemed promising as of 1929. The Locarno treaties signed four years earlier indicated that Germany had reconciled itself to the Versailles peace settlement. European prosperity not only lessened dissatisfaction within Germany but helped lubricate points of friction between other nations. Germany and Soviet Russia had joined the League of Nations, which now included all the major powers except the United States. Japan appeared to have abandoned military adventurism in favor of peaceful economic expansion. And the Kellogg-Briand Pact, though lacking sanctions, suggested that the Great War had impressed upon governments everywhere the futility of armed conflict. That all these conditions rested upon fragile underpinnings is more obvious today than it was at the time.

There were also less auspicious developments. Most of the European nations had embarked upon rearmament programs of varying magnitude, though each justified its action as defensive. In some cases, this was manifestly true, as when France began constructing the Maginot line in 1929. A naval conference held in Geneva in 1927 failed to produce an agreement over extending ship ratios to classes not included at the

Washington Conference. And in 1929, shortly after the Kellogg-Briand Pact became operative, China and Russia clashed over railroad concessions in Manchuria. Although both governments professed a desire to settle the affair by peaceful means in deference to Kellogg-Briand, they also invoked the right to act in self-defense. Fighting was brief and ended when the Chinese gave in.

The evaluation of some of these situations depended on one's political views. Conservatives regarded the Bolshevik government in Russia as a menace to civilized societies, through subversion for the time being and through conquest should it become capable of aggression. Opinions on the Left, however, ranged from qualified optimism to euphoria. Not only was Soviet Russia striving to attain true democracy internally, the more hopeful argued, it was a force for world peace because, as a Socialist government, it lacked the imperial designs of capitalist powers.

Events in Italy stirred opposite reactions, though with less intensity. Italy had emerged from the Great War in political and economic disarray, despite being on the winning side. It had suffered heavily in military campaigns and was denied its most cherished territorial ambitions at Versailles. Disgusted by the existing government's inadequacy and frightened by extremism on the Left, many Italians welcomed the seizure of power in 1922 by Benito Mussolini and his Fascist organization. Few Americans endorsed fascism as such, but some praised Mussolini for having rescued Italy from disintegration. "He made the trains run on time," became a popular refrain. Liberals denounced him, of course, though his appearance and bombastic conduct inspired as much ridicule as fear.

Public opinion in the United States was as mixed at the end of the decade as it was at the start, but disillusionment about world affairs seemed to have grown despite gestures like the Kellogg-Briand Pact. Bickering among European nations and between some of them and the United States over matters such as debt payment and tariffs reawakened traditional suspicions. Nativist movements and immigration restrictions reflected a growing distrust of all things foreign. In the late 1920s, a spate of books and articles challenged the assumption that Germany had caused the Great War. If the Allies bore as much or more responsibility, the entire Versailles peace settlement was based on deception. A corollary to this interpretation was the idea that the United States had been tricked into war, not to make the world safe for democracy but merely to further the aims of one imperialist bloc against the other. Many Americans became determined that this should never be permitted to happen again.

SELECTED BIBLIOGRAPHY

Adler, Selig. *The Isolationist Impulse: Its Twentieth-Century Reaction* (New York: Abelard-Schuman, 1957).

Brandes, Joseph. *Herbert Hoover and Economic Diplomacy: Department of Commerce Policy, 1921–1928* (Pittsburgh, Pa.: University of Pittsburgh Press, 1962).

Buckley, Thomas H. *The United States and the Washington Conference* (Knoxville: University of Tennessee Press, 1970).

Chatfield, Charles. *For Peace and Justice* (Knoxville: University of Tennessee Press, 1971).

Cohen, Warren I. *America's Response to China: An Interpretive History of Sino-American Relations* (New York: J. Wiley, 1971).

———. *Empire Without Tears* (Philadelphia, Pa.: Temple University Press, 1986).

Costigliola, Frank. *Awkward Dominion: American Political, Economic, and Cultural Relations with Europe, 1919–1933* (Ithaca, N.Y.: Cornell University Press, 1984).

Diggins, John P. *Mussolini and Fascism: The View from America* (Princeton, N.J.: Princeton University Press, 1972).

Dingman, Roger. *Power in the Pacific* (Chicago: University of Chicago Press, 1976).

Ferrell, Robert H. *Peace in Their Time* (New Haven, Conn.: Yale University Press, 1952).

Hawley, Ellis. *The Great War and the Search for a Modern Order: A History of the American People and Their Institutions, 1917–1933* (New York: St. Martin's, 1979).

Hoff-Wilson, Joan. *American Business and Foreign Policy* (Lexington: University Press of Kentucky, 1971).

Hogan, Michael. *Informal Entente: The Private Structure of Cooperation in Anglo-American Economic Diplomacy, 1918–1928* (Columbia: University of Missouri Press, 1977).

Iriye, Akira. *After Imperialism: The Search for Order in the Far East, 1921–1931* (Cambridge, Mass.: Harvard University Press, 1965).

Kennan, George F. *Russia and the West Under Lenin and Stalin* (New York: New American Library, 1962).

Kitchen, Martin. *Europe Between the Wars: A Political History* (New York: Longman, 1988).

Leffler, Melvin. *The Elusive Quest: America's Pursuit of European Stability and French Security, 1919–1933* (Chapel Hill: University of North Carolina Press, 1979).

Maddox, Robert James. *William E. Borah and American Foreign Policy* (Baton Rouge: Louisiana State University Press, 1969).

Maier, Charles. *Recasting Bourgeois Europe* (Princeton, N.J.: Princeton University Press, 1975).

Marks, Sally. *The Illusion of Peace: International Relations in Europe, 1918–1933* (London: St. Martin's, 1976).

Parrini, Carl. *Heir to Empire* (Pittsburgh, Pa.: University of Pittsburgh Press, 1969).

Rochester, Stuart I. *American Liberal Disillusionment: In the Wake of World War I* (University Park: Pennsylvania State University Press, 1977).

Silverman, Dan P. *Reconstructing Europe After the Great War* (Cambridge, Mass.: Harvard University Press, 1982).

Sontag, Raymond J. *A Broken World, 1919–1939* (New York: Harper & Row, 1971).

Trachtenberg, Marc. *Reparations and World Politics* (New York: Columbia University Press, 1980).

Ulam, Adam. *Expansion and Coexistence: The History of Soviet Foreign Policy, 1917–1967* (New York: Praeger, 1968).

3
The Collapse of Order
(1931–1935)

Europe had avoided a general war for nearly one hundred years before August 1914. But agreements made at Versailles and at the Washington Conference began to break down after only ten. The single most important cause was the onset of a world depression in the early 1930s. Nations dissatisfied with the existing order had grudgingly abided by it during the prosperous 1920s, but they were no longer willing to do so in the wake of economic disaster. They now sought to revise this world order, regardless of consequences. Ironically, the depression also sapped the resolve to defend the system in those nations responsible for creating it. The result was world war.

THE MANCHURIAN CRISIS

Japan raised the first major challenge to the principle of collective security in Manchuria during the autumn of 1931. The depression had been devastating to the Japanese economy, which relied heavily on overseas trade, and there had been crop failures, as well. Developments on the Asian mainland threatened to make matters worse. In China, a revolution that had begun in 1911 appeared to be consolidating in a manner that threatened Japan's interests. The Chinese had started boycotting Japanese goods during the late 1920s and continued to do so after the depression began. More important, they indicated that they meant to reassert control over Manchuria, long regarded by Japan as a special preserve. Manchuria offered markets and agricultural and mineral resources that Japan lacked, and it might even have served as a safety valve for overpopulation on the home islands. Its absorption by China was unthinkable to many Japanese.

Strains within Japanese society made the situation more combustible. Superficially, the government resembled a Western-style parliamentary system with an emperor who reigned without ruling. But the structure had been engrafted upon a people without democratic tradition. Ultranationalists wished to "restore" the emperor to complete authority and to cleanse Japan of corrupting foreign influence. Elements within the army were particularly zealous. Many younger officers, supported by some senior men in Tokyo, adopted what became known as the "imperial way." They despised the government for having accepted humiliating restrictions on military strength and held it responsible for Japan's economic plight. They were willing to defy and if necessary to kill civilian and military superiors who stood in their way.

On the night of September 18, 1931, an explosion reportedly took place along the South Manchuria Railway near the city of Mukden. Spokesmen for the Kwantung Army, as Japanese forces in Manchuria were called, accused the Chinese of sabotage. Japanese troops began spreading out along the rail line, ostensibly as a precautionary measure. In reality, the incident was staged by officers of the Kwantung Army, who used it as a pretext to eventually occupy all of Manchuria during the winter of 1931–1932. They installed a puppet regime in the area, which they renamed Manchukuo. The civilian government in Tokyo, cowed by popular support for the army's conduct, went along, and many officials welcomed the result, if not the methods used.

Japanese behavior in Manchuria called into question a number of international agreements: the League of Nations Covenant, the Nine Power Pact providing for an Open Door in China, and the Kellogg-Briand Pact. Now, the issue was what the "peace-loving" nations would do collectively or individually. The league withheld recognition from Manchukuo and appointed a commission to study the matter. An impartial assessment was desirable, of course, but the move also was designed to gain time. The commission's report, submitted in early fall of 1932, found Japan guilty of aggression, although it acknowledged Chinese boycotts as provocation. The league assembly subsequently passed a resolution condemning Japan's conduct without imposing sanctions of any kind. Its only discernible effect was to insult the Japanese, who served notice of their intent to withdraw from the organization.

Article 10 of the league covenant obligated members "to respect and preserve as against external aggression" each other's "territorial integrity and political independence." Article 16 provided for a range of sanctions that the league might invoke. But why did it fail to go beyond the useless gesture of a verbal reprimand? Its two most influential members, Great Britain and France, refused to support stronger measures proposed by other nations because they concluded that their own interests were not worth risking in China's behalf. Challenging the Japanese over Manchuria might push them into retaliating against British possessions such as Hong Kong and Singapore or against French Indochina. Some leaders in both nations thought even the mild league resolution was unnecessarily provocative, and they issued statements of confidence in Japan's peaceful intentions.

Japan's seizure of Manchuria had special significance for the United States. Since the turn of the century, the U.S. had championed the Open Door in China, which Americans regarded as an enlightened policy compared with European and Japanese imperialism. Woodrow Wilson had protested Japan's Twenty-One Demands against China in 1915, and Charles Evans Hughes had guided the Nine Power Pact through the Washington Conference. By accepting Japanese aggression, the U.S. would shatter any pretensions that it was China's benefactor and undermine the Kellogg-Briand Pact.

Secretary of State Henry L. Stimson did nothing at first because he hoped that moderate elements in Japan would settle affairs in Manchuria peacefully. When continued Japanese military operations extinguished this hope, Stimson began searching for ways to influence the situation. The United States could not appear to condone aggression, he believed, even though American economic interests were far greater in Japan than in Manchuria. His discussions with President Hoover, who was preoccupied by the depression, revealed the differences between the two men. The secretary was willing to consider economic sanctions against Japan, preferably in collaboration with other powers. Hoover, on the other hand, feared that any action beyond an expression of disapproval might set in motion a train of events that would lead to war. Hoover, as president, set policy.

On January 7, 1932, Secretary Stimson sent identical notes to Japan and China, which he first read to a gathering of ambassadors from those nations that had signed the Nine Power Pact. He stated that the United States would not recognize "any treaty or agreement" between Japan and China that violated existing American rights, the Open Door policy, or the Kellogg-Briand Pact. This message became known as the Stimson Doctrine, a phrase Hoover resented because he regarded himself as at least its coauthor. It also angered the Japanese without deterring them in Manchuria or elsewhere. On the contrary, three weeks later, on January 28, the Japanese navy bombed and shelled the Chinese city of Shanghai in retaliation for continued boycotts and landed marines, who committed numerous atrocities against civilians and troops.

The threat that Japan might launch a full-scale war against China prompted Stimson to renew his campaign for more vigorous measures. He argued again for sanctions and proposed sending American naval vessels to Shanghai. His efforts to enlist British support failed, and Hoover remained adamantly opposed to economic, let alone military, moves. After securing Hoover's approval, a frustrated Stimson resorted to another pronouncement, this time in the form of an open letter to William Borah, chairman of the Senate Foreign Relations Committee, on February 24. In it, he emphasized that the Washington Conference treaties were interrelated: A party to the arrangements could not ignore one agreement and still expect to benefit from the others. Without explicitly saying so, Stimson was warning the Japanese that if they continued to violate the Nine Power Pact providing for the Open Door in China, the United States might consider itself released from the Five Power Pact in terms of naval strength and the fortification of island possessions in the Pacific. He closed with an eloquent statement of American commitment to "fair play" in China.

Stimson hoped to impress several audiences besides the Japanese. He sought to bolster morale in China, encourage the British to take a more active part, and justify the administration's policy to the American people. As with his original statement of nonrecognition, however, the only obvious results of his veiled threat were a stiffening of Japanese resolve and a reinforcement of their belief that the United States stood as the major obstacle to their ambitions. In conversations with the president and in public speeches, Stimson tried to focus attention on Manchuria during the following months but with little success. Domestic issues, the presidential campaign, and the administration's lame duck status after the election of Franklin D. Roosevelt (FDR) in November precluded further action. Stimson's last contribution, if it can be called that, was to convince president-elect Roosevelt to publicly endorse the nonrecognition policy on January 17, 1933.

The response to events in Manchuria had ominous implications. The principle of collective security embodied in the League of Nations required that members form a united front against aggression and that they be willing to ensure its failure by whatever means necessary. But the principle broke down when individual nations placed their own immediate interests above those of an aggressor's victim. Whether U.S. membership in the league would have produced a different result cannot be known, but it must be doubted because President Hoover was no more willing than his European counterparts to risk confrontation. Ultimately, the league's failure to act decisively served notice that it might be defied without serious retaliation.

Hindsight knowledge of the events that led to World War II invites harsh judgments on the shortsightedness of politicians during the Manchurian crisis. How could they have failed to realize that retreat before aggression in one place merely encouraged it elsewhere? Clearly, they *were* shortsighted, but they obviously lacked an ability to read the future and were profoundly influenced by the conditions and assumptions of the times. Like the people they represented, leaders in Great Britain, France, and the United States were absorbed by the struggle to prevent economic collapse—and compared to that, the fate of distant Manchuria seemed a minor concern. Moreover, memories of the Great War were still fresh, and few were willing to advocate measures that might lead to even a smaller version of that discredited nightmare. How much more prudent it seemed to act cautiously and hope for the best. Unfortunately, the best was not to come.

THE RISE OF ADOLF HITLER

The depression proved fatal to the Weimar Republic. Germany's economy already was shaky by the autumn of 1929. More than 1 million people were out of work, and farm income had been low for several years. The Wall Street crash of October 24 dealt a crippling blow by abruptly terminating the loans that Germany had used to finance growth and the payment of reparations. Economic collapse soon led to political radicalization and a loss of confidence in a parliamentary system that had existed for only ten years. The republic may not have survived in any case, but the *way* it ended was determined by one man, Adolf Hitler.

Hitler was born in Austria on April 20, 1889. Difficult as a child, he developed into a moody, withdrawn teenager who dropped out of school with vague aspirations of becoming an artist or an architect, though he lacked real talent in either field. In 1907, he moved to Vienna, first living off modest family inheritances and then eking out a precarious existence selling paintings and doing odd jobs. He moved to Munich in 1913 and, a year later, enlisted in the army when the Great War broke out. He served with distinction on the western front, though never rising above the rank of corporal because his lack of rapport with other men made him seem unsuited for leadership.

News of the armistice in November 1918 filled him with rage over Germany's defeat, which he vowed to avenge. Remaining in Germany's reduced army after the war, he was posted to Munich, where he observed firsthand the activities of various ultrapatriotic political groups. His increasing involvement with one of them, the German Workers' Party, revealed him to be an able organizer and a superb orator. In April 1920, Hitler left the army to follow his true calling. It took him little more than a year to become the undisputed leader of the organization, which was renamed the National Socialist German Workers' Party, or Nazis.

Scholars have subjected Hitler's early years to relentless scrutiny in efforts to understand this complex man. Childhood traumas, ideas he picked up in Vienna, and his army experiences have received varying emphases. What may be said is that by the early 1920s, he had accumulated all the ideas, prejudices, and aspirations that, with only minor variation, would inform his behavior until his death. He had a mystical faith in the destiny of the German nation (as distinct from any particular German government); he detested and feared Jews, whom he regarded as a racial and cultural threat to Germany's "Aryan" stock; and he believed that the world was an arena in which superior individuals, groups, and nations must battle without mercy against those who stood in their way. Finally, he believed himself to be the chosen instrument of German salvation.

The Nazis remained little more than a splinter group throughout most of the decade. In 1923, following a botched attempt to overthrow the government by force—the so-called "beer hall putsch"—Hitler spent a year in jail, where he wrote *Mein Kampf* (My Struggle). The book consisted largely of unoriginal theories about race, Marxism, and nationalism, but it provided a remarkably accurate forecast of his conduct after he attained power. By the time he was released from prison, Hitler had concluded that the Nazis had to work within the system even if their ultimate goal was to destroy it. He spent the next four years trying to create a truly national movement, but by 1928, the Nazis won less than 3 percent of the vote in elections to the Reichstag (legislature).

The year 1929 marked the turning point for Hitler. Nazi membership doubled that year, profiting from unstable economic conditions and from national exposure gained by the group's participation in a referendum on the Young Plan. Then, as the effects of the depression spread, support for the party began to mushroom. Rising unemployment and bankruptcies, coupled with an even further lowering of farm income, created an atmosphere of resentment and desperation that was ripe for exploitation. All along, Hitler had accused Jews and Communists of having stabbed Germany in the back by accepting a humiliating peace in November 1918 and the equally humiliating Versailles treaty a few months later. He had blamed them for foisting upon the nation a corrupt political system that, in turn, encouraged social decadence and the loss of patriotic values. To these charges, which were gaining wider acceptance, the Nazis added responsibility for Germany's economic plight. Hitler promised to restore prosperity and national honor and to build a society untainted by influences alien to Germanic values. The elections held in July 1932 marked the crest of the Nazis' popularity as they became Germany's largest party, with 37 percent of the popular vote.

Ironically, Hitler obtained the coveted chancellorship just as Nazi fortunes began to wane. The party lost strength in a series of elections

Hitler at Nazi party rally, Nuremberg, Germany, ca. 1928. (National Archives photo no. W&C 981)

in November and December, it was beset by financial problems and
internal factionalism, and its appeal was further diminished by improving
economic conditions. The government was paralyzed by the incompatibility of left and right, however, and efforts to break the impasse played
into Hitler's hands. One intriguer, Franz von Papen, worked out a deal
with Hitler whereby the latter agreed to become chancellor, with Papen
as vice chancellor, in a cabinet dominated by conservative non-Nazis.
Papen believed this arrangement would harness Nazi mass support to
a coalition which he himself would dominate by virtue of his majority
in the cabinet. He persuaded President Paul von Hindenburg, an aging
and increasingly senile hero of the Great War, to name Hitler chancellor
on January 30, 1933.

Papen was neither the first nor the last to underestimate Hitler, who
never intended to play a subordinate role. On the grounds that the new
government did not have a functioning majority in the Reichstag, new
elections were scheduled for March. In the meantime, Hindenburg gave
Hitler ever broader powers through presidential decrees, which Hitler
then used to harass and muzzle opposition parties, particularly the
Communists. When a fire destroyed the Reichstag building late in
February, the Nazis exploited the incident by depicting it as the beginning
of a Communist revolution. Hindenburg responded to the "emergency"
by granting greater authority to Hitler, which he used to break up trade
unions, ban opposition political parties, and institute the first measures
to drive Jews out of civil service. During 1934, he purged radical Nazis
to placate the army and, following Hindenburg's death, assumed virtually
complete dictatorial powers.

In 1935, having consolidated his position in Germany, Hitler became
more adventuresome in foreign affairs. The year began auspiciously
when a plebiscite in the Saar region, mandated by the Treaty of Versailles,
revealed that 90 percent of the voters opted to become part of Germany.
During a two-week period in March, Hitler revealed that Germany
already possessed an air force, then denounced all military restrictions
imposed by the Allies at the end of the Great War. He proclaimed his
intention to increase the German army to more than five times the limit
stipulated in the Versailles settlement. In June, he concluded a naval
agreement with the British that permitted Germany a surface fleet that
was 35 percent of the size of Britain's and gave it equality in submarines.

In defending his actions, Hitler at all times denied any aggressive
intent; on the contrary, he repeatedly asserted Germany's devotion to
peace. He also condemned the Versailles treaty as an intolerable insult
to a proud nation. Unwilling to accept inferiority, Germany, he said,
demanded its place among equals and its right to bring back under its
flag the Germanic peoples who had been alienated by the Versailles

On April 1, 1933, the boycott announced by the Nationalsocialistic party began. Placard reads, "Germans! Defend yourselves! Do not buy from Jews!" at the Jewish Tietz store, Berlin. (National Archives photo no. W&C 985)

settlement. If those goals were met, he insisted, Germany posed no threat to anyone.

ATTITUDES AND RESPONSES IN THE DEMOCRACIES

The single most important factor in determining the responses of Germany's former enemies was the widespread determination that there be no repetition of the Great War. Revulsion to that slaughter shaped perceptions of every event, giving rise to attitudes that, in hindsight, are easy to criticize as based on false hopes. Hitler exploited the situation adroitly. By alternating provocative actions and soothing explanations of them as reasonable steps to rectify injustices, he sought to assure the many people who desperately wanted to believe him.

Ideology helped shape attitudes in the democracies. More than any other group, the conservatives tended to voice approval of Hitler's conduct. Often contemptuous of "the masses" at home, they were likely to justify Hitler's dictatorship, if not its violence, by noting that the German people, by their very nature, required a firm hand. It was commonplace for conservatives to say that although they did not approve of his methods, they approved of the results. Some made it clear that this approval extended to Nazi anti-Semitic legislation. Hitler had gotten Germany back on its feet economically, conservatives liked to point out, without having resorted to the socialistic programs they so loathed. Above all, to many on the Right, Nazi Germany stood as a bulwark against the Soviet Union (USSR), which they regarded as a far greater threat. If Hitler contained communism—or, better yet, destroyed it by war—his excesses would seem insignificant.

People on the Left were most critical of Nazi behavior in Germany, especially the oppression of Jews, but few advocated outright opposition to Hitler in foreign affairs. On the contrary, leftist leaders and organizations took the lead in condemning all wars; hence, they opposed measures against aggression by the dictators. Some professed to "understand" Hitler's actions. Disillusioned by what they regarded as the unnecessarily punitive Versailles treaty, they expressed sympathy for Hitler's desire to escape its humiliating terms. According to this view, he was doing what any patriotic German leader would, if somewhat more crudely. A few denied Hitler's actions were threatening almost until World War II began. Such sentiments, it must be emphasized, reflected the overwhelming desire to avoid reactions that might result in renewed armed conflict.

Divisions between the Right and Left were most pronounced in France but less so in Great Britain and the United States. The reactionary Right in France was sympathetic to fascism, so much so that when a mild Socialist named Leon Blum attained the premiership, "better Hitler than Blum" became a popular slogan. Pro-Fascist groups never attained wide support in either Britain or the United States. In the U.S., the German-American Bund and William Pelley's Silvershirts attained notoriety, but they were widely regarded as crackpot groups and never attained large membership.

Special mention must be made of the Communists, who were most influential in France. The Communist parties in all three countries operated under orders of the Soviet Union. Soviet dictator Josef Stalin initially displayed little concern over Hitler's rise to power, even when the latter annihilated the German Communist party. But eventually, Nazi rearmament and repeated denunciations of communism caused a reevaluation of Soviet security needs. Hesitantly at first, then more boldly, the Soviet Union moved to make accommodations with the "capitalist imperialism" that it had previously denounced. In what became known as the popular front, begun in 1935, Moscow ordered Communists everywhere to cooperate with all groups deemed anti-Fascist.

In the United States, the determination to avoid involvement in foreign disputes was strengthened by the emergence of the "merchants of death" interpretation of the Great War and America's subsequent involvement. A rash of books and articles appeared in the early 1930s emphasizing the role of arms and munitions makers in causing war. The most sensationalistic of these publications alleged that there was an international conspiracy dedicated to promoting "bloodshed for profits." This conspiracy was said to promote war during times of peace and make war more hideous when it came through its traffic in the instruments of destruction.

Peace groups used the indignation aroused by the "merchants of death" theme to campaign for Senate approval of a resolution to investigate munitions makers. The resolution, introduced by Senator Gerald S. Nye of North Dakota, probably would have remained in committee had it not been for this well-orchestrated pressure. The resolution passed in April 1934, and a Senate committee was formed, with Nye as its chairman. Hearings began in the latter half of the year.

The Nye investigating committee, as it came to be known, produced shocking evidence of profiteering and shady business practices by the munitions makers. But Nye was after bigger game. Often going far beyond what the facts warranted, he made extravagant allegations about the role arms makers had played in bringing on war. His statements were widely printed in newspapers across the country and seemed to confirm the most lurid accusations of the influence wielded by the "merchants of death." During the hearings and in press conferences, the senator claimed that the United States would have avoided war with Germany in 1917 had it not been for the exportation of armaments to the Allies.

Nye's charges appeared to be substantiated, though in less emotional fashion, by an influential book entitled *Road to War: America, 1914–1917*, published in 1935. Written by a well-known journalist, Walter Millis, the book sold widely and became a Book-of-the-Month Club selection. In calm, dispassionate prose, Millis argued that the United States had been drawn into war by British propaganda, President Woodrow Wilson's pro-Allied maritime policies, and America's economic reliance on British and French war orders. Millis suggested that an impartial arms embargo might have kept the United States out of a war it never should have fought, and he warned against repeating such folly. The "merchants of death" publications, the Nye investigation, and Millis's book greatly reinforced traditional American attitudes about remaining aloof from foreign quarrels.

MUSSOLINI INVADES ETHIOPIA

Italy, not Germany, was the first European nation to commit military aggression. Benito Mussolini had boasted he would restore to his country the glory of the once-mighty Roman Empire. In reality, Italy was a third-rate power: Its military forces were inefficient, its industrial base was inadequate, and it lacked natural resources. Although given to illusions about the future, Mussolini was sufficiently aware of Italy's limitations at the time to seek acquisition at small risk. Taking advantage of a December 1934 border clash in east Africa between Italian Somaliland and Ethiopia, he spurned compromise and began a military buildup in the region. Everyone assumed he was preparing for war against Ethiopia.

Surprisingly, in view of this and subsequent actions, Mussolini continued to be regarded by many in the democracies as a man dedicated to European stability. He was given credit for having saved Italy from chaos (read communism) and for having restored a measure of discipline and prosperity to a people devastated by the Great War, despite the fact that they had been on the winning side. Mussolini's fear of German intentions toward Austria, it was hoped, might make him a good counterweight to Hitler.

Mussolini's actions in 1935 lent support to the optimistic view with regard to Europe. Even while sending troops to Ethiopia, he responded to Hitler's March 1935 announcement of German rearmament by partially mobilizing Italian forces and by inviting Great Britain and France to a conference at Stresa, Italy, the following month. The resulting Stresa Front ultimately proved meaningless, but at the time, it seemed to place Mussolini with those who sought to curb German aggrandizement.

Great Britain and France faced a dilemma with regard to Italy. If Mussolini violated the League of Nations Charter by attacking Ethiopia, failure to respond might encourage aggression elsewhere. Yet, Germany was seen as the greater threat, and attempts to punish Italy might throw Mussolini into Hitler's arms. This is exactly what the Italian dictator counted on. He did fear Hitler's intentions, but he also sought British and French acquiescence in his Ethiopian adventure. This he achieved in substance. When Italy launched its long-awaited invasion on October

3, 1935, the League of Nations Council denounced the act as a violation of the league charter. The committee formed to decide on penalties gave the game away. It declared an arms embargo and several other restrictions against Italy. At British and French insistence, however, it refrained from taking the one step that might have crippled the Italian war effort—banning the exportation to Italy of vitally needed oil and other strategic raw materials.

In the United States during August 1935, Mussolini's anticipated attack against Ethiopia brought to a climax a long-simmering congressional debate over the proper response to foreign conflict. The debate was conducted within the context of attitudes about American involvement in the Great War and was greatly influenced by the "merchants of death" publications and by the Nye investigation. All participants sought legislation on issues such as the sale of arms and restrictions on shipping, but there was vehement disagreement over how this legislation should be applied.

The struggle approximated the division over membership in the League of Nations. Advocates of collective security wished to use neutrality legislation selectively. In the event of hostilities, they wanted to give the president the discretion to determine responsibility. He then could declare an arms embargo and other sanctions against the transgressor but freely supply the victim. If this were done in collaboration with other "peace-loving" nations, they argued, aggression would become too costly to pursue. Furthermore, they believed that remaining aloof from such matters would encourage international lawlessness that ultimately would involve the United States.

Opponents blamed such sentiments for having gotten the United States into war in 1917. Sympathy for the Allies had resulted in nonneutral policies, they contended, thereby forcing Germany to resort to unrestricted submarine warfare. To avoid repeating this error, the United States should maintain complete impartiality toward all belligerents, regardless of actual or assumed culpability. Advocates of this position did not want to grant the president discretionary powers. Rather, they wanted legislation that would go into effect mandatorily at the outbreak of hostilities, applying equally to all combatants. They got most of what they wanted. A bill providing for a mandatory arms embargo, with a few discretionary features on other matters, passed both houses of Congress in late August.

President Roosevelt, who would have preferred receiving full discretionary powers, reluctantly signed the bill into law on August 31. He complained that its "inflexible provisions might drag us into war instead of keeping us out," but agreed to accept it provided it had a six-month time limit. He compromised for several reasons. First, he did not want to jeopardize several important pieces of domestic legislation that the administration had pending. Second, he viewed the mandatory/discretionary issue as relatively unimportant with regard to a war between Italy and Ethiopia because the latter had no means of obtaining arms from the United States in any case. Finally, Roosevelt believed the six-month limit would free his hands for the future.

During his first two years in office, Roosevelt seemed to have been unsure what, if anything, the United States could do to promote peace in Europe and Asia. As assistant secretary of the navy during World War I and as a Democratic candidate for the vice presidency in 1920, he had been an ardent Wilsonian with regard to the League of Nations. American membership was out of the question by the time he became president. In 1933 and 1934, he had followed a mildly internationalist policy but understandably devoted most of his energies to combating the debilitating depression. His response to the Ethiopian conflict signaled a greater willingness to take steps that he hoped would deter aggression but within the constraints imposed by massive isolationist and pacifistic sentiment in the nation. Always the pragmatist, he tried to do what he could without risking repudiation of his leadership.

Two days after Italian troops pushed into Ethiopia, FDR directed Secretary of State Cordell Hull to proclaim an arms embargo. The president wanted to go further. He suggested publicizing the names of American citizens who traveled on ships owned by Italy or Ethiopia and of companies who did business with either nation. Hull at first agreed, but other officials argued that, because Ethiopia had neither ships nor ports, such an action would be criticized as a blatant attempt to punish Italy. A compromise was reached whereby the administration merely warned against travel and invoked what became known as a "moral embargo," stating that exporters would conduct business "at their own risk."

Roosevelt hoped to accomplish two purposes by acting so quickly. He wanted to signal the League of Nations that he supported economic penalties against Italy within the limits imposed on him. He also wished to head off criticism at home by making it clear that the administration was acting independently of the league. He accomplished little, and the steps he took had no discernible influence on league decisions. Indeed, his inability to impose a legal embargo on sales of materials such as oil was used as an argument against the league doing so. Nonetheless, he was criticized for cooperating with the organization in adopting nonneutral policies against Italy. Most important, the moral embargo did not work: Sales of oil to Italy increased threefold over previous averages.

Whatever hopes Roosevelt had of working with the league collapsed in mid-December with the revelation of a British and French proposal to end the Italian-Ethiopian war. The Hoare-Laval Plan (named after British Foreign Secretary Sir Samuel Hoare and French Premier Pierre Laval) so favored Italy in the disposition of territory and economic rights that it was widely condemned as a cynical betrayal of Ethiopia. The plan was withdrawn, but in the United States it helped discredit the notion of working with the league powers. Far from gaining the freedom of action he had hoped for when the original neutrality act expired in February 1936, FDR, under pressure from Congress, signed an even more comprehensive bill against involvement of any kind. Without serious hindrance, Mussolini completed his conquest of Ethiopia three months later.

Reaction to Italy's aggression resembled the response to Japan's actions a few years earlier, and it had similar results. In both cases, the League of Nations abandoned the idea that an attack on one member constituted an attack on all. The league's dominant powers, Great Britain and France, blocked strong measures out of concern for "larger" interests, thereby abandoning weaker peoples to their fate. The United States did likewise, failing to accompany verbal condemnation with meaningful steps. Irresolute action had two consequences: It offended but did not deter the guilty parties, and it served notice to all that further aggression might also go unpunished. Shortly after Italy's invasion, the emperor of Ethiopia, Haile Selassie, appeared before the league assembly for help. He warned the delegates that failure to respond might delay but ultimately would not prevent international violence that would engulf them all. His words were prophetic.

SELECTED BIBLIOGRAPHY

Bullock, Alan. *Hitler: A Study in Tyranny* (New York: Harper & Row, 1964).

Burns, James MacGregor. *Roosevelt: The Lion and the Fox* (New York: Harcourt, Brace, and World, 1956).

Cohen, Warren I. *The American Revisionists: The Lessons of Intervention in World War I* (Chicago: University of Chicago Press, 1967).

Cole, Wayne C. *Roosevelt and the Isolationists* (Lincoln: University of Nebraska Press, 1983).

Current, Richard N. *Secretary Stimson: A Study in Statecraft* (New Brunswick, N.J.: Rutgers University Press, 1954).

Dallek, Robert. *Franklin D. Roosevelt and American Foreign Policy, 1932–1945* (New York: Oxford University Press, 1979).

Divine, Robert A. *The Illusion of Neutrality: Franklin D. Roosevelt and the Struggle over the Arms Embargo* (Chicago: University of Chicago Press, 1962).

Doenecke, Justus D. *When the Wicked Rise: American Opinion Makers and the Manchurian Crisis of 1931–1933* (Lewisberg, Pa.: Bucknell University Press, 1984).

Ferrell, Robert H. *American Diplomacy in the Great Depression* (New Haven, Conn.: Yale University Press, 1957).

Fest, Joachim. *Hitler* (New York: Harcourt, Brace, Jovanovich, 1973).

Harris, Bryce, Jr. *The United States and the Italo-Ethiopian Crisis* (Stanford, Calif.: Stanford University Press, 1964).

Ienaga, Saburo. *The Pacific War: World War II and the Japanese, 1931-1945* (New York: Pantheon Books, 1978).

Jonas, Manfred. *Isolationism in America* (Ithaca, N.Y.: Cornell University Press, 1966).

Mack Smith, Denis. *Mussolini* (New York: Knopf, 1982).

Maier, Charles S., Stanley Hoffman, and Andrew Gould (eds.). *The Rise of the Nazi Regime: Historical Reassessments* (Boulder, Colo.: Westview, 1985).

Morley, James William (ed.). *Japan Erupts: The London Naval Conference and the Manchurian Incident, 1928-1932* (New York: Columbia University Press, 1984).

Rappaport, Armin. *Henry L. Stimson and Japan, 1931-1933* (Chicago: University of Chicago Press, 1963).

Spielvogel, Jackson J. *Hitler and Nazi Germany: A History* (Englewood Cliffs, N.J.: Prentice-Hall, 1988).

Turner, Henry A. *German Big Business and the Rise of Hitler* (New York: Oxford University Press, 1985).

Ulam, Adam B. *Expansion and Coexistence: The History of Soviet Foreign Policy, 1917-1967* (New York: Praeger, 1968).

Weinberg, Gerhard. *The Foreign Policy of Hitler's Germany: Diplomatic Revolution in Europe, 1933-1936* (Chicago: University of Chicago Press, 1970).

Wiltz, John E. *In Search of Peace: The Senate Munitions Inquiry, 1934-1936* (Baton Rouge: Louisiana State University Press, 1963).

4
Descent into Chaos
(1936–1939)

The failure of the League of Nations to do more than slap Mussolini's fingers, as it had done to the Japanese several years earlier, was inauspicious for the future of world peace. Those who would challenge existing arrangements by force realized the organization was no stronger than its leading powers, Great Britain and France, which meant it was not very strong at all. Both nations had proven irresolute in the face of challenges to collective security. The United States was little more than an interested spectator with regard to developments in Europe, and President Roosevelt had limited maneuverability in the Far East. From the mid-1930s on, fascism in Europe and Japanese militarism in Asia appeared to many as the wave of the future. Only in 1939 did the democracies begin to realize that appeasement of aggression only brought more aggression. Ultimately, their efforts to stop it resulted in the war they had sought desperately to avoid.

THE SPANISH CIVIL WAR

After centuries of a monarchical government in Spain, a republic was established in the early 1930s. The new government's efforts to weaken the influence of the Roman Catholic church in Spain and to institute other reforms stirred resentment among church leaders, large landowners, and conservatives in general. The elections of 1936 resulted in the formation of a popular-front government that was more left-leaning than its predecessor. This touched off a civil war between rightist insurgents, led by General Francisco Franco, and those loyal to the Spanish Republic.

The Spanish Civil War took on international overtones from the start as Franco appealed to Germany and Italy for help. Mussolini, anxious to aid the Fascist cause, responded immediately with 50,000 troops and supplies. Hitler moved more cautiously. Spain was a source of vital raw materials that a presumably grateful Franco, if victorious, would make available to Germany in time of war. Yet, Hitler did not want the conflict in Spain to spread because he believed Germany was not yet prepared. He therefore limited German aid to equipment, advisers, and an air squadron. Both he and Mussolini deliberately used the Spanish conflict as a proving ground for their own armor and air tactics.

The Soviet Union provided modest aid to the Loyalists after some delay. Although loyalty to causes or groups was not one of Stalin's strong suits, he probably thought it advisable to support a leftist regime against Fascist rebels backed by Fascist nations. He also was motivated by the desire to keep the civil war going as long as possible. The Soviet Union during these years was in the throes of Stalin's purges and could only profit if Europe's attention was centered on Spain. Stalin sent military experts and equipment and had the Comintern raise volunteer groups from other nations. These groups most often were manipulated by Soviet agents. Communists came to dominate the Spanish government because of Soviet assistance, but Stalin had no wish to see them victorious. He was afraid a Communist Spain might push Great Britain and France closer to Germany.

The democracies, as in previous crises, waffled. Great Britain and France adopted policies of noninterference in hopes of keeping the conflict localized. They formed a nonintervention committee to prevent sales of military supplies to either side, even though this meant equal treatment for both a government they recognized and the rebels who sought to overthrow it. The United States acted similarly. Secretary of State Hull quickly announced a "moral embargo" on arms, and a few months later, Congress enacted legislation designed specifically for Spain. Although public sentiment split along left/right lines, a near consensus existed that the United States should not get involved. Such policies ensured Franco's victory by default because Germany and Italy provided far more help to him than the Soviets did to the government. The Spanish Republic ceased to exist in April 1939.

To some Americans, as well as to people in other nations, the civil war in Spain seemed to be a preview of an apocalyptic world struggle. Those on the Right tended to regard Franco as a defender of Christianity and private property against the atheistic forces of communism as represented by the Soviet-backed republic. Leftists regarded the rebels as yet another manifestation of fascism that had prevailed in Germany, Italy, and several east European countries: If not stopped in Spain, it might spread across Europe and further. Several hundred idealistic young men volunteered for the Comintern-sponsored "Abraham Lincoln brigade" to fight the Fascists. The brigade suffered terrible casualties in combat, and some members grew disillusioned by the cynicism and cruelty of Soviet agents. Ironically, during the McCarthy era of the 1950s, brigade survivors were characterized as "premature anti-Fascists."

JAPAN INVADES THE CHINESE MAINLAND

After establishing the puppet state of Manchukuo in the early 1930s, Japan began trying to pry away China's northern provinces by diplomatic pressure and by fomenting separatist movements. In February 1936, a coup in Tokyo led by young army officers succeeded in killing several cabinet ministers and seizing some government buildings. The coup was put down but led to almost complete military domination of the Japanese government. In August, the cabinet adopted a plan entitled the Fundamental Principles of National Policy, providing for a military buildup, expansion in China and to the south, and repudiation of the various treaties negotiated at the Washington Conference of 1921. Three months later, Japan signed an anti-Comintern pact with Germany, containing a secret protocol aimed against the Soviet Union. Developments in Europe and Asia, never entirely without influence on one another, were drawing together.

On the night of July 7, 1937, a skirmish took place between Chinese and Japanese units near the Marco Polo Bridge, twenty miles west of Peking. The Japanese had not staged this clash as they had the Mukden incident in Manchuria years earlier, but militants were quick to exploit it. Initial plans to send three divisions to Peking were revised upward when Chinese Nationalist forces began moving toward northern China. By the end of the month, Japanese troops already stationed in the north, joined by reinforcements sent from Japan, began offensive operations that resulted in the seizure of Peking. The Japanese expanded the conflict in mid-August when they besieged and captured the southern port city of Shanghai.

President Roosevelt, who had hoped the fighting might be ended by Sino-Japanese negotiations, moved to help the Chinese. Existing neutrality legislation provided that it must be invoked whenever the president "found" that a state of war existed. This included an embargo on arms and a cash-and-carry policy on other goods. Invoking the act would aid Japan because it manufactured its own arms and had the money and ships to benefit from cash-and-carry. China, on the other hand, needed to import weapons and to purchase on credit. Taking advantage of the fact that neither side had issued a formal declaration of war, FDR simply chose not to find that a state of war existed. His critics accurately charged that he violated the spirit of the legislation, but they could do nothing about it.

Although Japanese actions in China clearly violated the Kellogg-Briand and Nine Power pacts, Roosevelt did nothing more for several weeks. Then, when the League of Nations began considering the issue in September, he permitted an American representative to take part as an "unofficial observer." On October 5, one day before the league issued a condemnation of Japan, Roosevelt made a speech in Chicago that seemed to herald a dramatic change in administration policy. Denouncing "the present reign of terror and international lawlessness," he likened it to an epidemic that communities fought by isolating those infected under quarantine.

Roosevelt's "quarantine speech," as it came to be called, was a shocker. He clearly was referring to the Japanese, although he did not mention them by name. Did his reference to a quarantine mean that he was proposing economic sanctions against Japan to isolate it from the world community? If this were done, the Japanese might be provoked into seizing by force what was denied them by normal trade. Reactions were predictable. Advocates of collective security praised the speech, indicating as it did a willingness to collaborate with other democratic nations. But isolationists responded with anger, charging that FDR was abandoning all pretense to neutrality and advocating a policy that would lead to war.

FDR's real intentions were never clear. At a press conference the next day, while the furor raged, he blandly denied he had any specific plans in mind when he made the speech. Some historians have suggested that he was testing the waters of public opinion and might have moved ahead had the response been favorable. Strong opposition instead caused him to back off. The following month, Roosevelt sent a delegation to a conference of Nine Power Pact signatories in Belgium but "without any commitments on the part of this government to other governments." Japan refused to attend, and the conference adjourned without taking action.

In mid-December, Japanese aircraft attacked and sank the U.S. gunboat *Panay* in the Yangtze River. The incident revealed both administration and public attitudes. Although evidence indicated the attack was premeditated, the administration accepted Japan's apology and an indemnity, and no cries of "remember the *Panay*" arose from the public. That same month, the Japanese captured the Chinese capital of Nanking and began a butchery of some 200,000 men, women, and children that was so barbaric that even the Nazis complained. The *Panay* incident and the "rape of Nanking" confirmed America's abomination of the Japanese and sympathy for China, but it brought no demand for a change in U.S. policies.

HITLER TAKES THE INITIATIVE

Hitler sent German troops into the Rhineland on March 7, 1936. According to the Versailles treaty, this area had remained part of Germany, but it had been demilitarized to provide a buffer for France. Hitler earlier had planned to wait until 1937 when Germany would be better prepared if the French decided to fight. But the league's token response to Italy's Ethiopian adventure had persuaded him he could move ahead of schedule without fear of reprisal. He guessed correctly. Although a few French leaders sought to block the intrusion, grossly exaggerated estimates of German troop strength and the British failure to offer support undermined the will to resist. German troops and policemen, under orders to pull back if they encountered opposition, occupied the Rhineland without firing a shot.

Hitler's successful bluff had wide impact. The league once again had proven to be a frail reed in the face of threat, its leading powers unwilling to do more than offer verbal protests. Meanwhile, Hitler's assertion of German "rights" greatly increased his popularity at home. The fact that German generals had opposed the move reinforced his view that he alone possessed the boldness and perceptivity to direct foreign affairs without hindrance. He further strengthened Germany's position by concluding a treaty with Italy in October—which Mussolini began referring to as the "Rome-Berlin axis"—and the Anti-Comintern Pact with Japan a month later. He accompanied these achievements with his usual claims of peaceful intentions as long as Germany was permitted to take its rightful place among nations.

Hitler made no overt moves in 1937, leading some in the democracies to believe he had achieved his goals. That was a mistake. In November, he held a secret meeting with his foreign minister, war minister, and top military leaders, during which he outlined plans that threatened to set Europe aflame. He told those present that Germany must secure its living space in the east, just as he had written in *Mein Kampf*. This would have to be accomplished by force of arms, he said, and might result in war with France and Great Britain. To prepare for this eventuality, Austria and Czechoslovakia on Germany's flank would have to be subdued first. He also said he might be ready to move by 1938 if conditions warranted. He set 1945 as the deadline for attaining his objectives because by that time, both German military strength and his own physical and mental powers would have peaked and would decline thereafter.

Three of those in attendance expressed strong reservations about Hitler's program: War Minister Field Marshal Werner von Blomberg; Foreign Minister Konstantine von Neurath; and General Werner von Fritsch, commander in chief of the army. Hitler, whose past successes had made him increasingly contemptuous of doubters, moved quickly to purge them. He replaced Neurath with a rabid Nazi, Joachim von Ribbentrop. Still wary of the army, Hitler acted more deviously to get rid of Blomberg and Fritsch. The discovery of police files showing that Blomberg's wife once had been a prostitute took care of the former, and trumped-up charges of homosexuality, the latter. Hitler increasingly surrounded himself with men whose loyalties were to him personally.

Hitler had reason to believe that he would encounter no strong opposition to Germany's absorption of Austria, provided it were carried out with a minimum of decorum. In late 1937, representatives from both Great Britain and France told him as much in private conversations, and Mussolini, who by now regarded Hitler as an ally and a man of destiny, made it clear that Italy would pose no obstacle. Alone, Austria stood little chance against German military and economic might.

Austrian Chancellor Kurt von Schuschnigg, aware of Hitler's intentions, tried to compromise. In early 1938, he proposed economic and military integration with Germany and even offered to appoint an Austrian Nazi, Arthur Seyss-Inquart, as head of the powerful ministry of the interior. Hitler was unimpressed. Trying to stave off complete absorption, on March 9 Schuschnigg called for a plebiscite on Austrian independence. Hitler thereupon threatened to use force unless the plebiscite were canceled and Schuschnigg replaced as chancellor by Seyss-Inquart. Schuschnigg caved in and resigned. On March 12, the new chancellor, Seyss-Inquart, invited German troops into Austria to quell internal disturbances—which Austrian Nazis had caused in the first place. Hitler proclaimed the annexation the next day. Whether Austrians were Hitler's first "victims" or, given the degree of collaboration, his willing accomplices is debatable.

In 1931, Great Britain and France, working through the World Court, had prevented Germany and Austria from forming a customs union, but now, they accepted formal annexation with scarcely a murmur. Reaction in the United States was equally forbearing. "It was natural for Hitler to take Austria," Senator Borah wrote, "Austria was really a German state and the Versailles peacemakers had ruined, crippled, and dismembered it, and it could not stand alone." Comforted by Hitler's refrain that he was only trying to bring Germanic people into the Third Reich where they belonged, many others convinced themselves that what had been done was "natural."

THE ROAD TO MUNICH AND BEYOND

Having correctly anticipated the French and British passivity over Austria, Hitler turned to Czechoslovakia during the summer of 1938. Created at the Versailles conference out of portions of the Austro-Hungarian Empire, Czechoslovakia projected like a thumb into Germany's southeastern flank. To give the fledgling nation economic coherence and defensible borders, the peacemakers had included in it an area known as the Sudetenland, which contained large numbers of Germanic peoples. This fact permitted Hitler to sound a familiar theme: He sought no foreign territory but would protect the interests of ethnic Germans whatever the consequences. Actually, he already had decided to "smash Czechoslovakia by military action in the near future."

Hitler carried out his plan in stages. First, he had Sudetenland Nazis mount a campaign against the alleged mistreatment of the region by the Czechoslovakian government. They were to make demands they knew would be refused, thereby enabling Hitler to pose as the defender of persecuted Sudeten Germans. Under intense pressure from Hitler and denied support by France and Britain, the Czech government granted the region almost complete autonomy in late summer. But this was not enough. In September, Hitler informed British Prime Minister Neville Chamberlain that Czechoslovakia must cede the Sudeten to Germany or there would be war. Chamberlain flew to Prague and persuaded the hapless Czechs to give in. Hitler responded with an even more humiliating ultimatum: Germany must be permitted to occupy the Sudetenland, with its fortifications left intact, by October 1. When resolution against this latest outrage appeared to stiffen, Mussolini suggested a last-minute conference in Munich to avoid war.

The Munich Conference, attended by Hitler, Mussolini, Chamberlain, and French Premier Edouard Daladier, began in late September. The participants hastily agreed to the dissection of Czechoslovakia and so informed a Czech delegation that had not been permitted to take part in the negotiations. Hitler received all he had asked for, with the slight concession that occupation would not be completed until October 10. Czechoslovakia had been eviscerated: It lost the formidable military installations on its frontier, a major part of its industrial base (including the Skoda armament works), and much of its natural resources.

The appeasement of Hitler at Munich has caused scholars to speculate on alternatives. The Czechs had a small but well-equipped and disciplined army, defending mountainous terrain. If Great Britain and France had supported Czechoslovakia, would Hitler have launched a two-front war? And would he have won if he had done so? A group of German generals and diplomats, convinced he was leading the nation to catastrophe, planned to arrest him, provided Great Britain and France stood firm. The conspirators tried to notify London and Paris of their intentions, but they were unable to influence policymakers there. In the end, Czechoslovakia was sacrificed in the forlorn hope of gaining "peace in our time," in Chamberlain's phrase.

The initial response to Munich in the West was one of great relief that the crisis had passed without war. Attitudes began to harden during the following months, however, especially after Hitler seized and dismembered what remained of Czechoslovakia in March 1939: The argument that he was merely trying to redress the grievances of Versailles no longer carried weight. In response, France and Great Britain stepped up their rearmament programs and gave guarantees to several nations that Hitler already was making demands on, such as Poland and Romania. The signing of the Pact of Steel between Germany and Italy in May made the situation even more alarming.

A growing number of Americans became convinced during this period that the United States had an interest in bolstering the Western powers against aggression. President Roosevelt, who had expressed satisfaction over the outcome of the Munich Conference, now tried to instill in the public a greater awareness of the threat Germany and Italy posed. In April, he publicly asked Hitler and Mussolini to guarantee the safety of some thirty-one nations. He also began to push for the revision of neutrality legislation. The most important change he sought was the repeal of the arms embargo provision, thereby allowing the United States to sell military supplies on a cash-and-carry basis in time of war. As Great Britain and France would benefit most, FDR hoped such a revision would act as a deterrent to the dictators.

At the same time, isolationist sentiment remained strong. FDR's critics charged him with advocating nonneutral policies that would drag the United States into conflict. His campaign to revise neutrality laws was stalled in mid-July, when the Senate Foreign Relations Committee voted against reconsidering the matter. In an effort to avoid defeat, the president invited congressional leaders of both parties to meet with him at the White House on the evening of July 18.

Roosevelt opened the session with an appeal for revision, then had Secretary of State Hull try to convince his listeners that war in Europe was imminent. Several individuals disputed Hull's version of events, and heated arguments followed. A poll of those present, taken by Vice President John Nance Garner, revealed insufficient support to reopen the question. Roosevelt adjourned the meeting, and on the following day, he announced publicly that nothing more could be done until the next session of Congress. His defeat was less important than he thought: There is no reason to believe that neutrality revision would have affected Hitler's conduct in the slightest.

THE NAZI-SOVIET PACT

The Soviet Union also began to alter its policy toward Nazi Germany in the spring and summer of 1939 but in the opposite direction. During the Popular Front period of the mid-1930s, it routinely exchanged the most vile denunciations with Germany. The USSR was the only nation to support the Spanish Republic against rebels backed by Hitler and Mussolini, and the Soviet delegate to the League of Nations repeatedly spoke in behalf of collective security. Then, on March 10, 1939, Stalin made a speech in which he criticized the democracies for their appeasement and suggested that they wanted to promote conflict between Germany and the Soviet Union. But, he said, the USSR would not "pull the chestnuts out of the fire for them." In early May, Maxim Litvinov, an advocate of collective security and a Jew, was replaced as minister for foreign affairs by V. M. Molotov—a move that was widely interpreted as a placatory gesture toward Hitler.

Hoping to get the best deal he could, Stalin opened simultaneous negotiations during the summer with Great Britain and France and with Germany. Prospects for agreement with the former Allies were slim. The Western nations were suspicious of the Communists, who, in turn, could not have had much trust in those who had so recently sold out democratic Czechoslovakia. What proved fatal to the negotiations was Stalin's insistence that in case of war with Germany, Soviet troops would be permitted to cross the territories of Poland and Romania. Both nations refused because they feared that if the Soviets entered they would never leave. "With the Germans we risk losing our liberty," the Polish foreign minister stated, "with the Russians we lose our soul."

Hitler, who had more to offer, was anxious to reach agreement quickly. He already had decided to crush Poland and wanted to proceed before bad weather hampered operations. To avoid a general two-front war, therefore, it was essential to assure Soviet neutrality should Great Britain and France choose to fight over Poland. He was willing to cede a generous sphere of influence to the Soviets in eastern Europe, he offered badly needed credits in exchange for strategic raw materials, and he promised to use his influence to restrain the Japanese, who recently had clashed with the Soviets along the Mongolian and Manchurian borders. Above all, he proposed a twenty-five-year nonaggression pact between Germany and the Soviet Union. Stalin hesitated, then accepted the German terms with Hitler's prodding.

Foreign ministers Ribbentrop and Molotov hammered out three agreements in Moscow between August 19 and 23. Two were made public: a trade treaty and a nonaggression pact. The third was kept secret, and until recently, Soviet authorities denied it existed. This secret protocol provided for spheres of influence as follows: Eastern Poland, Latvia, and Estonia would go to the Soviets; western Poland and Lithuania to the Germans. The nonaggression pact and the protocol granted the Soviet Union time and space as opposed to a possible war with Germany in the future. At a ceremony on the evening of August 23, however,

Soviet Foreign Minister Molotov signs the German-Soviet nonaggression pact, Moscow, August 23, 1939. Joachim von Ribbentrop and Josef Stalin stand behind him. (National Archives photo no. W&C 990)

there were only professions of friendship. Stalin toasted Hitler, proclaiming, "I know how much the German people love their Fuhrer." Later, defending the pact, Molotov said that fascism, after all, was "just a matter of taste."

News of the Nazi-Soviet pact fell like a bombshell on the West. Hitler was now free to move against Poland without fear of having to fight the Soviet Union along with Great Britain and France should the latter nations decide to intervene. The failure of Western leaders to persuade the Soviets to join an anti-German coalition had resulted in the realization of their worst nightmare. Communists in the West also were shocked. Literally overnight, they had to switch from reviling "Fascist dogs" to mouthing the new party line, which was that "capitalist imperialism" was the real threat to world peace. Some quit the party in disgust, but most followed orders, as they were used to doing.

BLITZKRIEG

Hitler had begun making demands on Poland during the autumn of 1938 regarding what was known as the Polish corridor and the city of Danzig. Allied statesmen at the Versailles conference had created the corridor, which separated East Prussia from the rest of Germany, to guarantee Poland an outlet to the Baltic Sea. Danzig, a German city at its terminus, was made a free city to provide port facilities. Hitler insisted upon the return of Danzig and that Germany be permitted to construct road and rail facilities across the corridor to East Prussia. The Poles, horrified at the thought of conceding to Germany control over their access to the Baltic, had responded with compromise offers that were rejected. Following the Nazi-Soviet pact, Hitler's demands were presented to the Poles in the form of an ultimatum: Give in at once or face invasion. They refused.

Hitler probably hoped that France and Great Britain would fail to honor their pledges to Poland if war came. For months, Nazi propagandists and their allies in the Western nations had been circulating the phrase "Why die for Danzig?" as a means of weakening resolve. Hitler prepared to go ahead anyway, at one point telling subordinates that he only feared "some swine or other" would propose mediation. Danzig was his excuse for making war on Poland, not its cause. In truth, it provided a fig leaf for his continued pretense that he was merely trying to bring Germanic peoples under the protection of the Third Reich.

Hitler preceded his assault against Poland with a ruse. Concentration camp inmates were dressed in Polish uniforms and killed, and their bodies were then deposited near a radio station in the border town of Gleiwitz on August 31. Ostensibly reacting to this Polish "outrage," Germany invaded Poland at dawn on September 1. British Prime Minister Chamberlain's reluctance to declare war in response to Polish pleas that Britain live up to its pledges precipitated a crisis in the House of Commons, and opposition in both parties to further appeasement forced him to declare war on September 3. The French followed suit a few hours later. World War II had begun.

Poland's position was hopeless from the start. With East Prussia on its northern flank, Germany to the west, and German protectorates on

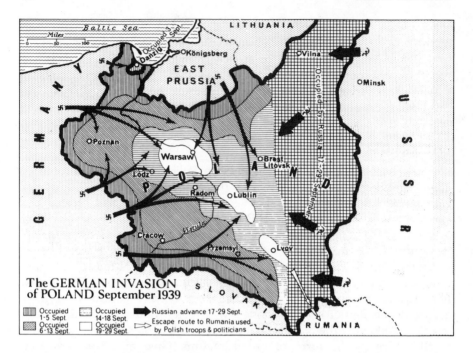

The GERMAN INVASION
of POLAND September 1939

▦ Occupied 1-5 Sept.	▦ Occupied 14-18 Sept.	➡ Russian advance 17-29 Sept.
▨ Occupied 6-13 Sept.	▢ Occupied 19-29 Sept.	⇨ Escape route to Rumania used by Polish troops & politicians

the southern flank, the western half of Poland was virtually surrounded.
German columns plunged into Poland from all three directions. The
Poles would have been better off had they concentrated their forces
along more defensible positions to the east, but instead they chose to
defend impossibly lengthy borders. This meant that when the Germans
broke through in any sector, there were no reserves to meet them.

Better strategy would have prolonged the fighting, but it would not
have changed the outcome. Against sixty German divisions, nine of
them panzer (armored), the Poles had only thirty-nine divisions, mostly
infantry and cavalry. Poland had begun to mobilize its trained reserves
after the Nazi-Soviet pact, but the French and British had pressured
them to rescind the mobilization order to avoid "provocation." The Poles
were also outclassed in every category of modern warfare: planes, tanks,
motorized transport, and communications. Despite their valiant resistance,
including several counterattacks, within two weeks they were falling
back on their capital city of Warsaw. By September 27, after several
days of devastating artillery and aerial bombardment, Warsaw capitulated.
Ten days earlier, the Soviets had invaded Poland from the east to get
their share of the spoils. Although pockets of resistance held out longer,
Poland had ceased to exist by the end of September.

The ease with which Germany crushed Poland shocked and frightened
many in the West. The term "blitzkrieg" (lightning war) suddenly became

popular. German armor, supported by aircraft, spearheaded the attacks, followed by motorized infantry, then conventional ground troops. Air attacks were made against rail and communication centers in the rear to disrupt the flow of troops, supplies, and information. Population centers also were bombed so that refugees would clog the roads that the Poles needed to deploy their forces. Stuka dive-bombers, with shrieking sirens affixed to their wings, were particularly valuable in creating panic. Although much of the equipment Germany employed was less than formidable by later standards—older tanks were armed only with machine guns, for instance, and the slow Stukas were vulnerable to fighters—it was overwhelming against the poorly armed Poles. To those in the democracies who had been claiming all along that Germany was invincible, the Polish campaign appeared to provide proof.

THE "PHONY WAR" AND THE WINTER WAR

France and Great Britain reneged on their promises to aid Poland as Hitler's blitzkrieg tore it to pieces. The French mounted a limited offensive against German territory but quickly retreated before any major collisions took place. Thus, another opportunity was missed to inflict upon Hitler a two-front war he was not militarily prepared to fight. The British response was even more pathetic: Royal Air Force planes dropped leaflets denouncing Hitler's actions on a few German cities. Sentiment remained strong in both governments for reaching some sort of accommodation to prevent general war. Meanwhile, the only fighting that took place in Europe during the first months after the fall of Poland occurred when the Soviet Union invaded Finland.

Hitler, buoyed by the swift defeat of Poland, had directed his subordinates to prepare for offensives against the West as quickly as possible. At the same time, he stated publicly that there were no irreconcilable differences between Germany and the Allies. Whether he genuinely hoped the sentiment for peace would bring Britain and France to the negotiating table on his terms or whether he merely wished to shift blame to them for continuing the war is unclear. In any case, stalemate resulted. Despite the Allied failure to respond to his overtures, Hitler did not attack. His generals warned him against further operations so soon after the Polish campaign because equipment of all kinds, particularly tanks, had to be replaced and refitted. Besides, they said, the approaching winter would hamper blitzkrieg-type assaults. For once, he accepted their advice.

When news of Germany's attack on Poland reached Washington, President Roosevelt prepared to summon a special session of Congress to change the neutrality laws, particularly the arms embargo. He delayed naming a date while he sounded out opinion in the Senate and House. He would have preferred outright revocation of the Neutrality Act, but he learned that enough support could be mustered to place the sale of arms on a cash-and-carry basis only if other provisions remained intact. He concluded that he had no choice but to seek the obtainable, a decision bolstered by word from Great Britain that Prime Minister Chamberlain believed failure to revoke the arms embargo would be "sheer disaster" for Great Britain and France. The special session was called for September 21.

FDR appeared before Congress the opening day to make a fervent appeal for revoking the arms embargo. His speech, frequently punctuated by applause, emphasized his determination to keep the nation out of war. To confound his critics, he professed to see the arms embargo as a perversion of traditional American policy and its repeal as a "return" to practices that had worked in the past. When debate got under way, opponents stressed the theme that repeal would be nonneutral in its effects, but they failed to get the necessary support. Public opinion and newspaper polls taken during this period revealed a majority of those surveyed favored Roosevelt's position. A bill repealing the embargo and placing the sale of arms on a cash-and-carry basis passed the Senate on October 27; the House concurred a few days later. Ironically, although France began purchasing war materials on a large scale almost immediately, Great Britain did not do so until after the fall of France in June 1940.

Even before Congress met, a prominent isolationist senator had floated an interpretation of the situation in Europe that became popular in the following months. Commenting on the absence of large-scale battles in the West like those that had characterized the early weeks of World War I, Senator Borah of Idaho told a reporter there was "something phony" going on. He suggested that France and Great Britain had declared war on Germany merely as a face-saving gesture. Then, after a decent interval during which they could boast of having lived up to their obligations, they would negotiate terms with Hitler, as they had known they would do all along. If this were the case, he concluded, recent events meant that "the chances are increased for peace." The senator was clutching for straws in an attempt to undermine Roosevelt's contention that the emergency required neutrality revision, but the phrase "phony war" caught on.

But there was nothing "phony" about the war the Soviets launched against Finland a month after the fall of Poland. In October, Stalin extracted from the three Baltic states mutual assistance pacts, boundary revisions, and rights to construct bases. (In a revision of the nonaggression pact, Hitler had consigned Lithuania to the Soviet sphere in exchange for territory elsewhere.) Finland, however, proved less compliant to similar demands made to protect the exposed Russian city of Leningrad. During weeks of negotiations, Finland made some concessions but refused most of what the Soviets asked for. Taking a page from Hitler's book, Stalin staged a border "incident" as an excuse to launch a Soviet invasion of its smaller neighbor in late November.

The Winter War at first went badly for the Soviet Union. Purges and an unwieldy command system had reduced the quality of its officer corps, and its troops were poorly equipped and trained for fighting in heavy snow at subzero temperatures. The Finns, by contrast, were in their element. Fighting on their own terrain, using skis and sleds for mobility and white clothing for camouflage, they fended off much larger attacking forces. They also reduced Soviet air superiority by outfitting their aircraft with skis, which permitted them to operate even when enemy planes had to be grounded. But they could not prevent their cities from being bombed, nor could they do more than delay ultimate defeat without help from other powers.

Sympathy for Finland ran strong in the West. The League of Nations expelled the Soviet Union two weeks after the war began, and volunteers from Western nations joined the beleaguered Finns to fight the Russian bear. There was sentiment among some in the British and French governments to send expeditionary forces across Norway and Sweden to join the Finns. This operation, it was argued, would serve two purposes: It would bolster the Finnish struggle against Soviet aggression; at the same time, it would cut off German access to Sweden's high-quality iron ore. This scheme was as much born of the desire to do something against Germany on the cheap as it was designed to combat Soviet aggression. Germany would not have remained idle, and the Allies had no troops capable of fighting in Finland's winter weather. Fortunately for the Allies—and probably for Finland—it was discarded.

Public opinion in the United States also favored the Finns. It was compounded of sympathy for the underdog, anticommunism, and admiration for the one European nation that had continued to make payments on its debts from the Great War. Nonetheless, the desire to stay out of the conflict ran even stronger. Although President Roosevelt condemned the Soviet invasion as "wanton disregard for law," he was unable to do more than declare a moral embargo on war materials, which had no effect on the situation. Equally irrelevant, Congress made available to the Finns a small loan for purchases of nonmilitary goods. Such impotent gestures did nothing to help Finland and served merely to poison American relations with the Soviet Union.

Prospects for avoiding a global conflagration looked bleak by the end of 1939. Fighting raged in Finland and in the Far East, and it was no secret that Hitler was building up German strength for a massive attack against the West. The Allies and Germany waged war at sea, as each side sought to damage the other by naval blockade. For the United States, it seemed like the Great War all over again, only larger. Although some Americans held to the notion of a "phony war," most found no such comfort. They wished to help the democracies but not at the cost of American involvement. President Roosevelt took it upon himself to educate the public and Congress and convince them that American security would be threatened if the aggressor nations prevailed.

SELECTED BIBLIOGRAPHY

Bethell, Nicholas. *The War Hitler Won: The Fall of Poland* (New York: Holt, Rinehart and Winston, 1972).

Borg, Dorothy. *The United States and the Far Eastern Crisis of 1933–1938* (Cambridge, Mass.: Harvard University Press, 1964).

Brooke-Shepard, Gordon. *Anschluss: The Rape of Austria* (London: Macmillan, 1963).

Burns, James MacGregor. *Roosevelt: The Lion and the Fox* (New York: Harcourt, Brace, 1956).

Compton, James V. *The Swastika and the Eagle: Hitler, the United States and the Origins of World War II* (Boston: Houghton Mifflin, 1967).

Dallek, Robert. *Franklin D. Roosevelt and American Foreign Policy, 1932–1945* (New York: Oxford University Press, 1979).

Divine, Robert A. *The Illusion of Neutrality: Franklin D. Roosevelt and the Struggle over the Arms Embargo* (Chicago: University of Chicago Press, 1962).

Guttmann, Allen. *The Wound in the Heart: America and the Spanish Civil War* (New York: Free Press of Glencoe, 1962).

Jakobson, Max. *The Diplomacy of the Winter War, 1939–1940* (Cambridge, Mass.: Harvard University Press, 1961).

Little, Douglas. *Malevolent Neutrality: The United States, Great Britain, and the Origins of the Spanish Civil War* (Ithaca, N.Y.: Cornell University Press, 1985).

Lukacs, John. *The Last European War* (Garden City, N.Y.: Doubleday, 1976).

MacDonald, C. A. *The United States, Britain and Appeasement, 1936–1939* (New York: St. Martin's, 1981).

Mack Smith, Denis. *Mussolini's Roman Empire* (New York: Viking, 1976).

Marks, Frederick W., III. *Wind over Sand: The Diplomacy of Franklin Roosevelt* (Athens: University of Georgia Press, 1987).

Murray, Williamson. *The Changes in the European Balance of Power, 1938–1939: The Path to Ruin* (Princeton, N.J.: Princeton University Press, 1984).

Rich, Norman. *Hitler's War Aims: Ideology, the Nazi State and the Course of Expansion* (New York: W. W. Norton, 1973).

Schmitz, David F. *The United States and Fascist Italy* (Chapel Hill: University of North Carolina Press, 1988).

Tanner, V. A. *The Winter War: Finland Against Russia, 1939–1940* (Stanford, Calif.: Stanford University Press, 1957).

Taylor, Telford. *Munich: The Price of Peace* (Garden City, N.Y.: Doubleday, 1979).

Thomas, Hugh. *The Spanish Civil War* (New York: Harper & Brothers, 1961).

Thorne, Christopher. *The Approach of War, 1938–1939* (London: St. Martin's, 1967).

Traina, Richard P. *American Diplomacy and the Spanish Civil War* (Bloomington: Indiana University Press, 1968).

Watt, Donald Cameron. *How War Came: The Immediate Origins of the Second World War, 1938–1939* (New York: Pantheon Books, 1989).

Weinberg, Gerhard. *The Foreign Policy of Hitler's Germany: Starting World War II, 1937–1939* (Chicago: University of Chicago Press, 1980).

5
The Dark Days
(1940–1941)

The early months of 1940 produced great apprehension in Europe and in the United States. The Winter War dragged to its inevitable conclusion in March when Finland had to give the Soviets much greater concessions than originally demanded. What would happen next? Some in the West still held to the forlorn belief in a "phony war." Without abandoning the slender hope that accommodation might be reached, the governments of France and Great Britain prepared for war and strengthened their naval blockade of Germany. Hitler, after some indecision, ended the uncertainty. Germany struck against Denmark and Norway in April and against France one month later. The success of the blitzkrieg exceeded expectations as France was knocked out of the war in a matter of weeks. Failure to subdue Britain in the months following, however, led Hitler to his most fateful decision: the invasion of Soviet Russia. As these events unfolded, President Roosevelt led a deeply divided nation into ever-greater support for Hitler's enemies.

SECURING THE NORTHERN FLANK

Hitler originally had planned to concentrate his forces for massive assaults against Holland, Belgium, and France as soon as weather permitted. Some of his advisers warned that a failure to seize Norway and Denmark first would leave the German right flank exposed. They also advised him that British occupation of these nations would threaten access to Swedish iron ore and deny Germany U-boat and air bases from which to harass Allied shipping. After some hesitation, Hitler decided to secure the Scandinavian countries before launching his major offensive.

On April 10, Germany invaded Denmark and put troops ashore in several places along the Norwegian coast. The Danes surrendered almost immediately as their tiny, lightly armed militia put up only sporadic resistance. Norway proved less obliging. Although initially unprepared for landings and parachute drops, the Norwegians regrouped around the king and the government in the northern part of the country. The British, who had no coherent plan despite repeated discussions on the subject, mounted hastily devised operations to bolster this resistance. Under trying circumstances (British troops were untrained and ill equipped for winter fighting), the Anglo-Norwegian forces acquitted themselves well. In late May, they succeeded in recapturing the key port city of Narvik. Norway was lost by default in early June, however, when Allied troops were withdrawn in the futile effort to stave off defeat in France.

Victory in Scandinavia contributed to the aura of German invincibility. With few exceptions, their campaigns were conducted efficiently, particularly with regard to coordination of sea, land, and air power. Hitler had secured his northern flank, as well as bases and access to raw materials. But his success came at a price. Germany suffered heavy naval losses it could ill afford, and, less obvious at the time, the occupation of Norway and Denmark pinned down several hundred thousand German troops for most of the war.

British errors and setbacks in Norway precipitated a debate in the House of Commons that led to the downfall of Neville Chamberlain's Conservative government even before the campaign ended. Winston S. Churchill was named prime minister of an all-party government on May 10. Sixty-five years old, the controversial Churchill had been a prominent public figure for forty years. Having switched parties several times, he had a reputation for inconsistency, but he had adamantly opposed Chamberlain's policy of appeasement toward Hitler. Considered by some to be a warmonger during peacetime, Churchill's forceful character made him an appealing choice when the threat he predicted became real. Although unable to alter the course of events in the short run, he proved to be an able, energetic, and inspiring wartime leader.

WAR IN THE WEST

As the fighting for Norway went on, French and British forces moved into defensive positions. The southern portion of France's eastern frontier was protected by the Maginot line, a massive system of fortifications in depth that was considered impregnable to assault. The Maginot line ended along the border with Luxembourg, but that region was deemed unsuitable for large-scale German offensive operations because of the heavily forested Ardennes mountains. Allied military leaders expected the main German thrust to come through Holland and Belgium to the north, as had happened at the beginning of the Great War. Documents obtained when a German plane crashed in Belgian territory the previous January bolstered this assumption.

Hitler originally had approved just such a plan of battle, but the loss of those documents helped convince him to adopt an alternative advocated by General Erich von Manstein. Manstein argued that to do what the British and French expected would play to their strength. He believed that a major offensive could be launched through the allegedly impassable Ardennes and proposed that the most powerful German forces, especially armor, be concentrated there. The invasion of Holland and Belgium, according to his plan, would draw French and British troops northward, while the main attack from the Ardennes drove toward the English Channel, cutting Allied defenses in two. A third army group would move against the Maginot line. Its mission was not to breach the line by headlong assault but to keep French troops stationed behind it in place. Manstein's strategy posed greater risks, but it also promised huge rewards at a low cost if successful.

Hitler's long-awaited invasion, launched on May 10, exceeded expectations. The Germans smashed across Holland and, through the imaginative use of parachutists and glider-borne troops, took Belgian fortresses that were counted on to block them until relief arrived. The British Expeditionary Force (BEF) and seventeen of the most mobile French divisions moving into Belgium and Holland advanced with great difficulty, due to the canals and other obstacles. Vainly trying to protect their neutrality, the Dutch and Belgians had refused to permit Franco-British forces to cross their borders before the invasion began, and they lacked coordinated defensive plans. By May 15, the Dutch surrendered, and the Germans had driven a large wedge into Belgium.

The war was won in the central sector. Powerful German panzer divisions plunged west against light opposition, then swung north to trap Anglo-French forces moving into Belgium and Holland. Only ten days after the battle began, spearheads had reached the Channel. The Germans spent the next two weeks strengthening their flanks against counterattacks and preparing offensives against the bulk of French forces to the south. On June 5, coordinated thrusts sent French forces reeling, and by June 14, German troops entered Paris. Fighting continued for several days, but the French government (now located in Bordeaux) was ready to capitulate. On June 22, at the very location where the armistice of 1918 was signed, French representatives accepted German terms. The Great War had lasted more than four years; Hitler's blitzkrieg succeeded in only forty-two days.

Belgian refugees, ca. 1940. (National Archives photo no. W&C 995)

At the outset, the opposing armies had seemed more or less evenly matched. Combined Allied forces outnumbered the Germans in manpower and in tanks (though they possessed fewer modern aircraft) and presumably enjoyed the advantage of holding defensive positions. German equipment was superior in most categories but not overwhelmingly so. In reality, Germany won so easily because of superior planning, imaginative leadership, and the quality of its troops. France and Great Britain had reacted to Manstein's plan just as expected and were unable to adjust as the situation unfolded. The French commander in chief, General Maurice Gamelin, was indecisive and out of touch with his subordinates most of the time. He was sacked nine days after the fighting began,

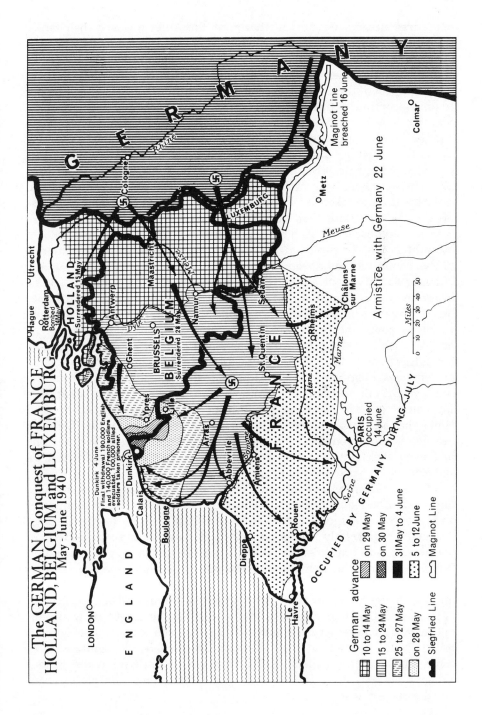

The GERMAN Conquest of FRANCE
HOLLAND, BELGIUM and LUXEMBURG
May – June 1940

German advance

10 to 14 May	
15 to 24 May	
25 to 27 May	
on 28 May	
on 29 May	
on 30 May	
31 May to 4 June	
5 to 12 June	
Maginot Line	
Siegfried Line	

OCCUPIED BY GERMANY DURING JULY

Armistice with Germany 22 June

Maginot Line breached 16 June

Miles
0 10 20 30 40 50

Dunkirk 4 June
Final withdrawal 190,000 English
and 140,000 French soldiers
evacuated. 100,000 allied
soldiers taken prisoner.

HOLLAND Surrendered 15 May
Rotterdam Bombed 14 May

BELGIUM Surrendered 28 May

PARIS occupied 14 June

but it was already too late. Furthermore, the Allies misused their tanks, throwing them piecemeal against massed German armor. Finally, although many French divisions fought well, others proved unreliable in combat and left gaping holes that the Germans were quick to exploit.

One aspect of the German campaign remains unclear. Had the advance columns continued pushing nort.. ¬fter they reached the Channel on May 20, they might have destroyed Allied forces caught between them and the army group pushing down from Belgium and Holland. On May 24, however, Hitler ordered his armored units to stand in place. This pause permitted the BEF to reach Dunkirk on the Channel. From May 27 to June 4, a massive evacuation of British, French, and other Allied troops was undertaken by ships of the British Home Fleet and countless private vessels. More than 338,000 soldiers, about two-thirds of them British, were rescued. This heroic endeavor under fire, though necessitated by military defeat, provided a boost to badly damaged British morale in the trying months ahead.

Hitler's motives for stopping his tanks can only be surmised. Some historians have suggested that he deliberately spared the BEF in hopes he could gain a negotiated peace with Great Britain. Hitler had mixed emotions about the British and on several occasions indicated that he had no wish to destroy their overseas empire, provided they would give him a free hand in Europe. Another explanation is that he underestimated his enemies' demoralization and feared that counterattacks from the south might fall on his tanks, striking from the rear. Finally, some have suggested that Hermann Goering, head of the Luftwaffe, convinced Hitler that air strikes alone could destroy Allied forces on the Dunkirk beaches without committing armor across difficult terrain. Neither one had even the faintest notion that British rescue operations could be carried out on such a scale.

The fall of France had worldwide implications. Hitler now dominated Europe and had gained access to enormous new reservoirs of manpower and resources. Italy joined the war by attacking France after the German onslaught began. Italy was not a first-class power, but an Italo-German partnership posed a threat to the entire Mediterranean region, including Britain's lifeline through the Suez Canal. The third member of the Tripartite Pact, Japan, clearly intended to exploit the Allied defeat in Europe, though precisely how was not known. If it moved against British, French, and Dutch possessions in the Far East, it might deny Britain raw materials necessary for survival. And as the already beleaguered British could not defend their interests everywhere, the United States confronted a painful dilemma. Inaction would undermine the British and give the Japanese a free hand in Asia. Greater involvement, however, ran the risk of war.

British prisoners at Dunkirk, France, June 1940. (National Archives photo no. W&C 999)

THE BATTLE OF BRITAIN

Great Britain stood alone against the Nazi war machine that had swept all before it. Fortifications against invasion were nonexistent, and British army units were stationed in various parts of the world defending the empire. The BEF had returned from France but had lost its tanks and other heavy equipment at Dunkirk. Consequently, the defense of the home islands depended on the English Channel, the Royal Navy, and the Royal Air Force (RAF).

Hitler in Paris, June 23, 1940. (National Archives photo no. W&C 998)

Hitler might have accepted British offers of accommodation during the summer of 1940, but none was forthcoming. In the interim, he ordered preparations for an invasion without committing himself to it: There were too many imponderables. German admirals, for instance, protested that their navy lacked the strength—especially after the Norwegian campaign—to protect an invasion armada against the Royal Navy unless the Luftwaffe attained complete air superiority. The same argument was made against the potential success of a naval blockade. Germany had fewer than sixty submarines available, only half of which could be operational at any given time. An effective blockade required both U-boats and surface raiders. And surface raiders were prey to superior British naval forces, as proven earlier by the loss of the pocket battleship *Graf Spee* in late 1939.

Massive air attacks, strongly advocated by Marshal Goering, appeared to provide the solution. At best, these alone would bring Great Britain to the peace table on Hitler's terms. Failing that, they still could serve a crucial function. If the British used up their fighter strength against enemy bombers, Luftwaffe air supremacy would enable Hitler to launch an invasion, institute a more damaging naval blockade, or both. He accepted Goering's advice.

Fortunately for Britain, the Luftwaffe was unsuited for the task. Created as a component of blitzkrieg, it possessed no heavy bombers. Medium and light bombers and the dreaded Stuka had proved devastating in support of ground operations, but in attacking cities such as Rotterdam and Warsaw, they encountered little or no opposition in the air. Relatively slow and lightly armed and armored, all were extremely vulnerable to modern fighters like the British Spitfires and Hurricanes. Nor was Germany's basic fighter, the Messerschmidt 109, designed for strategic bombing. It was equal to the Spitfire and better than the Hurricane, but its short range limited its effectiveness as a bomber escort.

On July 10, the Luftwaffe began attacking shipping in the English Channel, partly to determine British air strength and tactics. In mid-August, operations were broadened to include airfields and radar stations. What fighter strength the Germans could not destroy on the ground they hoped to lure into the air for decisive battles. This strategy promised success. The Royal Air Force shot down roughly twice as many German planes as it lost but suffered more heavily in the all-important category of fighters. By the end of August, losses threatened to outstrip production, and trained pilots were in short supply.

At the end of the first week in September, Germany switched its emphasis from attacking airfields to bombing London and other British cities. (Sorties against radar stations had ended several weeks earlier.) This decision appears to have been made for two reasons. Wildly exaggerated estimates of British losses led Goering and Hitler to believe that the RAF's Fighter Command had been depleted, and a British raid on Berlin, ineffective though it was, goaded Hitler into retaliation. It was a case of error piling upon error, for the British had responded to an unintended raid on London that had been caused by navigational miscalculation. In any case, the change in strategy may be regarded as one of the major German mistakes of the war. Indeed, some historians believe the RAF would have been rendered ineffective had the Germans continued focusing on airfields, command posts, and radar installations.

This picture of London's dock area, taken during the first mass air raid on London, September 7, 1940, describes more than words ever could. Tower Bridge stands out against a background of smoke and fire. (National Archives photo no. W&C 1004)

The Battle of Britain lasted little more than a month, peaking in the last weeks of September with huge raids on London and other cities. By this time, Fighter Command had fewer than 300 operational fighters to send against the Germans. But the Luftwaffe caved in first under the constant hemorrhaging of planes and men. Morale plummeted as losses mounted, and pilots became exhausted from the number of sorties they were ordered to fly. Unlike the British, who could parachute to safety from damaged planes, German pilots and crews knew that, at best, they could expect to be interned for the duration. Worst of all, from the standpoint of Luftwaffe personnel, their sacrifices bore no fruit. British resolve did not weaken, and the much-awaited invasion never was launched. Hitler postponed the operation several times, then canceled it altogether. Germany continued nighttime bombing but on a far smaller scale. Britain had won its battle in the air.

Credit for victory belonged to many, the courageous and skilled RAF pilots being only the most obvious. A sophisticated system of radar installations and coastal observation posts gave Fighter Command the information necessary to locate and intercept German bomber formations. And the strategy adopted by Fighter Command's leaders, air marshals Hugh Dowding and Keith Park, also contributed. Quite aware that the

Germans were trying to destroy British fighter strength by attrition, Dowding and Park resisted the temptation to put as many planes in the air as possible to defend their people. Unfortunately, their conservation of aircraft and pilots earned them criticism rather than praise at the time, and both were forced out of their posts.

THE BATTLE AT SEA AND AMERICAN INVOLVEMENT

Though it was less spectacular than the air battle over Britain, Germany's U-boat campaign proved to be the greater threat in the long run. The German navy lacked enough submarines at the start of the war for quick results, but increased production in the following months resulted in grievous losses to British shipping. With their possession of the western coasts of France and Norway, the Germans were able to construct submarine bases and sow mines, provide relatively safe haven for surface raiders, and greatly extend the scope of air reconnaissance and attack. In addition to vessels sunk by U-boats, British shipping was further strained by having to make long detours to reduce losses around Channel ports.

President Roosevelt was moved by Britain's plight to render aid that caused great controversy in a still badly divided United States. On June 10, 1940, in Charlottesville, Virginia, Roosevelt stated publicly that the United States could not remain a "lone island in a world dominated by the philosophy of force." He went on to say that he intended to make American resources available to the opponents of aggressors. This he proceeded to do in a series of steps, the most explosive of which was the destroyer-for-bases deal in September. Responding to Winston Churchill's pleas for help against U-boats, Roosevelt, by executive agreement, turned over to Great Britain fifty World War I destroyers in return for ninety-nine-year leases on naval and air bases in British possessions such as Newfoundland and Jamaica. The administration naturally emphasized the value of the bases to the United States, rather than the nonneutrality of giving one side military equipment in the midst of war. Such actions, together with the passage that month of the selective service act—the draft—convinced many that Roosevelt was leading the nation into war.

FDR's critics were a mixed bag of traditional isolationists, pacifists, and some anti-Semites who blamed the war on an alleged Jewish conspiracy. The America First Committee embraced these groups. It counted among its members powerful senators and newspaper publishers, and its leading spokesman was Charles A. Lindbergh, "The Lone Eagle," who had attained heroic stature by making the first solo flight across the Atlantic. Because the Nazi-Soviet pact was still in effect, pro-Communists joined with pro-Fascists to deny aid to Britain.

The America Firsters were opposed by the awkwardly named Committee to Defend America by Aiding the Allies, headed initially by the well-known journalist William Allen White. The organization, as its title suggests, supported Roosevelt's contention that the best way to keep the United States out of war was by supporting the democracies in Europe. The majority of Americans supported this view. Despite the destroyer-for-bases deal's blatant violation of neutrality, a Gallup poll taken at the time revealed that 62 percent of those queried supported it; 38 percent opposed it.

The presidential election of 1940 failed to provide a referendum on the issue because the Republicans nominated a liberal, Wendell Willkie, who also supported sending aid to the Allies. Both candidates promised to keep the United States out of the fight. Only toward the end of the campaign, when Roosevelt's reelection to a third term seemed assured, did Willkie challenge him directly by promising never to send American boys to fight in a European war. Roosevelt was stung to respond, pledging to the American people that "your boys are not going to be sent into any foreign wars." His words did not reassure those who believed his policies made war inevitable.

Roosevelt's victory in November encouraged him to believe the people supported his foreign policies thus far and emboldened him to do more. In late December, he referred to the United States as the "arsenal of democracy," and a week later, he sent to Congress what became known as the lend-lease bill, significantly numbered H.R. 1776. Calling for an original appropriation of $7 billion—astronomical for the time—this bill would enable Roosevelt to "lease, lend, or otherwise dispose of" supplies and equipment, including military hardware, to those nations whose defense he deemed vital to American security.

The significance of the lend-lease bill is difficult to exaggerate, amounting as it did to a declaration of economic warfare against the Axis powers. Opponents responded with fury, denouncing the bill as a giant step down the path to full involvement. They had reason. FDR must have known lend-lease would increase the chances of being dragged in, but he believed that America's stake in Britain's survival justified the risk.

Roosevelt's handling of the campaign for passage was superb. He emphasized that lend-lease would provide others with the means necessary to fight the aggressors, thereby keeping the war far from American shores. He defused the issue of repayment, which had caused so much bitterness after the last war, with a homely example: He likened his program to lending a garden hose to a neighbor whose house is on fire, the spread of which threatens one's own home; the hose is returned after the fire is put out. His analogy was simple but misleading. Planes and tanks are destroyed or worn out in combat, and their return or replacement during peacetime would be of little value. One senator put it more accurately when he said that lending military supplies was like lending chewing gum: "You don't want it back." But such complaints were made in vain. Both houses of Congress passed the bill by large majorities, and polls revealed strong public support. Roosevelt signed the lend-lease bill into law on March 11, 1941.

Roosevelt's dubious claim that lend-lease decreased the chances of involvement typified his leadership in the months following. He sought public and congressional support for his policies and usually won it through justifications he knew were disingenuous, if not completely false. Afraid of being repudiated if he went too far, he also kept some of his actions hidden from scrutiny. During the weeks when lend-lease was being debated, for instance, British and American military planners held secret talks in Washington. They discussed aid requirements and military coordination if the United States joined the Allies, and they agreed that the defeat of Germany would be the first objective, even if Japan entered the conflict. It must be emphasized that Roosevelt did not seek war, but he was prepared to take whatever steps necessary to prevent an Axis victory because he believed it would jeopardize the vital security interests of the United States.

OPERATION BARBAROSSA

In *Mein Kampf* and in conversations with subordinates, Hitler made it clear that his ultimate territorial goal was to acquire lebensraum (living space) in the east. The Nazi-Soviet pact of 1939 was a tactical move to avoid a two-front war while he dealt with the Western Allies. Hitler would have been free to invade the Soviet Union at his pleasure had the British caved in after the defeat of France. But their refusal do to so convinced him that they hung on in anticipation of Soviet and American help. He therefore decided to invade Russia first. Soviet defeat not only would secure Germany its lebensraum, it would also free Japan to act more boldly in the Far East, which he believed would divert American attention from Europe. Deprived of both its erstwhile allies, Great Britain would become an easy prey. In December 1940, Hitler issued a directive for the invasion of the Soviet Union the following May. The operation was designated BARBAROSSA, after a medieval German emperor.

Hitler anticipated the invasion would succeed in a matter of months, despite the vast distances involved. He regarded Slavic peoples as inferior and was contemptuous of their "Jew-Bolshevik" leadership. He knew, moreover, that Stalin had instituted massive purges of the Soviet officer corps during the 1930s; that these purges had crippled military effectiveness seemed obvious during the botched war against Finland. Events would show that Hitler underestimated his enemy's productive capacity and the quality of its military equipment. He envisioned a repetition of the campaigns against Poland and France on a larger scale: Rapid thrusts spearheaded by armor would penetrate, isolate, and destroy Soviet armies, after which territory could be taken at will.

Hitler's schedule was thrown off by his ally, Benito Mussolini, who would prove a burden through most of the war. Mussolini, jealous of Hitler's triumphs and anxious to share the spoils, had launched an invasion of Greece in October 1940. Hitler initially approved of Mussolini's action but quickly regretted it when the Greeks sent Italian armies staggering in retreat. British aid to Greece prompted Hitler to rescue his ally, even though this meant diverting forces. Efforts to protect the German flanks for the campaign in Greece led, in turn, to a confrontation with Yugoslavia. In April 1941, Hitler invaded and quickly overwhelmed both Greece and Yugoslavia. The campaign may have been far more costly than he could have imagined for it delayed the launching of BARBAROSSA more than a month.

German preparations for the massive assault against Russia soon became obvious: Troop movements, the massing of armor and supplies, and the preparation of airfields could not be concealed. Through a variety of intelligence sources, the United States and Great Britain learned of the buildup and, as the time drew near, even knew the date on which BARBAROSSA would begin. Roosevelt and Churchill repeatedly tried to impress upon Stalin the danger he faced, to enable him to prepare for the onslaught, and Moscow received the same information independently, including reports from its own agents. Stalin's refusal to act on the signals he received from so many quarters has intrigued historians ever since.

Stalin was a treacherous man who assumed everyone else was equally treacherous. He did not trust Hitler, but he so feared war with Germany that he convinced himself it could be prevented in the immediate future, provided the Soviet Union gave Germany no cause. Despite friction over boundaries and spheres of influence, for instance, Stalin scrupulously adhered to agreements providing for shipments of raw materials to fuel the Nazi war machine. Indeed, Soviet freight trains were puffing westward on the day BARBAROSSA was launched. Unwilling to recognize the obvious, Stalin chose to believe the preposterous German disinformation that Hitler intended to invade Great Britain and was building up forces in the east merely to keep them outside British bombing range. All the signs pointing to a German assault on the Soviet Union, he concluded, were part of a monstrous Anglo-American plot to provoke war between his nation and Germany. As BARBAROSSA approached, interrogations of German deserters and increased Luftwaffe flights over Soviet territory appeared to confirm the earlier information, but they still failed to puncture Stalin's illusions.

In the early hours of June 22, 1941, German forces, augmented by Hungarian, Romanian, and Finnish allies, launched the most massive military operation in history until that time. More than 3 million men, as well as thousands of tanks, aircraft, and artillery pieces, were thrown against Soviet Russia in a three-pronged invasion across a front of almost two thousand miles. Army Group North, under Field Marshal Ritter von Leeb, crashed through the Baltic states toward Leningrad; Field Marshal Fedor von Bock's Army Group Center advanced on Smolensk and Moscow; and Army Group South, commanded by Field Marshal Gerd von Rundstedt, moved into the southern regions that contained important sources of grain, coal, and oil. As in Poland and France, panzer spearheads pierced defensive lines, isolating Soviet forces into pockets to be overwhelmed by the advancing German infantry. Hitler's goal was to destroy Russian armies as far west as possible, thereby preventing them from regrouping in the interior.

German offensives exceeded expectations during the first four weeks of fighting. The Soviets outnumbered the Germans in almost every category, especially manpower, but many divisions were poorly trained, and large numbers of tanks and aircraft were obsolete. Soviet officers and their troops were taken by complete surprise when the invasion began, and units under attack were at first denied permission to return fire. The speed of German thrusts disoriented the Soviets, preventing efforts to coordinate defensive operations. Meanwhile, the Luftwaffe destroyed huge numbers of aircraft on the ground and in the air and created havoc with enemy communications. Russian troops suffered enormous casualties and surrendered by the hundreds of thousands. But this was not to be a repetition of the campaign in France. Despite hideous losses, the Soviets continued to hurl men, tanks, and planes against the invaders with dismaying ferocity.

Beginning in mid-July, the Germans paused for almost a month to reconsider their strategy. Several problems had become obvious: Rapid advances stretched supply lines and widened the length of the front, fast-moving panzer units in many areas were far ahead of supporting infantry, and some of the larger Soviet pockets of resistance still had not been destroyed. German armor commanders wanted to continue their offensives, especially against Moscow, to keep the Soviets off balance. But Hitler and some of his more cautious generals were worried

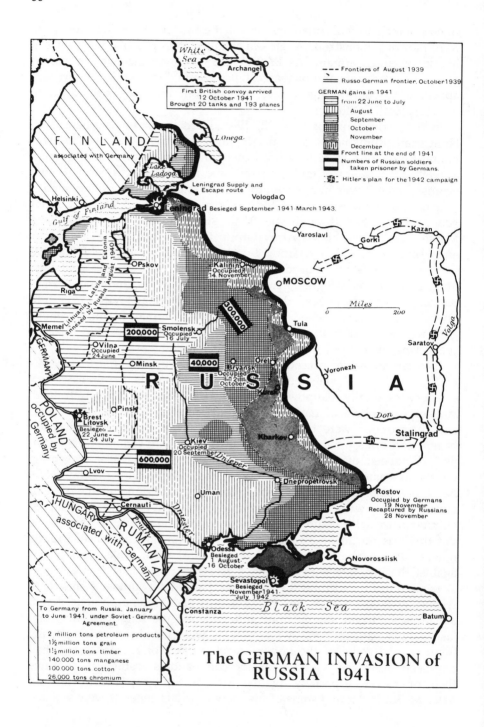

White Sea

Archangel

FINLAND
associated with Germany

L. Onega

Lake Ladoga

First British convoy arrived
12 October 1941
Brought 20 tanks and 193 planes

Leningrad Supply and
Escape route

Helsinki

Vologda

Gulf of Finland

Leningrad Besieged September 1941-March 1943.

- - - Frontiers of August 1939
≡≡≡ Russo-German frontier, October 1939
GERMAN gains in 1941
from 22 June to July
August
September
October
November
December
Front line at the end of 1941
Numbers of Russian soldiers
taken prisoner by Germans.
Hitler's plan for the 1942 campaign

Yaroslavl
Gorki
Kazan

Pskov

Kalinin
Occupied
14 November

MOSCOW

Miles
0   200

Riga

Lithuania, Latvia and Estonia
annexed by Russia August 1940

Memel

200,000

Smolensk
Occupied
16 July

Tula

Saratov

Vilna
Occupied
24 June

300,000

40,000

Orel

Voronezh

Volga

Minsk

R   U   S   S   I   A

Bryansk
Occupied
in 2nd
October

Kursk

GERMANY

Pinsk

Brest
Litovsk
Besieged
22 June-
24 July

Kharkov

Don

Stalingrad

POLAND
occupied by
Germany

Lvov

Kiev
Occupied
20 September

Dnieper

Rostov
Occupied by Germans
19 November
Recaptured by Russians
28 November

600,000

Dnepropetrovsk

HUNGARY
associated with Germany

Cernauti

Uman

Dniester

RUMANIA

Prut

Odessa
Besieged
1 August-
16 October

Novorossiisk

To Germany from Russia. January
to June 1941. under Soviet-German
Agreement.

2 million tons petroleum products
1½ million tons grain
1½ million tons timber
140 000 tons manganese
100 000 tons cotton
26 000 tons chromium

Constanza

Sevastopol
Besieged
November 1941-
July 1942

Black   Sea

Batum

The GERMAN INVASION of RUSSIA 1941

that the Soviets might drive wedges between the forward panzer units and their support and use guerrilla warfare to cut off supply and communication lines.

Hitler acted indecisively at this juncture. First, he weakened the Army Group Center by diverting most of its armor, sending part of it north toward Leningrad and part of it south to the Ukraine. A few weeks later, he sent it back again and ordered simultaneous drives in the center and south. The renewed offensives temporarily threatened to overwhelm the battered Soviet defenders, but the pause may have been decisive. Heavy autumn rains turned roads into quagmires that bogged down German armor and transport. Then, temperatures dropped suddenly, creating subzero conditions for which neither the German troops nor their equipment had been prepared. During this time, Stalin, having been persuaded by Soviet intelligence that Japan would not attack in the east, transferred divisions from the crack Siberian army to throw into the struggle. By December, the Germans had bogged down only 20 miles from Moscow, and the Soviets began launching counterattacks in several sectors. The Nazi juggernaut had suffered its first major setback of the war.

Hitler had expected the Soviet Union to fall apart when he kicked it. He was mistaken. In some areas, such as the Ukraine, many inhabitants welcomed German troops as liberators from the tyranny of Moscow, but such notions were quickly disabused by the savage treatment they received, particularly at the hands of SS (Schutzstaffel) units. On the whole, the Soviet people and armed forces proved willing to endure unbelievable hardships and losses. They did so out of patriotism, not a belief in communism—a fact that Stalin recognized early on when he appealed to them publicly as "brothers and sisters," rather than as "comrades." The Soviet Union not only inflicted upon Hitler his first defeat in the winter of 1941–1942 but it bore the brunt of the fighting throughout the war.

THE UNITED STATES MOVES CLOSER TO WAR

Germany's invasion of the Soviet Union emboldened President Roosevelt to take further steps against Nazi Germany. Senator Harry S. Truman voiced a common sentiment when he stated that the United States should let the dictatorships fight it out, only helping whichever side was losing. Roosevelt knew better. If Hitler subdued Russia, he would have the resources of the continent at his disposal to use against Great Britain. The president therefore resolved to provide what support he could to the Soviets as well as to the British, within the limitations imposed by a still-divided public and Congress. On occasion, he proved willing to exceed these limitations.

Roosevelt quickly extended lend-lease to Russia after Hitler's invasion. Though months would elapse before the pipeline could begin providing materials in quantity and though his military advisers doubted the Soviets could hold on that long, he hoped even the gesture of support would boost morale. This move at first sparked controversy because many Americans, in addition to being anti-Communist, were repelled by Soviet acts like the pact with Germany and the war against Finland. Attitudes began to change as Russia's heroic resistance continued, but a residue of distrust remained.

In August, FDR met with Prime Minister Churchill off the coast of Newfoundland. At the end of the conference, the two men issued what became known as the Atlantic Charter, a statement of general principles reminiscent of Woodrow Wilson's Fourteen Points. It called for self-determination, freedom of the seas, equal access to world trade and resources, and an end to the use of force in international affairs. It also proclaimed as a goal "the final destruction of the Nazi tyranny." Because the charter was not a formal treaty providing for specific actions, Roosevelt could proclaim American solidarity with Great Britain without requiring congressional approval.

During the last six months of 1941, FDR led the United States into virtual cobelligerency with Great Britain in the battle of the Atlantic. He did so in stages, often using incidents resulting from one stage to gain support for the next. American naval vessels had for some time been tracking U-boats and radioing their whereabouts to the British. In July, the United States occupied Iceland and began convoying merchant vessels to adjacent waters. When a German submarine fired two torpedoes at the American destroyer *Greer* in September, Roosevelt used this as a pretext to announce a "shoot-on-sight" policy. He neglected to mention that the *Greer* had been tailing the U-boat for several hours. He similarly manipulated American opinion following an attack on the destroyer *Kearny* and the sinking of the *Reuben James* in October. In the next month, he succeeded in having Congress remove virtually all restrictions on American shipping. His critics protested in vain.

By December 1941, the United States was involved in an undeclared shooting war at sea. Under any measure of traditional neutrality, Roosevelt had given Hitler ample provocation for a declaration of war. Germany protested American actions, of course, but refrained from doing more. Locked in the enormous struggle with Russia, Hitler had no wish to confront the United States, as well. The issue was resolved when the Japanese attacked Pearl Harbor on December 7.

SELECTED BIBLIOGRAPHY

Bailey, Thomas A., and Paul B. Ryan. *Hitler vs. Roosevelt: Undeclared Naval War* (New York: Free Press, 1979).

Bialer, Seweryn (ed.). *Stalin and His Generals: Soviet Military Memoirs of World War II* (Boulder, Colo.: Westview, 1984).

Calvocoressi, Peter, and Guy Wint. *Total War* (New York: Penguin, 1979).

Chapman, Guy. *Why France Fell: The Defeat of the French Army in 1940* (New York: Holt, Rinehart and Winston, 1968).

Clark, Alan. *Barbarossa: The Russian-German Conflict, 1941–1945* (New York: William Morrow, 1965).

Cole, Wayne S. *Charles A. Lindbergh and the Battle Against American Intervention in World War II* (New York: Harcourt, Brace, Jovanovich, 1974).

———. *Roosevelt and the Isolationists* (Lincoln: University of Nebraska Press, 1983).

Deighton, Len. *Fighter: The True Story of the Battle of Britain* (New York: Knopf, 1977).

Dziewanowski, M. K. *War at Any Price*, 2d ed. (Englewood Cliffs, N.J.: Prentice-Hall, 1990).

Ellis, John. *Brute Force: Allied Strategy and Tactics in the Second World War* (New York: Viking, 1990).

Erickson, John. *Stalin's War with Germany: The Road to Stalingrad* (Boulder, Colo.: Westview, 1975).

Fleming, Peter. *Operation Sea Lion* (New York: Simon & Schuster, 1957).

Fraser, David. *And We Shall Shock Them: The British Army and the Second World War* (London: Hodder and Stoughton, 1983).

Fuller, J.F.C. *The Second World War: A Strategic and Tactical History* (New York: Meredith, 1968).

Gilbert, Martin. *The Life of Winston Churchill*, 8 vols. (Boston: Houghton Mifflin, 1966–1986).

———. *The Second World War: A Complete History* (New York: Henry Holt, 1989).

Guderian, Heinz. *Panzer Leader* (London: Michael Joseph, 1952).

Horne, Alistair. *To Lose a Battle: France, 1940* (New York: Macmillan, 1969).

Hughes, Terry, and John Costello. *The Battle of the Atlantic* (New York: Dial, 1977).

Keegan, John. *The Second World War* (New York: Viking, 1990).

Kimball, Warren. *The Most Unsordid Act* (Baltimore, Md.: Johns Hopkins University Press, 1969).

Kitchen, Martin. *A World in Flames: A Short History of the Second World War in Europe and Asia, 1939–1945* (New York: Longman, 1990).

Leutze, James R. *Bargaining for Supremacy* (Chapel Hill: University of North Carolina Press, 1977).

Liddell Hart, Basil. *History of the Second World War* (New York: Putnam, 1971).

Lukacs, John. *The Last European War* (Garden City, N.Y.: Doubleday, 1976).

———— . *The Duel, 10 May–31 July 1940: The Eighty-Day Struggle Between Churchill and Hitler* (New York: Ticknor and Fields, 1991).

Petrow, Richard. *The Bitter Years: The Invasion and Occupation of Denmark and Norway, April 1940–May 1945* (New York: William Morrow, 1979).

Seaton, Albert. *The Russo-German War, 1941–1945* (New York: Praeger, 1970).

Stokesbury, James L. *A Short History of World War II* (New York: William Morrow, 1980).

Taylor, Telford. *March of Conquest: The German Victories in Western Europe, 1940* (New York: Simon & Schuster, 1958).

———— . *The Breaking Wave* (New York: Simon & Schuster, 1965).

Terraine, John. *A Time for Courage: The Royal Air Force in the European War, 1939–1945* (New York: Macmillan, 1985).

Wheatley, Ronald. *Operation Sea Lion: German Plans for the Invasion of Britain* (New York: Oxford University Press, 1958).

Wilmot, Chester. *Struggle for Europe* (New York: Harper & Row, 1952).

Wilson, Theodore. *The First Summit* (Boston: Houghton Mifflin, 1969).

Wright, Gordon. *The Ordeal of Total War* (New York: Harper & Row, 1968).

Ziemke, E. F. *The German Northern Theater of Operations, 1940–1945* (Washington, D.C.: Department of the Army, 1959).

6
Japan Strikes
(1939–1941)

The Japanese invasion of China in 1937 had failed to bring victory. Their armed forces had won almost every battle, and by 1939, they held most of North China and port cities on the east coast. But they were stymied by the vast distances involved, rather than by military opposition, as the Chinese government retreated to the remote city of Chungking in the interior, beyond the reach of Japanese ground forces. Meanwhile, militants in Tokyo sought to exploit European distress both to end the Chinese resistance and to expand the Japanese empire. President Roosevelt's unwillingness to acquiesce in the face of Japan's actions ultimately led to war. And the attack on Pearl Harbor fused what had been two separate wars into a truly global conflict.

JAPANESE-AMERICAN RELATIONS DETERIORATE

Polls revealed that most Americans opposed Japan's bloody war against China, but disagreement existed over what course the United States should follow. Many people expressed sympathy for the Chinese, but above all, they did not want to be dragged into any conflict. FDR's refusal to invoke neutrality legislation in 1937 had come under attack because it clearly was intended to assist China. Roosevelt himself vacillated during the following years, but he was determined to keep China afloat. As in the case of aiding Great Britain, however, he had to move cautiously to avoid alienating public and congressional support.

China's ability to continue the war depended heavily upon supplies imported from abroad. Most of the material flowed through French Indochina, British Hong Kong, and over the Burma Road. Successive crises in Europe encouraged the Japanese to move against these routes without worrying about French or British reprisals. Following the Munich crisis of September 1938, the Japanese seized China's southern ports, and a few months later, after Hitler destroyed what remained of Czechoslovakia, they occupied the Chinese island of Hainen in the Gulf of Tonkin in order to interdict shipping from French Indochina. One by one, China's lifelines were being cut.

Roosevelt was caught in a bind. Aside from words, which had been unavailing, the only tool he had to use against the Japanese was an economic one. Yet, his failure to invoke neutrality legislation cut both ways. Although the Chinese were able to secure badly needed goods in the United States, Japan also was buying enormous amounts of oil, gasoline, and scrap metals for its war effort. Restrictions applied exclusively against the Japanese would have violated the existing Japanese-American commercial treaty. In July 1939, therefore, Roosevelt took the significant step of notifying Japan that he was unilaterally abrogating the treaty. As provided for in the agreement, abrogation would take effect six months later, on January 26, 1940. He intended to serve notice to Japan that continued provocation might lead to economic sanctions.

The wisdom of imposing trade restrictions or embargoes against Japan would be debated through 1940 and 1941, as it had been during the Manchurian crisis. Advocates of such a policy based their arguments on two grounds. First, they said, it was immoral to sell strategic supplies that would be used to wage war against innocent people. On a more practical level, they hoped that denying these materials would so damage the Japanese economy as to make obvious the folly of continued aggression. Critics of sanctions predicted the opposite effect. To the extent that the Japanese economy suffered, they warned, militants would be strengthened in their determination to end Japan's reliance on imported raw materials. Their nation would be encouraged to acquire its own sources by conquest, even if this meant risking a general war. Events would prove the latter group correct.

Roosevelt hesitated to invoke sanctions after the commercial treaty expired in January 1940. He hoped that forbearance would strengthen moderate elements in Tokyo who opposed further adventures. However, his belief that Japanese policies depended on what the United States did or did not do was exaggerated. The struggle in Europe again proved decisive. Soon after the fall of France and the Netherlands, Japan made threatening moves against French Indochina and the Dutch East Indies. In response, on July 25, FDR announced restrictions on the sale of scrap metal and petroleum. A week later, he banned the exportation of aviation gasoline outside the Western Hemisphere.

The president's attempt to restrain Japan by economic pressure failed. If anything, it nourished the belief that the United States wanted to prevent the Japanese from achieving their destiny in creating what they liked to call the "greater East Asian co-prosperity sphere." In September, Japan secured from Vichy France the rights to construct military bases in northern Indochina and signed what became known as the Tripartite Pact with Germany and Italy. Roosevelt retaliated by making a new loan to China and by banning entirely the sales of scrap metals, rather than merely restricting them.

The alliance Japan entered with Germany and Italy designated their respective spheres of influence. It also provided that if one of the signatories were attacked by a nation not presently at war, it would receive all possible "political, economic and military" assistance from the other two. The United States and the Soviet Union were the only major powers not then at war. Because of the Nazi-Soviet nonaggression pact, the Tripartite agreement appeared to be aimed at the United States.

The Tripartite Pact was not a master plan for conquest, as some American officials thought, but it had ominous implications nonetheless. In Japan, the army had long agitated for alignment with Nazi Germany. The navy opposed such a step because it feared war against the combined fleets of Britain and the United States. The army prevailed, but at no time was there thought of creating a functioning partnership in which Japan would plan and coordinate strategy with its allies. Those who supported the treaty reasoned that fear of a two-front war would weaken American determination to thwart Japanese aspirations in Asia. And if war did come, it was assumed that the United States would be unable to devote all its resources to fighting Japan.

Japan's pact with Germany and Italy underlined the need for the United States to develop a coherent strategy in the event of war with the combined Axis powers. In November 1940, Chief of Naval Operations Admiral Harold Stark submitted a plan to President Roosevelt. Listing several options the United States could follow, Stark recommended that the major effort be directed toward winning the war in Europe, while maintaining defensive operations in the Pacific. His chief justification was that Germany presented the greater and most immediate menace to America's vital interests. When Army Chief of Staff General George C. Marshall concurred, the Roosevelt administration adopted Stark's plan, and it became the basis of secret Anglo-American military discussions held during the early months of 1941.

In February, Tokyo dispatched a new ambassador, Admiral Nomura Kishisaburo, to Washington. The following month, he began talks with Secretary of State Cordell Hull that would last until the day Pearl Harbor was attacked. Nomura, who genuinely wished to prevent a rupture between his nation and the United States, was in some respects a decoy. Although the Japanese had not yet determined a fixed course of action, internal debates during the following months concerned *where*—not whether—expansion should take place. Of course, the militants would have been delighted had the United States acquiesced in whatever they chose to do, but they were determined to go ahead regardless of the consequences.

By this time, the Japanese government was almost completely dominated by the military, which itself was divided. Some elements in the army wished to move north against Japan's historic enemy, Russia. (Japan had suffered humiliating defeats at the hands of the Soviets in a series of clashes along the Manchurian border in 1938 and 1939.) Other army officers, supported by the navy, advocated a "southern advance" to secure the rubber, tin, and oil of areas such as Malaya and the Dutch East Indies. In April, Japan's erratic foreign minister, Matsuoka Yosuke, shocked other government officials by concluding a nonaggression pact with the Soviet Union. Matsuoka was quickly dumped, but the treaty benefited those who argued in favor of the southern strategy. That strategy was given priority by the summer of 1941.

In July, Tokyo demanded from the reluctant French the rights to build naval and air bases and to station troops in southern Indochina. The French gave in after appealing in vain to both Germany and the United States for intercession: Hitler had no wish to block a move that would further divert American attention to the Far East, and Roosevelt lacked the authority to do more than protest. The president regarded the Japanese action with great apprehension because Japan's leaders had secured an excellent staging area to strike out against targets in Southeast Asia. On July 26, he issued an executive order freezing all Japanese funds and assets in the United States.

FDR's response had unforeseen consequences. He believed sanctions should be applied gradually to enable the Japanese to weigh the effects without provoking them to rash action. He had intended his freeze order to further limit sales of strategic materials through licensing, not to cut them off altogether. But his zealous subordinates interpreted his order to mean banning entirely all exports of oil and gasoline to Japan. FDR was dismayed by this construction when he learned of it but did not rescind it because he was afraid he would appear irresolute. The Japanese were shocked by his action, which, as one newspaper put it, amounted to "a declaration of economic war." The freeze not only strengthened the argument that Japan must seize its own resources but emphasized the need to do so quickly, before existing stocks became depleted.

Roosevelt took another step during these days that would have far-reaching consequences. He recalled to active duty former Army Chief of Staff General Douglas MacArthur to head a newly formed command, U.S. Armed Forces, Far East (USAFFE), consisting of the Philippine army and American army units in the Philippines. The flamboyant, controversial

MacArthur had served as military adviser to the Philippine government for the previous five years. The creation of USAFFE indicated to the Japanese that the United States was preparing for war. MacArthur's appointment was doubly significant because he had boasted for years that the Philippines could repel an invasion, provided necessary military measures were taken. And there was only one nation capable of mounting such an invasion.

American-Japanese relations continued to unravel. Four days after Roosevelt's freeze order, a Japanese aircraft dropped several bombs on an American gunboat anchored at Chungking. Tokyo issued an apology that the State Department accepted, but the incident stirred more bitterness. In August, the United States sent a lend-lease mission to China, thereby expanding its commitment to furnish the Chinese with supplies and equipment. Roosevelt also permitted some pilots and ground personnel to resign from the services to join the American Volunteer Group in China, an organization quickly dubbed the Flying Tigers. In September, he turned down a proposal from the Japanese premier, Konoye Fuminaro, for a summit conference in the Pacific. FDR at first was tempted to attend, but subordinates persuaded him that the gulf between Japan and the U.S. was too wide to be bridged by personal diplomacy. When the Konoye cabinet fell a month later, General Tojo Hideki became the new premier. His nickname, ominously, was "the Razor."

Unknown to the United States, the Japanese already had taken a fateful step on September 3. They had agreed that if by early October it did not appear that Japanese demands would be met, "we shall immediately decide to open hostilities against the United States, Great Britain, and the Netherlands." Negotiations would continue after that time, but unless an unexpected breakthrough occurred, Japan would strike during the last ten days of the month. This decision was not conveyed to Ambassador Nomura, who earnestly continued to seek accommodation.

American-Japanese negotiations during 1941 involved a tangle of issues, complicated further by outside factors such as well-meaning but bungling efforts by two Catholic priests with Japanese connections to act as go-betweens. Nomura, joined in November by special envoy Kurusu Saburo, met with Secretary of State Hull almost daily during the last weeks. Hull, an elderly, moralistic Tennesseean, doggedly sought compromise. The discussions, however, were fruitless. The minimum terms each side found acceptable remained far apart. Barring almost complete capitulation by the United States, Japan's timetable made war inevitable.

Japan stated its final demands on November 20. The most important of them required the United States to restore commercial relations as they existed before the freeze, supply Japan with the necessary quantities of oil, and refrain from any interference in Japan's efforts to subdue China. In return, the Japanese would remove their troops from southern Indochina immediately and from the north following peace in China. By this point, Roosevelt and Hull, who would have refused to abandon China under any circumstances, distrusted any promises Japan might make. They considered offering a three-month truce during which limited amounts of supplies would be made available to Japan, but they withheld this offer in the face of British and Chinese protests. FDR feared that concessions to Japan might destroy China's will to go on fighting.

On the afternoon of November 25, Secretary of War Henry L. Stimson sent the president an intelligence report disclosing that a Japanese troop convoy of more than thirty ships had been spotted off the island of Formosa (Taiwan), apparently heading for Indochina. The next morning, Stimson telephoned Roosevelt to ask whether he had seen the report. FDR said no and "fairly blew up" when Stimson told him what it said. According to Stimson's notes of the conversation, Roosevelt stated that "that changed the whole situation because it was evidence of bad faith on the part of the Japanese that while they were negotiating for an entire truce—an entire withdrawal—they would be sending this expedition down there to Indo-China." Later in the morning, Secretary Hull and other State Department officials began preparing the American response to Japanese demands.

That afternoon, November 26, Hull met with Nomura and Kurusu. He handed them two documents: a statement of general principles and a list of specific steps to resolve the issues. The general principles stipulated, among other things, that Japan should remove all troops from Indochina *and* China, support the Chinese government, and enter a multilateral nonaggression pact for the Pacific. Hull had no illusions that the Japanese would accept this proposal, given their previous actions, but he wished to place the American position on record. His Ten Point Program, as it became known, was in no sense an ultimatum as some critics have charged. Rather, as Robert H. Ferrell has written in *American Diplomacy*, it was "little more than a restatement" of the Nine Power treaty the Japanese had signed in Washington in 1921.

Twenty-four hours before Hull met with Nomura and Kurusu, a Japanese task force consisting of six aircraft carriers, two battleships, two heavy cruisers, nine destroyers, and supporting tankers had left home waters and was plowing across the Pacific. Its target was the American Pacific Fleet stationed at Pearl Harbor in Hawaii. Submarines, due to their slower speeds, had been dispatched even earlier. None of these movements were detected by American intelligence. The task force, commanded by Admiral Nagumo Chuichi, took a roundabout route to avoid commercial shipping lanes and maintained radio silence. The attack was scheduled for Sunday, December 7, at 8:00 A.M. Hawaiian time (1:30 P.M. Washington time). If an unforeseen diplomatic breakthrough occurred by noon on December 1, the task force would be ordered to return. After that, as one Japanese admiral put it, "the situation would be placed in the lap of the gods."

"THIS IS NOT DRILL"

The attack on Pearl Harbor was conceived by Admiral Yamamoto Isoroku, commander in chief of Japan's Combined Fleet. Conventional wisdom held that if war came, the United States would send a mighty armada across the Pacific to destroy Japan's navy. The correct strategy was to have submarines strike at American ships along the way, while the Japanese surface fleet remained in its home waters, close to supplies and land-based air support. Under such conditions, the Japanese should triumph in a massive naval battle. Yamamoto doubted that the Japanese navy could provide support for the far-flung military operations then being planned and at the same time prepare for an all-out slugging match. He reasoned that if a surprise attack crippled the American Pacific Fleet, Japan would gain six months or more to complete its conquests without naval interference. He had no wish to go to war with the United States, and he knew Japan lacked the population or resources to win a long war. At best, he hoped, a shattering defeat would so demoralize the United States that it would accept Japan's "co-prosperity sphere."

Only Yamamoto's enormous prestige enabled him to begin preparations in early 1941 against strong opposition within the navy. Critics protested that if the Americans learned of the operation, whether through a breach of security or accidental sighting, they might ambush and annihilate the task force. They also complained that assigning precious aircraft carriers to a strike against Pearl would deny other operations adequate air cover. There were objections on technical grounds, as well: Existing torpedoes ran too deeply to be used in the shallow waters of Pearl Harbor, and even if new ones could be developed, torpedo nets would render them useless. Yamamoto doggedly lobbied other high-ranking officers for support while he put together a superb staff to begin training and to solve mechanical problems.

Operation HAWAII did not receive official approval by the Japanese navy's General Staff until late September, after an elaborate series of war games had demonstrated its feasibility. By that time, most technical problems had been overcome. Torpedoes rigged with special fins, dropped at the proper altitude and angle, had proven effective in shallow water. Armor-piercing shells from heavy naval guns had been modified into bombs for use against American battleships. And intense training of pilots and crews had improved accuracy rates in all categories. Refueling at sea still remained unsatisfactory, but this, too, was worked out in the following weeks. The task force approaching Pearl Harbor in the early days of December was a formidable weapon.

President Roosevelt and his advisers had been pessimistic about Japan's intentions since the fall of the Konoye cabinet in mid-October. By late November, after Japan had submitted its final demands, they feared war might break out in the near future. American cryptographers had broken Japan's highest-level diplomatic code through what became known as the Magic intercepts. These intercepts revealed that Tokyo repeatedly had warned Ambassador Nomura that he must conclude negotiations by a certain deadline. Although the deadlines had been advanced several times, on November 22 a final date was set—November 29: "This time we mean it, that the deadline absolutely cannot be changed." Even more ominously, "after that, things are automatically going to happen." What the Magic intercepts did not reveal, however, was when or where the threatened action would commence.

On November 27, the day after a Japanese troop convoy was sighted south of Formosa and Hull delivered his Ten Points, Army Chief of Staff Marshall advised the army commander at Pearl Harbor, Lieutenant General Walter C. Short, that negotiations "for all practical purposes had been terminated." "Japanese future action unpredictable," Marshall continued, "but hostile action possible at any moment." That same day, the Navy Department sent a message to Pearl for Admiral Husband E. Kimmel, commander in chief of the United States Fleet. It began, "This despatch is to be considered a war warning." But neither of these communications, nor any others sent out from Washington, referred specifically to the danger of an air attack against Pearl Harbor. Some measures were taken, but the installation remained unprepared for what was about to descend upon it.

The architects of Operation HAWAII, from Yamamoto down, hoped to achieve complete surprise but did not count on it. The task force was prepared to fight its way in, if necessary. As it turned out, there was no need. Through careful planning and good luck, the task force had escaped detection throughout its long voyage. American battleships and other vessels were berthed just where espionage reports had placed them, with three significant exceptions. No aircraft carriers were at Pearl: The *Enterprise* and *Lexington* and their escorts were at sea, and the *Saratoga* was on the American West Coast undergoing repairs.

Shortly after 6:00 A.M. Hawaiian time on December 7, about 200 miles north of Pearl Harbor, Nagumo's six aircraft carriers turned into the wind for launching. Plane after plane flew off the decks, rose, and circled in formation until the rest were airborne. This, the first wave, consisted of 183 aircraft almost evenly divided by type: torpedo planes, dive-bombers, high-level bombers, and fighters. At 6:20, the signal was given to make for the target. An hour later, the second wave began to launch. There were 177 planes in this group: 77 dive-bombers and 54 high-level bombers, escorted by 36 fighters. Of the total number of aircraft scheduled to take part, only two had to be scratched because of malfunctions, and one crashed into the sea. It was a near-perfect operation.

No one at Pearl Harbor was prepared for the attack, which began a few minutes before 8:00 A.M. More than half an hour earlier, two enlisted men at a radar station north of Pearl noticed blips on the screen indicating a large flight of incoming planes. They called the information center, but the officer on duty there, thinking it was a flight of American B-17s from the mainland, told them, "Don't worry about it." An even earlier report of a submarine sighting brought no response because it had not been confirmed and because such reports were commonplace. As a result, when the first Japanese planes appeared many who saw them believed they were part of an American flight exercise. Others, noticing the Rising Sun insignia, sounded the alarm. Minutes later, radio messages went out: "Enemy air raid, Pearl Harbor. This is not drill."

What followed was a disaster for the Pacific Fleet. Except for sporadic firing by hastily formed gun crews and individuals with small arms, there was virtually no opposition to the Japanese attack. Few American fighters got into the air, and many were destroyed on the ground, where they had been parked in clusters for protection against sabotage. Even the vulnerable Japanese torpedo planes were able to make their runs under ideal conditions. The Americans were better prepared when the second wave hit about half an hour after the first departed, but the resulting damage was still enormous. When it was all over, 6 battleships were on the bottom or headed there, 2 more were badly damaged, and 3 cruisers and 3 destroyers were also hit. Both the navy and the army suffered heavy losses in aircraft, and nearly 3,000 men were killed, another 1,000 wounded.

Of the 350 Japanese planes that had taken part in the attack, only 9 were lost from the first wave, and another 20 went down in the second. Some of Nagumo's subordinates argued that the task force should remain to launch further attacks and to seek the missing American carriers, but the cautious admiral refused to alter his plans. His mission was accomplished, in his mind, and he was unwilling to expose his

The *Arizona* burning after the Japanese attack on Pearl Harbor, December 7, 1941. (National Archives photo no. W&C 1136)

ships to possible attacks from land-based planes at Pearl or from the carriers he believed might be nearby. In the long run, it was a costly decision.

"A DATE WHICH WILL LIVE IN INFAMY"

On December 6, Ambassador Nomura had been notified by Tokyo that a fourteen-part message would be sent in reply to Secretary Hull's Ten Points. Thirteen parts were received by early evening, which, unknown to Nomura, the Americans were busily decoding. Shortly after 9:00 P.M., a courier began delivering copies of the message to the president and other top officials. When Roosevelt read it, he said something to the effect that "this means war." He telephoned Admiral Stark but directed no particular action because there was nothing in the message indicating the time or place that hostilities would begin.

Early the next morning, December 7, the fourteenth part arrived and was decoded. It ended with the statement that the Japanese government considered it "impossible to reach an agreement through further negotiations." There was no declaration of war, nor even a notification of a break in diplomatic relations. If anything, this part seemed less threatening than the earlier installments had.

What rang alarm bells in the minds of two intelligence officers, Colonel Rufus S. Bratton and Lieutenant Commander Alwin D. Kramer, was another message received that morning. It directed Nomura to present the fourteen-part reply to the State Department (preferably to Hull himself) by 1:00 P.M. that afternoon. Why, they asked themselves, would he deliver the message on a Sunday, when the department usually was closed, and why place such importance on the time of delivery? Bratton and Kramer believed that 1:00 constituted a deadline, at which time or soon after the Japanese would strike at some American installation in the Pacific. Bratton persuaded General Marshall to issue urgent warnings, which went out shortly after noon, but the one intended for Pearl was delayed in transmission and did not arrive until the Japanese attack had begun.

As instructed, Ambassador Nomura had asked to meet with Secretary Hull at 1:00. Because of security precautions, he used only a small staff to decode the fourteen-part message and to type it up in presentable form for submission. Unable to meet the deadline, Nomura asked for an hour's postponement. By the time he met with Hull, the secretary of state already knew that Pearl Harbor had been attacked. Scarcely looking at the document Nomura handed him, which he already had read through intercepts, Hull characterized the message as despicable. In all his years of public service, the secretary stated, he had never seen such "infamous falsehoods and distortions on a scale so huge that I never imagined until today that any government on this planet was capable of uttering them." Disdaining a reply, he motioned Nomura and Kurusu to leave.

Shortly after noon the next day, Roosevelt appeared before a joint session of Congress. His speech was brief and emotional: "Yesterday, December 7, 1941, a date which will live in infamy, the United States was suddenly and deliberately attacked by naval and air forces of the Empire of Japan." He did not request a declaration of war; rather, he asked for recognition that a state of war had "been thrust upon the United States." The resolution was passed with one dissenting vote. On December 11, Germany and Italy declared war on the United States, and the Congress responded in kind. This time, however, there were no opposing votes. Now, virtually the entire world was at war.

CONSEQUENCES AND CONTROVERSY

The attack on Pearl Harbor radically altered the course of world history. In one stroke, it had united a divided nation in support of the

President Franklin D. Roosevelt signing the declaration of war against Japan, December 8, 1941. (National Archives photo no. W&C 743)

war. And instead of demoralizing the American people, it instilled in them a deep commitment to defeat the enemy at all costs. This was a kind of struggle that Japan could never win. Once placed on a wartime basis, America's industrial capacity, technological superiority, and large population created a military juggernaut the Japanese could not halt, no matter how hard they fought. By triggering German and Italian declarations of war, the attack also produced a consensus behind American entry into the European conflict. The Japanese had scored a victory that, in the long run, led to the downfall of all the Axis powers.

Scholars have debated the wisdom of the strike against Pearl both in conception and execution. Had the Japanese restricted their targets to British and Dutch possessions, some have argued, it would have been difficult, if not impossible, for President Roosevelt to convince Congress and the public that it was in the national interests to intervene. Had he committed American forces, he would have aggravated an already potent opposition to his leadership. With regard to the military aspects of the raid, a number of historians have emphasized Japan's failure to focus on repair facilities and fuel storage farms as well as the fleet. Destruction of these installations would have forced the American navy back to the West Coast of the United States, thereby delaying offensive operations by many months.

Greater controversy surrounds the conduct of American civilian and military officials during the period before December 7. From the day of the attack until the present, people have asked how this military base could have been so woefully unprepared to defend itself. The deterioration of relations between the United States and Japan was no secret, after all, and Japan had a history of initiating hostilities without prior warning. Several official hearings and a flood of books and articles over the years have failed to satisfy those who believe the American people have been misled as to what actually happened.

The most dramatic and provocative explanation is that President Roosevelt and those around him engaged in a conspiracy to withhold crucial information that would have alerted commanders at Pearl to the impending danger. FDR believed the United States should be in the war, the argument runs, but most Americans disagreed. Having failed to provoke Hitler into retaliation for blatantly anti-German acts in the Atlantic, Roosevelt turned to Japan. He deliberately refused accommodation with the Japanese in favor of economic pressures he knew would force them to fight. Then, having learned from various sources about the planned strike against Pearl, he permitted it to take place without warning because he knew such a tragedy would thrust a unified nation into the conflict. According to this theory, Admiral Kimmel and General Short were made the scapegoats to conceal a plot devised in the White House.

There is no question that Roosevelt knew his policies toward Japan risked war. He also regarded Asian affairs as having a direct bearing on the conflict in Europe. The Chinese government might have collapsed if the United States had abandoned it, as the Japanese demanded, which would have freed a large portion of Japan's military forces for operations in Southeast Asia. Moreover, if Japan had seized the raw materials in that area, those resources would not have been available to the British, with possibly disastrous effects. Nonetheless, available evidence indicates that Roosevelt sought to avoid a break for as long as possible. His military advisers were unanimous in declaring that American armed forces were unprepared for war and in recommending that he buy time through diplomacy. Equally important, he had no wish to divert American resources to Asia when the outcome in Europe remained in doubt. And he could not have known that Hitler and Mussolini would declare war on the United States.

That FDR sought war against Japan is dubious. But the theory that he "set up" Pearl Harbor verges on the grotesque. The popularity of such a view provides testimony to the gullibility of segments of the American public, as well as to their fascination with the idea of conspiracy in high places. Acceptance of such a theory presupposes a belief that Roosevelt, together with top military and civilian leaders (and a number of key subordinates), agreed among themselves to sacrifice thousands of American lives. Unlikely on its face, the "conspiracy" theme is supported by no hard evidence. Rather, as Gordon Prange, who spent thirty years researching the subject, has written in *Pearl Harbor: The Verdict of History*, it is based on a "tissue of unsupported assumptions and assertions."

Those who have advanced the conspiracy theory dismiss the lack of documentation by pointing out that people engaged in skulduggery do not write memos to one another describing their misdeeds. Instead, the "evidence" cited generally falls into two categories. First, by stringing together every clue or hint that Pearl Harbor was the target, they try to make the conclusion appear so obvious that the failure to convey it to the local commanders seems to have been deliberate. In so doing, they neglect to mention the thousands of pieces of information pouring across intelligence desks that had to be evaluated: Many of these—some put out as disinformation by the Japanese—indicated that Japan would strike elsewhere. The second approach is to accept as fact the testimony of a few lower-echelon officials, as well as some unnamed "sources," that they had heard one or another revealing Japanese message that the policymakers pretended not to have known about. Such claims have not been corroborated sufficiently to inspire confidence.

Responsibility for the disaster at Pearl Harbor rests on many shoulders but not equally. During the final weeks before the attack, administration officials received a number of indications that the Japanese had decided upon war. None specified the target nor, until the very last moment, the timing. Army Chief of Staff Marshall and his navy counterpart, Admiral Stark, sent repeated messages to Pearl Harbor, warning that hostilities were likely. They and Roosevelt, to whom they reported, can be faulted for not conveying more specific instructions and for failing to insist that the local commanders report what measures they had taken. In view of the information that *was* sent to them, however, Kimmel and Short showed very poor judgment in not taking the maximum precautions, rather than the minimum. Many scholars agree that *all* the individuals involved shared one tragic misperception: They simply did not believe the Japanese would dare attack Pearl Harbor.

THE RISING TIDE

The United States was unprepared for war in December 1941. The draft had been in effect little more than a year, and much of the military hardware that had been produced had been sent overseas as lend-lease. During the first months of fighting in the Pacific, American servicemen generally found themselves opposing an enemy who was better trained and equipped. These months would see a string of unbroken Japanese successes as Tokyo expanded its empire by conquest and sought to protect it by creating an impenetrable defensive perimeter.

Japan's first seizures of American possessions occurred at Guam and at Wake Island (actually a cluster of three tiny islands) in the western Pacific. Unfortified Guam fell quickly, but the defenders of Wake provided more trouble than the Japanese had bargained for. Part of a marine battalion and a marine squadron of only twelve obsolete fighters, assisted by several hundred construction workers, held out for two weeks against bombing, shelling from naval vessels, and amphibious landings. The initial attempt to put Japanese troops ashore on December 11 was beaten off by accurate fire from shore batteries, and the few remaining fighters inflicted further damage on the fleeing Japanese ships. The second assault, ten days later, was made by a much larger contingent, supported by two aircraft carriers. An American task force built around the carriers *Saratoga* and *Lexington* had been sent to relieve Wake, but the overcautious admiral who was temporarily appointed to replace Kimmel ordered it back. When the officers at Wake learned that no help was coming, they surrendered their men to overwhelming Japanese strength.

The defense of Wake Island became a symbol of heroism in defeat for the Americans, much as Dunkirk had been to the British. A widely circulated story reported that the marine commander at Wake, Major James P.S. Deveroux, when asked by radio what he needed, replied, "Send us more Japs." Deveroux, who survived as a prisoner of war, later denied saying any such thing—there already were more than enough Japanese for the marines to handle. A similar myth involved an American bomber pilot who allegedly ordered his men to bail out before diving his plane into and sinking a Japanese battleship. There were many documented acts of individual heroism, but the American people were eager to believe anything that gave inspiration in the midst of successive disasters.

Japan's next target was the Philippines, which had not figured prominently in American contingency planning for a war with Japan before the summer of 1941. Defensive forces were to be concentrated on the main island of Luzon. If initial landings could not be beaten off by air attacks, these units were to retreat west to the Bataan Peninsula across the bay from Manila; their objective would be to prevent Japan from using Manila as a naval base. Ideally, the troops on Bataan (and on Corregidor, the fortress island in the mouth of the harbor) could hold out until the American navy, fighting its way from Pearl, could bring reinforcements and supplies, but none of the planners actually believed they could do so. Estimates of the time it would take the navy to push back the Japanese ran as high as two years, and no provisions had been made for staging and transporting reinforcements from the West Coast of the United States. It was assumed that the Philippines would be an early casualty in the event of war with Japan.

Such pessimistic estimates were quickly revised when General MacArthur assumed command of the American forces in the Far East on July 26, 1941. MacArthur had had a brilliant career as a West Point cadet and as a commissioned officer. Wounded twice in World War I, he had come home a brigadier general. Subsequently, he had become superintendent of West Point and had several tours of duty in the Philippines, where his father, General Arthur MacArthur, had served with distinction. In 1930, Douglas MacArthur had been named chief of staff of the army, a post he held for five years. He retired from active duty in December 1937 to become a field marshal in the Philippine army and adviser to President Manuel Quezon. His obvious abilities and his stature with the people and government of the Philippines made him the logical choice to command the defense of the islands. MacArthur immediately set about to convince his superiors in Washington that the islands could be defended successfully.

The general was aware that U.S. military strength in that region was pitifully insufficient to stop what the Japanese could throw against it; his forces in all branches were undermanned and poorly equipped. His plans were predicated on two assumptions: that he would receive massive injections of new equipment and that there would be sufficient time to mobilize a potent Philippine army of ten divisions. If these criteria were met, he predicted that by April 1942, American and Philippine forces could defeat Japanese assaults on the beaches.

MacArthur gained the support of Army Chief of Staff Marshall and Secretary Stimson. They respected his leadership, and both were optimistic about the use of air power in defeating an invasion. They were particularly impressed with the capabilities of the new American heavy bomber, the B-17. If they could supply MacArthur what he requested and if he had time to put it to use, perhaps the Philippines could be held after all. Throughout the summer and fall, Marshall and Stimson did what they could to meet MacArthur's requirements. Unfortunately, the American economy was then only in the process of gearing up to wartime production, and there were numerous demands for what was available. The delivery of aircraft was typical. Of the 340 B-17s and 260 fighters earmarked for the Philippines, only 35 and 100, respectively, were in place when war broke out.

At 2:30 A.M., December 8 (the time differential is due to the international date line), a naval radio operator in Manila picked up the report of the attack on Pearl Harbor. The information was quickly forwarded to MacArthur's headquarters, then down through the echelons. Everyone expected the Japanese to launch strikes against the airfields on Luzon at dawn or shortly thereafter. About 8:00 A.M., reports of an incoming Japanese flight caused a flurry of activity. Fighters were sent up from various bases, and the 16 B-17s at Clark Field were ordered into flight patterns to avoid being caught on the ground. When no contact was made—the Japanese formation altered course—American aircraft returned to their bases. Aside from refueling, there seemed nothing to do except wait. At that very time, a flight of 108 Japanese bombers and 84 Zeros was heading toward Clark and Iba Field, a nearby fighter base. The Japanese *had* intended to strike at dawn, but heavy fog over their bases on Formosa had delayed takeoff.

Shortly before 11:30 A.M., radar reports indicated that an enemy formation was approaching the northern coast of Luzon. The information was relayed to all nearby bases except one—Clark. By the time alarms sounded there, it was too late. Approaching unopposed from the northwest were two Vs of bombers and their fighter escorts, plainly visible in the blue sky. The Japanese, who had expected to meet heavy opposition, flew on as though in a training exercise. The bombers dropped their loads in a single pass, then flew off as quickly as they had come. The fighters stayed. Concentrating on the parked airplanes, they poured fire into everything with wings. Eventually, in order to avoid hitting one another, they formed a large circle. Each plane made its run, flashing in and out of the rising smoke columns, then banked and got in line for its next turn. By the time they were through, all the bombers and most of the fighters had been destroyed.

That MacArthur's planes had been caught on the ground ten hours after the raid on Pearl Harbor has caused controversy ever since. His air commander, Major General Lewis H. Brereton, blamed MacArthur. According to Brereton, he repeatedly requested permission to launch the

B-17s against Formosa, but his requests were denied, first on the grounds that actual attacks on the Philippines had to occur before retaliation could be permitted, then with the explanation that photo reconnaissance would have to be completed. If Brereton's account is correct, the B-17s not only would have been able to strike against the Japanese but they would have been aloft when the attack on Clark took place.

MacArthur, supported by his chief of staff, Major General Richard K. Sutherland, contradicted Brereton's version of events. They claimed Brereton had been ordered to send all the B-17s south to the island of Mindanao the day before and professed surprise that he had sent only half. Furthermore, they contended, a raid against Formosa without aerial photos and fighter protection (American P-40s lacked the range) would have been suicidal and without effect. They placed responsibility for the loss of the B-17s entirely on Brereton. Both accounts are self-serving, of course, and the truth probably will never be known.

MacArthur's plans for defending the Philippines proved unrealistic. Creation of the Philippine army was barely under way by late 1941. Even if more equipment had been made available, it is unlikely he could have realized his goal in only four additional months. As it was, except for the professional Philippine Scouts, troops were virtually untrained, and units existing on paper were unable to function effectively in combat when war came. Nor were the B-17s as formidable a weapon as had been hoped. As shown later in Europe, they could be enormously destructive when used in large masses. But the number available at the time, even if losses on that first day had been avoided, could not have materially altered the course of events.

The general's tragic error was that he deployed his troops and supplies for defending the beaches long before they were capable of doing so. When the main Japanese landings on Luzon took place on December 22, it quickly became clear that they could not be thrown back. MacArthur was forced to adopt the very strategy he had earlier opposed: retreat to the jungles of Bataan and fight a delaying action. However, because supplies and equipment had been dispersed, instead of stockpiled there, American and Philippine troops lacked adequate food and medicine from the beginning. As a result, hunger and disease took as great a toll as did the Japanese.

MacArthur appealed to Washington for relief for his beleaguered command. It never came. Despite their anguish over the sacrifice of so many men, the chiefs of staff and Stimson concluded that the United States lacked the naval strength, especially after Pearl Harbor, to mount a relief operation. An enormous commitment of carriers, battleships, and supporting craft would have been required to convoy the necessary troop transports and cargo vessels across Japanese-controlled waters to

Japanese troops on Bataan, the Philippines, ca. 1942. (National Archives photo no. W&C 1140)

the Philippines with any chance of success. Anything less would fail to reach its destination and entail further losses to an already depleted navy. Unable to save MacArthur's troops, President Roosevelt decided that the general himself must not be captured or killed. On February 22, he ordered MacArthur to proceed south to Mindanao, then to Australia. Lieutenant General Jonathan M. ("Skinny") Wainwright assumed command.

The defenders of Bataan held out doggedly against air attacks, artillery bombardments, and infantry assaults. At last, weakened by malnutrition,

U.S. soldiers and sailors surrendering to Japanese forces at Corregidor, the Philippines, May 1942. (National Archives photo no. W&C 1143)

exhaustion, and disease, they surrendered in early April. From the southern tip of Bataan, the Japanese were able to concentrate punishing artillery fire on Corregidor, adding to the destruction caused by the bombing. Finally, after pounding the island for weeks, the Japanese launched amphibious assaults on the night of May 6. By late morning of the next day, it was all over. Almost out of ammunition, water, and supplies, Wainwright decided to end the hopeless struggle. "With profound regret and with continued pride in my gallant troops," he notified Washington, "I go to meet the Japanese commander."

MacArthur's management of the Philippine campaign had shown poor judgment. To begin with, he was almost universally detested by the troops he commanded. During the battle for Bataan, he had made the short trip from Corregidor to visit them only once, thereby earning himself the contemptuous nickname "Dugout Doug." Then, before leaving for Australia, he had accepted President Quezon's gift of $500,000 for his services, a highly irregular act for an army officer on active duty. None of this was known to the American public; for morale purposes, Roosevelt, Stimson, and Marshall helped create an image of MacArthur as the gallant leader in a lost cause. He was lionized in the press, and in March, he received the Congressional Medal of Honor for his "heroic conduct."

The loss of the Philippines, like Wake Island, was presented to the American people in the most favorable light. Defenders of Bataan and Corregidor had bought precious time against the Japanese, the official version ran, and they had been defeated only because they faced vastly superior forces. In reality, Japan's timetable was scarcely affected by the campaign, and Japan's forces were outnumbered by those of its opponents. Only two Japanese divisions took part in the invasion, one of which was replaced after the first weeks by a brigade of second-line troops. The truth was that the Americans and their Philippine allies were doomed from the start, just as the prewar planners has assumed. Nevertheless, their courageous perseverance inspired the war effort.

Had the American public known the aftermath of Bataan, it would have been stimulated to fury. Prior to attacking Corregidor, the Japanese evacuated American and Filipino prisoners to a camp many miles to the north. This was the infamous "Bataan death march," a journey of death and suffering during which about 600 Americans and as many as 10,000 Filipinos died. The Japanese, thinking that the main battle would be fought in front of Manila—not in Bataan—had made no provisions for the long trek, nor had they anticipated that the troops would be so debilitated by malaria, dysentery, and starvation; these factors alone would have caused extreme suffering. In addition, many (though not all) Japanese soldiers treated the prisoners barbarically. Men who could not keep up the pace or who accepted food and water from civilians were routinely bayoneted or hacked to death with swords. Some Japanese guards killed or maimed for no reason at all. American officials learned of the march only after three prisoners escaped in the summer of 1943, and they did not release the story until early in 1944.

Meanwhile, if Americans could take pride in their armed forces even in defeat, the British were denied such consolation. Their garrison on Hong Kong, a small island off the coast of China, surrendered in less than two weeks, and British Borneo fell almost as quickly. These posts were not expected to hold out long, but Singapore, a large island at the southern tip of the Malayan peninsula, was another story. The British had invested money and resources to build Singapore into an Asian Gibraltar, a stronghold they thought would ensure their military position in the region. It was supposed to provide an impregnable base for the British navy, enabling it to project its strength where it chose. Instead, the defense of Singapore became, in Churchill's words, "the worst disaster and largest capitulation of British history."

Shortly before Pearl Harbor, the battleship *Prince of Wales* and the battle cruiser *Repulse* were dispatched to Singapore. Three days after war began, these two ships were sunk at sea by Japanese torpedo planes, a graphic example of how vulnerable capital ships were without air cover. Japan already had begun landing troops in northern Malaya, and they were advancing south toward Singapore. The British, who had regarded the Malayan jungles as virtually impenetrable—certainly for armor—put up weak resistance. The Japanese outflanked hastily improvised defenses and repeatedly got behind the British by leapfrogging troops down the coast via amphibious landings. Though without experience in jungle fighting, Japanese soldiers adapted quickly. One of their most potent weapons in this campaign was the bicycle, which enabled them to travel quickly over the most primitive roads and paths. By the beginning of February, they stood poised at the tip of the mainland, separated from Singapore by a short stretch of water.

The island fortress held out for only two weeks. Its mighty guns, pointing to the sea, could not be moved out of fortified emplacements. Men who had retreated down the peninsula were demoralized, and bad feelings between British and Australian units hampered coordination. The commanding general, A. E. Percival, was incapable of organizing a coherent defense to fend off multiple landings. Lackluster at best, he was virtually paralyzed by the successive defeats his units had suffered. All hope was lost when the Japanese seized the island's source of water. Percival requested and received permission to surrender his troops, which he did on February 15. Adding to the tragedy, reinforcements had arrived at Singapore only to become prisoners without having fired their weapons. Ultimately, a garrison of 80,000 soldiers capitulated to an invading force less than half its size.

The Japanese seemed invincible during the first five months of war. By April, they had pushed the British out of Burma and had taken the Dutch East Indies. Beyond that, their success against the Western powers had more than military significance: It destroyed the myth of white supremacy over Oriental peoples. The Japanese were welcomed at first by many Asians as liberators from the yoke of colonialism. In fact, their rule turned out to be far more brutal than that of their predecessors, but they inadvertently nurtured independence movements that would continue to grow after the war ended.

SELECTED BIBLIOGRAPHY

Allen, Louis. *Singapore, 1941–1942* (Newark: University of Delaware Press, 1976).
Butow, Robert J.C. *Tojo and the Coming of the War* (Princeton, N.J.: Princeton University Press, 1961).
Calvocoressi, Peter, and Guy Wint. *Total War* (New York: Penguin, 1979).
Costello, John. *The Pacific War, 1941–1945* (New York: Rawson Wade, 1981).
Divine, Robert. *The Reluctant Belligerent: American Entry into World War II* (New York: J. Wiley, 1965).

Fehrenbach, T. R. *FDR's Undeclared War* (New York: David McKay, 1967).

James, D. Clayton. *The Years of MacArthur* 3 vols. (New York: Macmillan, 1970–1985).

Kahn, David. *The Codebreakers* (New York: Macmillan, 1967).

Lewin, Ronald. *American Magic: Codes, Ciphers, and the Defeat of Japan* (New York: Farrar, Straus, and Giroux, 1982).

Manchester, William. *American Caesar* (Boston: Little, Brown, 1978).

Mintz, Frank P. *Revisionism and the Origins of Pearl Harbor* (Washington, D.C.: University Press of America, 1985).

Morison, Samuel Eliot. *The Two Ocean War* (Boston: Little, Brown, 1963).

Morton, Louis. *The Fall of the Philippines* (Washington, D.C.: Department of the Army, 1953).

Petillo, Carol Morris. *Douglas MacArthur: The Philippine Years* (Bloomington: Indiana University Press, 1981).

Prange, Gordon. *At Dawn We Slept: The Untold Story of Pearl Harbor* (New York: McGraw-Hill, 1981).

_____ . *Pearl Harbor: The Verdict of History* (New York: McGraw-Hill, 1986).

Schaller, Michael. *Douglas MacArthur: The Far Eastern General* (New York: Oxford University Press, 1989).

Spector, Ronald. *Eagle Against the Sun: The American War with Japan* (New York: Vintage Books, 1985).

Toland, John. *But Not in Shame: The Six Months After Pearl Harbor* (New York: Random House, 1961).

_____ . *Rising Sun: The Decline and Fall of the Japanese Empire* (New York: Random House, 1970).

_____ . *Infamy: Pearl Harbor and Its Aftermath* (Garden City, N.Y.: Doubleday, 1982).

Utley, Jonathan. *Going to War with Japan* (Knoxville: University of Tennessee Press, 1985).

Weber, Ralph E. *United States Diplomatic Codes and Ciphers* (Chicago: University of Chicago Press, 1978).

Wohlstetter, Roberta. *Pearl Harbor: Warning and Decision* (Stanford, Calif.: Stanford University Press, 1962).

7
Japan at Bay
(1942)

No blueprint guided the Japanese in their conduct of the war. Plans were made as new situations arose, frequently representing compromises within or between the armed forces. All of Japan's early objectives had been achieved with surprising ease following the attack on Pearl Harbor. What could be expected next? Perhaps the only consensus within the military services was that Japan should not sit back while the United States and its allies regrouped and prepared to take the offensive. Some Japanese naval officers wanted to seize Hawaii, others coveted Australia, and still others advocated moving west into the Indian Ocean for a possible linkup with Germany. The army vetoed any large-scale commitment of troops because an invasion of Siberia remained a possibility as long as the German-Soviet war remained in doubt. In the midst of such conflicting views, decisions were made for operations that would mark the turning of the tide against Japan.

WAGING WAR AGAINST JAPAN

Japan's enemies had a vested interest in cooperating with one another, but a coalition among equals was unrealistic. With British capacity already stretched thin, other European nations under German occupation, and China barely holding on, the United States assumed leadership of the Allied war effort in the Pacific. Roosevelt and the Joint Chiefs of Staff insisted that the direction of the war should rest in American hands to avoid endless debate over priorities. Other nations reluctantly consented to become junior partners because the United States would have to supply the major share of men and resources. The arrangement worked, although friction occurred.

Like Japan, the United States was beset by interservice rivalries. The nature of the Pacific conflict guaranteed that these rivalries would generate strong disagreement over the way it should be fought. The admirals regarded it as a naval war and, although some were slow to grasp the point, a naval war for air supremacy in which carriers would be the dominant weapon. Ground operations would be impossible unless the American navy could convoy troops, protect their landings, and keep them supplied. This required tactical supremacy at points of attack and, for final victory, destruction of the Japanese fleet. Navy officers were loath to entrust such a task—let alone their ships—to the army.

The army and its air corps disagreed. The defeat of Japan could only be achieved, they said, by getting close enough to employ strategic bombing against its home islands and then invading them. Objectives along the way would have to be seized by ground forces, which would also bear the brunt of fighting on Japanese shores. That these operations should be under the control of anyone other than those who were trained to carry them out was folly to the generals. In addition to honest differences, both sides were determined to gain as much credit as possible for the ultimate victory.

If the army had the weaker argument, it had a trump card in the person of Douglas MacArthur. The best-known military figure in the United States even before the war, MacArthur had attained mythic proportions as the hero of Bataan and Corregidor. To have made him subordinate to some obscure admiral would have caused great furor in Congress and with the public. Largely due to MacArthur's prestige, a compromise was worked out whereby the Pacific was divided into two theaters. He was given command of the Southwest Pacific Area, composed of Australia, the Philippines, the Solomon Islands, and most of the Dutch East Indies. The rest, designated the Pacific Ocean Area, was placed under Admiral Chester W. Nimitz. This violation of the principle of unified command was dictated by political expedience, not military realities, and it resulted in a lack of coordination and wasteful duplication of scarce resources.

MacArthur and Nimitz possessed radically different personalities. The general was a mercurial, arrogant figure who was virtually unapproachable except to the small circle of sycophants he kept around him. He demanded unquestioning obedience from his subordinates but showed no reluctance to argue with or ignore orders he himself received from Washington. He took full credit for every success and blamed others for every failure. Nimitz, by contrast, was an unpretentious man of unflappable temperament. He had an inner confidence and a strong ego that required no massaging, which, in turn, inspired confidence in those who served under him. His most obvious fault was his reluctance to relieve officers from command until their incompetence became glaring. Lacking MacArthur's monstrous ego, Nimitz was largely responsible for what cooperation existed between the two theaters.

THE BATTLE OF THE CORAL SEA

Australia, which lay along the eastern flank of Japan's newly acquired sphere, appeared likely to be Tokyo's next objective. Although it posed no threat to the Japanese at the time, if it were left in Allied hands it could become a base for operations against lines of communication and supply and, ultimately, a staging area for an invasion of the home islands. Australia could not be defended without American help, especially after part of its army had been lost at Singapore. The United States had been sending troops and equipment to Australia and to islands along the route leading to it since early 1942. But even with the addition of three Australian divisions returned from the Middle East, this buildup probably would have been inadequate against a large-scale invasion.

The Japanese decided not to try to conquer Australia because the army objected to the necessary commitment of men and materials. Instead, they sought to neutralize it by seizing bases from which they could attack harbors and landing fields by air. One of the most important of these bases would be Port Moresby at the southeastern end of New Guinea, a huge island just to the north of Australia. During the first week in May, a Japanese invasion force, protected by two large carriers and one small one, steamed toward New Guinea.

The Americans were ready—or as ready as they could be given the scarcity of available ships. Analysts at Pearl Harbor had succeeded in breaking Japanese naval codes sufficiently to read parts of messages. These bits, together with other sources, convinced them that the Japanese were preparing to take Port Moresby. Admiral Nimitz ordered a task force built around the carrier *Lexington* to proceed to the Coral Sea, southeast of New Guinea, to join the *Yorktown* task force already there. This situation provided an early example of the problems caused by divided authority. The area lay in MacArthur's theater, yet the carriers belonged to Nimitz's command. As a consequence, coordination in air reconnaissance between MacArthur's land-based planes and those of the navy was poor.

The Japanese assumed the United States would send naval forces to defend Port Moresby, but they did not know how strong those forces might be. By May 7, each side was probing to find the other. Strikes were made against ships comprising other groups—the Japanese small carrier was sunk and an American tanker was crippled—but the main forces did not locate one another until the next day. The Americans

112

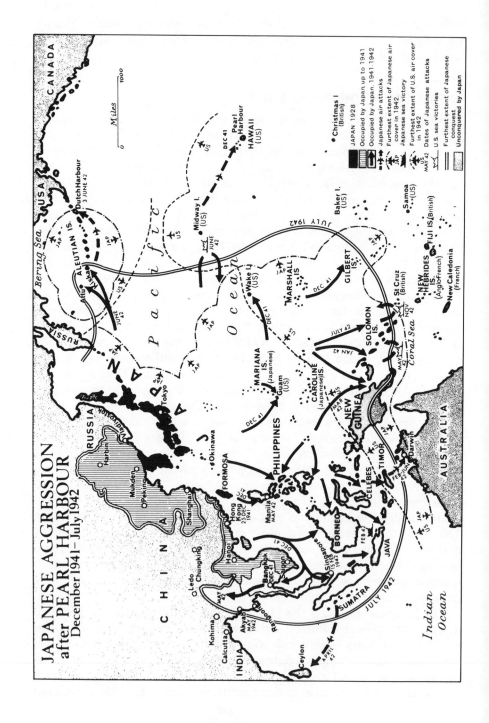

JAPANESE AGGRESSION
after PEARL HARBOUR
December 1941–July 1942

Legend:
- Christmas I 1928 (British)
- JAPAN 1928
- Occupied by Japan up to 1941
- Occupied by Japan, 1941-1942
- Japanese air attacks
- Furthest extent of Japanese air cover in 1942
- Japanese sea victory
- Furthest extent of U.S. air cover in 1942
- Dates of Japanese attacks
- U.S. sea victories
- Furthest extent of Japanese conquest
- Unconquered by Japan

Miles
0   1000

CANADA

USA

Bering Sea

Pacific Ocean

ALEUTIAN IS.
Attu Kiska
JUNE 42
Dutch Harbour 3 JUNE 42

Midway I. (US) JUNE 42

Pearl Harbour
HAWAII (US)
DEC 41

RUSSIA

Tokyo
JAPAN

Harbin
Mukden
Peking
Shanghai

CHINA

Ledo
Chungking
Hanoi
DEC 41
Bangkok DEC 41
Saigon
Rangoon
Kohima
Akyab MAY 1942
Calcutta

INDIA

Ceylon APRIL 42

Okinawa

FORMOSA

Hong Kong 25 DEC 1941

PHILIPPINES
Manila MAY 42

MARIANA IS. (Japanese)
Guam (US) DEC 41

CAROLINE IS. (Japanese)

MARSHALL IS. DEC 41

Wake I. (US) DEC 41

GILBERT IS.

Baker I. (US)

Samoa (US)

NEW HEBRIDES (Anglo-French)
FIJI IS (British)
St Cruz (British) NOV 42
New Caledonia (French)

SOLOMON IS. JULY 42

Coral Sea

NEW GUINEA
JAN 42
MAR 42
MAY 42

BORNEO
CELEBES
TIMOR
FEB 42
Darwin
FEB-JUNE 42

SINGAPORE 15 FEB 1942
SUMATRA
JAVA
FEB 42
JULY 1942

AUSTRALIA

Indian Ocean

MAY 42
JULY 1942

struck first, damaging the carrier *Shokaku* but losing track of the *Zuikaku* in a sudden rainstorm. The Japanese fared better. The *Yorktown* was hit by only one bomb, but the *Lexington* took two torpedoes and suffered bomb damage. The latter continued to function and appeared to be out of immediate danger until a series of gasoline explosions tore it apart internally. The *Lexington* was soon abandoned and sunk by an American destroyer. The American task force commander, Rear Admiral Frank Jack Fletcher, unsure of what ships the Japanese still had and not wanting to risk his remaining carrier, received permission from Nimitz to break off the action and return to Pearl.

The Japanese pulled out as well. The damaged *Shokaku* had to go to port for repairs, and the *Zuikaku* emerged from battle with only half its air strength. What remained was deemed insufficient to provide air cover for the invasion against land-based planes operating from Australia and New Guinea. The United States paid dearly with the *Lexington*, but it had prevented the seizure of Port Moresby and had inflicted heavy losses on precious aircraft and crews. The Battle of the Coral Sea marked the first time a Japanese offensive had been thwarted, and their two carriers were unable to participate in operations against Midway Island the following month.

MIDWAY

Midway Island (actually two small islands) lies 1,100 miles northwest of Pearl Harbor. It was valuable property. If it remained in American hands, it could become, at some future date, a stepping-stone along the way to the Japanese home islands. Japanese possession, on the other hand, would threaten Hawaii. For months, Admiral Yamamoto had advocated attacking Midway, arguing that its importance would lure the remaining American naval forces to their destruction in battles against the superior Japanese fleet. Such a victory would then enable Japan to roam freely in the Pacific. Even if the Americans did not respond as he hoped, the seizure of Midway would strengthen Japan's defensive perimeter. Although the admiral's plan was criticized by the army and within the navy as unsound and fraught with danger, an apparently unrelated event, the "Doolittle raid" on Tokyo, resolved the debate in Yamamoto's favor.

The idea of bombing Japan to provide a morale boost for the American people originated with President Roosevelt. Naval air officers devised a plan to use army bombers operating from an aircraft carrier deep in Japanese waters. After dropping their loads, the aircraft would fly to safety in China. Army Air Forces General H. H. ("Hap") Arnold concurred and selected Lieutenant Colonel James H. Doolittle, a famous aviator

An Army B-25 takes off from the deck of the *Hornet* on its way to participate in the first U.S. air raid on Japan, April 1942. (National Archives photo no. W&C 1148)

during peacetime, to lead the raid. Doolittle and handpicked air crews trained for a month, flying modified B-25 medium bombers off carrier-length runways. In early April, they and their aircraft were loaded aboard the carrier *Hornet*. The *Hornet* and its escort joined the *Enterprise* task force near Midway and proceeded toward Japan.

On April 18, while still more than 650 miles from the target, the B-25s had to take off earlier than intended when Japanese picket boats were sighted. They reached Tokyo, dropped their bombs, and headed for China without losses. Fifteen of the sixteen planes reached China (one landed in the Soviet Union), but they barely made it because the extra distance exhausted their fuel supplies. Some crews had to bail out when fuel tanks ran dry, and others landed where they could. Unfortunately, eight men came down in Japanese-held territory, three of whom were later shot for war crimes. The daring operation inflicted miniscule damage, but it provided the psychological lift Roosevelt had intended. He delightedly announced that the raid had originated from "Shangri-La," alluding to a fictional Himalayan retreat in the then-popular novel *Lost Horizon*.

The Doolittle raid had far more momentous consequences than Roosevelt knew. Yamamoto and other high Japanese military leaders were humiliated that enemy planes had been permitted to hit Tokyo, residence of the emperor himself. A decisive victory over the American fleet would help to atone for this, and Midway had become a special prize. In fact, it had played no part in the bombing attack, but it might have—the Japanese could not have known. Its capture would deepen the Japanese perimeter, thereby reducing the chances that another raid could be mounted successfully. Opposition to Yamamoto's plan collapsed overnight.

The attack on Tokyo may even have determined the outcomes of the Coral Sea and Midway battles. Because of preparations for the latter operation, only two Japanese carriers were made available for the invasion of Port Moresby. Had three or four been used, they might have sunk the *Yorktown* as well as the *Lexington*, while sustaining less damage and fewer losses of aircraft and crews. As it turned out, the *Yorktown* was hurriedly repaired at Pearl Harbor and participated in the battle of Midway; the *Shokaku* and the *Zuikaku* did not. The net difference of three carriers may have been decisive.

The battle plan for Midway devised by Yamamoto's staff was complicated, involving almost the entire Japanese navy, divided into numerous separate groups. It provided for a diversionary attack against the Aleutian Islands in the North Pacific to divide American naval strength, then an invasion of Midway. The Strike Force of four large carriers, commanded by Admiral Nagumo, would open the assault with an air attack against Midway from one direction. Battleships, cruisers, and a small carrier would escort troop transports in from another. The Main Force, grouped around battleships and another small carrier, would lie in wait to destroy American ships when they arrived. In addition to having overall command of the operation, Yamamoto himself would lead the Main Force, which he mistakenly believed would be the decisive factor.

American cryptanalysts again proved invaluable. Delay in scheduled codebook changes enabled the navy intelligence unit at Pearl, headed by Commander Joseph J. Rochefort, Jr., to conclude in late April that a major assault against Midway was being planned. Japanese message traffic during the first weeks of May convinced them they were right about the target and provided detailed information about the plan of battle. By mid-May, Rochefort had persuaded Admiral Nimitz, who later stated that "had we lacked early information of the Japanese movements, and had we been caught with carrier forces dispersed . . . the Battle of Midway would have ended differently."

Nimitz acted decisively. Reinforcements of all kinds were sent to Midway, and the marines stationed there beefed up defenses against air attack and amphibious landings. Task Force 16, comprised of the *Enterprise* and the *Hornet*, was recalled to Pearl from the South Pacific for refueling and headed for Midway in late May. Its commander, the colorful and experienced Vice Admiral William F. ("Bull") Halsey, had to be hospitalized at Pearl for a debilitating skin disease, but he was replaced by Rear Admiral A. Spruance. Spruance had never commanded carriers before, but he proved to be an excellent choice. Task Force 17, consisting of the *Yorktown* and an escort, left Pearl a few days later. The *Yorktown*, badly damaged in the Coral Sea, was temporarily patched up in less than a week. It was commanded by Rear Admiral Fletcher, who was given overall charge of the American carriers. In essence, the Japanese, believing they were mounting a surprise attack, instead were heading into an ambush.

Despite their knowledge of Japanese intentions, U.S. naval forces and the men at Midway faced heavy odds. The *Yorktown* operated at less than full efficiency and had received new, inexperienced air crews at Pearl. The *Hornet* had never seen combat. Against them, the Japanese would have four large carriers and two small ones in the waters around Midway, as well as a strong force of battleships. (A lack of fuel had caused the United States to send its battleships back to the West Coast.) The odds were lessened by three American advantages: long-range reconnaissance from Midway; Japan's lack of radar; and Yamamoto's dispersion of his strength, which prevented his battleships and the two small carriers from taking part.

At 9 A.M. on June 3, an American PBY flying boat sighted the invasion convoy. A flight of B-17s and four flying boats from Midway attacked it without inflicting any damage. Unaware that the disposition of their forces was already known, the Japanese maintained radio silence in hopes the Americans would think the convoy was operating alone. When Nagumo launched his attack on Midway early the next morning, therefore, he assumed he had the advantage of surprise. And if his bombers caught the defenders unprepared, the island's air strength could be destroyed at a single blow.

Alerted the previous day, planes from Midway and the American carriers sought Nagumo's Strike Force. The incoming attack wave was spotted first, then the carriers themselves. The Japanese soon found the Americans waiting for them over Midway. Obsolete Brewster Buffaloes and Grumman Wildcats were outmatched by Japanese fighters, but, together with antiaircraft fire, they destroyed or badly damaged more than sixty-five Japanese aircraft. American torpedo planes and bombers of all types had gotten off the ground before the strike began and were heading for the Japanese Strike Force. Six American torpedo planes and four medium bombers attacked Nagumo's ships first. They scored no hits, but their appearance confirmed an earlier report that "there is need for a second attack" on Midway's airfields.

What followed confused the Japanese. No enemy ships had yet been reported in the area, so Nagumo gambled on mounting a second raid against Midway before his first wave had returned. This meant removing torpedoes and armor-piercing bombs from his reserve aircraft and replacing them with high-explosive bombs. Fifteen minutes after he gave the order, a Japanese scout plane reported sighting ten enemy surface vessels. Afraid one or more of them might be carriers, Nagumo stopped the rearming and requested clarification. At that point, American planes from Midway began piecemeal attacks on the Strike Force. They were beaten off, but the Japanese carriers had to commit their available fighters and resort to evasive action. Then came word that "what appears to be" a carrier was among the American ships. Not knowing what he faced, Nagumo decided to recover all his aircraft before going after the American ships.

Admiral Spruance's Task Force 16 had begun steaming toward the enemy carriers as soon as they were sighted. He launched his aircraft at maximum range to catch the Japanese in the act of refueling and rearming the Midway attack group on deck; Admiral Fletcher later sent his planes from the *Yorktown*. Heavy clouds caused American formations to become separated en route. Some never found the Japanese Strike Force, which had altered course; others located it at different times. Torpedo squadrons from the *Hornet* and the *Enterprise* struck first, then another from the *Yorktown* went in. They suffered appalling losses without inflicting any damage: Thirty-five of forty-one torpedo planes were lost.

Though futile themselves, the attacks proved crucial. Almost all the Japanese fighters had gone down after the low-flying torpedo planes, and they lacked the altitude to provide protection when dive-bombers swooped down from 14,000 feet a few minutes later. Two squadrons from the *Enterprise* quickly turned the *Akagi* and the *Kaga* into burning hulks. Another squadron from the *Yorktown* came out of the sun at the *Soryu* and set it ablaze. The Japanese carriers, their decks laden with aircraft, aviation fuel, bombs, and torpedoes, blew themselves apart.

Only the *Hiryu*, which had become separated during evasive action, remained of the mighty Japanese Strike Force. It launched a strike against the *Yorktown*, which one of its scout planes had located. The *Yorktown*'s fighters and antiaircraft guns shot down some of the attackers, but the carrier took three hits from dive-bombers, and two torpedoes tore gaping holes in its hull. It had to be abandoned. The *Hiryu*'s turn came next. Twenty-four dive-bombers from the *Enterprise*, some of which originally had belonged to the *Yorktown*, set the last Japanese carrier on fire. The *Kaga* and the *Siryu* sank that evening, and the *Akagi* and the *Hiryu* went down the next day. The *Yorktown* remained afloat, but a

Navy fighters during the attack on the Japanese fleet off Midway, June 4–6, 1942. To the right of center a burning Japanese ship is visible. (National Archives photo no. W&C 972)

later attempt to tow it back to Pearl failed when a Japanese submarine torpedoed it.

Admiral Yamamoto still hoped to accomplish his goals of invading Midway and smashing American naval strength in the Pacific. His battleships of the Main Force, together with the fighting ships from the two other groups, still had overwhelming firepower. He planned to intercept and attack the American carriers that night. Admiral Spruance, to whom Fletcher had turned over tactical command after the *Yorktown* was abandoned, avoided such an encounter by ordering his ships to retire from the area. He knew through intelligence that the Main Force existed, and he did not want to risk his remaining carriers in a night engagement. Yamamoto ordered his fleet back to base, his opportunity missed.

The battle had enormous consequences. Japan could ill afford to lose four large carriers, more than 250 aircraft, and, not least, veteran pilots and crews. Moreover, Midway remained in American hands. Most important was the psychological shock inflicted upon the Japanese leaders. They took extreme measures, such as isolating the returning wounded, to keep knowledge of the disaster restricted to the highest echelons.

But within these echelons, confidence in naval offensives was destroyed, perhaps unnecessarily. Although a formidable fleet still existed, Japanese strategists relinquished the initiative at sea. What resulted was a war of attrition that Japan could not win. The Americans had won a victory even more decisive than they could have known, at the cost of only one aircraft carrier. Mitsuo Fuchida and Masatake Okumiya's book title says it best: *Midway: The Battle That Doomed Japan.*

THE UNITED STATES TAKES THE OFFENSIVE: GUADALCANAL

On July 2, two days before the carrier battle at Midway, the Joint Chiefs of Staff approved a plan for offensive operations in the South Pacific. Thrashed out in the midst of jurisdictional disputes between the army and navy, the plan was divided into three stages: landings in the southern Solomon Islands east of New Guinea; advances up the Solomons and along the northeastern coast of New Guinea; then an attack on Rabaul, a powerful Japanese base further to the east on the island of New Britain. Accomplishing these tasks would remove the threat to Australia and pierce the Japanese defensive perimeter. The first stage, under Admiral Nimitz's control, had as its targets Tulagi, Guadalcanal (where the Japanese were constructing an airfield), and several lesser islands.

A powerful fleet rendezvoused in the Fiji Islands on July 25, commanded by Admiral Fletcher. There were three carriers, one battleship, a division of cruisers, and destroyers to convoy the invasion force's transports and cargo vessels. Rear Admiral Richmond Kelly Turner had charge of the amphibious landings, and Major General Alexander . A. Vandegrift controlled the ground forces, which consisted of the First Marine Division augmented by a regiment from the Second. The operation did not begin auspiciously. Fletcher, worried about endangering his carriers, informed Turner and Vandegrift that the flattops would remain for only two days and overrode their angry objections that it would take longer than that to unload all the supplies and equipment.

On August 7, eight months after the attack on Pearl Harbor, American marines landed on Japanese-held territory. By the following day, they had overwhelmed light defenses and controlled the nearly completed air base, which they named Henderson Field after a marine pilot shot down at Midway. Fletcher again infuriated Turner and Vandergrift when he departed with his carriers that evening, twelve hours before his own deadline. At that very moment, a Japanese fleet of cruisers and destroyers was approaching Guadalcanal from Rabaul. Eluding patrolling destroyers, it struck what remained of the covering force during the early morning hours of August 9, with devastating effects. One Australian and three American cruisers were sunk; another was badly damaged. The Japanese commander withdrew instead of going after the sitting transports because he feared daylight would bring air attacks from the carriers he thought were still nearby. He did not know they had departed hours earlier.

The Japanese army, occupied elsewhere and underestimating the number of marines put ashore, lost its opportunity to recapture Guadalcanal. The first Japanese landing did not take place until August 18, by which time the marines had dug in and had made Henderson Field operational. The Japanese force, consisting of only 1,000 men, was all but wiped out when it attacked marine defenses. By the time the Japanese were capable of larger assaults, aircraft flown in from a small carrier gave the Americans air superiority over the island. Enemy fighters from Rabaul could not remain in combat for long because of the distance they had to fly.

The Guadalcanal campaign developed into a drawn-out struggle fought under debilitating conditions. The island was covered by tropical jungle ill suited for human habitation. Men on both sides suffered from heat, damp-rot, malaria, and dysentery, not to mention a rich assortment of insects and snakes. There were chronic shortages of food, medicine, and supplies, and equipment was difficult to maintain. The nearly impenetrable jungle inhibited movement and observation. Firefights erupted when patrols stumbled upon one another, and the Japanese harassed the marines with mortars, grenades, and small arms fire almost nightly.

The Japanese landed fresh units to rebuild their shattered forces during the weeks following the first battle. They attacked again on the night of September 13; by this time, they had about 6,000 men on the island. Marine lines bent under repeated assaults, but they did not break. Americans, who suffered nearly 20 percent casualties, killed or wounded more than half the enemy attack force. Again, the Japanese had to await reinforcements before mounting a new offensive. The next attack came in late October, and the Japanese were hurled back yet another time with the loss of more than 3,000 men. This was to be their last major effort.

The struggle for Guadalcanal also was waged at sea as each side sought to reinforce and provision its own troops and to prevent the other from so doing. No less than seven naval battles took place in the waters near Guadalcanal between August and November. Most of them were fought at night because American air power at Henderson forced the Japanese to bring their convoys in under cover of darkness. Battleships and cruisers often were sent to bombard the airfield. In most cases, the Japanese navy proved superior in night encounters, despite its lack of radar. A daylight battle between carriers occurred in October, when the

A Japanese bomb splashes astern of a U.S. carrier during the Battle of Santa Cruz, October 26, 1942. (National Archives photo no. W&C 977)

Enterprise and the *Hornet* intercepted an enemy task force approaching Guadalcanal to support the Japanese ground offensive. Two Japanese carriers were badly damaged, but so was the *Enterprise*. Worse still, the *Hornet* was sunk.

The Japanese tried to rebuild their strength on the island in November. In mid-month, however, a large convoy of troop transports was virtually annihilated by American bombing and strafing attacks. Meanwhile, the United States was pouring in fresh units and equipment, and by December, the original marine units had been replaced by one marine and two army divisions. The Japanese, caught in a competition they could not win, decided not to send any more men into the meat grinder. In late December, orders were issued to evacuate the island, which was done during the first week of February 1943.

The battle for Guadalcanal was a turning point. It provided a psychological boost to the United States and its allies, marking the first time Japanese troops had suffered defeat after an unbroken string of victories throughout east Asia. It also denied Japan a key air base from which to strike at Australia and New Guinea. The American navy, though bested in most of the engagements, profited from the experience, particularly with regard to the use of radar. Most important, the United States could replace its losses of ships, aircraft, and trained crews much more rapidly than could Japan.

The victory paid another dividend. Two weeks before American marines went ashore at Guadalcanal, the Japanese made another attempt to capture Port Moresby. Unwilling to risk the losses earlier sustained in the Coral Sea, this time they landed at Buna and Gona on the northern coast of the Papuan peninsula, which forms the eastern "tail" of New Guinea. The overland distance to Port Moresby is not great, but the area is bisected by the Owen Stanley Mountains, a nearly impassable range of jungle-covered peaks and gorges. Outnumbered Australian troops tried to block Japanese passage, but they had to retreat southward toward Port Moresby. As Guadalcanal began to absorb more and more Japanese troops and supplies, however, the Port Moresby operation died on the vine. By late fall, the Japanese had fallen back on Buna and Gona and were besieged by American and Australian forces. The threat to Australia was over for good.

THE FIRST YEAR AT WAR

The disaster at Pearl Harbor had propelled the United States into a war it had only begun preparing for. During the following months, Japan defeated all of the Western powers that had possessions in the Far East, at times with remarkable ease. But the Japanese aura of invincibility came to an abrupt end in the Coral Sea and at Midway, and the loss of Guadalcanal placed Japan on the defensive for the remainder of the war. Years of hard fighting lay ahead, but the United States and its allies possessed such superior human and material resources that the outcome was inevitable.

War in the Pacific was a racist war on both sides. Unfavorable stereotypes of Orientals in general had a long history in the United States. At best, the Japanese were regarded as a quaint people given to floral arrangements, tea ceremonies, and colorful kimonos. At worst, particularly after their savage treatment of the Chinese was widely reported in the American press, they were considered treacherous barbarians. Their attack on Pearl Harbor confirmed the latter belief.

Racial attitudes at first caused Americans to belittle the Japanese as inept. Due to the low intelligence of these people, one popular myth had it, only Japanese officers were capable of independent thought: Kill the officer and his men would mill helplessly about in confusion. Another myth was that their pilots were incompetent because, having been carried on their mothers' backs as babies, they lacked a sense of balance. Their reputation for exporting cheaply made consumer goods to the United

States before the war also led to the assumption that their military hardware must be imitative and inferior. Of course, ridiculing the enemy was, in part, a way of compensating for humiliating defeats.

As the war went on, Japanese fighting men were depicted less as incompetent soldiers and more as sadistic beasts. Political cartoonists drew them as bowlegged, buck-toothed individuals with glasses, grinning obscenely as they bayoneted babies or decapitated women. They were similarly portrayed in motion pictures, comic strips, and popular fiction. Their actual behavior toward civilians and captured military personnel in many instances closely resembled the popular image. In reports of battles, Japanese troops were referred to as "fanatics" who attacked in "hordes," as opposed to the Americans who invariably fought bravely against superior numbers.

The Japanese were equally racist. Although professing to be the protectors of Oriental peoples against the hated white colonialists, they treated the Chinese, Koreans, and other Asians they conquered with contempt and often with great cruelty. Japanese education, particularly during the 1930s, stressed the superiority of their people, the divinity of their emperor, and their destiny to dominate Asia. Military doctrine taught that to give one's life for the emperor was the highest honor and to surrender for any reason was the worst disgrace. Those who did not abide by similar codes were, by definition, inferior and unworthy of humane treatment.

Racism and cultural differences ensured that war in the Pacific would be waged with greater ferocity than that between Americans and Germans or Italians in Europe. There is a tendency among fighting men to dehumanize the enemy, in order to make the act of killing him less repugnant; this is easier to do when the opponent is of a different race. To many Americans, the Japanese were "Japs" or "monkeys," who were little better than wild animals to be exterminated. The fact that they fought so tenaciously and seemed so willing to die, often committing suicide when unable to offer further resistance, only strengthened the view that they were of a lower order than people of European stock. Atrocities on both sides were commonplace.

Americans, who prided themselves on technological competence, were surprised to learn that Japanese military equipment was superior in a number of categories. The Japanese Zero initially outperformed even first-line American fighters such as the Grumman Wildcat and the P-40, let alone the many obsolete craft still being flown. American pilots compensated by using tactics that avoided individual dogfights when possible. Japanese torpedo planes were also better, as were the torpedoes they carried. American torpedoes, on the other hand, were wildly inaccurate and often failed to explode. They not only hampered naval air power but rendered U.S. submarines virtually ineffective until improved models were available.

By far the greatest advantage enjoyed by the United States during the first year of war, aside from some good luck in key situations, was in the area of intelligence. Through code-breaking and traffic analysis, Japanese intentions and dispositions were known beforehand in the Coral Sea, at Midway, and at Guadalcanal. The battles still had to be fought, but such knowledge enabled the Americans to make the best use of their resources. In contrast, Japanese intelligence often was faulty and based on little more than guesswork. At Midway, for instance, Admiral Yamamoto had been led to believe that American carriers were operating far to the south. Had he known that four were being sent against him, let alone the direction from which they were coming, he probably would have been able to achieve a decisive victory. Although the United States began to produce better planes and ships as time went on, intelligence played a vital role throughout the war.

SELECTED BIBLIOGRAPHY

Buell, Thomas B. *The Quiet Warrior: A Biography of Admiral Raymond A. Spruance* (Boston: Little, Brown, 1974).
Dorwart, Jeffrey M. *Conflict of Duty: The U.S. Navy's Intelligence Dilemma 1919–1945* (Annapolis, Md.: U.S. Naval Institute, 1983).
Dower, John W. *War Without Mercy: Race and Power in the Pacific War* (New York: Pantheon Books, 1986).
Dyer, George C. *The Amphibians Came to Conquer: The Story of Admiral Richmond Kelly Turner*, 2 vols. (Washington, D.C.: Department of the Navy, 1969).
Frank, Richard B. *Guadalcanal* (New York: Random House, 1990).
Friend, Theodore. *The Blue-Eyed Enemy: Japan Against the West in Java and Luzon* (Princeton, N.J.: Princeton University Press, 1988).
Fuchida, Mitsuo, and Masatake Okumiya. *Midway: The Battle That Doomed Japan* (Annapolis, Md.: U.S. Naval Institute, 1955).
Griffith, Samuel B. *The Battle for Guadalcanal* (Philadelphia, Pa.: J. B. Lippincott, 1963).
Hagan, Kenneth J. *This People's Navy: The Making of American Sea Power* (New York: Free Press, 1991).
Hiroyuki, Agawa, *The Reluctant Admiral: Yamamoto and the Imperial Navy* (Tokyo: Kodansha International, 1979).
Hough, Richard. *The Battle of Midway* (New York: Macmillan, 1970).
Hoyt, Edwin Palmer. *Blue Skies and Blood: The Battle of the Coral Sea* (New York: Eriksson, 1975).
Iriye, Akira. *Power and Culture: The Japanese-American War, 1941–1945* (Cambridge, Mass.: Harvard University Press, 1981).
Leckie, Robert. *Challenge for the Pacific: Guadalcanal, the Turning Point of the War* (Garden City, N.Y.: Doubleday, 1965).

Lundstrom, John. *The First South Pacific Campaign: Pacific Fleet Strategy, December 1941–June 1942* (Annapolis, Md.: U.S. Naval Institute, 1976).

Potter, E. B. *Nimitz* (Annapolis, Md.: U.S. Naval Institute, 1976).

Prange, Gordon W. *Miracle at Midway* (New York: Penguin, 1982).

Tregaskis, Richard, *Guadalcanal Diary* (New York: Random House, 1955).

Tulegja, Thaddeus. *Climax at Midway* (New York: Norton, 1960).

8
War in North Africa
(1940–1944)

The war in North Africa was not the product of some master plan, as Hitler's invasion of the Soviet Union was. It began as a struggle between Italy and Great Britain, escalated when Germany sent in what became known as the Afrika Korps, and was decided when the United States launched its first offensive operation in the west. Never large, compared with the battle for France or the eastern front, it nonetheless came to have an important influence on Allied grand strategy against Germany. And it was fought under conditions unlike those on any other front.

BEGINNING OF THE DESERT WAR

Benito Mussolini was an opportunist who sought to make the most of his alliance with Germany. He hoped that if Hitler restricted his ambitions to western Europe and Russia, Italy could one day dominate the entire Mediterranean region in the manner of Imperial Rome. He acted shrewdly during the 1930s, exploiting the British and French fear of Hitler to get away with aggression that otherwise might have been blocked. When war came in September 1939, he stayed on the sidelines at first because he did not want to be on the losing side. Evidence indicates he had decided even before Hitler's invasion of France to enter the war at some point, and apparently he anticipated a negotiated settlement in which he would take part to Italy's advantage. The success of German arms during the first weeks of fighting persuaded him to advance his schedule to get in on the kill before it was too late. He declared war on June 10, just six days before the French government asked for a cease-fire.

Mussolini did have one glaring blind spot, which proved fatal. In his zeal to make Italy a first-class power, he persistently exaggerated the strength of his military forces. He was bedazzled by numbers of tanks, aircraft, and ships, without ascertaining their combat effectiveness. The truth was that although Italy possessed modern equipment in a few categories, most of its weaponry was hopelessly inadequate. Nor was that all. The Italian army was badly led, poorly trained, and almost entirely lacking in fighting spirit. Finally, Italy's industrial base was too primitive to sustain a wartime economy.

Although Mussolini mounted some ineffective operations against the French after they had requested a cease-fire, his real interests lay in the Mediterranean. His first target was Egypt, defended by a skeleton British force. In Libya, which bordered Egypt on the west, Italy had an army of more than 250,000 men. Soon after France collapsed, Mussolini began urging his commander in Libya, Marshal Rudolfo Graziani, to attack the outnumbered British. Graziani, who had made his military reputation fighting Ethiopians armed with spears, was out of his league. He also appreciated, as Mussolini did not, that despite its numerical superiority, the army he commanded was poorly prepared to challenge the British. Italian aircraft were virtually inoperable in desert conditions, the tanks lacked adequate armor and cannon, and the infantry lacked sufficient transportation. Only after repeated prodding by Mussolini did a reluctant Graziani move east.

Great Britain, already beset by Germany in the air and at sea, reacted hastily to bolster its tiny garrison. An Italian victory in Egypt threatened the Suez Canal, through which passed strategic raw materials that the British desperately needed. Loss of the canal, together with U-boat depredations in the North Atlantic, might deny Britain the ability to continue the war. Despite the emergency, Winston Churchill was able to scrape together only enough reinforcements to create a defense force of 30,000 men against an army many times its size.

Graziani's apprehensions were fully justified. In mid-September, he cautiously moved into Egypt against little opposition. After advancing only fifty miles, he stopped and began establishing defensive positions while awaiting supplies for the next push forward. The British, commanded by General Sir Archibald Wavell, did not wait. On December 9, a mixed force including Indians, Australians, and New Zealanders launched devastating armor attacks that quickly overran Italian fortifications. Italian forces retreated in disarray, leaving behind 40,000 prisoners of war. The quality of the British troops and equipment was overwhelming, particularly the armor. British tanks, especially the Matildas, were virtually impregnable to Italian cannon; Italian tanks were little more than tinderboxes.

Wavell's field commander, General Richard O'Connor, pressed his advantage and chased the fleeing Italians into Libya. Before the end of January 1941, British forces had taken several fortified ports, including Tobruk. Two weeks later, Italian troops retreating along the coast were trapped between British units pursuing them and others that had driven straight across the desert. They surrendered in droves. At the cost of 2,000 casualties, the British had taken more than 125,000 Italian prisoners since the desert war began.

Great Britain halted its offensive in mid-February because of developments elsewhere. One month after his invasion of Egypt, Mussolini had launched an attack against Greece from Albania. After initial successes, the Italians had been pushed back into Albania, where the struggle had turned into a stalemate. Having staved off the immediate threat to the Suez Canal, the British decided that the war in Greece should have priority. Wavell was ordered to stand in place while part of his forces were sent across the Mediterranean.

Hitler, chagrined by Mussolini's blunders, chose to help his ally even though the forthcoming invasion of Russia had first claim on German military reserves. He sent two undermanned divisions—one armored, one motorized infantry—to North Africa under the command of General Irwin Rommel. Rommel had attracted attention for his exploits as a young infantry officer during World War I. Later, he became a favorite of Hitler and, convinced that armor would play a major role in modern warfare, had used the latter's influence to gain command of a panzer division. His excellent performance in the French campaign earned him further advancement. His assignment to North Africa soon became a nightmare for the Allies. Rommel was the perfect choice to lead the Afrika Korps, and he became a legend during the next few years.

Although ordered only to take up defensive positions in support of his Italian ally, Rommel attacked the British in late March. General Wavell had learned of the Afrika Korps's arrival, but he did not think it was capable of offensive operations so quickly. The surprised British fell back against Rommel's well-timed attacks all the way to Egypt, and the capture of General O'Connor during one engagement added to the British humiliation. Rommel had failed to take the fortified port of Tobruk, however, which posed a threat on his flank and denied him an advance base. With his forces now at the end of a supply line stretched beyond capacity, he had to abandon further advance.

The British push against the Italians, followed by an equally long retreat before the Afrika Korps, set a pattern for the campaign. Fixed lines could be bypassed or outflanked. Armored and motorized infantry units maneuvered over vast expanses of barren land, at times restricted only by their ability to sustain themselves. The availability of supplies,

General Rommel with the 15th Panzer Division between Tobruk and Sidi Omar, Libya, January or November 24, 1941. (National Archives photo no. W&C 1016)

fuel, and spare parts often dictated strategy as much as did enemy strength. Meanwhile, the desert took a terrible toll on men and equipment. Blasted by heat in daytime and chilled at night, soldiers also had to endure the swirling sand that penetrated everything they wore and clouds of flies that would blanket the contents of a mess kit in seconds. Engines overheated quickly, and sand clogged moving parts of machines and weapons.

The need to send provisions from Europe via the Mediterranean resulted in a naval war between Great Britain and Italy, which was assisted by German U-boats and air power. The British were numerically inferior to the Italians and, because of the distances involved, had to divide their forces. One fleet operated out of Gibraltar at the western end of the sea; another was based in Alexandria on the eastern shores. Fortunately for the British, however, Italy's navy was as timid and inept as its army.

The Italian navy was virtually eliminated as a factor by March 1941. There were several minor engagements during the summer and early fall of 1940. Then, in November, the British mounted a daring nighttime attack by carrier-based torpedo planes against the Italian naval base at Taranto. One battleship was disabled, and two others and several cruisers were badly damaged. In March 1941, when an Italian task force tried to intercept a British convoy of reinforcements to Greece, a battle took place off Cape Matapan at the southern tip of the peninsula. Italy's most powerful battleship sustained a few hits, and three heavy cruisers and two destroyers were sunk. For the remainder of the war, Italy's larger warships stayed close to port and offered no further challenge. Torpedo boats and submarines continued to operate.

The quality of forces aside, the British possessed an enormous advantage over Axis forces in the Mediterranean area through their code-breaking capabilities. The most important source, kept from public knowledge for twenty-five years after World War II ended, became known as the Ultra secret. During the 1920s, the Germans had constructed a sophisticated enciphering machine called Enigma, which they believed gave them absolute security of communications at the highest levels throughout the war. They did not know that an Enigma machine had fallen into the hands of Polish authorities in 1929 and was replicated before being delivered to its destination. Within a few years, Polish mathematicians discovered how to break Enigma's complicated patterns and later made their knowledge available to the British. Of limited use in the French campaign and the Battle of Britain, Ultra became a key factor in the desert campaign and for the remainder of the war.

Enigma messages took time to decode, and the system was used only for communications between Rommel's headquarters and Berlin. They did not, therefore, provide the British with day-to-day operational information or Rommel's tactical plans. What they did reveal was significant: shipping dates of supply convoys destined for North Africa (enabling the British to attack them with devastating results) and the condition and location of German ground units at the time of decoding. The testimony of General Wilhelm Ritter von Thoma, who assumed command of the Afrika Korps when Rommel fell ill in September 1942, provided a graphic account of Ultra's value. Captured a few weeks later, Thoma was invited to dinner by British General Bernard Montgomery. "Instead of asking me for information," Thoma told an interviewer shortly after the war, "he said he would tell me the state of our forces, their supplies and dispositions. I was staggered at the exactness of his knowledge, particularly of our deficiencies and shipping losses. He seemed to know as much about our position as I did myself." In addition to Ultra, the British also had broken Italian naval codes, which supplied information crucial to the attack on Taranto and the Battle of Matalan.

THE CAMPAIGN RESUMES

Between the end of Rommel's offensive in April and the autumn of 1941, the Afrika Korps and the British Eighth Army, as it was now designated, engaged in inconclusive battles while both sides brought in additional men and equipment. During this period, General Claude Auchinleck replaced Wavell as commander in chief of the Middle East because Churchill did not think the latter was sufficiently aggressive.

Like Wavell, however, Auchinleck delayed mounting an offensive until he believed his forces were sufficiently augmented and trained to prevail over the Afrika Korps. Finally, in mid-November, Auchinleck moved. The Eighth Army was numerically superior to its enemy in men, tanks, guns, and trucks. But Rommel was the superior tactician, his men were better trained, and his tanks for the most part were superior than those he faced. He made devastating use of dug-in antitank guns against advancing armor and was quick to launch counterattacks that repeatedly caught the British by surprise. Auchinleck's offensive gained some ground but failed in its objective, which was to smash the Afrika Korps. In the process, much of his armor was destroyed. The Eighth Army's strength was further sapped after December, when the Japanese went to war in the Far East. Australian divisions already stationed in North Africa were sent back to defend their homeland, a British division earmarked for the Eighth Army was diverted to Singapore, and other scheduled reinforcements were sent elsewhere.

The Afrika Korps, reinforced and reequipped during the lull following Auchinleck's offensive, struck at the depleted Eighth Army in May 1942. Armored thrusts at several targets simultaneously kept the British off balance and sent them reeling back, despite fierce resistance at several points. In June, Rommel captured the strategic port of Tobruk, seizing huge amounts of fuel and supplies that his forces badly needed. Taking advantage of British disorder, he renewed his drive only a week after taking Tobruk and pushed the British deep into Egypt. They fell back to El Alamein, only sixty miles from Alexandria.

British defenses at El Alamein enjoyed a rare advantage in the desert war. Between the Mediterranean to the north and the impassable Qattora Depression (a moonscape of rocky canyons and salt marshes) to the south, they occupied a passage only forty miles wide. Within that strip, furthermore, steep ridges restricted the number of attack routes. Rommel was unable to utilize his genius for maneuver in such a situation. And when he launched his assault on July 1, the British employed their armor more flexibly than they had in the past. Several seesaw battles took place, with both sides incurring heavy losses. Finally, in late June, an exhausted Afrika Korps paused before an equally exhausted Eighth Army. Hitler, obsessed with the war against Russia, had refused to send Rommel the resources that might have ensured victory.

Despite Auchinleck's successful defense of El Alamein, he was removed from his position in August by an interfering Churchill, who blamed him for reaching a stalemate instead of victory. General Harold Alexander became commander in chief of the Middle East, and the Eighth Army was taken over by General Montgomery, Churchill's third choice for the position. "Monty," as he became known, was an eccentric, egotistical

General Bernard L. Montgomery watches his tanks move up, North Africa, November 1942. (National Archives photo no. W&C 1017)

loner whose abilities have been the subject of controversy ever since. Barely two weeks after taking command, Montgomery had to face a new offensive by Rommel. The British had several advantages. During the lull, the Eighth Army had received far more men, tanks, and supplies than had the Afrika Korps, and it had air superiority. Thanks to Ultra, Montgomery also knew where and with what forces Rommel planned to strike. The attack, launched on the night of August 30–31, gained some ground but had to be abandoned after a few days, partly because of fuel shortages. The British defensive strategy had been devised by Auchinleck, but Montgomery took the credit himself.

Churchill's hope that Montgomery would quickly go on the offensive was misplaced. Instead, the general waited until late October, by which time the Eighth Army had attained overwhelming strength: a 2 to 1 advantage in men, tanks, and guns, and 530 serviceable planes against 350. Montgomery also had improved morale and discipline among the mixed forces he commanded. On October 23, after an immense artillery barrage, his offensive began. Rommel, who had flown to Germany for medical treatment, returned two days later. The Afrika Korps and its

Italian allies offered stiff resistance, but they were chewed up by superior numbers. On November 2, Rommel requested permission to retreat but was turned down by Hitler, who ordered him to fight to "victory or death." Rommel disobeyed his orders, and, gathering all available transport, he began to fall back, leaving the Italians to fend for themselves. Montgomery pursued, but cautiously. Some military experts believe he lost a good chance to annihilate the Afrika Korps.

GRAND STRATEGY

While the Eighth Army was pursuing the remnants of Rommel's Afrika Korps into Libya, Allied landings began on November 8 in the French colonies of Algeria and Morocco to the west. American troops, who made up the bulk of the invasion force, were about to go into action against Germany and Italy for the first time. The operation would have important ramifications for the course of the European war and for relations with the Soviet Union. It would also raise questions in the United States about the purposes for which the war was being fought.

Almost as soon as the United States entered the war, Soviet leader Joseph Stalin began importuning Churchill and Roosevelt to open a second front against Hitler by invading Nazi-occupied France from across the English Channel. The Soviet Union was bearing the entire weight of German arms, he pointed out, and had suffered enormous casualties and devastation. He warned that Russia might not be able to continue the struggle if the United States and Great Britain failed to relieve the pressure in time.

Soviet pleas for an early cross-channel invasion were congenial to American army planners and to President Roosevelt. They believed that the best way to achieve victory in the least time and with fewest casualties was to engage Germany in large-scale land battles as quickly as possible. They were worried that delay might force Russia out of the war, thereby enabling Hitler to transfer powerful forces from the eastern front to defend against an Allied invasion of France.

Churchill and most British military leaders disagreed. They were committed to what became known as the "peripheral" strategy, which meant attacking Hitler around the borders of Germany's sphere and forcing him to commit men and resources to several places at the same time. They believed that such harassment, together with strategic bombing (stressed especially by the airmen) and the demands of the eastern front, would erode Germany's strength. A direct thrust should be made only when it became clear that Germany was already crumbling.

Probably the most important reason for the difference in strategic views lay in the experience each nation had had in World War I. Great

Britain had lost almost an entire generation of its young men in the horrible slaughters of trench warfare on the western front. Consequently, Churchill and his generals had no wish to repeat such bloodletting. American troops, on the other hand, had fought in large numbers only during the final months of the war. Then, going against a badly depleted German army, they had participated in successful offensives that led to Germany's request for an armistice. The perception of American generals, most of whom had served in France as junior officers, was that boldness in the attack brought results. They tended to believe that the British now suffered from an excess of caution because of what they had gone through twenty years earlier.

The American Joint Chiefs of Staff were not united on this matter. The naval chief of staff, Ernest J. King, a dour and arrogant man who was ardently disliked by many who had to deal with him, consistently emphasized the Pacific war and dragged his feet on diverting resources to Europe. "Hap" Arnold of the Air Forces was lukewarm about invasion, predicting that strategic bombing alone might defeat Germany. The Army chief, George Marshall, carried the burden of argument for an early cross-channel operation. Marshall was a man of commanding presence and unbending integrity who came to be Roosevelt's most trusted military adviser. Winston Churchill did not exaggerate when he later referred to Marshall as the "architect of victory" in World War II.

Roosevelt had another reason for wanting to open a second front as soon as possible. Assuming eventual victory, he realized that the Soviet Union would play a major role in postwar Europe. He wished to assure Stalin and other Soviet leaders that, despite earlier differences, the United States would be a good ally during the war and that collaboration should continue after the fighting ended. Although FDR endorsed the United Nations, he believed that only large-power cooperation could ensure a peaceful world. He sought to establish a basis for trust, therefore, by aiding Russia during its greatest hour of need.

During the months following Pearl Harbor, Roosevelt endorsed a plan drawn up by General Marshall's staff, providing for a 1943 cross-channel invasion of France. The plan also contained provisions for an emergency assault in 1942 should that appear necessary to prevent a collapse of the Soviet Union. FDR seized on the latter proposal as a means of assuring the Soviet Union of American good faith. He cabled Stalin, asking him to send Foreign Minister V. M. Molotov to Washington to discuss "a very important military proposal involving the utilization of our armed forces in a manner to relieve your critical western front." Molotov arrived in late May after talks with the British. In response to his direct query about a second front, Roosevelt told him that he could "inform Mr. Stalin that we expect the formation of a second front this year." Molotov understandably took this to mean an invasion of the European mainland.

Roosevelt's pledge shocked and alarmed Churchill, who thought such a scheme would lead to disaster. He hurried to the United States to dissuade FDR from a premature cross-channel operation and to convince him that North Africa was the most feasible target. Roosevelt, to the great dismay of Marshall and other army leaders, eventually went along with Churchill's strategy. He knew a cross-channel attack could not be staged without British support, and he was anxious to open a second front somewhere before the end of the year. He also believed American morale required taking the offensive in the near future. Just as important, he hoped the diversion of German troops to North Africa would mollify Stalin.

Roosevelt's endorsement of the North African campaign also reflected his deep respect for Winston Churchill and his commitment to Anglo-American unity. He and the prime minister had begun a secret correspondence with one another soon after the fall of Poland, when Churchill was first lord of the Admiralty. Their relationship was cemented by personal meetings. Despite different temperaments—Churchill was given to pomposity and solemn declarations, but Roosevelt preferred a lower-key, lighter approach—they established a partnership that survived numerous disagreements over policy. Although the balance changed later as the United States assumed an ever-larger role in the war effort, FDR at this stage was inclined to defer to Churchill's judgment.

The decision to mount TORCH, the code name for the North Africa operation, continues to be questioned. Churchill was almost surely right that a cross-channel attack at that time would have failed, with great losses. Some have argued that an invasion in 1943 would have had a good chance of success—and of shortening the war—if Anglo-American resources had been devoted exclusively to it. But TORCH diverted these resources and strongly influenced subsequent decisions to strike at Sicily and other parts of Italy. As a result, the cross-channel invasion was put off until 1944. The effect of all this on Stalin can only be guessed, but he must have suspected that his Western allies were dragging their feet while the Soviet Union bore the brunt of German might.

EISENHOWER AND THE DARLAN DEAL

The North African campaign catapulted General Dwight D. Eisenhower from relative obscurity into a position of importance that grew as the war progressed. It also enmeshed him in a controversy that jeopardized his career and raised questions about the Roosevelt administration's conduct of the war.

Eisenhower was born in Kansas, attended West Point, and, after graduation, acquired a reputation as a brilliant staff officer and planner. He had served in this capacity under several influential generals, such as John J. Pershing and Douglas MacArthur. At the time of Pearl Harbor, Eisenhower had recently been promoted to the rank of brigadier general and was chief of staff of the Third Army, stationed in Texas. General Marshall, who kept tabs on promising officers, immediately summoned Eisenhower to Washington to head the War Plans Division (soon renamed the Operations Division) of the General Staff.

Eisenhower's performance in his new position so favorably impressed Marshall that it appeared he was doomed to spend the war in Washington. "Ike" longed for a command assignment, but he accepted Marshall's judgment that he was more valuable where he was. When the general who was sent to Great Britain to preside over the American buildup there (designated BOLERO) proved inadequate, however, Marshall gave the job to Eisenhower. Although this was technically a command assignment, with the title of Commanding General, European Theater of Operations, Eisenhower's position was largely administrative in nature. Many, probably including Marshall, regarded Eisenhower as "Marshall's man in Great Britain." They assumed that when an invasion was scheduled, a new commander (likely Marshall himself) would be appointed, with Eisenhower becoming his chief of staff.

The Combined Chiefs of Staff agreed that an American should command TORCH, largely because of French dislike for the British. (Shortly after the fall of France, Churchill had ordered an attack on French warships moored near Oran to prevent them from falling into German hands; more than 1,000 Frenchmen were killed.) Eisenhower was the logical choice because he already was in place, and the logistical requirements of TORCH bore directly on the progress of BOLERO. Most important, he had Marshall's confidence. Ike learned of his appointment in an unusual fashion. Summoned to Marshall's hotel room in London, he arrived when the chief of staff was in the bathroom. He was told through the closed door that he was in charge of planning for TORCH and probably would command the operation. A few days later, this was made official.

Eisenhower's command of TORCH was doubly ironic. He had been sent to Britain in the first place for his organizational and planning skills, not because of any accomplishments as a commander of troops. Furthermore, when he was head of the Operations Division and at later times, he had vigorously opposed the North African operation because he knew it would delay a cross-channel invasion of France. Characteristically, he plunged into his new assignment with enthusiasm, and in the course of preparations, he established a policy he enforced throughout the war. Aware of how coalition warfare in the past had been hindered by national rivalries, he insisted that whatever personal differences arose, they would not be rooted in any Americans-versus-British ethic. As a result, American officers who were heard to disparage their British counterparts because of nationality were quickly relieved.

The most baffling problem confronting Eisenhower was how the French would respond. Landings could be expected to proceed efficiently if they welcomed the invasion. Their opposition, on the other hand, would have serious repercussions. There were 120,000 French troops in Morocco, Algeria, and Tunisia at this time. Although these were occupation forces rather than combat units, they might seriously disrupt an operation manned largely by troops that were inexperienced in amphibious landings and combat. Fighting the French would not be popular either in Britain or the United States, and it might throw the collaborationist Vichy government completely into the arms of Germany.

Although most French officers and men felt no love for Germany, they had at least nominal loyalty to Vichy. And members of the Vichy government, whatever their sentiments, could not openly defy Hitler. Eisenhower's task, therefore, was to find a Frenchman with sufficient stature to persuade French troops in North Africa not to fight the Allies.

One individual was dismissed at the outset—General Charles de Gaulle. De Gaulle had fled France after its defeat and had established in Great Britain what he called the Free French movement, with himself as its head. He and the Vichy government exchanged charges of treason. But Roosevelt, who disliked de Gaulle personally, excluded him as having little influence in North Africa. Another individual, a retired general named Henri Giraud, was brought out of unoccupied France, but his initial demand for supreme command of the operation caused delay. Giraud had no official position within the Vichy government, and when he finally did issue an appeal, it had no effect. When Allied landings began on November 8, the troops soon encountered French resistance at Oran and Algiers and especially at Casablanca.

Admiral Jean Darlan, commander in chief of the French armed forces, happened to be in Algiers visiting his hospitalized son when the invasion began. Frantic negotiations with Darlan resulted in his November 10 order to French troops to cease their resistance. The next day, when Hitler declared his intention to move into unoccupied France, Darlan announced that he would assume power in behalf of the Vichy government because it no longer had freedom of action. Two days later, Eisenhower concluded an agreement recognizing Darlan as commander in chief of French military forces and as head of the civil government. Giraud was relegated to a subordinate position.

News of the deal caused a sensation in Great Britain and the United States. The Vichy regime was quasi-Fascist and anti-Semitic. For an American general to recognize one of its former officials as the legitimate head of government seemed to many a betrayal of what the war was supposed to be all about. It also constituted a slap at the Free French, and, some pointed out, it would cause Stalin to wonder whether the Americans might make a similar deal with the Nazis if the opportunity arose.

Eisenhower defended himself in a long telegram to Washington on November 14. He noted that casualties would have been much greater if the French had continued resisting. As conquerors, the Allies would have had to occupy French North Africa militarily and create a civil government to administer a hostile population. The costs in men and resources would have been staggering. Darlan was the only man who could have gained a cease-fire, Eisenhower pointed out, and the only person the French in North Africa would have regarded as the legitimate successor to the Vichy government.

Roosevelt remained silent for four days while the uproar grew over the collaboration with Darlan. The political embarrassment must have tempted him to repudiate both the deal and Eisenhower. Finally, after prodding by Secretary of War Stimson, General Marshall, and others, FDR reluctantly issued a statement supporting what Ike had done. The president emphasized repeatedly that the arrangements had been made to save lives and that they were purely temporary measures "justified by the stress of battle." Darlan's assassination in December and the subsequent inclusion of General de Gaulle in the North African government muted criticism, but Eisenhower probably was lucky he did not spend the rest of the war as a staff officer back in Washington.

FIGHTING THE AXIS

The day after Allied forces went ashore in Morocco and Algeria, Hitler began sending troops from Sicily to ports in Tunisia, 400 miles east of Algiers. The British had wanted to seize the Tunisian ports of Bizerte and Tunis in the initial landings to deny them to the Germans, but General Marshall disagreed. He thought it too dangerous to expose Allied convoys to German air strength so far east, and he feared that the expeditionary forces would be cut off if Spain entered the war and seized Gibraltar. He insisted on a "safe" port (Casablanca) fronting on the Atlantic and sought to limit the landings to French Morocco. Because there were not enough troops or air cover to do everything, Eisenhower proposed a compromise: Casablanca would be occupied to satisfy Marshall, and Algerian ports would be occupied to placate the British.

The decision not to land in Tunisia may have been a major mistake of the war. Germany built up a defensive perimeter around Tunis and Bizerte far more quickly than Allied planners had assumed. The eastward thrust from Algiers into Tunisia bogged down in December due to a lack of men, equipment, supplies, and advance air bases. Only half a dozen trains a day were available to transport men and materials over the increasingly long distance. Meanwhile, Hitler was pouring German and Italian troops into Tunisia, and Rommel was approaching from Libya. The failure to seize Tunisia quickly actually prolonged the North African campaign for months, thereby delaying the cross-channel invasion of France. One of Eisenhower's biographers, Stephen E. Ambrose, suggests that the general bore partial responsibility because his preoccupation with the Darlan mess prevented him from assuming decisive leadership in time.

THE CASABLANCA CONFERENCE

Roosevelt and Churchill, together with their military staffs, met from January 13–24, 1943, at Casablanca. They had invited Stalin to attend, but he said he could not leave Russia "even for a day" because important military operations demanded all his time and energies. He stressed the need for an invasion of western Europe during that year to relieve the enormous pressures on the Soviet Union. The decisions reached at Casablanca would disappoint the Soviet dictator yet again.

The most immediate issues that had to be dealt with involved North Africa. To coordinate operations between General Alexander's command in the east and Eisenhower's, the latter was made supreme commander, with Alexander as his deputy in charge of all ground forces. Air Marshal Arthur Tedder was placed in command of the air unit, and Admiral Andrew B. Cunningham, also British, remained in charge of naval operations. The British agreed to Eisenhower's appointment because they recognized his organizational abilities and his gift for working with others and because they retained effective control of day-to-day operations. Ike asserted himself on some of the broader issues, but he gave great latitude to his more experienced subordinates.

The second local issue involved creating a stable French government in the wake of Darlan's assassination. General Giraud was an ineffectual leader with no base of support. Roosevelt detested de Gaulle personally, perceiving him to be an egotistical martinet, but he was persuaded by Churchill that the general was necessary to give legitimacy to the government in North Africa. Besides, bringing in the Free French would help deodorize the Darlan deal. An arrangement was worked out whereby Giraud and de Gaulle would share responsibilities, but in the following months, de Gaulle maneuvered himself into complete control. The general was on his way to prominence in the future of France, and he never forgot what he regarded as Roosevelt's shabby treatment of him.

When negotiations turned to matters of strategy, Roosevelt disappointed his military advisers, especially General Marshall, by agreeing with Churchill that the next target would be Sicily. This meant putting off a cross-channel invasion until 1944, and it was sure to deepen Soviet suspicions. FDR kept his own counsel, so it is difficult to determine his motives precisely. He tended to yield to Churchill at this stage of the war, as in the case of TORCH, and he must have been impressed by the prime minister's persuasive and oft-repeated arguments that the Mediterranean region constituted the "soft underbelly" of Europe. The fact that the Sicilian operation could be mounted soon after North Africa was cleared and that the invasion of France lay many months in the future must also have appealed to the president. His concern for American morale predisposed him toward an operation that promised quick dividends.

At a press conference held at the end of the Casablanca meeting, Roosevelt announced a doctrine that has remained controversial to this day. With Churchill at his side, FDR told reporters that the Allies would prosecute the war to the "unconditional surrender of Germany, Italy, and Japan." Critics have claimed that the unconditional surrender formula prolonged the fighting in Europe because it permitted the Nazi propaganda minister, Joseph Goebbels, to convince the German people that the Allies meant to enslave them. It also was said to discourage those who later might have unseated Hitler if they had had reason to believe they could secure a negotiated peace. The doctrine also prolonged Japanese resistance, according to this view, because it dashed hopes that they would be able to retain their emperor. Such allegations cannot, of course, be proven.

Roosevelt later said that the idea of unconditional surrender "popped" into his mind at the moment, and Churchill claimed that the announcement took him by surprise. But both men dissembled: The formula had been worked out well in advance of the Casablanca Conference and had been cleared with Churchill. FDR proclaimed it for several reasons in addition to the hope that it would become an inspirational phrase. Peace negotiations at the end of World War I had given rise to the "stab in the back" version of events that Hitler had used so effectively to discredit the Weimar Republic, and Roosevelt was determined to avoid that mistake and to inflict decisive defeat upon the Axis powers. He also wished to assure Stalin there would be no "deal" with Hitler, as there had been with Darlan, and to dissuade the Soviets from making a separate peace with Germany.

Allies' grand-strategy conference in North Africa, 1943: *seated,* E. J. King, Mr. Churchill, President Roosevelt; *standing,* Maj. Gen. Sir Hastings Ismay, Lord Louis Mountbatten, Field Marshal Sir John Dill. (National Archives photo no. W&C 748)

END OF THE DESERT WAR

By the time the Casablanca Conference met, there was little question that the Allies eventually could overwhelm German-Italian forces. How long this would take was another matter. The petering out of the eastward advance into Tunisia from Algeria gave the Germans time to place powerful formations, designated the Fifth Panzer Army, in their bridge-head around Tunis and Bizerte. This, in turn, meant that the retreating Afrika Korps was approaching a German stronghold rather than the other jaw of a vise being closed by Montgomery's Eighth Army. By late January 1943, after retreating 2,000 miles, Rommel reached Tunisia and occupied the Mareth line, a defensive system the French had built against an Italian invasion from Libya. Although still plagued by shortages of fuel and other materials, the Afrika Korps was replenished with new tanks and guns.

The German position was hampered by rivalry between Rommel and General Jurgen von Arnim, commander of the Fifth Panzer Army. Though ill and exhausted, Rommel devised a bold plan. After taking the Libyan

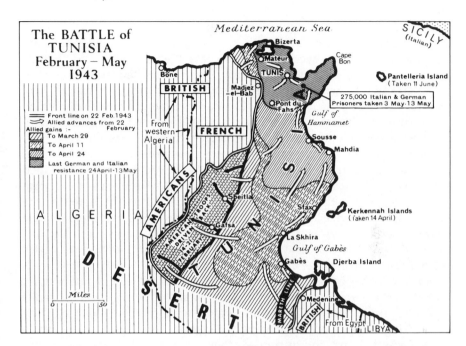

The BATTLE of
TUNISIA
February – May
1943

Front line on 22 Feb.1943
Allied advances from 22 February
Allied gains :-
To March 29
To April 11
To April 24
Last German and Italian resistance 24 April-13 May

Mediterranean Sea

SICILY (Italian)

Bizerta
Mateur
Cape Bon
TUNIS
Bône
BRITISH
Madjez-el-Bab
Pont du Fahs
FRENCH
From western Algeria
Gulf of Hammamet
Sousse
Mahdia

Pantelleria Island (Taken 11 June)

275,000 Italian & German Prisoners taken 3 May-13 May

A L G E R I A

AMERICANS

AMERICAN TROOPS DRIVEN BACK 14-21 FEBRUARY

Speitla
Gafsa

Sfax
Kerkennah Islands (Taken 14 April)

La Skhira
Gulf of Gabès
Gabès
Djerba Island

D E S E R T

Miles
0   50

MARETH LINE
BRITISH
Medenine
From Egypt LIBYA

port of Tripoli, the main body of the Eighth Army had paused while the harbor was made operational for stockpiling supplies and equipment. Rommel wanted to use this time to strike west against the inexperienced Allied forces under Eisenhower and Alexander. A penetration to key points behind their lines might push them back into Algeria and render them ineffective for months. Meanwhile, he could return to the Mareth line to await Montgomery without having to worry about his rear. His strategy might have worked had Arnim provided the Afrika Korps with more armor and mounted coordinated attacks. Arnim did not cooperate.

Rommel's offensive, launched in mid-February, succeeded at first. He broke through Allied lines at the Kasserine Pass, where the Afrika Korps routed elements of the American II Corps and sent them retreating in disarray. He lacked sufficient strength, however, to penetrate deeply enough to seize his maximum objectives. He had bought enough time to meet Montgomery before the Allies in western Tunisia could regroup and attack his rear, but he had not eliminated them as a threat to the Tunis-Bizerte bridgehead. Rommel returned to the Mareth line and, in early March, mounted an attack against the Eighth Army, units of which were still arriving from Libya. Montgomery hurried tanks and artillery forward to strengthen his forces already in place, and the Afrika Korps was thrown back with heavy losses. A sick, broken Rommel returned to Germany.

On March 20, Montgomery struck at the Mareth line. Repulsed at the center, elements of the Eighth Army outflanked the defenders and sent them retreating back along the coast toward Tunis and Bizerte. Then, after a number of veteran divisions were detached from the Eighth Army and sent to beef up the still-green Allies in the west, attacks were mounted all along the shrinking German perimeter. After being pried out of Tunis and Bizerte, Axis troops ran out of food, fuel, and ammunition, and more than 150,000 finally surrendered to the Allies on May 13.

Victory in the desert was, above all, a British victory. General Montgomery had transformed the Eighth Army into a proud, disciplined force that had chased the already legendary Afrika Korps more than 2,000 miles across the wastes of North Africa. Before El Alamein, the British had known only defeat; Churchill now said, with pardonable exaggeration, that after El Alamein, they would know only victory. Coupled with the defeat at Stalingrad, German capitulation in Africa spelled the end of Hitler's dreams of conquest.

For the Americans, North Africa brought knowledge, rather than military achievement. American troops, equipped with the best tanks and other hardware, had gone into battle with great confidence. Their humiliating defeat at Kasserine revealed how unprepared they really were. Badly led and poorly trained, they were no match for the enemy.

Responsibility for the fiasco rested on many shoulders. Eisenhower never fully grasped control of the campaign, and his desire to mediate between subordinates who disagreed with one another often resulted in half-measures when decisive action was called for. Many American officers, from the II Corps commander on down, performed ineptly. Undisciplined troops had failed to dig in properly, and many simply assumed American superiority over the enemy.

Eisenhower, stung by the defeat, began acting more forcefully. He relieved the timorous commander of II Corps and replaced him with the aggressive George Patton. Eisenhower resolved to become more ruthless with incompetents himself, and he encouraged Patton to clear out the deadwood in II Corps. He also urged Patton, who scarcely needed any urging, to instill discipline in the troops under him and to toughen them with realistic training exercises. Although no overnight miracles occurred, the performance of American units improved markedly during the remaining months of fighting in Africa. The "blooding" at Kasserine in the long run helped to create an army fit for combat.

SELECTED BIBLIOGRAPHY

Ambrose, Stephen E. *The Supreme Commander: The War Years of General Dwight D. Eisenhower* (Garden City, N.Y.: Doubleday, 1970).

Barnett, Corelli. *The Desert Generals* (London: Kimber, 1983).

Blumenson, Martin. *Kasserine Pass* (Boston: Houghton Mifflin, 1967).

Braddock, D. W. *The Campaigns in Egypt and Libya, 1940–1942* (Aldershot, U.K.: Gale and Polden, 1964).

Carell, Paul. *Foxes of the Desert* (New York: Dutton, 1961).

Carver, Michael. *Dilemmas of the Desert Wars: A New Look at the Libyan Campaign, 1940–1942* (Bloomington: University of Indiana Press, 1986).

Chalfont, Alan. *Montgomery of Alamein* (New York: Atheneum, 1976).

Chase, John L. "Unconditional Surrender Reconsidered," in *Causes and Consequences of World War II*, Robert A. Divine (ed.). (Chicago: Quadrangle, 1969).

Cray, Ed. *General of the Army: George C. Marshall, Soldier and Statesman* (New York: W. W. Norton, 1990).

Cruikshank, Charles. *Greece, 1940–1941* (London: Davis-Pointer, 1976).

Divine, Robert A. *Roosevelt and World War II* (Baltimore, Md.: Johns Hopkins University Press, 1969).

Funk, Arthur Layton. *The Politics of Torch* (Lawrence: University of Kansas Press, 1974).

Garlinski, Jozef. *The Enigma War* (New York: Scribner, 1979).

Hamilton, Nigel. *Monty's War Years, 1942–1944* (New York: McGraw-Hill, 1983).

Hart, B.H. Liddell (ed.). *The German Generals Talk* (New York: William Morrow, 1948).

Heckmann, Wolf. *Rommel's War in Africa* (Garden City, N.Y.: Doubleday, 1981).

Higham, Robin. *Diary of a Disaster: British Aid to Greece, 1940–1941* (Lexington: University Press of Kentucky, 1986).

Howard, Michael, and J.R.M. Butler (eds.). *Grand Strategy, August 1942–September 1943* (London: Her Majesty's Stationery Office, 1972).

Jackson, W.F.G. *The North African Campaign, 1940–1943* (London: Batsford, 1975).

Lewin, Ronald. *Montgomery as Military Commander* (New York: Stein and Day, 1971).

_____. *Life and Death of the Afrika Korps* (London: Batsford, 1977).

_____. *Ultra Goes to War* (London: Hutchinson, 1978).

Lucas, James. *War in the Desert: The Eighth Army at Alamein* (New York: Beaufort Books, 1983).

Matloff, Maurice, and Edwin M. Snell. *The War Department: Strategic Planning for Coalition Warfare, 1941–1942* (Washington, D.C.: Office of the Chief of Military History, Department of the Army, 1953).

Moorhead, Alan. *The Desert War* (London: Hamish Hamilton, 1965).

O'Connor, Raymond G. *Diplomacy for Victory: FDR and Unconditional Surrender* (New York: W. W. Norton, 1971).

Parrish, Thomas. *Roosevelt and Marshall: Partners in Politics and War* (New York: William Morrow, 1989).

Pogue, Forrest. *George C. Marshall: Ordeal and Hope, 1939–1942* (New York: Viking, 1966).

_____. *George C. Marshall: Organizer of Victory, 1943–1945* (New York: Viking, 1973).

Sainsbury, Keith. *The North African Landings, 1942* (Newark: University of Delaware Press, 1976).

Smith, Gaddis. *American Diplomacy During the Second World War, 1941–1945,* 2d ed. (New York: Knopf, 1985).

van Creveld, Martin. *Supplying War* (Cambridge: Cambridge University Press, 1977).

9
Attacking the Underbelly (1943–1945)

Planning for the invasion of Sicily, code-named HUSKY, had begun well before North Africa was cleared. From beginning to end, the campaign would reveal the difficulties of conducting a coalition war, as national rivalries precluded unified command in fact as well as in name. The conquest of Sicily would give the Allies undisputed mastery of the Mediterranean and might even push Italy out of the war. These goals were accomplished but, much to the dismay of General Marshall and other American military leaders, the occupation of Sicily also strengthened the case for invading Italy at the expense of the buildup for a cross-channel invasion of France. The Italian campaign subsequently became one of the most criticized of the war.

SICILY

As originally drawn, HUSKY called for seven separate landings along the east, south, and north coasts of Sicily. General Montgomery objected strongly to this dissipation of forces and argued for a single, concentrated assault on the southeastern shore. He believed his experienced Eighth Army should dominate the operation, with the American II Corps under his command in a subsidiary role. His plan was militarily sound but politically divisive, especially in view of his own abrasive nature and condescending attitude toward his allies. That U.S. forces should serve as a supporting cast to the Eighth Army was unacceptable to the Americans.

A compromise was worked out whereby the many landings were reduced to two: the Eighth Army in the southeast and the American forces, reconstituted as the Seventh Army, in the southwest. General Alexander, as Eisenhower's deputy, was nominally in charge of the entire campaign. He proved unable to impose his will on subordinate commanders, and Ike was too concerned about maintaining the facade of unity to interfere. The result was two almost independent operations with leaders that rarely cooperated with one another and at times quarreled over jurisdictions and objectives.

British intelligence staged a clever ruse to conceal Allied intentions. A corpse, dressed in a British uniform, was set afloat in a life preserver off the coast of Spain, ostensibly a courier whose plane had crashed at sea. A briefcase chained to the body contained documents indicating that the Allies planned to invade Greece and Sardinia. Spanish officials turned these papers over to the Germans, who believed them to be authentic, and defenses were beefed up in Greece and Sardinia at the expense of Sicily.

Shortly before dawn on July 10, Allied armies began putting troops on the beaches of Sicily. The two available German panzer divisions were located many miles away, with the result that the invaders had to face only surprised Italian coastal defense units of inferior quality. Airborne landings inland fared less well. Inexperienced pilots, flying in high winds, made drops far away from assigned zones. Still, during the first few days, eight divisions had been put ashore, and all objectives were secured. The heaviest Allied casualties resulted from German air attacks against inadequate fighter cover.

The key to the Sicilian campaign was Messina, which lay at the northeastern tip of the island only two miles from the toe of Italy. If Messina could be taken quickly, Axis forces in Sicily would be prevented from escaping across the narrows to the mainland. Although American advances had been slowed by the first Axis counterattacks, including one by the crack Hermann Goering Panzer Division, British troops had moved forward quickly against light opposition. Buoyed by such easy success, Montgomery concluded that the Eighth Army could drive directly northward to Messina along the east coast, while the Seventh Army provided flanking cover in the center of the island.

Montgomery erred badly. The road to Messina ran through Catania, about halfway up the coast. The proximity of Mount Etna to the west made the Catania area a natural bottleneck with terrain well suited for defense. Montgomery, with Alexander's permission, launched a two-pronged offensive against Catania: a drive along the coast and what he called a "left hook" to the west of Etna. The Germans and Italians, meanwhile, had concentrated their forces to deny the British access to Messina. After initial successes, Montgomery's offensives bogged down against determined opposition, and his divided forces lacked sufficient strength on either wing to punch through. Usually criticized for being overcautious, Montgomery in this instance acted too boldly.

SWITZERLAND

GERMANY

The ALLIED INVASION
of ITALY
1943 – 1945

Mussolini executed by
Italian partisans
28 April 1945

Brenner
Pass

US
troops
met 4 May

Vipiteno

Dongo
L. Como

New Zealand troops
entered 2 May 1945

Milan
26 April

Salo

L. Garda

Verona

Trieste

Turin

Allied Advances
20-30 April 1945

Venice
29 April

YUGOSLAVIA

Genoa

Bologna

Ravenna

Zara

US Advance
20-30 April 1945

WINTER LINE JAN-APRIL 1945

Florence

Adriatic Sea

Liberated by Free
French forces
September 1943

by 4 August

Elba
Occupied
18 June

CORSICA
Revolt of Resistance
Movement, summer 1943

by 9 June

Termoli

ROME
Entered
4 June

Monte
Cassino
18 May

WINTER LINE 1943-44

by 8 October

Bari

Anzio
Beachhead
22 Jan-
22 May 1944

Naples

Brindisi
by 14
Sept

Occupied by
Anglo-American
troops,
autumn 1943

Salerno

Taranto

by 25 September

SARDINIA

Tyrrhenian
Sea

9 Sept 1943

by 14 Sept

9 Sept 1943

Mussolini overthrown 25 July 1943
Italy surrendered 3 September 1943
Germans occupied Italy September 1943
Italy declared war on Germany 13 Oct 1943
Germans in Italy surrendered 29 April 1945

Entered 17 Aug

Messina

Palermo

3 Sept

Miles

0   100

by 23 July

by
17 August

Catania

Licata
by
15 July

Syracuse

ANGLO-AMERICAN
occupation
See Map 78

Tunis

AMERICANS

10 July 1943
Landings from
NORTH AFRICA

BRITISH

Being relegated to a covering role infuriated the impetuous Patton, who longed for military glory for himself and his command. Insult was added to injury when highways previously assigned to the Seventh Army were taken over by the British to sustain Montgomery's "left hook." Even the normally unflappable General Omar Bradley, who now commanded II Corps, was outraged.

Patton refused to stay put. Leaving II Corps to advance through central Sicily along the British flank, he sent the rest of the Seventh Army plunging toward Palermo, on the extreme northwestern tip of the island. This meant these units were heading *away from* Axis troops, who were withdrawing east to face Montgomery. Palermo had no strategic value, but its capture would bring Patton the headlines he sought. He next intended to pivot eastward and "beat" Montgomery to Messina. That Alexander and Eisenhower permitted such personal motives to dictate military strategy does not reflect well on their leadership.

As Montgomery continued to slug upward through the Catania region, Patton took Palermo on July 22. In a series of poorly coordinated but aggressive attacks, including three ineffective amphibious landings behind retreating Axis lines, Patton began driving along the northern coast toward Messina. Montgomery, unwilling to sacrifice troops needlessly and deeply involved in preparations for invading Italy, conceded the "race" for Messina to Patton. Advance units moved into the city on the night of August 16, and others were held back so that Patton himself could make a triumphal entry. Unfortunately, more than 100,000 Axis troops, together with guns, tanks, and equipment, had already been ferried across the Strait of Messina to fight another day. Montgomery's overconfidence and Patton's ego precluded the kind of cooperation that would have enabled Messina to be taken before evacuation was possible. As a military operation, the best thing that can be said about the operation in Sicily is that it provided experience.

During the final days of the Sicilian campaign, General Patton became involved in several incidents that brought him great notoriety and almost ended his career. Visiting an army hospital on August 3, he became enraged at an American soldier with no visible wounds who said he "couldn't take it" in combat anymore. Patton screamed curses at the young man, slapped his face, and threw him out of the tent. A week later, he repeated his performance at another hospital, this time waving his pistol and threatening to shoot the offending soldier.

When he learned of these events, Eisenhower wrote Patton a personal reprimand and had him apologize to the men involved, to the divisions from which they came, and to the doctors and nurses at the hospitals. Reporters who learned about the incidents agreed to keep silent after Eisenhower appealed to them, saying that Patton would be "indis-

Lt. Col. Lyle Bernard, CO, 30th Inf. Regt., a prominent figure in the second daring amphibious landing behind enemy lines on Sicily's north coast, discusses military strategy with Lt. Gen. George S. Patton, near Brolo, 1943. (National Archives photo no. W&C 1024)

pensable" to the Allied war effort in the months to come. Three months later, however, a popular American newspaper columnist broke the story, which caused a flurry of demands for Patton's relief. Eisenhower and Marshall rode out the storm because they believed that, whatever Patton's faults, his aggressiveness and drive would be sorely needed in defeating the Germans. It would not be the last time Patton's ungovernable behavior would cause embarrassment.

ITALY LEAVES THE WAR

Neither the Italian people nor their armed forces had been as enthusiastic about the war as had their German allies, and Mussolini never had attained the kind of personal loyalty Hitler commanded. The Duce had led Italy to disasters in Greece and North Africa, and the invasion of Sicily presaged the invasion of the Italian peninsula itself. The Italians had neither the resources nor the will to resist. Most wanted Italy out of the war and Mussolini out of power.

Two weeks after the first landings in Sicily, the Italian Grand Council repudiated Mussolini, and the king dismissed him the following day. Mussolini was put under arrest and spirited away to a series of secluded hideaways. Although German intelligence had failed to give Hitler any warning of these developments, he learned where Mussolini was being kept and had him rescued by a daring SS commando operation. Hitler installed Mussolini as head of a "government" in northern Italy, but it never really functioned as such. The Duce by this time was a broken figurehead. During the last months of the war in Europe, as German forces in Italy retreated north, he was captured and executed by Italian partisans.

Far more important than Mussolini's fate was the position of the new Italian government, headed by Field Marshal Pietro Badoglio, former commander of the Italian army who had been dismissed by Mussolini after his defeat in Greece three years earlier. Hitler had begun sending divisions to Italy as soon as he heard of Mussolini's downfall. If, in defense of their own country, Italian troops fought alongside the Germans, there was a good chance the invasion would be thrown back into the sea. But prospects would improve vastly if the Italians could be persuaded to join with the Allies or at least offer passive resistance to German operations.

Negotiations between Eisenhower's headquarters and the Badoglio government, begun through intermediaries in mid-August, were enormously complicated. The Allies wished to get all the help they could, but they were wary of entering into another Darlan deal with Badoglio and of compromising the unconditional surrender doctrine. The Italians, on the other hand, were frightened of antagonizing the Germans, who might retaliate harshly for the double-cross, particularly against Rome. Finally, on the evening of September 8, just hours before the main Allied landing at Salerno, the armistice was announced. Eisenhower's hopes of gaining Italian support were dashed. The king and Badoglio fled from Rome, and Italian military forces laid down their arms before advancing German troops. Meanwhile, the Germans had used the time consumed by negotiations to pour reinforcements into Italy.

THE INVASION OF ITALY

There were disagreements among the Allies over strategy in Italy. Churchill, wavering again about a cross-channel invasion, wanted a large-scale offensive that would take Rome quickly and drive the Germans out of Italy. To help achieve this goal, he spoke of turning the "fury" of the Italian population and armed forces against Germany, an absurd notion, as it turned out. Marshall, supported by FDR, had more modest goals. Although willing to accept any Italian aid that might be forthcoming, he was opposed to committing large forces that would detract from the buildup for the invasion of France, now code-named OVERLORD. His immediate objective was to seize the Foggia air base in the southeast, from which bombers could operate against Austria and the Balkans as well as the Germans in Italy. Eisenhower, harassed by conflicting messages from London and Washington, muddled along as best he could.

There were differences among German leaders about how best to defend Italy. Rommel, having recovered his health after the North African campaign, had been given command of German forces in northern Italy. He recommended pulling back to defensive positions north of Rome. Field Marshal Albert Kesselring, commander in the south, believed all of Italy should be defended. Hitler at first agreed with Rommel, then adopted Kesselring's strategy. The delay proved costly.

The first Allied landings were made on September 3 by elements of the British Eighth Army, which crossed the Strait of Messina to the toe of Italy. The appearance of Allied troops on the mainland helped convince the Badoglio government to accept an armistice. British units met only light opposition because German forces were in the process of withdrawing to the north. Montgomery, cautious as usual, paused to build up his bridgehead before moving forward. He did not know that the Germans had temporarily decided to abandon the south, and he was afraid premature advances might be thrown back by counterattacks in force. Besides, to his great chagrin, Montgomery had been given no clear-cut objectives other than to engage enemy forces and to move north if they retreated. He later contemptuously referred to his orders as "a unique incident in the history of War."

The main landings were made by General Mark Clark's Fifth Army, consisting of the British X and the American VI Corps, on September 8 in the vicinity of Salerno, about 30 miles south of Naples. Clark, who had served as Eisenhower's deputy, had no combat experience but opposed the selection of Salerno because nearby hills would permit defenders to pour down fire on the exposed beaches. He was overruled for Sicilian-based fighters could not provide air cover any farther north. The operation was made even more risky when shoreline conditions forced the British to make three separate landings, the nearest almost 10 miles north of the American beachhead. The Germans had a panzer division in the vicinity and could bring other units into the fighting in a matter of days.

After initial success, the invading forces encountered mounting opposition: Kesselring had five additional divisions in place two days after the assault began. The British X Corps was taking particularly heavy casualties, and efforts by the Americans to close the gap by moving laterally were impeded. Heavy German attacks on September 12 threatened to prevent the linkup and get behind exposed American units. Disaster was averted by throwing in an airborne division previously slated to drop near Rome, together with heavy air and naval bombardment and Montgomery's advance from the south. On September 15, forward units of the Eighth Army arrived, and the crisis was over. Kesselring broke off his attacks and began withdrawing. Allied soldiers, too exhausted to follow up, did not take Naples until October 2.

As with the North African and Sicilian campaigns, recriminations between the British and Americans quickly developed. Montgomery, smarting under the subsidiary role assigned his forces, regarded the Salerno operation as amateurish and claimed credit for bailing it out. The Americans, on the other hand, blamed Montgomery for jeopardizing Clark's Fifth Army by his slow advance up the Italian boot. Eisenhower, as usual, tried to paper over the differences.

The original objectives of the Italian campaign, at least in Marshall's view, had all been obtained by early October. Italy had been knocked out of the war, the Foggia airfields had been seized by a third landing at the instep of the boot, Naples had been captured, and the Germans had committed a total of more than twenty divisions to Italy's defense. Political, more than military, considerations dictated what followed. The seizure of Rome, capital city of one of the Axis powers, was a powerful magnet that attracted both Churchill and Roosevelt. Instead of consolidating in the areas already occupied, therefore, the Allies began preparing to drive on Rome. The only military justification for such action was that it would continue to tie up German forces and make them unavailable for redeployment elsewhere. Of course, Allied personnel and resources also would be expended.

OVERLORD AND ITALY

If the cross-channel invasion were to constitute the decisive Anglo-American thrust against Germany, as Roosevelt and Marshall insisted, its requirements would determine what could be allocated to the Italian campaign. Offensives by the Eighth and Fifth armies in mid-October brought only limited gains against determined opposition on terrain that was well suited for defense. Rugged mountains running down the Italian peninsula and frequently swollen rivers crossing it laterally provided the Allies with few options except to punch forward. Renewed offensives in November again achieved modest successes, but they had to be called off when winter rains made the roads impassable. By the end of 1943, Allied forces stood before the Gustav line, a system of fortifications running from about 80 miles below Rome on the west coast across Italy to the Adriatic.

As overall commander of Allied forces in Italy, Eisenhower argued vigorously that they should be strengthened as much as possible. Offensive operations in Italy, he contended, would help ensure the success of OVERLORD. They would keep twenty-five German divisions pinned down and, if successful, would threaten southern France by spring 1944. He met opposition from two sides. Churchill, still enamored of avoiding OVERLORD by attacking the "soft underbelly," wanted to detach divisions from Italy to attack elsewhere in the eastern Mediterranean. Marshall, on the other hand, resisted any measures that would delay or weaken OVERLORD.

In November, Roosevelt, Churchill, and Stalin, together with their civilian and military advisers, held a conference in Teheran. FDR, who had never met Stalin before, regarded this as an opportunity to convince the Soviet dictator that his Western allies meant to collaborate fully in winning the war and in creating a lasting peace. He went out of his way throughout the conference to demonstrate American goodwill. In response to Stalin's inquiry about the long-awaited cross-channel invasion, FDR assured him it would take place no later than spring 1944. When told that no one had yet been selected to command the operation, however, Stalin expressed doubt that the British and Americans were acting in good faith. Eager to please the Soviet leader, Roosevelt replied that he would decide on a commander, with British concurrence (they already had agreed to accept an American), during the next few days.

FDR, who frequently put off making hard choices, could delay no longer. Many people, probably including Roosevelt himself, had assumed that General Marshall would command OVERLORD, with Eisenhower replacing him as army chief of staff. The president gave Marshall the opportunity by asking him personally to make the selection. With characteristic unselfishness, Marshall declined to name himself to a position he undoubtedly coveted and told Roosevelt he would abide by whatever decision was made. With Marshall's refusal to take him off the hook, FDR at last named Eisenhower. On his way back to Washington, Roosevelt met with Eisenhower in Tunis. His first words to the general were, "Well, Ike, you are going to command OVERLORD."

Roosevelt later said he selected Eisenhower because he would not have been able to sleep at night with Marshall out of Washington. But there were other considerations. Eisenhower had demonstrated his ability to get along with the British, especially Churchill; Marshall might not have been as diplomatic. Marshall, on the other hand, probably exercised more influence on both the Joint Chiefs of Staff and the Combined Chiefs of Staff than Eisenhower would have been able to attain. Finally, Marshall handled the always difficult MacArthur about as well as anyone could. As MacArthur's former aide, Eisenhower might not have fared as well.

The commitment to OVERLORD rendered the Mediterranean a secondary theater. Eisenhower was replaced by British General Henry Maitland Wilson, with Alexander remaining in command of ground forces. Along with Eisenhower, American generals Bradley and Patton and the airman Carl Spaatz were reassigned to England. To command the British contingent in OVERLORD; Churchill picked Montgomery, who turned over the Eighth Army to General Oliver Lease. Those who remained in Italy had to fight constantly to get resources diverted from the cross-channel invasion. They found that Eisenhower, in his new position, was far less sympathetic than he had once been to Allied requirements in Italy.

ANZIO

One of Eisenhower's legacies to the Italian campaign was Operation SHINGLE, scheduled for late January 1944. SHINGLE provided for an amphibious landing behind German lines at Anzio, a coastal town 30 miles south of Rome. If Allied forces drove inland to the Alban hills 20 miles away, they could cut supply and communication lines between Rome and the Gustav line. Offensives by the Fifth and Eighth armies, set to begin a week earlier, would provide diversion. Success on both fronts would force the Germans to abandon their strong defensive positions and retire north, leaving Rome to the Allies. Few at Eisenhower's headquarters had been enthusiastic about the plan, but he had bowed to Churchill's desire for a bold stroke to end the stalemate.

Landings at Anzio began on January 22. VI Corps, a mixed force of British and Americans commanded by General John Lucas, went ashore unopposed. SHINGLE achieved complete tactical surprise. The Germans had believed that if the Allies mounted an amphibious operation, it would take place north of Rome. However, the inexperienced and cautious Lucas, with Clark's concurrence, failed to exploit the opportunity. Determined to avoid a repetition of Salerno, when Allied forces had almost been pushed back into the sea, Lucas sat tight until tanks and artillery could be brought in during the next several days. Kesselring used the time to patch together what became XIV Army and surrounded the beachhead.

Finally, on January 30, when Lucas at last decided to move ahead, the recently arrived Germans inflicted heavy casualties on Allied advance units. In early February and again a week later, the Germans mounted counterattacks that almost destroyed VI Corps. Lucas was replaced by the more aggressive Lucian Truscott, but all he could do was hang on. "I had hoped that we would be hurling a wildcat ashore," Churchill commented, "but all we got was a stranded whale." Instead of a threat to the German rear, SHINGLE had become instead a besieged outpost that had to be rescued months later by Allied forces advancing from the south. Despite Lucas's initial hesitation, the Anzio operation might have succeeded had it been mounted on a much larger scale. However, this could not be done because so many landing craft, always in short supply, had been designated for use in OVERLORD. Ironically, because there were no port facilities around Anzio, the beachhead had to be supplied by these craft until the Fifth Army reached it.

MONTE CASSINO

Offensives by the Fifth and Eighth armies in mid-January 1944 penetrated but failed to break through the Gustav line, which lay behind deep and fast-flowing rivers. The major German strongpoint was Monte Cassino, an imposing mountain overlooking miles of river valley. Flanking attacks made some advances, but the U.S. II Corps, moving directly against Monte Cassino, was stopped cold, with extremely heavy losses. The battered Americans were replaced in early February by a New Zealand corps commanded by General Bernard Freyberg. What followed provided yet another example of how difficult it was to conduct coalition warfare.

The plans for a renewed offensive provided that an Indian division under Freyberg's command would attempt to storm Monte Cassino while other units struck at the flanks. The Indian general complained that the Germans were using a Benedictine monastery on top of the mountain as an observation post, enabling them to direct accurate fire on attackers. He demanded that the monastery be bombed before the assault began. Freyberg supported him against General Clark, who did not believe the Germans were using the monastery and opposed its destruction. The issue was debated through General Alexander's headquarters to General Wilson's, where Clark was overruled. In mid-February, hundreds of Allied bombers blasted the ancient and famous monastery to rubble.

The Allied high command knew there would be enormous criticism over the bombing of the abbey but went ahead primarily for political reasons. There had been a growing demand in New Zealand that its troops be pulled out of the Italian campaign, and Wilson and Alexander were afraid that if they opposed Freyberg's demand, he would take his troops off the line. Ironically, the Germans had not been using the monastery but moved in after the bombing because the ruins provided excellent fortifications. Subsequent attacks by New Zealanders and Indians were repulsed. Critics later charged that repeated head-on assaults against Monte Cassino were unnecessary and that it would have been wiser and less costly merely to have bypassed it.

Renewed attempts to storm Monte Cassino were made in mid-March, preceded by heavy bombing of the town lying at the foot of the mountain. Again, they were repulsed with heavy losses and were called off after a week. Finally, after Allied forces regrouped by moving units of the Eighth Army west to reinforce those in the Monte Cassino area, a massive offensive began on May 11 along a 20-mile front. Breakthroughs elsewhere rendered Monte Cassino untenable, and it was finally taken by the Polish II Corps after fierce fighting. Kesselring was forced to retreat north of Rome, which he declared an open city to avoid its destruction.

Having broken through the Gustav line, General Clark made a decision that has been criticized ever since. German concentration on defending Monte Cassino at last permitted VI Corps to break out of the Anzio perimeter. Earlier plans called for the two forces to link up and then swing east behind the Germans to trap them against the advancing Eighth Army. But Clark instead chose to head north for Rome, which the first American troops entered on June 4. The psychological boost derived from having captured the first Axis capital scarcely compensated for permitting the Germans to retire in good order to prepared positions north of the city. Even the propaganda value was diminished by the fact that, two days later, the Allied invasion of France pushed the capture of Rome off the headlines.

ANVIL (DRAGOON)

Generals Marshall and Eisenhower had long advocated that OVER-LORD be complemented by a simultaneous invasion of southern France, code-named ANVIL. Such an operation, they argued, would divert German forces and secure the ports of Toulon and Marseilles. Churchill and his military people opposed ANVIL because seven divisions would be taken from the Italian campaign. Better to strengthen Allied armies in Italy, they claimed, enabling them to advance through northern Italy to strike at Vienna and Budapest. As the United States was providing the bulk of men and resources in Europe by this time, the American view prevailed. A disgruntled Churchill insisted that the operation be renamed DRAGOON because he had been dragooned into it.

Due to the delay in reaching Rome, landings in southern France did not begin until August 15. Obviously, this was too late to divert enemy forces during the early stages of OVERLORD. ANVIL-DRAGOON met light opposition, which was quickly forced to withdraw. Marseilles and other ports soon began handling Allied supplies and equipment, and more than a third of all tonnage shipped to Europe during the latter months of 1944 passed through them. Their importance diminished when new harbor facilities became available.

Meanwhile, in Italy, reduced Allied forces continued to hammer away at German defenses ranged across the Gothic line, about 100 miles north of Rome. Not as formidable as the Gustav system, the line was breached by late August, but the Germans continued to make the Allies pay for every mile they advanced. Finally, after the fall rains began, offensive operations were called off until spring 1945. Both sides settled in for another muddy, cold winter.

The drive north resumed in early April. Employing a two-pronged offensive by the Fifth and Eighth armies, supported by overwhelming air power, the Allies forced the Germans to retreat into the Po Valley. By late April, the Germans were finished, having been forced to abandon their tanks and heavy equipment when crossing the Po River. On April 29, the German commander agreed to an unconditional surrender, effective May 2. That week, elements of the Fifth Army linked up with Allied units advancing from the west. The Italian campaign, at long last, was over.

A STRANGE INTERLUDE

Events in Italy were to have unanticipated consequences for the relations between the Western Allies and the Soviet Union. Stalin accused Roosevelt and Churchill of bad faith in dealing with German forces in Italy. His charges fed the increasing mistrust on both sides that was becoming evident during the spring of 1945, on the eve of victory over Germany.

In February, the American Office of Strategic Services (OSS) in Switzerland received word that a German SS officer, Major General Karl Wolff, sought a meeting with Allied authorities. Wolff believed he could influence Field Marshal Kesselring to surrender the troops under his command. The British and Americans notified the Soviets but did not invite them to participate in preliminary talks with Wolff, to be held in a Swiss city. When the Soviets protested, they were told that it was a local military matter but that they would be invited to attend if negotiations progressed to a formal stage—that is, if someone actually representing Kesselring appeared at Allied headquarters in Italy.

Moving up through Prato, Italy, men of the 370th Infantry Regiment have yet to climb the mountain that lies ahead, April 9, 1945. (National Archives photo no. W&C 1030)

On March 22, Soviet Foreign Minister V. M. Molotov handed the American ambassador in Moscow a note stating that the Soviet government regarded what was being done as "not a misunderstanding but something worse." To Roosevelt's denial of wrongdoing, Stalin replied that the Germans were using the talks as a cover to transfer divisions from Italy to the eastern front (this was false). When FDR protested that this allegation was untrue, Stalin became even more insulting. On April 3, he claimed that an agreement already had been reached with the Germans to open the Italian front in exchange for favorable peace terms. Knowledge of this arrangement had spread, Stalin continued, causing the Germans to stop fighting in the west while continuing to resist the Soviets.

Roosevelt, who previously had treated Stalin with great deference, responded sharply. He had a message drafted that not only rejected Stalin's charges but expressed his "bitter resentment" of those Soviet officials who had made such "vile misrepresentations" of Anglo-American actions. On April 7, Stalin retreated. Without retracting his allegations, he informed Roosevelt and Churchill that he had not doubted their trustworthiness and professed to see the matter as one of disagreement over proper procedures. Roosevelt had no wish to belabor the issue but repeated his contention that the fault lay with Soviet misinformation, rather than Anglo-American betrayal. Whether Stalin actually believed his charges or if he made them for other reasons is unknown. The effect was to deepen suspicions on both sides.

THE ITALIAN CAMPAIGN: AN ASSESSMENT

Critics of the campaign in Italy range all the way from those who say it never should have been mounted at all to others who believe a greater commitment would have brought enormous gains, possibly even rendering OVERLORD unnecessary. No one can be sure what would have happened had alternative courses been followed, and it must be remembered that political considerations influenced military decisions. What can be said with some confidence, however, is that the path actually taken represented a compromise that brought a poor return on the investment made.

Almost all American military planners and many of the British tacticians opposed the invasion of Italy as a wasteful diversion of men and resources from OVERLORD. They were overruled by Churchill's vigorous advocacy and by Roosevelt's acquiescence. FDR seems to have agreed for two reasons. He went along with the prime minister in the matter of Italy in return for the latter's firm commitment to a cross-channel invasion later. He also believed that domestic enthusiasm for the war in Europe could best be maintained by a successful offensive against Italy months before OVERLORD could be launched. Whether his concern for American morale was justified can never be known.

Operations in Italy never went according to expectations. Montgomery, partly because his objectives were not clearly defined, dithered in southern Italy while the Salerno landings were almost annihilated. Similarly, Anzio came close to ending in disaster. Although it is tempting to place the blame on one or another general for lost opportunities, the fact is that tenacious German opposition made a mockery of Churchill's image of a "soft underbelly."

Churchill later claimed that the real tragedy of the Italian campaign is that it never received the priority that would have enabled it to succeed properly. Given enough strength, he wrote, Allied forces could have thrust north through Italy and burst out onto the Hungarian plains. Not only would this have ended the war sooner, it would have permitted Anglo-American armies to meet the Soviets far to the east of where they actually did, thus sparing millions of people from Soviet occupation.

Churchill's scenario is fanciful. At the time, he argued in purely military terms, without any reference to the political implications of denying territory to the Soviets. Had Allied forces in Italy been reinforced, the Germans undoubtedly would have sent more divisions to bolster their defenses. And even if the Anglo-American armies had cleared Italy sooner, their ability to penetrate north into the heartland would have been limited by extended supply lines over rugged terrain, as well as by German resistance.

If Italy had to be invaded at all, General Marshall's recommendation that occupation should be limited to the southern portion probably would have been the wisest course. The Allies would have secured the Loggia airfields, enabling them to dominate the skies over Italy and to bomb Austria and the Balkans. They would have pinned down almost as many German divisions with fewer of their own. Air superiority and Ultra would have rendered surprise counterattacks next to impossible. That the capture of Rome and the long struggle northward was worth the additional expenditures of men and resources has to be doubted.

SELECTED BIBLIOGRAPHY

Blumenson, Martin. *Anzio: The Gamble That Failed* (London: Weidenfeld & Nicolson, 1963).
_____ . *Salerno to Cassino* (Washington, D.C.: Office of the Chief of Military History, Department of the Army, 1969).
Bradley, Omar, with Clay Blair. *A General's Life: An Autobiography* (New York: Simon & Schuster, 1983).

Clark, Mark. *Calculated Risk* (New York: Harper, 1950).

Deakin, F. W. *The Brutal Friendship: Mussolini, Hitler and the Fall of Italian Fascism* (New York: Harper & Row, 1962).

Gilbert, Martin. *Winston S. Churchill: Road to Victory, 1941–1945* (Boston: Houghton Mifflin, 1986).

Hapgood, David, and David Richardson. *Monte Cassino* (New York: Congdon and Weed, 1984).

Higgins, Trumbull. *Soft Underbelly: The Anglo-American Controversy over the Italian Campaign* (New York: Macmillan, 1968).

Jackson, W.G.F. *The Battle for Italy* (New York: Harper & Row, 1967).

———. *The Battle for Rome* (New York: Bonanza Books, 1969).

Kesselring, Albert. *Kesselring: A Soldier's Record* (Westport, Conn.: Greenwood, 1954).

Linklater, Eric. *The Campaign in Italy* (London: Her Majesty's Stationery Office, 1951).

Matloff, Maurice. *Strategic Planning for Coalition Warfare, 1943–1944* (Washington, D.C.: Office of the Chief of Military History, Department of the Army, 1959).

Pond, Hugh. *Sicily* (London: Kimber, 1962).

Smith, Howard M., and Albert N. Garland. *Sicily and the Surrender of Italy* (Washington, D.C.: Office of the Chief of Military History, Department of the Army, 1965).

Stoler, Mark. *The Politics of the Second Front: American Military Planning in Coalition Warfare, 1941–1943* (Westport, Conn.: Greenwood, 1977).

10
Occupied Areas

At the peak of their expansion, Germany and Japan controlled large portions of the globe and many millions of people. Leaders in both nations stressed the mutual benefits that would flow from these arrangements. Nazis boasted of a "new order" that would guarantee a prosperous and integrated Europe under German auspices. The Japanese, using the more pretentious phrase "greater East Asian co-prosperity sphere," promised not only material progress but liberation from European colonialism. The reality turned out to be something else. People in occupied areas were, at best, exploited economically; at worst, they were victims of repressive policies as brutal and murderous as any in recorded history.

THE GERMAN "NEW ORDER"

Adolf Hitler's racial theories guaranteed that German occupation policies would vary by region. They were relatively light-handed in the west. The Germanic peoples of Denmark, Norway, and the Netherlands fared best. They were encouraged to become partners in the new order and actively recruited by various Nazi groups, such as the military arm of the SS. Thousands responded, especially among the Dutch. Hitler apparently intended that, some day, the Scandinavian countries and Holland would become integral parts of the Third Reich.

Means of exercising influence over these nations differed according to circumstances. Hitler permitted the Danish government to continue functioning with a measure of independence for several years, though it was subject to overall German control. Norway, because of its struggle against invasion in 1940 and widespread anti-German feelings, was at first ruled by a Nazi collaborationist regime headed by Vidkun Quisling. Quisling's ineptitude and unpopularity with the Norwegian people caused Hitler to force him offstage for a while, but he was reinstated as prime minister in 1942 and remained in that position until the end of the war. Whatever form German domination took, its purpose was to place human and material resources at the disposal of the Nazi war machine. Overt resistance in any area, of course, was countered with quick and savage reprisals.

Hitler had mixed feelings about the French. As Latin people, they were, he felt, inferior to Aryans, but he admired some aspects of their culture (others he regarded as degenerate). The two-thirds of France occupied as a result of the 1940 armistice was run by the German army, though with considerable interference by competing Nazi bureaucracies. Unoccupied France was governed by a collaborationist regime, with its seat in the resort town of Vichy. The Vichy government, as it became known, was subservient to Germany in the realm of foreign affairs, but it exercised nearly full civil authority until the Germans moved in after the Allied invasion of North Africa. Even then, the Vichy regime served as the conduit through which German policies were carried out.

Vichy France, unlike other collaborationist governments that were run by Nazi stooges, was nominally led by a man of national stature. Marshal Henri Pétain, hero of the Great War, had been appointed vice premier shortly before the fall of France in 1940 and became Vichy's head of state after the armistice. He believed that, to survive, France had to accommodate itself to a German-dominated Europe. No democrat himself, Pétain was surrounded by a gaggle of authoritarians and pro-Nazis who represented the most reactionary elements in France. Men like the vicious anti-Semite Pierre Laval actually formulated and carried out policies, as the old marshal became increasingly senile.

During its short life, the Vichy regime inflicted wounds upon France that fester to this day. It existed, after all, at the pleasure of the detested Germans, who had battered the French so badly during the Great War and humiliated them in 1940. Yet, it was the "legitimate" successor to the Third Republic and exercised at least the appearance of a national government. Those who served in or supported it wrapped themselves in the flag, while denouncing Charles de Gaulle and his Free French as traitors. Vichy collaborators were treated roughly when France was liberated, and the entire sordid episode still evokes deep emotions among those who lived through it.

German policies in the east varied by area, but on the whole, they were much harsher than those in western nations. The Czechs were Slavic people for whom Hitler had contempt, but their docility and productivity at first earned them mild treatment. The British-engineered assassination of "reich protector" Reinhard Heydrich in the town of Lidice brought barbaric reprisals. Lidice and another village were completely destroyed: The men were shot out of hand, and the women and children were sent to concentration camps. The Slovaks also fared relatively well until increasing German pressures sparked a revolt in 1944 that was suppressed with great bloodshed.

Nazi barbarism was revealed most nakedly in Poland and in occupied Soviet lands. Polish intellectuals and religious leaders were murdered by the SS, millions of Poles were forcibly resettled, and millions more were sent to Germany as slave laborers. German rule was equally harsh in Soviet territory, even in areas such as the Ukraine where many inhabitants initially welcomed the Germans as liberators. Known Communists were executed as a matter of policy. The SS carried on a reign of terror designed to keep the population submissive, and large numbers of people were deported to labor camps. The treatment of Soviet prisoners of war was especially brutal. An estimated 3 million perished in German captivity: Some were worked to death, some were subjected to hideous "scientific" experiments, and others died of starvation or of untreated diseases. In all, the Nazis killed as many as 9 to 10 million Europeans, excluding the Jews and Gypsies, who occupied a special category.

THE HOLOCAUST

Anti-Semitism has a long history in Europe. Adolf Hitler imbibed it deeply during his years in Vienna, subsequently making it a central part of his life. "Today I believe that I am acting in accordance with the will of the Almighty Creator," he wrote in *Mein Kampf, "by defending myself against the Jew, I am fighting for the work of the Lord"* (his emphasis). His evil crusade against Jews reached its depths in what was euphemistically called the "final solution"—that is, the systematic extermination of all Jews unfortunate enough to find themselves within reach of the Third Reich. He croaked out his message of hatred until the very end, even blaming "international Jewry" for Germany's fate in the last will he composed before committing suicide in his Berlin bunker.

Following his accession to power in 1933, Hitler moved in stages to remove Jews from participation in German society, thereby forcing them to emigrate. Between April and October of that year, a series of laws were enacted barring "non-Aryans" from various professions and occupations and limiting the number who could pursue higher education. In 1935, the screws were tightened through what became known as the "Nuremberg laws," stripping Jews of their citizenship and forbidding them to marry or to have sexual relations with "subjects of German or kindred blood." A lull followed, partly because of domestic considerations and partly to present a better face to foreigners visiting Germany during the 1936 Olympics.

By 1938, about 150,000 German Jews had emigrated, some 60,000 going to British-held Palestine. The absorption of Austria in March, however, brought 200,000 more Jews into the reich. The Nazis inaugurated a reign of terror during the summer and fall, beating some Jews and sending others to concentration camps. In November, using as an excuse the assassination of a minor German official in Paris by a young Jewish student, Propaganda Minister Joseph Goebbels orchestrated an orgy of destruction against synagogues and Jewish homes and shops. During what became known as *Kristallnacht* ("night of glass," because of the many broken windows), more than 100 Jews were killed, others were beaten and humiliated, and 20,000 males were sent to concentration camps. Throughout this period, Jews were stripped of their remaining privileges, and the SS established a special department to facilitate the policy of forcibly expelling them from Germany.

Hitler dallied with several schemes for relocating Jews after the war began. At first, he seemed to have intended to create a German-dominated Jewish region in the eastern part of the territory seized from Poland. By late September 1939, the SS began transporting Jews from all over Poland to crowded ghettos in eastern cities. In 1940, after defeating France, Hitler briefly considered a plan to transport Jews to the island of Madagascar, a French colony off the coast of southern Africa. Somewhere along the way—historians do not agree precisely when—the policy of resettlement was replaced by one of total annihilation.

The "final solution" initially was entrusted to special SS units, *Einsatzgruppen*, sent close on the heels of German armies invading the Soviet Union. The *Einsatzgruppen* killed an estimated 1 million Jews (and many others) during operations in 1941 and 1942, usually dispatching their victims by rifle or machine-gun fire. However, this method, appropriate when carried out in rear areas of combat zones, would not suffice for the extermination of the additional millions of Jews in areas controlled by Germany and its allies. Six death camps were created in eastern Poland—Auschwitz and Treblinka being the most notorious— to which Jews from all over Europe were shipped to be gassed and their bodies burned in crematoria. About 1 million Gypsies met the same fate because they, too, were of "alien blood."

Approximately 90 percent of the Jewish population of Germany, Poland, the Baltic nations, and occupied Soviet territory was murdered. The fate of those who lived elsewhere was mixed, usually depending upon the degree of control exercised by Germany. In Holland, under the iron hand of the reich commissioner, Arthur Seyss-Inquart, an estimated 75 percent of Holland's 140,000 Jews perished. Similar percentages went to the death camps from Greece and Yugoslavia and from Hungary after Germany occupied it in 1944. The Danish people and government,

These are slave laborers in the Buchenwald concentration camp near Jena, Germany, April 16, 1945; many others had died from malnutrition by the time U.S. troops of the 80th Division entered the camp. (National Archives photo no. W&C 1105)

on the other hand, conspired to save as many Jews as possible. Though anti-Semitic, the Vichy government of France placed various impediments in the way of deportations, with the result that about 75 percent of Jews there survived. Italian Jews fared about the same; they were treated harshly, but deportations did not begin until Germany occupied Italy in 1943. All told, some 5 to 6 million Jews died at the hands of Nazi butchers and their accomplices.

Controversy persists about the Holocaust. The claim by a small fringe element that it never happened is absurd and can be dismissed out of hand—there were too many witnesses, and too much supporting evidence survives to permit any doubts. A larger group, citing the fact that no direct order from Hitler has ever been found, has argued that the extermination policy was implemented without his knowledge by over-zealous officials, such as SS leader Heinrich Himmler, or that it resulted from frustration over Germany's failure to defeat the Soviet Union.

That Hitler could have remained ignorant of such an enormous undertaking is a dubious proposition, if for no other reason than that the Nazi hierarchy was so faction ridden it is unlikely Himmler's enemies

Bones of anti-Nazi German women remain in the crematoriums in the German concentration camp at Weimar, Germany, taken by the 3rd U.S. Army, April 14, 1945. Prisoners of all nationalities had been tortured and killed. (National Archives photo no. W&C 1122)

would have refrained from immediately making it known that he was exceeding his authority. The second theory requires one to overlook the copious documentary evidence and eyewitness reports that *Einsatzgruppen* began killing Jews virtually from the day German troops crossed the Soviet border. The most plausible interpretation is the simplest one: that Hitler made his wishes clear to subordinates, who proceeded to carry them out in murderous good faith.

Responsibility for the Holocaust rested upon those who ordered and carried it out. The reactions of others to the plight of Jews before and after the final solution became known, however, provided a sorry spectacle. Germans at least had the excuse that opposition would have been suicidal and futile in any event, but people in other countries had no such alibi. During the 1930s, when the Nazis were actively promoting Jewish emigration, few nations were willing to accept more than a handful. The United States was no exception. Anti-Semitism, indifference, and fear that Jewish refugees would add to unemployment during the depression combined to prevent any serious revision of existing immigration laws. Even Jewish groups soft-pedalled the issue in public for fear of stirring up anti-Semitism in the United States. Instead, they vainly tried to influence policies through personal contact with government officials.

Information about the death camps began arriving in London and Washington soon after the extermination policy got under way. Such stories were doubted at first. Nazi anti-Semitism was well known, but the fact that they intended to annihilate entire Jewish populations seemed too fantastic to be believed. Anti-Semites in both the British Foreign Office and the U.S. State Department were quick to label these reports as Jewish propaganda. By 1942, sufficient evidence had accumulated to verify the situation, and in December of that year, the United States and Great Britain formally accused Germany of genocide.

At that time, they were powerless to do more. Even after Allied bombers were able to penetrate deeply enough to reach the death camps, however, no action was taken to destroy them despite appeals by Churchill and others. Both the Royal Air Force and the United States Army Air Forces stonewalled, claiming that they could not spare bombers and crews for missions against targets of such low military priority. Besides, the bomber generals argued, Auschwitz and the other camps lay in the Soviet zone of operations. Roosevelt refused to join Churchill in overruling them, and as a result, German trains continued rolling eastward virtually until the camps were overrun by advancing Soviet forces. Although Jews themselves on occasion rose up against their tormentors, they fought alone. The world had forsaken them.

RESISTANCE MOVEMENTS

The numerical strength and the effectiveness of those who overtly resisted Nazi occupation are difficult to estimate. Few records were kept at the time by individuals or groups, in order to maintain secrecy. After Germany's defeat, it became fashionable for many to claim they had been resistance fighters when, in fact, they had not, and for those who were to exaggerate their accomplishments. As might be expected in such a situation, a very few heroic men and women risked their lives to fight the Nazis. But more than a few actively collaborated with the Nazis, some out of fear or avarice, others because they believed in Nazi ideology or because they detested their own governments. Fighting units were formed by the Germans even in the Soviet Union, although their military value was negligible. Most people merely hunkered down and got by the best they could.

A number of factors affected the nature of resistance organizations and their methods of operation. In urban areas, for instance, members stayed separated except for furtive meetings, to avoid detection. Missions, usually involving sabotage or assassination, were carried out by small groups. In more remote regions, especially where mountains or forests afforded protection, guerrilla bands might operate, provided they had the support of villagers and farmers to keep their whereabouts unknown. Although the Allies tried to provide arms, most often through airdrops, these forces were no match for regular troops even in approximately equal numbers, and they resorted mostly to ambushes and harassment of enemy communications and supply lines.

The French resistance movement was most important to Allied victory because it helped facilitate the cross-channel invasion by disrupting German transportation and communications. The movement was slow in building for two reasons: German occupation policies were at first relatively civilized, and many people were reluctant to oppose the collaborationist Vichy government. Germany's occupation of all of France in 1942 and its increasingly harsh treatment brought more recruits, though precise numbers are unknown. Many Frenchmen also joined the resistance to avoid being sent to Germany as laborers. In 1943, General de Gaulle was able to consolidate numerous groups into the National Resistance Council. Its military arm was designated the French Forces of the Interior in early 1944.

Communists played an important part in the French resistance movement, as they did in almost all others. They were tightly disciplined, used to clandestine activities, and dedicated to their cause. They did not join the anti-Nazi coalition until June 1941, however, when Germany invaded the Soviet Union. From the time the Nazi-Soviet Pact was signed in 1939, they had actively worked to sabotage the French war effort, and many collaborated with the Nazis after the fall of France in 1940. They pursued their goal of creating a Communist France even after they joined the resistance, and only astute political maneuvering by de Gaulle (backed by Great Britain and the United States) kept them from seizing power.

The French underground, in particular, faced a dilemma that never was fully resolved. Should it attempt to harass the Germans on an ongoing basis, or should it husband its strength until the invasion? In practice, it did both. Some Germans were killed—a drunken soldier knifed in a subway, a truck convoy ambushed—but these were exceptions due to the harsh reprisals. More common were activities such as sabotaging factories, distributing anti-German leaflets, collecting military information, and acting as a conduit for escaped prisoners of war (POWs) and others seeking passage to England. Resistance groups began functioning more openly after the invasion, destroying communication lines and blowing up bridges and railway trestles. Their overall contribution cannot be measured, but it was critical at certain junctures. In one instance, they kept an SS panzer division from reaching the Normandy beaches for more than a week.

Resistance movements in other Western nations followed a similar pattern. Propaganda and sabotage were the main activities until the invasion, and then overt military operations were launched against German forces fighting Allied armies. Special mention should be made of the Norwegians who put a heavy-water plant near Oslo out of production for five months and later sank a ferry transporting fourteen tons of the stuff. (Heavy water was used in the German atomic research program.) Toward the end of the war, resistance groups also engaged in antisabotage activities to stop retreating Germans from demolishing facilities of various kinds. The Belgians, for example, were able to see to it that the port of Antwerp was captured by the Allies virtually intact.

Resistance movements in the more rugged areas of Greece, Yugoslavia, Poland, and occupied Russia were able to mount guerrilla operations against the Germans. Too lightly equipped to engage major enemy forces, they ambushed troop and supply convoys and cut communications lines. In several countries, Greece and Yugoslavia especially, resistance forces were bitterly divided between Communists and those who supported governments in exile. In addition to fighting Germans, they waged civil wars to determine who would dominate after the Germans left. In Yugoslavia, Great Britain and the United States first backed General Draza Mihailovich, a Royal Army officer who had organized a group known as the Chetniks. Later, when it became known that the Chetniks had, on occasion, collaborated with occupying forces, support was thrown to Tito (Josip Broz) and his "partisans," even though he and those around him were Communists. The partisans helped drive the Germans out of Yugoslavia and took over the nation at war's end. Ironically, it has since been revealed that Tito also collaborated with the Axis in order to improve his position against the Chetniks.

In 1940, the British organized the Special Operation Executive (SOE) to work with and encourage resistance movements. Two years later, the United States formed the Office of Strategic Services under General William ("Wild Bill") Donovan, so named because of his exploits during World War I. These two organizations, though often disagreeing over tactics and objectives, supplied large amounts of arms and equipment to underground movements. They also sent thousands of agents into occupied Europe to gain intelligence and to throw as many monkey wrenches as possible into the enemy war machine. Some of these agents performed valuable services; others were quickly captured and executed.

When the SOE was set up, Winston Churchill said he hoped it would help "set Europe ablaze." This was wishful thinking. Until D Day, the most valuable contribution of resistance movements in the west was the collection and transmission of intelligence. Guerrilla operations in eastern and southern Europe were more formidable militarily, but even they could only harass and interfere. Resistance groups nonetheless served two very valuable purposes. They helped maintain morale and national pride during the long, bleak months of occupation, and they pinned down hundreds of thousands of Axis troops who otherwise would have been available to fight the Allied armies.

THE GREATER EAST ASIAN CO-PROSPERITY SPHERE

Japan also attempted to create a "new order" in areas it occupied in Asia. Like the German version, Japan's system was designed to create a self-sustaining economic bloc for its own benefit. Japan's method of exercising control varied from place to place: In some, it permitted existing governments a measure of independence in domestic affairs; in some, it set up puppet regimes; and in others, it ruled subject peoples directly. The Japanese initially enjoyed the advantage of appearing as liberators, freeing Asians from the yoke of European imperialism. Their weakness lay in the fact that resources from overseas possessions had to be carried by surface vessels, which became more vulnerable to air and submarine attack as time wore on.

Japan's conduct in Manchuria and in China proper did not augur well for the populations it acquired after Pearl Harbor. At best, its rule was harsh; at worst, it was barbarous. Some Japanese in civilian ministries genuinely sought to befriend local peoples, if for no other reason than that such treatment would encourage cooperation in the economic realm. Whatever tentative steps were taken usually were undermined by the army, which viewed such "softness" with disdain. Japanese soldiers and lower-echelon officers contributed to the estrangement on a daily basis. They habitually slapped or beat civilians for the slightest offense and showed contempt for native cultures.

Burma's experience under Japanese occupation was typical of how smaller nations fared. Long restive under British control, many Burmese welcomed Japan as the nation that would deliver Asia to the Asians. The Japanese, issuing vague assurances of ultimate independence, installed as leader a man named U Ba Maw, who previously had been prime minister under the British. In a later account of his experience, Ba Maw wrote that he genuinely believed that the Japanese had good intentions. As time wore on, however, their conduct in Burma became increasingly arrogant and rapacious. They arbitrarily seized crops and livestock and impressed an ever-larger number of Burmese into forced labor. The Japanese, he concluded, were "devoid of judgement in their dealings with others" and "domineering and blinded by delusions of their own racial grandeur." Toward the end of the war, Burmese nationalist forces that had been organized to help eject the British instead began fighting the Japanese.

The Philippines proved unique. Japanese attempts to play upon Asian solidarity there bore little fruit. Filipinos had fought Japan's invasion and had seen firsthand the barbaric treatment of soldiers and civilians. Although part of the prewar elite collaborated, the regime installed by Japan received little support as most Filipinos remained loyal to the commonwealth's president, Manuel Quezon, who had fled to Washington. Resentment against Japanese occupation was so great that guerrilla movements flourished in the major islands from the very beginning. The fact that some of the largest were led by American army officers testified to where Filipino loyalties lay. These movements could not have survived had it not been for the active and passive support of the people. As in the case of European resistance groups, they were unable to mount large-scale military operations but challenged civil control, helped keep up morale, and provided intelligence to the Allies.

French Indochina also was unique in that it was the only area in which the Japanese permitted a European government to continue functioning, albeit in a reduced role. Just as the Vichy regime collaborated with Germany, its counterpart in Saigon exercised civil administration under Japan's overall control. Nominally loyal to Vichy through most of the war, French colonial leaders began to tilt toward General de Gaulle after the liberation of France, by which time the Japanese were being pushed back across the Pacific. The British SOE began parachuting supplies, equipment, and French agents into Indochina to promote the creation of an anti-Japanese underground. To forestall such a development, the Japanese overthrew the French government in March 1945 and disarmed or defeated all but a few French troops who escaped to China.

American conduct in Indochina caused controversy. In northern Vietnam, there was a strong resistance movement known as the Viet Minh. Originally formed to gain independence from France, the Viet Minh continued its struggle against the Japanese. It was a Communist-dominated organization headed by Ho Chi Minh, but it downplayed its ideological orientation to maintain a united front with other nationalist groups. The OSS supplied and worked with the Viet Minh to harass the Japanese and to gain intelligence about their troop movements. President Roosevelt envisioned a United Nations trusteeship for Indochina after the war, and some OSS agents may have given Ho Chi Minh reason to believe that the United States intended to support complete independence. The French subsequently blamed the United States for strengthening the Viet Minh and for nurturing its opposition to French reoccupation after Japan's surrender.

CHINA

The Roosevelt administration and most of the media assured the American public that China was a staunch ally in the war against Japan. Chiang Kai-Shek, head of the Chinese Nationalist government, was depicted as a strong leader who had rallied the long-suffering Chinese masses against Japanese militarism. With American assistance, according to this view, prospects were good that a democratic, progressive China would emerge from the war. The facts were otherwise. China was less an ally than a dependent, with key areas of its territories dominated by the Japanese. China contributed little to the war effort other than pinning down occupation troops, and Chiang presided over an uneasy coalition government that was challenged by a vigorous Communist movement.

The Sino-Japanese War had settled into a stalemate after the fighting of 1937–1938. The Japanese, who controlled large portions of northern China as well as all the coastal cities, had been unable to defeat the Nationalists decisively after the latter's withdrawal to Chungking in the interior. The Nationalists, on the other hand, were incapable of mounting offensive operations to dislodge the enemy. Cut off from lend-lease supplies by sea, they had to rely on what could be brought in overland via a long, tortuous route from Burma.

Japan's attack on Pearl Harbor greatly increased American interest in keeping China afloat. President Roosevelt was more aware of Chiang's weaknesses than he let on publicly. Still, he hoped the regime might be shored up by material and technical assistance. Then, if reconciliation with the Communists could be affected, a unified China might contribute more effectively to the conflict. Successful campaigns against the Japanese could result in China providing bases for bombers and becoming a major staging area for the final assault against Japan's home islands. Finally, China could play a part in the stable, postwar world that Roosevelt sought.

Chiang viewed the situation differently. Assuming the United States and its other allies would bear the burden of defeating the Japanese, he was more interested in making sure the Nationalist government extended its control over all China after the war ended. He had no intention of dissipating his strength in a struggle the Americans would wage regardless of what he did. There followed a clash of wills that manifested itself virtually from Pearl Harbor to V-J Day: The Americans constantly prodded Chiang to engage the Japanese, while he did just enough to stave off a rupture that would cut off lend-lease aid.

China's military liabilities were made manifest in the months following Pearl Harbor. In early 1942, Roosevelt sent General Joseph W. ("Vinegar Joe") Stilwell to China in a variety of capacities, among them military adviser to the Nationalist government and commander of U.S. forces in the China-Burma-India theater. Stilwell's introduction to the Chinese military situation was a rude one. Named chief of staff by Chiang and placed in charge of Chinese troops assisting the British in Burma, Stilwell was appalled by the incompetence and lack of fighting spirit among Nationalist commanders. The Japanese not only succeeded in cutting off the Burma road but got behind Chinese lines, compelling Stilwell and his staff to beat an arduous retreat to safety to India. The United States had to mount a massive airlift over the Himalayas from India to keep lend-lease supplies flowing and began constructing an alternative route from the Indian town of Ledo.

Stilwell had been chosen for the mission to Chungking because he had served in China earlier, he spoke the language, and he was an extremely able officer. As his nickname suggested, however, he was no diplomat. Unable to persuade Chiang to take the initiative against Japanese forces, Stilwell came to despise the Chinese leader and began referring to him as "the peanut" in his diary. Chiang reciprocated his dislike. Their relationship deteriorated to the point of alternating between icy correctness and bitter quarrels. Chiang was not to be moved. All he did was to demand ever-larger quantities of aid.

A more personable individual might have gotten along better with Chiang, but it is doubtful that the situation could have been altered significantly. Chiang not only was reluctant to commit his forces against the Japanese, he had few reliable forces to commit. The Chinese army, huge on paper, was, for the most part, a shambles. Generals were paid directly for the forces under their command, encouraging them to pad numbers and to feed and clothe their troops with the minimum necessary for survival—sometimes not even that. The average Chinese division consisted of undernourished, badly trained, and poorly equipped troops who had little motivation beyond avoiding the beatings their regular officers and noncommissioned officers (NCOs) routinely inflicted.

Stilwell had almost as much trouble with U.S. Army Air Forces (USAAF) General Claire Chennault as he had with Chiang. After retiring as a captain in the 1930s, Chennault had been hired by Chiang to command the Chinese air forces. Even before Pearl Harbor, Chennault (then a colonel) had been permitted by FDR to form the American Volunteer Group (AVG), better known as the Flying Tigers, composed of pilots and ground personnel released from active army and navy

Gen. and Madame Chiang Kai Shek and Lt. Gen. Joseph W. Stilwell, commanding general, China Exped. Forces, on the day following Japanese bombing attack, Maymyo, Burma, April 19, 1942. (National Archives photo no. W&C 747)

service. Flying P-40s, which were far less maneuverable than the Zeros they fought, the Tigers nonetheless developed tactics that enabled them to achieve an impressive kill ratio during the months following Pearl. The AVG's exploits reached heroic proportions in the United States at a time when the nation was starved for encouraging news. Chennault was promoted to brigadier general in July 1942 when the AVG was incorporated into the U.S. Army Air Forces.

Wide publicity, his connections in the White House, and his relationship with Chiang gave Chennault far more clout than his rank or the importance of his command warranted. He pulled every string to get precious supplies and equipment diverted to his group at Stilwell's expense. In October 1942, he assured Roosevelt by letter that his operation could defeat Japan within a year if he were only given 105 fighters, and 30 medium and 12 heavy bombers. First he would gain air superiority, he boasted, then he would destroy Japanese shipping and industrial production. Meanwhile, his public relations officer, who also had lines to the White House, was promoting the notion that Stilwell's opposition stemmed from his inability to appreciate the significance of modern air power.

A Chinese soldier guards a line of American P-40 fighter planes, painted with the shark-face emblem of the "Flying Tigers," at a flying field somewhere in China, ca. 1942. (National Archives photo no. W&C 1149)

Chennault's absurd claims were seductive to Roosevelt, despite the reservations expressed by senior airmen in Washington. Stilwell's best efforts to reform the Chinese army had produced few results so far, and his ongoing friction with Chiang was embarrassing politically. Chennault's scheme held out prospects for a quick fix: carrying the war to Japan without relying on the Chinese ground forces that Chiang was so reluctant to commit. Chiang naturally supported Chennault to the utmost. By late spring 1943, Chennault was given command of the newly formed Fourteenth Air Force, as well as first priority on supplies coming in over the Himalayas—the "hump," as Americans called it.

Chennault's air offensive during the next months achieved far less than he had predicted. American fighter pilots continued to outperform the Japanese when confronting them in approximately equal numbers, but they failed to achieve control of the air. The actual shipping losses inflicted were only one-tenth of what the Fourteenth Air Force claimed. Heavy bombers consumed enormous amounts of scarce fuel and were difficult to service without sophisticated equipment. Most important, repeated Japanese bombing raids forced Chennault to evacuate his forward airfields.

In April 1944, the Japanese launched an offensive in eastern China, code-named ICHIGO. Its goals were to destroy Nationalist armies and to overrun not only the Fourteenth's air bases but those from which B-29 Superfortresses were beginning to operate. ICHIGO's initial success was so alarming that, in July, General Marshall prevailed upon Roosevelt to demand that Chiang delegate full military command to Stilwell. Chiang agreed in principle but stalled, requesting that FDR send a personal representative to discuss Stilwell's status. When the emissary arrived in Chungking several months later, Chiang told him that he was prepared to place Chinese forces under the command of an American general but not Stilwell.

FDR backed down. He was loathe to alienate Chiang and, aware of Stilwell's abrasiveness, chose to regard the matter as a clash of personalities. He recalled Stilwell, replacing him with the more diplomatic General Albert C. Wedemeyer. Good soldier that he was, Stilwell did not protest his own sacrifice on the altar of politics. Wedemeyer got along better with Chiang, to be sure, but he was no more successful in getting the Chinese armies to fight. The general quietly eased Chennault out of his command following FDR's death in April 1945.

The United States committed air units to China, as well as engineers and construction personnel, but only miniscule ground forces. Most notable was the 5307th Provisional Regiment, better known as Merrill's Marauders after its commander, General Frank Merrill. An all-volunteer unit, it was specially trained for long-distance penetration behind enemy lines in the manner of British General Orde Wingate's Chindits. The Marauders fought in several campaigns to help the British and Chinese clear northern Burma during 1944. Indeed, they were kept in combat so long without relief that the unit was reduced to a small fraction of its original size, with survivors debilitated by fatigue and sickness. A similar unit, called the MARs force, also saw action.

Several developments between late 1944 and early 1945 relieved the supply crisis in China. Allied success in north Burma permitted the airlift to fly a much shorter route into China. Tonnage also was increased by improvements in bringing materials to the Indian end of the line for transshipment. In mid-January 1945, the first truck convoy left India for China along the newly completed Ledo Road, with two pipelines paralleling the road carrying precious aviation fuel. These sources facilitated American air operations but, unfortunately, had little impact on Chinese military performance—or lack of it.

The U.S. involvement in China probably kept the Nationalist regime from collapse, thereby forcing the Japanese to continue expending men and resources they might have used elsewhere. Other than that, few military dividends were produced. However, the capture of the Mariana Islands in the central Pacific provided B-29 bases that were closer and more secure than those in China. (Military planners had abandoned the idea of using China as a staging area for the invasion of Japan's home islands long before atomic bombs rendered such an assault unnecessary.)

More important for the future, Chiang proved unwilling or unable to reform the Nationalist political and military structure despite massive American aid and advice. The regime was shot through with corruption and remained dependent upon regional warlords who ruthlessly exploited the Chinese peasantry. The Chinese Communists not only fought the Japanese more vigorously but attracted popular support in the areas they controlled. U.S. efforts to reconcile the two factions failed during the war and would continue to fail after Japan's defeat. A unified China would emerge four years later, as Roosevelt had envisioned, but by that time, the Communists had ousted Chiang's discredited regime from the mainland, forcing it to Formosa (Taiwan).

SELECTED BIBLIOGRAPHY

Arad, Yitzhak. *Belzec, Sobibor, Treblinka: The Operation Reinhard Death Camps* (Bloomington: Indiana University Press, 1987).

Bauer, Yehuda. *A History of the Holocaust* (New York: Doubleday, 1982).

Buhite, Russell D. *Patrick J. Hurley and American Foreign Policy* (Ithaca, N.Y.: Cornell University Press, 1973).

Dallin, Alexander. *German Rule in Russia, 1941–1945* (London: Macmillan, 1957).

Davidowicz, Lucy. *The War Against the Jews, 1933–1945* (New York: Holt, Rinehart and Winston, 1975).

———. *The Holocaust and the Historians* (Cambridge, Mass.: Harvard University Press, 1981).

Feis, Herbert. *The China Tangle: The American Effort in China from Pearl Harbor to the Marshall Mission* (New York: Atheneum, 1965).

Fleming, Gerald. *Hitler and the Final Solution* (Berkeley: University of California Press, 1984).

Foot, M.R.D. *Resistance: European Resistance to Nazism, 1940–1945* (London: Her Majesty's Stationery Office, 1978).

Gilbert, Martin. *The Holocaust* (New York: Holt, Rinehart and Winston, 1986).

Haestrup, Jorgen. *European Resistance Movements, 1939–1945: A Complete History* (Westport, Conn.: Meckler Publishing, 1981).

Hilberg, Raul. *The Destruction of the European Jews* (New York: Holmes and Meier, 1985).

Hinsley, F. H. *British Intelligence in the Second World War* (London: Her Majesty's Stationery Office, 1979).

Irving, David. *Hitler's War* (London: Hodder & Stoughton, 1977).

Jones, Francis Clifford. *Japan's New Order in East Asia: Its Rise and Fall* (London: Oxford University Press, 1954).

Lacqueur, Walter. *The Terrible Secret: Suppression of the Truth About Hitler's "Final Solution"* (Boston: Little, Brown, 1980).

Lacqueur, Walter, and Richard Breitman. *Breaking the Silence* (New York: Simon & Schuster, 1986).

Lees, Michael. *The Rape of Serbia: The British Role in Tito's Grab for Power, 1943–1944* (New York: Harcourt, Brace, Jovanovich, 1991).

Lukas, Richard. *Forgotten Holocaust: The Poles Under German Occupation, 1939–1944* (Lexington: University Press of Kentucky, 1986).

Morgan, Ted. *An Uncertain Hour: The French, the Germans, the Jews, the Klaus Barbie Trial, and the City of Lyon, 1940–1945* (New York: William Morrow, 1989).

Myers, R. H., and Mark R. Peattie (eds.). *The Japanese Colonial Empire* (Princeton, N.J.: Princeton University Press, 1984).

Ogburn, Charles. *The Marauders* (New York: Harper & Row, 1959).

Paxton, Robert O. *Vichy France and the Jews* (New York: Knopf, 1972).

Penkower, Monte Noam. *The Jews Were Expendable: Free World Diplomacy and the Holocaust* (Urbana: University of Illinois Press, 1983).

Petrow, Richard. *The Bitter Years: The Invasion and Occupation of Denmark and Norway, April 1940–May 1945* (New York: William Morrow, 1979).

Read, Anthony, and David Fisher. *Kristallnacht: The Nazi Night of Terror* (New York: Times Books, 1989).

Rich, Norman. *Hitler's War Aims: The Establishment of the New Order* (New York: Norton, 1973).

Schaller, Michael. *The U.S. Crusade in China, 1938–1945* (New York: Columbia University Press, 1979).

Smith, Bradley F. *The Shadow Warriors: The OSS and the Origins of the CIA* (New York: Basic Books, 1983).

Stafford, David. *Britain and European Resistance, 1940–1945* (London: Macmillan, 1980).

Steinberg, Jonathan. *All or Nothing: The Axis and the Holocaust 1941–1943* (London: Routledge, 1991).

Tsou, Tang. *America's Failure in China, 1941–1950* (Chicago: University of Chicago Press, 1963).

Tuchman, Barbara W. *Stilwell and the American Experience in China, 1911–1945* (New York: Macmillan, 1971).

Wedemeyer, Albert C. *Wedemeyer Reports* (New York: Henry Holt, 1958).

White, Theodore (ed.). *The Stilwell Papers* (New York: William Sloane Associates, 1948).

Winks, Robin W. *Cloak and Gown: Scholars in the Secret War, 1939–1961* (New York: William Morrow, 1987).

Wyman, David S. *The Abandonment of the Jews: America and the Holocaust, 1941–1945* (New York: Pantheon Books, 1984).

Yahil, Leni. *The Holocaust: The Fate of European Jewry, 1932–1945* (New York: Oxford University Press, 1990).

11
Americans at War

All the major nations faced similar problems in mobilizing people and resources to fight a total war, but not all responded similarly. Nazi ideology, for instance, inhibited Germany's employment of women in defense work and in the armed forces. The United States had unique concerns, in addition to the common ones. Except for those who served in combat zones, Americans did not share the immediate experience of war. No cities were bombed, no territories invaded. This fact, American leaders believed, required that special efforts be made to stimulate an ongoing commitment to the war effort. As the "arsenal of democracy," the United States also had to weigh the allocation of resources to the Allies against the needs of its own armed forces. Finally, the nation had to deal with contradictions between idealistic wartime slogans and the actual treatment of those Americans who belonged to minority groups.

WHY WE FOUGHT

The Japanese attack on December 7, 1941, in one stroke united a badly divided public. The slogan "remember Pearl Harbor" was spoken, printed, and shown in films countless times during the following years. Hitler's declaration of war on the United States relieved President Roosevelt of the need to convince the public that Nazi Germany was an even greater threat. But what, aside from defeating the enemy, was the war all about? What could the American people look forward to achieving by sending their young men to fight and die in faraway places no one had ever heard of before? And how could those not in uniform further the war effort?

FDR offered a brief definition of American aims even before the United States entered the conflict. In a speech before Congress on January 6, 1941, he called for a world that would be based upon what he referred to as the "four essential freedoms": freedom of speech, freedom of worship, freedom from want, and freedom from fear. In August, he and Winston Churchill proclaimed the Atlantic Charter, an eight-point statement combining two of the Four Freedoms (freedom from want and freedom from fear) with a list of goals closely resembling some of Woodrow Wilson's Fourteen Points, such as freedom of the seas and self-determination.

Roosevelt has been criticized for failing to pursue the Four Freedoms at home, as exemplified by his statement to reporters that "Dr. New Deal" was being replaced by "Dr. Win-the-War." The federal government took an active role in directing the war effort, but it did so by working within the confines imposed by traditional institutions. To achieve victory as quickly as possible, Roosevelt believed he needed the cooperation of Congress, the business community, labor, and farmers. The social and economic reforms that *were* undertaken either were pressed on him by his wife or a few advisers or were forced on him by groups threatening to mount embarrassing demonstrations.

FDR deliberately refrained from holding out inspirational visions that would produce disillusionment if unfulfilled. He was equally reluctant to embark upon crusades that might unleash passions with unforeseen consequences. He preferred instead that the war be depicted as a disagreeable but necessary task: to defeat the Axis powers and to render them incapable of threatening freedom and world peace in the future. The sooner the job was done, the sooner Americans could resume their normal way of life, though presumably under better conditions than had prevailed during the depression.

Although a number of federal agencies became involved in propaganda work, the Office of War Information (OWI) was created in June 1942 to coordinate the flow of information to the public and to stimulate support for the war effort. With few exceptions, OWI adhered to Roosevelt's modest version of war aims but nonetheless stirred controversy from the start. Its attempts to explain policies frequently elicited complaints from other bodies within the government—most often the State Department—that it was encroaching on their turf. Critics of the administration, on the other hand, accused it of playing politics by glorifying FDR and the Democrats. After only a year in existence, OWI's domestic operations were drastically reduced when opponents in Congress succeeded in having its appropriations slashed. Its most important contribution was that it exercised some influence on the content of motion pictures.

If the administration refrained from doing much to define war aims beyond stressing the need to achieve victory, it actively promoted the idea that every individual could contribute. The sale of government bonds provides a case in point. Although bonds were sold as much to curb inflation by sopping up excess purchasing power as they were to finance

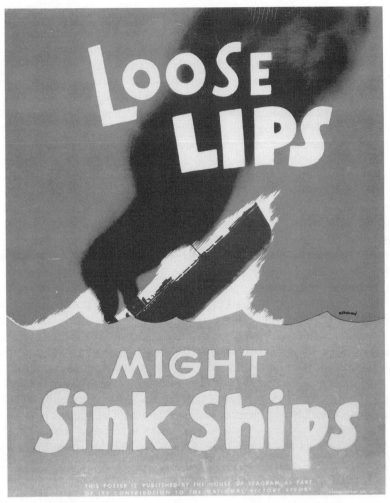

"Loose lips might sink ships." (National Archives photo no. W&C 830)

the war, people were led to believe that every one they bought helped to make available more guns, planes, and tanks to defeat the enemy. Scrap drives served the same purpose. Under the slogan "give till it hurts," the public was mobilized to collect and donate everything from cooking fats and paper to scrap metal and rubber goods. Some of these items actually were converted for use, and some moldered at collection centers or were sold to private dealers. Citizens also were urged to volunteer for civil defense groups and to grow victory gardens in their backyards.

Private enterprise also kept the war before the public. Advertising played an especially important role, as companies tried to outdo one another in showing how they were helping to win the war. Ads in newspapers and magazines showed smiling servicemen and defense workers drinking beverages to refresh themselves, chewing their favorite gum to relieve tensions, and smoking cigarettes to get deep satisfaction (what else they were getting was unknown at the time). Manufacturers of automobiles and durable consumer goods were undeterred by the fact that the production of these items was suspended for the duration. Soldiers in foxholes dreamed of the cars they would buy, and beaming housewives envisioned the refrigerators and stoves that would delight their returning husbands.

Many comic strips and books joined the war, as well. Joe Palooka, the prizefighter, and Popeye the Sailor began punching out enemies of freedom, as well as domestic bullies. Terry and the Pirates and Smilin' Jack fought the Japanese, while Superman used his powers against all minions of the Axis coalition. New heroes were created specifically to combat the enemy, some by companies mixing patriotism with self-promotion. The Bendix Aviation Corporation, for instance, published a strip featuring the conveniently named Captain Ben Dix.

Radio programs contributed in a number of ways. Sponsors, of course, larded their commercials with allusions to the war effort. Musical and variety shows often emanated from military bases or social centers such as United Services Organization (USO) canteens. Police, private detectives, and government agents began tracking down spies and subversives, instead of the usual assortment of murderers and bank robbers. Comedians made jokes about "Japs" and Nazis, and soap operas often involved situations in which one or more of the characters had loved ones in the armed forces.

World War I had its "Over There" and "Give My Regards to Broadway," but World War II produced nothing to compare. Older songs such as "I'll Be Seeing You" and "I'll Never Smile Again" regained popularity for obvious reasons, but those written for the occasion ran from dreadful to worse. Efforts to promote "Praise the Lord and Pass the Ammunition" as *the* war song were doomed. Some, such as "Johnny Got a Zero" and "You're a Sap, Mr. Jap," attained brief popularity. Others, among them "The Bigger the Army and Navy Is, the Better the Loving Will Be" and "We're Gonna Find a Feller Who Is Yeller and Beat Him Red, White, and Blue," mercifully sank without a trace.

Motion pictures provided the most promising vehicle for wartime propaganda. But despite OWI's efforts to inject some sophistication in the messages conveyed, the results usually were shallow and simplistic. A few of the many combat films strove for realism, but most depicted Americans performing improbably heroic deeds against overwhelming odds. One Hollywood cliché was to have each squad or crew composed of members representing a cross section of society. Often perpetuating vulgar stereotypes, a typical unit might contain a wisecracking Jew or Italian from Brooklyn, a drawling Southerner, a phlegmatic Swede from Minnesota, an older man invariably called "Pop," and a lovable youngster who had lied about his age to join up. Sometimes, even a black was included, though this required ingenuity for the armed forces remained largely segregated throughout the war. During the course of the film, these disparate individuals would learn to overcome their differences and prejudices to fight the common enemy.

The enemy usually appeared as a figure of pure cardboard. Malevolent Nazis, some with monocles, periodically clicked their heels and exclaimed, "Heil Hitler," as they coldly went about ordering atrocities or torturing prisoners. At times, distinctions were drawn between Nazis and "good" Germans who secretly worked for the underground or who experienced conversions when they learned the evil nature of the cause they served. No such contrasts were permitted the Japanese. To a man, they were depicted as depraved beasts who laughed maniacally while machine-gunning the wounded or raping nurses. Most commonly, they were referred to as "Nips," "dirty Japs," or "little brown monkeys."

Films made about America's allies often verged on the absurd. Actors wearing stage whiskers imitated Russians by shouting "tovarich" or saying "da" to indicate agreement. When not killing Germans, they sat around campfires or hearths discussing their longings to regain freedom from Nazi tyranny (Soviet tyranny went unmentioned). Movies about China were even more unbelievable. Chinese actors played the parts of Japanese, while Americans with pancake makeup and taped eyelids played stoic, noble Chinese peasants. In one film, the regal Katherine Hepburn, wearing elegantly cut designer pajamas, starred as a humble villager fighting for the right to till ancestral lands in freedom.

Due to the popularity of newspapers and magazines, widespread ownership of radios, and avid theater attendance, Americans arguably were subjected to more propaganda than any other people. Though not as heavy-handed as that issued by authoritarian governments, the material they encountered seldom rose above the level of institutional cheerleading. The United States had been attacked by barbaric enemies of freedom who must be defeated to protect the "American way of life." Questions about the inequities of this way of life were deferred for the duration.

A NATION UNDER ARMS

When Holland surrendered in May 1940, the United States Army became the nineteenth largest in the world. Widely scattered on posts across the nation (many created for the purpose of fighting Indians), its members were underpaid and held in low regard by the public. Equipment was in short supply and mostly obsolete. The basic tank, for example, was armed only with machine guns. Lacking a periscope, it was steered by a commander who sat in the turret with his head exposed, signaling changes of direction by kicking one or the other shoulder of the driver seated beneath him. The Army Air Corps was just as badly off. Despite the introduction of new models, many pilots still flew antiquated biplanes.

In September, Congress passed the Selective Service Act, the first peacetime draft law in American history. Men between the ages of twenty-one and thirty-one were to be conscripted for a period of one year. Those eligible would be selected by lottery number in a system administered by more than 5,000 local boards. Although fiercely contested by a coalition of isolationists, pacifists, Communists, and mothers concerned that their sons' morals would be corrupted by military service, the bill passed handily. False rumors that married men were to be exempted caused applications for marriage licenses to skyrocket, and a song entitled "Good Bye Dear, I'll See You in a Year" enjoyed a short-lived success.

The conscription system functioned poorly at first. Draft boards, staffed by volunteers, often were grossly inefficient, and sons of families with political clout frequently received exemptions for the flimsiest of reasons. Many boards simply ignored repeated pleas by the army that it preferred men from the lower end of the age spectrum. Those who were inducted at times reported to camps that were unprepared to handle them and spent weeks lounging around in the clothes they wore when they arrived.

The draft also revealed depressing facts about American society. Illiteracy rates were high, and a shocking number of young men had poor eyesight uncorrected by glasses, bad teeth caused by a lack of dental care, or a variety of ailments due to inadequate diet. When career soldiers mockingly told recruits, "You never had it so good," they were telling the truth regarding the health of many young Americans.

Selective service was renewed for a year in September 1941, then extended for the duration after Pearl Harbor. Eventually, all men between eighteen and forty-five became eligible. By war's end, more than 15 million men were conscripted, had volunteered, or entered the service through the activation of national guard units. Deferments continued to be given for physical disabilities or for employment deemed vital to the war effort, and married men with children could receive exemptions on the grounds of family need. There were abuses, of course, but on the whole, the system worked. Due to the war's popularity, healthy-looking young men often were reviled or even physically abused when they appeared in public wearing civilian clothes.

Some 300,000 women volunteered for the armed forces. Limited to noncombat roles, they usually served as nurses, clerks, and drivers. The army had its Women's Auxiliary Army Corps (WAACs, later shortened to WACs by dropping the "Auxiliary"), and the navy had its Women Accepted for Volunteer Emergency Service (WAVES). More than 1,000 Women's Auxiliary Service Pilots (WASPs) ferried bombers to Great Britain, towed targets for aerial gunnery practice, or charted weather. Only the marines resisted an acronym: Women marines were referred to simply as "marines."

Freedom from discrimination was not one of the Four Freedoms. Although blacks had fought in every American conflict, often with distinction, the armed forces remained largely segregated and unequal throughout the war. In 1944, tentative steps were taken to integrate some units, but most blacks served in segregated outfits officered by whites. Not surprisingly, morale usually was low as black divisions were relegated to doing construction work or other menial labor. There were exceptions. The all-black 761st Tank Battalion compiled an excellent record in Germany, for instance, and the 99th Pursuit Squadron became one of the most highly decorated in the Army Air Forces.

Blacks met discrimination everywhere. Facilities on military posts were segregated, and blacks were routinely harassed by military police. Race riots were commonplace. Blacks on pass could expect neither protection from abuse by civilian authorities nor exemption from local racist practices. One black soldier stationed in the South told of watching German prisoners of war being served at a lunch counter from which he was barred. The American Red Cross even kept separate supplies of blood plasma, despite the fact that it used a process for obtaining the plasma from whole blood that was invented by Dr. Charles Drew— a black.

Other groups fared according to the prejudices of the time. More than 25,000 Native Americans served, some in radio communications where they spoke to one another in their own languages to befuddle enemy listeners in combat. Spanish-speaking Americans, although not officially segregated as blacks were, often found themselves consigned to the least desirable duties and otherwise discriminated against. Despite this treatment, they earned a higher percentage of combat decorations than their numbers warranted. Similarly, the all-Japanese-American 442d Regimental Combat Team compiled a magnificent record in Italy, as did a battalion recruited from Hawaii. Military regulations barring homosexuals from the armed forces were often loosely enforced because of personnel shortages. A recent study based on interviews with veterans has concluded that, although there was some baiting of those individuals identified as homosexual, a "live and let live" attitude prevailed. Many

"For your country's sake today—For your own sake tomorrow / Go to the nearest recruiting station of the armed service of your choice." (National Archives photo no. W&C 730)

The 93rd Infantry Division, reactivated May 15, 1942, was the first all-black division to be formed during World War II. (National Archives photo no. W&C 731)

more gay men and lesbian women kept their sexual preferences hidden and performed their duties as well or as poorly as anyone else.

MOBILIZING THE ECONOMY

The American economy had been lifted from the doldrums of depression even before Pearl Harbor, and full wartime mobilization after Pearl produced spectacular results. FDR's call for the production of 50,000 airplanes a year in 1940 had seemed fantastic, but by 1944, the American aircraft industry built almost double that number. Similar results were obtained in the construction of ships, tanks, vehicles, and guns. Despite inefficiencies and widespread profiteering, the United States actually did become the arsenal of democracy. Alone, it produced more armaments than all the Axis powers combined.

Roosevelt's "Dr. Win-the-War" efforts were based on cooperation, rather than coercion. Business was encouraged to convert to war production through a variety of incentives. The government built many war plants, then leased them to private industry on favorable terms. What became known as "cost-plus" contracts guaranteed profits, as did liberal tax write-offs, and the enforcement of antitrust laws was suspended. The government agencies' employment of "dollar-a-year men"—executives who remained on company payrolls—ensured that industry would be treated generously. FDR's proposal that salaries be limited to $25,000 per year (worth many more times that today) was indignantly rejected by businessmen and their friends in Congress on the grounds that such a salary cap would destroy executive morale. (Servicemen, it may be noted, were never consulted as to the relationship between *their* pay and morale.)

Large companies benefited most. They had the political clout with Congress, their "dollar-a-year-men" occupied key positions, and it was easier to negotiate and supervise a few large contracts for a particular item than many small ones. The top 100 corporations received nearly two-thirds of the funds devoted to wartime production. Yet, most smaller firms still managed to do very nicely, either producing for the military or for an increasingly prosperous public. Net corporate profits increased a whopping 70 percent, despite the imposition of wartime taxes.

The rising tide raised all boats. Increased production meant more jobs at higher pay. In fact, average weekly wages doubled between 1939 and 1944, and time-and-a-half for overtime became commonplace. Because of the availability of work, many families had more than one member holding a job outside the home. Union membership rose dramatically, and when limits on wage increases were imposed, union leaders were able to negotiate fringe benefits that were virtually unheard of in peacetime. Most unions also adhered to the "no-strike" pledges they made after American entry into the war. Although some wildcat strikes occurred, the only major exception took place when the United Mine Workers' John L. Lewis ordered his men off the job several times in 1943. An outraged Congress retaliated by passing strong legislation to enable the federal government to seize and run striking industries if they were deemed essential to the war effort. Existing attitudes made it fairly easy to depict strikes as actions that undermined the war effort, rather than as attempts to obtain a more equitable share of swollen company income.

Farmers enjoyed unparalleled prosperity as agricultural prices shot upward. Military purchases and higher levels of consumption by other sectors of the society ended the problems of surpluses that had dogged the farming community since the 1920s. The process was self-reinforcing. As growers' incomes rose, they bought more agricultural machinery (partly to offset labor shortages) and better fertilizers, thereby increasing production per acre and enabling them to purchase more land. The United States soon became the granary of democracy, as well as its arsenal.

Government intervention in the economy took numerous forms. The allocation of resources was most important. Steel needed for tanks could not be wasted on private automobiles, nor could aluminum required for aircraft be devoted to pots and pans. The War Production Board (WPB) was created to distribute strategic materials and to control or suspend production of consumer goods. The National War Labor Board (NWLB) sought to balance the interests of business and labor, while the War Manpower Commission (WMC) tried to ensure the appropriate distribution of men and women in the military forces, industry, and agriculture. In late 1942, FDR appointed a former senator and Supreme Court justice, James F. Byrnes, to coordinate the activities of these and other agencies, an arrangement formalized by the creation of the Office of War Mobilization (OWM) in the spring of 1943. (Obviously, acronyms proliferated in this era.)

The combination of soaring personal income and shortages of many consumer goods raised the threat of runaway inflation. In addition to selling government bonds to absorb purchasing power, the government raised income taxes and levied others, such as an entertainment tax. The slogan "taxes to fight the Axis" was floated to make the medicine go down easier. The Office of Price Administration (OPA) also was created, both to curb inflation and to ensure equitable distribution of items that were in short supply.

The OPA relied on two basic tools. Empowered by Congress to set maximum prices, the agency issued the General Maximum Price Regulation in April 1942, freezing all retail prices at the highest level they had attained the previous month. Rationing was introduced not only as a hedge against inflation but to provide fair distribution with provisions made for special needs. Although instituted primarily to conserve precious rubber, gasoline rationing provided a case in point. Most automobile owners received an "A" sticker entitling them to four gallons a week. Those who had to drive long distances to work were given "B" stickers, which allowed them additional amounts based on mileage traveled. "C" stickers went to ministers, doctors (who actually made house calls in those days), and others who needed their cars to perform their duties. Patriotic congressmen voted themselves "X" stickers, which permitted them unlimited supplies. Other commodities were handled similarly. A variety of foods were rationed through a coupon system, with allowances made for those with special dietary needs.

The system worked about as well as could be expected. The freeze on prices was difficult to enforce, often resulting in under-the-counter payoffs and the substitution of inferior goods at prices fixed for those of higher quality. Rationing was cumbersome and hard to oversee. Some 5,600 boards, staffed by volunteers, distributed tons of ration books each month at local schools. Coupons were bought and sold illegally, and black marketeers flourished. Nonetheless, inflation *was* kept in check and, though inconvenienced, consumers did not suffer unduly. Indeed, in view of what we know about the effects of diet, the restricted intake of meat, butter, coffee, and sugar almost certainly was beneficial to public health.

SOCIAL CHANGE

The war had a great impact on American society. Most obvious was the fact that 15 million men and several hundred thousand women left their civilian lives for service in the military, with its emphasis on discipline, conformity, and hierarchical structure based on rank. Individuals who had never ventured more than short distances from home found themselves scattered all across the United States and shipped to various parts of the world, where they encountered cultures as alien to them as would be life on a different planet. The extended separation of those who entered the armed forces from those left behind profoundly altered traditional conventions of courtship and marital relations. It is no wonder that many people who came to maturity during that period continued to regard it, for ill or good, as the most memorable experience of their lives.

The creation of a wartime economy caused massive population shifts. Millions of Americans moved from rural areas to cities as burgeoning defense industries offered employment at wages that were previously unheard of. Manufacturing centers in the Midwest and along the West Coast (where most of the shipbuilding and aircraft industries were located) expanded at a dizzying pace. And such rapid and unplanned growth brought all kinds of strains. Families that had relocated in search of a better life often had to pay exorbitant rates for abominable housing and send their children to overcrowded schools. Other children were left unattended when both parents worked. Rates of crime, divorce, prostitution, and juvenile delinquency soared.

The demands of war opened new opportunities for some groups. Blacks who had worked as sharecroppers or farm laborers in the South began getting work for decent pay in urban areas for the first time in their lives. In addition to raising their standard of living, they were able to learn skilled trades previously denied them and to join unions from which they had been excluded. The transition was not easy. Blacks often were discriminated against on and off the job, and they were victims of race riots in a number of cities. For many, however, the chance to test their abilities and intelligence provided a sense of worth that could never again be taken away. Many blacks both in the military service and in civilian life grew increasingly determined to break down the barriers imposed by a racist society.

Even before Pearl Harbor, leaders of traditional black organizations, such as the Urban League and the National Association for the Advancement of Colored People, were joined by those representing new ones, such as the National Committee for the Participation of Negroes in National Defense, in demanding equal treatment in the armed forces and in civilian life. How, they asked, could the United States call upon black Americans to support national defense while relegating them to second-class citizenship?

President Roosevelt, loathe to alienate white Southern voters and congressmen and no great champion of racial equality himself, at first did no more than pay lip service to black demands. He needed prodding. A. Philip Randolph, head of the Brotherhood of Sleeping Car Porters and widely respected by other black spokesmen, provided it. In January 1941, he organized the Negro March on Washington Committee under the slogan "We loyal Negro American citizens demand the right to work and fight for our country." FDR continued to stall until Eleanor Roosevelt and the fiery mayor of New York City, Fiorello La Guardia, finally persuaded him that he had better meet with Randolph and "thrash it out right then and there."

After a meeting in the White House on June 18, during which Randolph threatened to bring 100,000 black protesters to Washington, Roosevelt capitulated. He issued what became Executive Order 8802, providing that "there shall be no discrimination in the employment of workers in defense industries or government because of race, creed, color, or national origin." A Fair Employment Practices Committee was set up to hear grievances and "take appropriate steps." His action provided no magic formula and was ineffective against subtler forms of discrimination, but it did at last place the United States government on the side of racial and ethnic equality.

Women constituted the largest group affected by the economic boom. Some 12 million women had jobs outside the home when the war began. Most were single and employed as clerks, teachers, waitresses, and salespersons. By contrast, many of the nearly 6 million who entered the labor force after Pearl Harbor were married and went to work in defense plants. Because the military siphoned off so many males, these women often became skilled machinists, welders, and truck drivers. The stereotypical "Rosie the Riveter" was depicted on the cover of the *Saturday Evening Post* as a proud, heavily muscled young woman in work clothes, eating a sandwich as she sat with a riveting gun across her lap. Yet, few of the "Rosies" received equal pay for equal work, and fewer still obtained supervisory positions.

Riveter at Lockheed Aircraft Corp., Burbank, California. (National Archives photo no. W&C 804)

The lasting effect that these new job opportunities had on the women involved is difficult to measure. Many reported a newfound sense of pride and independence when they realized they could handle traditionally male jobs as well or better than men. Others took no special satisfaction but became accustomed to the additional income. Still others longed to return to the home when the men returned. In most cases, the choices were not theirs to make: Women, along with blacks, were among the first to be fired after the war ended.

The most profound change to come out of the war was effected by the Servicemen's Readjustment Act, better known as the GI Bill of Rights, passed by Congress in June 1944. Among other benefits, the act provided for modest weekly payments to veterans until they found employment, preferences in hiring, and loan guarantees for the purchase of small businesses, farms, and homes. Most important, the GI Bill entitled veterans to full tuition payments plus living allowances upon enrollment in educational programs at any level. The bill enabled many young men and women to complete high school or to learn trades previously inaccessible to them. Others earned college or graduate degrees that allowed them to pursue careers they could only have dreamed of before. The overall impact of the GI Bill of Rights on equality of opportunity can only be described as revolutionary.

THE BROWN PERIL

During World War I, countless Americans with Germanic-sounding names were subjected to insults and indignities by fellow citizens acting in the name of "patriotism." All things German were deplored. Sauerkraut was renamed "victory cabbage," and dachshunds became an unpopular breed of dogs. No such hysteria developed during World War II, at least toward those of German or Italian origin. However, people of Japanese descent were less fortunate. Prejudice against Orientals had a long, dishonorable history in the United States. In popular literature and in films, they frequently were portrayed as men and women behind whose smiling faces lurked unimaginable evil. The surprise attack on Pearl Harbor appeared to confirm the worst suspicions about the Japanese.

Of about 127,000 people of Japanese ancestry in the United States at the time, 80,000 were native-born American citizens (nisei). Most of the rest (issei) had been rendered ineligible for citizenship by the Immigration Act of 1924. Some 112,000 lived on the West Coast, usually in communities segregated by white restrictions and by cultural preference. Barred from many desirable professions, they worked as farm laborers and domestic help, fished commercially, or ran small shops. Anti-Japanese sentiment ran strong even before the war began.

Panic swept the West Coast during the days following Pearl Harbor. Authorities were swamped with reports of incoming flights of Japanese planes or of submarines cruising in nearby waters. Some people claimed to have seen bonfires or automobile headlights being used at night to signal enemy ships offshore. Fear persisted despite the fact that no evidence of subversive activity was found. Japanese-Americans became scapegoats, as rumors spread that they were poisoning agricultural produce and water supplies and committing sabotage in defense industries. Whipped on by politicians and by groups such as the Native Sons and Daughters of the Golden West, a demand arose to evacuate everyone of Japanese ancestry to the interior. Citizenship provided no defense because, as one official put it, "A Jap is a Jap."

Dressed in a uniform marking service in World War I, this veteran enters Santa
Anita Park assembly center for persons of Japanese ancestry evacuated from the
West Coast, Arcadia, California, April 5, 1942. (National Archives photo no. W&C
775)

On February 19, 1942, President Roosevelt issued Executive Order
9066, authorizing the War Department to exclude from designated military
areas all those considered threats to national security. Lieutenant General
John L. DeWitt, head of the West Coast Defense Command, oversaw
the evacuation. He defended the policy with curious logic: "The very
fact that no sabotage has taken place to date is a disturbing and confirming
indication that such action will be taken." Some 110,000 Japanese-
Americans, more than 60 percent of them citizens and 40,000 of them
children, were transported to ten internment camps scattered across
seven states. Most families had been forced to sell what property or
possessions they had at scandalously low prices. In 1944, the United
States Supreme Court declared the evacuation constitutional.

Many of those officials who had a hand in the relocation policy later
expressed regrets. And well they might. No Japanese-American ever was
convicted of espionage or sabotage, and a number of them fought with
distinction in the European theater. Yet, from 1942 until late in the war,
when the program began to be phased out, thousands of people had
been forced to live behind barbed wire for no other reason than the
color of their skin. Suspicions about their loyalty followed them to the

camps. One story even had it that they were arranging the small gardens they were allowed to grow so that rows of plants pointed the way to defense installations for Japanese planes to follow!

In 1982, the fortieth anniversary of Executive Order 9066, Congress formed the Commission on Wartime Relocation and Internment of Citizens. In 1983, the bipartisan group issued a report condemning the relocation policy as a product of "war hysteria," "racial prejudice," and "failure of political leadership." The commission recommended that the United States government apologize for what had been done and offer reparations. Finally, in 1988, Congress voted to compensate internees with a payment of $20,000 each. But no amount could have made up for the injustice done.

ENLISTING SCIENCE AND TECHNOLOGY

Humans have shown remarkable ingenuity in devising more efficient ways of killing one another, and wars historically have stimulated rapid advances in weaponry and related systems. During World War I, airplanes evolved into fairly efficient killing machines, poison gas was used to lethal effect, and the first tanks trundled across battlefields. No genius was required to realize that science and technology would play a significant part in determining the outcome of World War II. As early as 1940, at the prompting of eminent scientists, President Roosevelt created the National Defense Research Committee (NDRC) to issue defense contracts to universities, research centers, and corporate laboratories. The following year, the much larger Office of Scientific Research and Development (OSRD) took over day-to-day operations, and the NDRC remained to exercise overall coordination.

The atomic bomb was by far the most dramatic and lethal weapon developed. The potential energy of atomic particles had been known for decades, and German scientists had successfully split uranium atoms in 1938. Perceptive physicists everywhere realized the dreadful implications: If a chain reaction could be induced in a sufficiently large amount of uranium, an explosion of unparalleled magnitude would result. Nazi Germany had the lead in nuclear research. It also had the industrial capacity and sufficient uranium deposits (located in occupied Czechoslovakia) to construct an atomic bomb.

Physicist Leo Szilard, who had earlier emigrated from Hungary, sought to alert President Roosevelt to the danger. In the summer of 1939, Szilard drafted a letter to FDR about the potential destructiveness of nuclear energy, warning him that the United States should immediately embark upon a program lest the Germans acquire such a weapon first. To ensure the president's attention, Szilard persuaded the world-famous theoretical physicist Albert Einstein to sign the letter. It was delivered on October 13 by Alexander Sachs, an acquaintance of both Einstein and Roosevelt. After reading the letter and accompanying documents, FDR asked, "Alex, what you are after is to see that the Nazis don't blow us up?" "Precisely," Sachs replied. Roosevelt thereupon called in an aide and told him that "this requires action."

Despite Roosevelt's apparent recognition of the threat, the atomic program did not get under way in earnest until 1942. The Manhattan Project, as it became known, ultimately required massive expenditures of resources, and, by the end of the war, it had employed some 120,000 people. The actual construction of the devices took place in a remote area of New Mexico, but huge plants were built in Oak Ridge, Tennessee, and elsewhere, and several leading universities participated. The first chain reaction, for instance, was achieved in a squash court under the football stadium at the University of Chicago in December 1942.

The acquisition of atomic bombs constituted a miracle of American technology and engineering, rather than one of theoretical abilities. German and other European physicists had led the way, British and Canadian scientists brought advanced techniques when the project became a joint one, and refugees from the Nazis such as Niels Bohr (Denmark), Enrico Fermi (Italy), and Szilard made invaluable contributions. The scientific director of "Manhattan," J. Robert Oppenheimer, although a brilliant physicist in his own right, deserves most of the credit for coordinating the work of a large group of often difficult individuals who were unused to working under supervision. The project's military director, Brigadier General Leslie J. Groves, was an unpleasant bully who moved heaven and earth to provide the scientists with equipment and facilities for their work.

During and after the war, Americans tended to take credit for a number of scientific achievements that actually originated elsewhere. Proximity fuses (radio devices within artillery shells that caused detonation anywhere near the target), radar, and sonar, for example, were British innovations. Penicillin was discovered in Great Britain, sulfa drugs and DDT in Germany. The United States lagged behind both nations in research on jet propulsion and solid-fuel rocketry.

What Americans were good at was improving designs and developing techniques for mass production. Inferior fighter aircraft were gradually replaced by improved types so that by war's end, American planes outperformed anything the Germans and Japanese flew against them (with the exception of German jets). Advances in radar technology greatly benefited the U.S. Navy in its war against Japan, as did construction of vastly superior aircraft carriers. U.S. jeeps (so named because of the designation "general purpose" vehicle) and trucks were the envy of other armies, and merchant vessels were turned out faster than anyone previously thought possible. The list can be extended. Aside from its fighting forces, America's greatest contribution to the Allied war effort was its ability to produce such vast quantities of everything from medicines to B-29 Superfortresses.

SELECTED BIBLIOGRAPHY

Anderson, Karen. *Wartime Women: Sex Roles, Family Relations, and the Status of Women in World War II* (Westport, Conn.: Greenwood, 1981).

Berube, Allan. *Coming Out Under Fire; The History of Gay Men and Women in World War II* (New York: Free Press, 1990).

Blum, John Morton. *V Was for Victory: Politics and American Culture During World War II* (New York: Harcourt, Brace, Jovanovich, 1976).

Brinkley, David. *Washington Goes to War* (New York: Knopf, 1988).

Campbell, D'Ann. *Women at War with America: Private Lives in a Patriotic Era* (Cambridge, Mass.: Harvard University Press, 1984).

Capeci, Dominic J., Jr. *The Harlem Riot of 1943* (Philadelphia, Pa.: Temple University Press, 1977).

Costello, John. *Virtue Under Fire: How World War II Changed Our Social and Sexual Attitudes* (Boston: Little, Brown, 1986).

Dalfiume, Richard M. *Desegregation of the United States Armed Forces: Fighting on Two Fronts, 1939–1945* (Columbia: University of Missouri Press, 1969).

Daniels, Roger. *Concentration Camps: North American Japanese in the United States and Canada During World War II* (Malabas, Fla.: R. E. Kriege, 1981).

Davis, Benjamin O., Jr. *An Autobiography* (Washington, D.C.: Smithsonian Institution Press, 1991).

Davis, Nuel. *Lawrence and Oppenheimer* (New York: Simon & Schuster, 1969).

Foner, Jack. *Blacks and the Military in American History* (New York: Praeger, 1974).

Gluck, Sherna B. *Rosie the Riveter Revisited: Women, the War, and Social Change* (Boston: Twayne, 1987).

Hewlett, Richard B., and Oscar E. Anderson, Jr. *A History of the United States Atomic Energy Commission, Vol. 1, The New World* (University Park: Pennsylvania State University Press, 1962).

Irons, Peter. *Justice at War: The Inside Story of the Japanese-American Internment* (New York: Oxford University Press, 1983).

Jones, Reginald V. *The Wizard War* (New York: Coward, McCann & Geoghegan, 1978).

Jones, Vincent C. *Manhattan: The Army and the Atomic Bomb* (Washington, D.C.: Center of Military History, United States Army, 1986).

Koppes, Clayton, and Gregory D. Black. *Hollywood Goes to War: How Politics, Profits and Propaganda Shaped World War II Movies* (New York: Free Press, 1987).

Lee, Ulysses. *The Employment of Negro Troops* (Washington, D.C.: Office of the Chief of Military History, Department of the Army, 1966).

Lichtenstein, Nelson. *Labor's War at Home: The CIO in World War II* (New York: Cambridge University Press, 1982).

MacPherson, Malcolm C. *Time Bomb: Fermi, Heisenberg, and the Race for the Atomic Bomb* (New York: Dutton, 1986).

Mazon, Mauricio. *The Zoot Suit Riots* (Austin: University of Texas Press, 1984).

Milkman, Ruth. *Gender at Work: The Dynamics of Job Segregation by Sex During World War II* (Urbana: University of Illinois Press, 1987).

Nalty, Bernard C. *Strength for the Fight: A History of Black Americans in the Military* (New York: Free Press, 1986).

Nash, Gerald D. *World War II and the West: Reshaping the Economy* (Lincoln: University of Nebraska Press, 1990).

Rhodes, Richard. *The Making of the Atomic Bomb* (New York: Simon & Schuster. 1987).

Rupp, Leila. *Mobilizing Women for War: German and American Propaganda* (Princeton: N.J.: Princeton University Press, 1978).

Terkel, Studs. *"The Good War": An Oral History of World War II* (New York: Pantheon Books, 1984).

Winkler, Allan. *The Politics of Propaganda: The Office of War Information, 1942–1945* (New Haven, Conn.: Yale University Press, 1978).

————. *Home Front USA: America During World War II* (Arlington Heights, Ill.: H. Davidson, 1986).

Wynn, Neil. *The Afro-American and the Second World War* (New York: Holmes & Meier, 1976).

12
The Eastern Front (1942–1944)

World War II was the most destructive armed conflict the world had ever seen. That part of it waged on the eastern front between Germany and the Soviet Union was by far the largest theater of the war. Huge armies, numbering millions of men, fought savagely back and forth over huge expanses of territory. And casualties were not limited to the armed forces. Millions of civilians also perished during the course of the fighting and by the brutal policies carried out by the Germans in territories they occupied. "The great patriotic war," as it became known to the Soviet people, remains a central event in their history.

THE STRUGGLE FOR SURVIVAL

The most remarkable aspect of the Soviet war effort was the people's tenacity against untold suffering and deprivation. Although the inhabitants of some non-Russian regions initially welcomed the Germans as liberators from Moscow's rule—until Nazi policies disabused them of any such notion—Soviet citizens on the whole remained loyal even during the darkest days of defeat. Their dedication, it must be emphasized, was not to communism but to the defense of their homeland against the invader. Stalin recognized this early on. Soviet propaganda throughout the war emphasized patriotism—love for "Mother Russia"—rather than sacrifice for a political and economic system. Reliance on the devotion to traditional values can also be seen in the suspension of efforts to suppress religious institutions for the duration.

Soviet tenacity was best expressed in the behavior of the inhabitants of Leningrad, which fell under German siege in September 1941. German Army Group North had advanced rapidly toward the city during the first weeks of BARBAROSSA, and panzer spearheads had gotten to within 60 miles by the end of July. Hitler was intent on the annihilation of this former capital of Russia, renamed after the founding father of the Bolshevik state. He did not want to employ his mobile armor in a set-piece battle, however, so he decided to besiege it and compel surrender through starvation and bombardment.

During the early weeks of the siege, Leningrad received supplies from only a single railroad running southeast to Moscow, more than 500 miles away. From November 9 to December 30, even that source was cut off by German advances, and the Soviets were forced to rely on shipments brought by rail to the tip of Lake Ladoga to the east, across the lake by boat (or by trucks when it was frozen), then another 35 miles by rail from the port to Leningrad. This trickle of supplies was sufficient to prevent total collapse but just barely.

The winter months of 1941–1942 were the worst. Troops and inhabitants of Leningrad suffered unimaginable horrors of subzero temperatures and hunger, as well as a lack of drinking water and medical supplies. Thousands perished each day from some combination of starvation, cold, and sickness. Those who lived resorted to eating anything that provided some nourishment: cats, dogs, rats, even, in some cases, human bodies. People died at home, in the streets, and at their places of work. Through it all, those who were able helped build fortifications, cleared rubble, and carried out whatever other duties they were assigned.

That first winter was the cruelest, but life in Leningrad remained hard even after construction of alternate supply routes eased the crisis. Soviet forces were unable to liberate the city until January 1944, some 900 days after the siege began. During that period, nearly a million people died in Leningrad—more than 600,000 from starvation or disease, the rest by air attack and artillery bombardment. Throughout, discipline was strict and punishment for infractions harsh, but none of it would have worked had it not been for the will of the citizenry to persevere.

Soviet determination also was shown, if less dramatically, by the speed with which industrial output revived following the German onslaught. Most of the nation's productive capacity had been located in precisely those areas that the Germans had overrun. Soviet efforts during the 1930s to develop coal, steel, and manufacturing centers in eastern regions paid unexpected dividends by providing bases for a colossal relocation of human and industrial resources out of German reach. Millions of people and thousands of tons of industrial equipment were transported to the interior during the first year of war.

This migration of people and machinery was carried out at great cost. Factory buildings and crude housing facilities were thrown up in bitterly cold weather by people chronically short of food, warm clothing, and medicine. Working hours were long, conditions unspeakable. As in

Leningrad, authorities in charge of these projects carried out their orders ruthlessly and brooked no complaints. Somehow, out of the confusion of hastily constructed factories staffed by underfed workers who often were poorly trained for their tasks, production was resumed. The continued resistance of Soviet armed forces would have been impossible had it not been for the stream of tanks, guns, and ammunition that began flowing to the fighting fronts by the early months of 1942.

HITLER'S SECOND OFFENSIVE

Hindsight makes it easy to see that Germany's failure to knock Russia out of the war in 1941 was a turning point. Yet, this was by no means obvious at the time. Failure to provide German troops with warm clothing and winterized equipment had been costly, and one might blame the generals (as Hitler usually did) for blunders or lack of aggressiveness in the field. Even so, terrible punishment had been inflicted on the Soviet armed forces. They had suffered an estimated 3 million casualties and lost nearly 20,000 tanks. It was reasonable to assume that new divisions and their commanders would be less effective and that the elimination of so much prewar industrial capacity would prevent the Soviets from making up equipment losses. Food shortages resulting from the German occupation of some of Russia's most fertile agricultural areas might also prove crippling. Such assumptions led Hitler to believe that a renewed effort in 1942 might finish the job.

His calculations rested upon false premises. The Soviet Union's population of 200 million permitted it to make up human losses that would have proved fatal to a smaller nation. Furthermore, the demands of war brought to command positions Soviet generals—some of whom had languished previously because they were politically suspect—who were the equals of any who fought in World War II. A large percentage of the tanks and aircraft lost during the first months of the fighting were obsolete, but replacements made possible by the relocation of manufacturing facilities often were of superior quality. The T-34 medium tank is a case in point. This heavily gunned, reliable machine was better than any the Germans were able to employ until late in the war. Just being introduced in 1941, the T-34 played a major part in Soviet battlefield success as more and more became available. The Soviet Union had been wounded but not as badly as Hitler imagined.

Despite the fate of BARBAROSSA, Germany appeared to hold the stronger hand going into 1942. Soviet counterattacks had bogged down by February, and German armies still sat deep inside Soviet territory. Hitler had sacked those generals he held responsible for failure, replacing them with men he assumed would perform more capably. Meanwhile,

Heinrich Himmler inspects a prisoner-of-war camp in Russia, ca. 1940–1941. (National Archives photo no. W&C 1275)

German forces were reinforced and reequipped during the early spring in preparation for new offensives when good weather permitted. They also enjoyed the advantage of choosing where to launch their attacks, while the Soviets had to disperse their forces along a very broad front. Less promising was the fact that Germany had lost some of its best, most seasoned men and officers the previous year. As a result, divisions from the satellite nations had been sent to the eastern front to maintain numerical strength, but they were poor substitutes for the crack units that had crossed the Soviet border in June 1941.

Hitler's 1942 offensive had more modest goals than had BARBAROSSA. New divisions were thrown against Leningrad, but the main effort would be directed south toward the oil fields of the Caucasus: Seizure of these fields would relieve Germany's chronic shortages of petroleum products and deny them to the Soviets. The campaign, consisting of several phased thrusts, began in late June, almost precisely a year after the start of BARBAROSSA. Advances at first went according to schedule, but later objectives took longer to attain than anticipated, causing Hitler to improvise. His altered plans initially appeared to produce results as Soviet forces withdrew from several defensive positions. However, Hitler misread these retreats as signs of collapse. His zeal to exploit the situation

The RUSSIAN ADVANCE
1942-1944

Miles
0   300

Russo-German Frontier October 1939
Front line November 1942
Russian gains to April 1943
Retaken by Germans June-July 1943
Russian gains from July 1943-April 1944
German Controlled territory April 1944

led him to divert elsewhere a panzer army scheduled to attack Stalingrad, leaving the mission to a slow-moving army mostly composed of infantry units. It was a costly mistake.

Stalingrad (since renamed Volgograd) is an industrial city located on the west bank of the Volga River. Its capture would enable the Germans to choke off Soviet use of both the river and several north-south railways. The city itself was of only modest military importance because the Germans could have achieved their main goal by cutting the river and rail lines south of it. But Hitler became obsessed with the idea of capturing a city named after his hated enemy. Stalin could not abide its loss.

The German Sixth Army, commanded by General Frederich von Paulus, neared Stalingrad in late August. Its slow progress enabled the Soviets to reinforce and fortify the city. By this time, Stalin had shaken up the Soviet command structure, and General Georgi Zhukov, responsible for the defense of Moscow in 1941, now took over the southern front. In September, General V. I. Chuikov was placed in command of the Sixty-second Army in the Stalingrad sector. Both were able, aggressive leaders who served with distinction throughout the war.

The battle for Stalingrad turned the city and its environs into a huge killing ground. Entire sections were reduced to rubble from block-to-block, building-to-building combat. Some areas changed hands several

German troops in Russia. (National Archives photo no. W&C 996)

times in a day, and on two occasions, German forces almost annihilated Soviet defenders fighting with their backs to the river. The Germans had local air superiority, but Soviet artillery on the east side of the Volga had more guns.

Zhukov fed just enough reinforcements into Stalingrad to defend it while amassing reserves for a counteroffensive. Meanwhile, some German generals warned that the Sixth Army was dangerously exposed and wanted to pull back from Stalingrad. Hitler refused, but he did send two Romanian armies to protect Paulus's flanks. It was against these inferior troops that Zhukov launched a two-pronged strike in mid-November. Both Romanian armies quickly fell apart, permitting Soviet forces to meet west of Stalingrad. More than 200,000 German troops were trapped.

On December 12, Field Marshal Erich von Manstein, commander of the newly created Army Group Don of which the Sixth Army was a part, sent a panzer army to relieve Stalingrad. Hitler refused to allow Paulus to attempt a breakout to meet the thrust, which bogged down forty miles short of the city. Reichsmarshal Herman Goering had rashly promised that the Luftwaffe could supply the beleaguered troops at Stalingrad by air: It never even came close. Lack of available aircraft, Soviet fighters and antiaircraft fire, and bad weather combined to prevent the German air force from providing more than a tiny fraction of the required supplies.

The Stalingrad pocket at first comprised an area of about 25 by 12 miles. Within it, when not fighting to repel attacks, German troops huddled in cellars and other shelters under almost constant shellfire. Medicine for the sick and wounded quickly ran out, and doctors performed emergency operations under the crudest of conditions. As food supplies dwindled, the men began slaughtering pack horses. Their suffering was intensified as winter set in, adding numbing cold to the agonies they had to endure. Some went mad, others committed suicide, and those who were able went on fighting. Still the perimeter shrank.

In early January, the Soviets called upon Paulus to surrender under honorable terms. Hitler, in turn, promoted Paulus to field marshal and ordered him to continue fighting to the last man. By this time, the German forces no longer were capable of even attempting to break out. Soviet attacks in late January split the pocket in two, and the men had gone beyond endurance. On February 1, Paulus agreed to surrender. Fighting continued another day in the northern sector because communications had been cut off, but the guns finally went silent on February 2.

German losses at Stalingrad were appalling. The Sixth Army, consisting of twenty-two frontline divisions and supporting units, had ceased to exist. About 30,000 wounded men had escaped through evacuation by cargo plane, another 30,000 had been taken prisoner during the fighting, and 90,000 survived to be placed in Soviet prison camps from which few returned. More than 70,000 Germans perished, many from starvation and cold. Even these staggering figures do not measure the battle's significance. German forces had been stopped and in some sectors pushed back during the winter of 1941–1942, but never had they suffered disaster on this scale. Psychological factors defy measurement, but Stalingrad surely hastened the decline of Hitler's physical and mental resilience, while it encouraged the Soviets to believe in eventual victory.

As the battle for Stalingrad developed during the autumn months, Germany's southern offensive bogged down. Hitler's penchant for splitting his forces and assigning them overly ambitious objectives lay at fault. Unwilling to recognize this, he responded to failure as he usually did— by sacking his generals. He replaced the army chief of staff with a younger, more compliant man and personally began directing operations on the eastern front. The situation in the south grew worse. German units at the end of long supply lines were scattered across a huge front. Ultimately, Soviet resistance, fuel shortages, rough terrain, and then the onset of winter precluded further advance.

In December, the Soviets launched a series of thrusts designed to entrap the entire southern army group. German commanders in the field narrowly escaped disaster by executing a series of well-coordinated retreats and even managed to regain some ground by counterattack.

Still, at great cost in men and equipment, Hitler's second great offensive had failed, and in some places, German forces had lost areas they occupied when it began.

Despite their failure to entrap the German southern army group, the Soviets had reason to celebrate their accomplishments. Even before the German surrender at Stalingrad, Stalin elevated several generals, including Zhukov, to marshal. A bit later, Stalin himself assumed the highest rank, marshal of the Soviet Union. Conferring these titles constituted part of a process that had begun earlier and would continue: recognition of Soviet armed forces as professional military organizations rather than as "revolutionary" units dominated by the Communist party. Designations of rank such as shoulder boards and gold braid, previously banned as symbols of the detested czarist regime, were reinstituted, as were standard forms of military address instead of the all-purpose "comrade." These changes represented yet another example of the way in which Soviet leaders relied on traditional institutions to help stimulate pride and discipline. By formally assuming military rank, Stalin also enhanced his personal power in his role as architect and hero of "the great patriotic war."

THE BATTLE OF KURSK

The German army had taken a beating during the winter of 1942–1943. In addition to the defeat at Stalingrad, it had lost ground to Soviet offensives on the central front and had been unable to prevent the opening of a supply corridor to Leningrad. The tide that had turned against Hitler was irreversible. Soviet forces grew stronger and better armed, while he was hard put to replace the lost men and equipment, as indicated by his use of inferior divisions provided by his allies. Military logic dictated that he try to salvage what he could. Strategic withdrawals, punctuated by counterattacks when opportunities appeared, would have shortened overextended German supply lines and permitted a concentration of forces along a narrower front. But such a course, amounting to an admission of failure, was unthinkable to Hitler. He still hoped for some masterstroke that would prove decisive.

Hitler chose as his target what became known as the "Kursk salient," a Soviet-occupied bulge in the front about 300 miles south of Moscow. Crushing the salient, he believed, would regain the initiative for Germany and boost morale both at home and in the armed forces. Two factors doomed the enterprise. Soviet intelligence learned through its spy network the full details of the operation, code-named CITADEL. Already knowing where the attack would take place, the Soviets were given time to prepare elaborate defenses. Ignoring advice that the operation should be mounted as early as April, Hitler decided to wait until what he regarded as overwhelming numbers of tanks (especially newer models) and troops could be brought into position. He did not know that the Soviets were just as busily building up their own strength.

The Battle of Kursk was impressive even by the standards of the eastern front. Nearly a million German troops, 2,700 tanks and assault guns, 1,800 aircraft, and 10,000 artillery pieces took part in a double envelopment to isolate and reduce the salient. Soviet figures were even more impressive; 1.3 million men, 3,300 tanks, and 20,000 pieces of artillery. During the interval Hitler had granted them, the Soviets had constructed successive defensive lines (in some places, to a depth of nearly seventy miles), all protected by extensive minefields.

Hitler launched his offensive on July 5, with simultaneous attacks from the north and south against the base of the salient. German tanks in groups sometimes numbering in the hundreds, followed by infantry, crashed into Soviet positions. Soviet armor moved up to block advances in what became by far the largest tank battle of the war. While aircraft fought in the skies above, the ground rocked with explosions from bombs, cannon, rockets, and mines at points of attack. The battlegrounds became nightmares of savage fighting amidst the smoke of burning wreckage. Men died by the tens of thousands.

The German offensive lasted only a week, but it had a far-reaching impact. After some initial penetration, deepest against the southern base, German units had stalled with their own flanks exposed to Soviet counterattacks, which began on July 12. Hitler might have persevered had he not learned that the Allies had invaded Sicily. He decided to cut his losses so that he could transfer a panzer corps to help defend Italy. The Germans conducted a fighting withdrawal that lasted until late August. Nearly fifty divisions (seventeen of them panzers) had been mauled in varying degrees, some shattered beyond repair. One panzer division that had gone into battle with 300 tanks emerged with only 30, some of which had to be scrapped. As many as 70,000 German officers and men had been killed. Hitler never again attempted a large offensive in the east after Kursk.

Through the summer and autumn of 1943, the Soviets mounted a series of attacks at various points that kept the Germans off balance and forced numerous retreats to prevent encirclement. Partisan operations behind German lines grew steadily more effective. In early September, field marshals Guenther von Kluge and Erich von Manstein appeared at Hitler's headquarters in an effort to alter a situation they felt sure was leading to disaster. First, they stressed the need for unifying the command system under a single person to achieve coordination between the various theaters in which German forces were stationed. Then, they urged Hitler to either greatly reinforce the eastern front from other areas or order large-scale withdrawals to defensible lines.

Hitler rejected their first request out of hand, implying as it did a criticism of his own military leadership. He was unwilling to concentrate so much power in the hands of another and insisted that he alone possessed the vision necessary to conduct grand strategy. However, he temporized with regard to the eastern front. He refused to strip other theaters for reinforcements but acknowledged that German forces in Russia were overextended by permitting retreats from exposed positions on the southern front. Beyond that he refused to go. Even though he had earlier directed that work begin on creating an "eastern wall" (designated WOTAN in the south and PANTHER in the central and northern zones), he could not bring himself to relinquish territory voluntary.

Hitler's response to the proposals made by Kluge and Manstein displayed a characteristic that became more pronounced as time wore on. He shrank from making painful decisions until they were thrust upon him, often with disastrous results. Had he authorized systematic withdrawals to WOTAN and PANTHER in early September, his forces might have been able to fortify them and hold off the Soviets indefinitely. German armies were pushed back during the next few weeks anyway, but they were so chewed up in the process that they were unable to hold the "eastern wall" when they reached it.

By the end of 1943, the Soviets had driven the Germans back an average distance of nearly 200 miles on the southern and central fronts and were threatening to lift the siege of Leningrad. (The city was liberated in January 1944.) German manpower shortages were becoming so acute that some staff officers wanted to conscript women into the armed forces in noncombat capacities. Hitler vetoed the idea because it violated his convictions about the proper roles for women. Instead, he sought to bolster frontline strength by drastically stripping rear echelon units, but this produced only modest numbers while reducing the efficiency of supply and support services. The quality as well as the numerical strength of German units had declined. By late 1943, divisions began to be rated in terms of their reliability in combat, and relatively few were judged to be of top quality. Those of Germany's allies grew worse.

In response to deteriorating conditions on the eastern front, Hitler issued a remarkable directive on November 3. The bulk of German resources since June 1941 had been devoted to the Russian campaign, he stated, but the situation had been changed by the prospect of an Anglo-American invasion. If necessary, Germany could buy time by giving up space in the east. Allied success in the west, however, would have "unforeseeable consequences in a short time." His conclusion was that efforts in western Europe had to receive priority, rather than be weakened by transferring troops to stiffen the resistance against the Soviets. In effect, he was conceding defeat in a struggle that was already going on in order to gamble on victory in one that had not yet begun. If Germany smashed the anticipated Anglo-American invasion, he reasoned, it could then turn its entire strength against the Soviet Union.

1944: HITLER AT BAY, STALIN ASCENDANT

The Soviets continued hammering away at retreating German armies during the first months of 1944. They persisted even after the arrival of spring thaws and rains, which usually impeded offensive operations. The wide-tracked Soviet T-34s and American four-wheel-drive trucks enabled them to move over terrain that was impassable to German vehicles. Soviet infantry hauled its equipment and supplies on small wagons called *panjes* that provided excellent mobility in muddy conditions. Aggressive Soviet generals fully exploited these advantages.

Hitler's directive of the previous November had implied a willingness to conduct fighting retreats in the east until the expected Anglo-American invasion had been dealt with. Such a strategy ran against his nature, as shown by his refusal to give up Stalingrad. Then, in March 1944, angered by the loss of several cities, Hitler reverted to type. He issued a directive designating nearly thirty cities and strongpoints as "fortified places." The commanders of these fortified places were ordered to defend them to the last man unless they received Hitler's personal permission to withdraw. The penalty for disobedience was death. His order undoubtedly stiffened resistance in some places, but it also resulted in the needless sacrifice of troops caught in hopeless situations.

In his monumental history of the German-Soviet war, historian John Erickson aptly titled his chapter on the period of April to August 1944, "Breaking the Back of the *Wehrmacht*." After a pause following spring operations, the Soviets mounted a series of offensives on June 22 that dwarfed what had gone before. By this time, their total troop strength outnumbered the Germans by nearly 3 to 1, and they had an overwhelming preponderance of tanks, aircraft, and artillery. Counting both Soviets and Germans, some 6 million men were involved. Coordinated with blows struck in the north and south, the Soviets launched a massive offensive on the central front that tore huge gaps in enemy lines. Within a week, in the central sector alone, 130,000 German soldiers were killed and 66,000 taken prisoner. Soviet forces had penetrated up to 350 miles in some sectors, and the nearest units were only 400 miles from Berlin by the same time the offensive was called off in late August.

Hitler had lost his gamble by this time. Allied landings in Normandy on June 6 had not been thrown back. By July, Anglo-American forces had broken out from the beachheads and were moving across France. On July 20, an attempt on Hitler's life carried out by army officers resulted in a purge of the army's higher echelons. Italy already had left the war, and Hitler's other European allies were searching for ways to get out, as well. Meanwhile, the Allied strategic bombing campaign was beginning to inflict crippling damage against German transportation and oil facilities. That German forces continued to fight on against such adversity was a tribute to their discipline, their patriotism, and, however misplaced, their loyalty to Hitler. But the outcome no longer could be in doubt.

As Soviet armies reached and crossed pre-1939 boundaries, military strategy became inextricably tied in with political questions. This was especially true with regard to Poland. All along, Stalin had made clear to Roosevelt and Churchill that he meant to establish the Soviet-Polish boundary as drawn in the Nazi-Soviet pact of September 1939. Because that line approximated what was known as the "Curzon line" (as suggested by the British after World War I), FDR and Churchill had no quarrel with it, although they hoped the Soviets would make some adjustments to favor the Poles. But what about the rest of Poland and, by extension, other nations such as Romania, Hungary, and Bulgaria? Would he permit these nations to exist independently, provided "friendly" governments were established, or did he intend to dominate them?

Both Roosevelt and Churchill had grown increasingly apprehensive about Stalin's intentions toward Poland. The United States and Great Britain recognized the London-based Polish exile government, which refused to accept the Curzon line. The chances for a compromise between the London Poles and Moscow were undermined in April 1943 by Germany's accusation that, in 1940, the Soviets had murdered more then 4,000 Polish officers, whose bodies had been found in the Katyn Forest near Smolensk. When the London Poles asked the International Red Cross to investigate in spite of indignant Soviet denials, Stalin branded the request an unforgivable insult to Soviet honor. (In April 1990 the Soviet government finally admitted responsibility for the atrocity and for killing 10,000 more Polish officers in other areas.) A few months later, the Soviets announced the formation of the Union of Polish Patriots in Russia, a puppet group that Churchill and Roosevelt feared Stalin might promote as the "legitimate" government of Poland.

Soviet actions as they moved into Poland in 1944 did not inspire confidence. Among several Polish partisan forces, the two most important were the *Armija Krajowa* (AK), loyal to the London Poles, and the Communist-dominated *Armija Ludowa* (AL). That the Soviets provided arms and supplies for the AL was understandable, but their treatment of the AK caused alarm. Reports from inside Poland indicated that advance Soviet units cooperated with the AK until the Germans had been cleared out. Then AK members, whose identities were now known, were arrested or shot out of hand. On July 22, the Soviets announced that the Polish Committee for National Liberation had been established in the Polish city of Lublin, and a few days later, they concluded an agreement with it in Moscow. The Lublin Committee, of course, quickly announced its support for the Curzon line as the Polish-Soviet boundary.

Soviet military operations during late summer appeared to confirm Anglo-American suspicions that Stalin meant to eliminate any opposition to his handpicked new "government." As Russian forces approached Warsaw during late July, the leaders of the Polish exile government and the AK planned an uprising to liberate the city. They wanted to demonstrate their strength and support among the Polish people, hoping it would encourage Great Britain and the United States to support them against Stalin's handpicked group.

The Warsaw uprising began on August 1 as elements of the AK, commanded by General Tadeusz Bor-Komorowski, began firing on German installations. The Poles achieved early successes through surprise, but the Germans quickly consolidated their forces in various sections of the city. The AK units, equipped only with light arms and homemade explosive devices, were relatively ineffective against fortified positions. Soon, the Germans began sending reinforcements to Warsaw, against which the Poles could not hope to prevail without outside help. And that help could come only from Soviet forces now occupying the east bank of the Vistula River, several miles away.

The Soviet failure to relieve Warsaw had been a subject of controversy for years. At the time, it seemed to the United States, Great Britain, and, of course, the Poles that Stalin deliberately refrained from advancing on the city because he wished to see the AK annihilated. The Soviets angrily denied the charge, claiming their divisions had exhausted their offensive capabilities in reaching the Vistula, where they faced strong German defenses. They, in turn, denounced the London Poles and the AK for having launched the uprising prematurely.

The truth appears to lie somewhere in between. Soviet forces probably were not in any condition to cross the Vistula at the time the uprising began, but they showed uncharacteristic tardiness in resuming operations during the following weeks. The few small thrusts they did attempt seem to have been intended primarily to encourage the Poles to keep on fighting. Furthermore, Stalin refused to allow American and British planes to use Soviet airfields as shuttle bases for supply drops into Warsaw until it was too late to affect the outcome. And toward the end, he began calling the Polish resistance fighters "criminals." Most likely he did not plan these events, but he was quite willing to take advantage of them.

On October 2, the Warsaw uprising collapsed after sixty-two days of appalling slaughter. The Germans had employed several SS and police brigades, whose reputation for brutality preceded them. Employing all kinds of incendiary and explosive devices, they burned and blasted Poles out of cellars and sewers without regard for civilian casualties. Those who surrendered, as well as the sick and wounded, were killed indiscriminately. In addition to 15,000 AK members, as many as 200,000 of a population of 1 million perished; the rest were deported or sent to gas chambers. To complete the disaster, Hitler ordered that what was left of Warsaw be razed as an example to other Nazi-occupied cities.

Elsewhere, Soviet forces advanced relentlessly during the autumn of 1944. By the end of the year, they not only had liberated the Soviet Union but had penetrated the Baltic states, compelled the surrender of Romania and Bulgaria, and laid siege to the capital of Hungary. Bulgaria's surrender had forced the Germans to evacuate their forces from Greece and Yugoslavia. Germany's military situation was hopeless, yet Hitler went on dreaming of some miracle that would redeem his fortunes.

SELECTED BIBLIOGRAPHY

Armstrong, John A. (ed.). *Soviet Partisans in World War II* (Madison: University of Wisconsin Press, 1964).

Carell, Paul. *Hitler's War on Russia* (London: Harrap, 1964).

————. *Scorched Earth* (London: Harrap, 1970).

Central Intelligence Agency. *The Rote Kappelle: The CIA's History of Soviet Intelligence and Espionage Networks in Western Europe, 1936–1945* (Frederick, Md.: University Publications of America, 1979).

Ciechanowski, Jan. *The Warsaw Rising of 1944* (London: Cambridge University Press, 1974).

Craig, W. *Enemy at the Gates: The Battle for Stalingrad* (New York: Reader's Digest Press, 1973).

Erickson, John. *Stalin's War with Germany: The Road to Berlin* (Boulder, Colo.: Westview, 1983).

Fitzgibbon, Louis. *Katyn: Crime Without Parallel* (London: Stacey, 1971).

Gouré, L. *The Siege of Leningrad* (Stanford, Calif.: Stanford University Press, 1962).

Higgins, Trumbull. *Hitler and Russia: The Third Reich in a Two-Front War* (New York: Collier-Macmillan, 1966).

Jukes, Geoffrey. *Kursk: The Clash of Armor* (London: Ballantine, 1969).

Korbonski, Stefan. *Fighting Warsaw: The Story of the Polish Underground State, 1939–1945* (New York: Minerva, 1956).

Mastny, Vojtech. *Russia's Road to the Cold War: Diplomacy, Warfare, and the Politics of Communism, 1941–1945* (New York: Columbia University Press, 1979).

Rozek, Edward J. *Allied Wartime Diplomacy: A Pattern in Poland* (New York: J. Wiley, 1958).

Salisbury, Harrison. *The 900 Days: The Siege of Leningrad* (New York: Avon, 1969).

Werth, Alexander. *Russia at War, 1941–1945* (New York: Avon, 1970).

Zawadny, J. K. *Death in the Forest: The Story of the Katyn Forest Massacre* (London: Macmillan, 1971).

_____ . *Nothing But Honor* (Stanford, Calif.: Hoover Institution Press, 1977).

Zhukov, Georgi. *Marshal Zhukov's Greatest Battles* (New York: Harper & Row, 1969).

_____ . *The Memoirs of Marshal Zhukov* (New York: Delacorte Press, 1971).

Ziemke, E. F. *Stalingrad to Berlin: The German Campaign in Russia, 1942–1945* (Washington, D.C.: Department of the Army, 1968).

13
Launching the Second Front (1944)

OVERLORD was to be the main offensive against Germany in the west. A cross-channel invasion of France, American military leaders had long believed, provided the best way to end the war as quickly as possible by defeating German armies in the field. Churchill, who continued to have doubts almost until the end, was tormented by visions of beaches "choked with the flower of American and British youth" and "tides running red with their blood." The operation *was* risky, with numerous factors beyond anyone's control. Failure would have disastrous consequences, at the very least prolonging the war in Europe by many months. That it did not fail was due more to General Eisenhower as supreme commander than to any other individual. Whatever his limitations as a strategist, his abilities to overcome national rivalries, interservice struggles, and the outsized egos of several subordinates made him a superb choice for the job.

PLANNING FOR OVERLORD

Determining the location and timing over Operation OVERLORD was, of course, crucial. Pas de Calais was the obvious choice for the landing. It was the shortest distance from England, and it lay near the excellent port of Antwerp. However, it was rejected because the Germans knew just how desirable a site it was and had stationed their strongest forces there. Other locations were passed over for various reasons, such as vulnerability to Atlantic storms or beaches that were unsuitable for landings. In the end, Normandy was chosen because it had the fewest disadvantages.

Timing was essential. Planners at Supreme Headquarters, Allied Expeditionary Force (SHAEF) wanted the invasion armada to cross the channel under cover of night, with the troops sent ashore at dawn to avoid confusion and to afford a full day to consolidate the beachheads. This also had to be done when the tide was low so that offshore obstacles planted by the Germans would be plainly visible. To complicate matters further, some moonlight was deemed necessary during the predawn hours to facilitate airborne operations inland. These conditions would obtain only during early May and in the first and third weeks of June. D Day, as it was called, originally was scheduled for May 1.

A costly error in channeling American productive capacity was the low priority assigned to landing craft. These unglamorous implements of war were in short supply worldwide. Eisenhower, convinced that the European theater should take precedence, unsuccessfully lobbied for a greater share of the precious vessels at the expense of operations in the Pacific. As commander of the European Theater of Operations as well as OVERLORD, he was able to squeeze some landing craft out of the Mediterranean, but this affected other plans such as ANVIL, the invasion of southern France. The lack of landing craft inhibited training opportunities and threatened to limit the number of divisions that could be put ashore at Normandy. As a result, D Day was postponed from May 1 to early June to obtain more ships from current production during the delay.

Eisenhower also had problems securing the air support he believed necessary for the success of OVERLORD, especially with regard to heavy bombers. SHAEF strategists wanted these aircraft used during the weeks before D Day to destroy French transportation facilities that the Germans could use to move troops and equipment. Unless this were done, Eisenhower warned, the Germans might throw sufficient reinforcements against the beachheads to push Allied troops into the sea.

Commanders of both the British Bomber Command and U.S. Strategic Air Forces (the United States Army Air Forces by this time was practically independent of the army) opposed the SHAEF plan. They argued that attacking oil-producing industries within Germany was the best way to help OVERLORD, and they were impervious to arguments that this would be of no immediate value because the Germans had stockpiled fuel supplies in France. Aside from their commitment to the theory that strategic bombing alone could defeat the enemy, it is difficult to avoid the conclusion that they also resented the notion of being an auxiliary arm of the ground forces. Churchill also resisted because he did not want Allied air forces inflicting casualties and devastation upon an occupied nation.

Eisenhower ultimately got most of what he wanted, although he had to threaten to resign in order to do so. He was willing to go so far because he genuinely feared the invasion would fail if the French transportation system were left intact. He was helped in his cause when, at Churchill's insistence, the commander of French forces in Great Britain was consulted. "This is war," the Frenchman replied, "and it must be expected that people will be killed." In view of how close the invasion came to being defeated during its early days, Eisenhower's determination may have provided the margin for success.

FORTITUDE

As in the Sicilian campaign, the Allies tried to mislead Germany as to their real objectives for OVERLORD. This time, they wanted to convince the enemy that they intended to launch a diversionary strike against Norway, then invade France at the Pas de Calais. British intelligence devised a plan, code-named FORTITUDE, to make the deception convincing. It provided for the creation of two fictitious armies: one in Scotland that supposedly would move against Norway and the more "powerful" First Army Group in southeastern England, destined for the Pas de Calais. An ingenious array of dummy tanks, vehicles, and buildings were set in place in the area around Dover; phony radio traffic was generated; and Allied intelligence organizations spread misinformation to confirm the ruse. The First Army Group was "commanded" by General George Patton, who had gained a measure of respect from the Germans for his aggressiveness in Sicily.

FORTITUDE had one unintended outcome that nearly ended Patton's usefulness, especially after the slapping incidents a few months earlier. To promote the fiction that the First Army Group was stationed nearby, Patton was encouraged to make frequent public appearances in the vicinity of Dover. Unfortunately, he spoke at some of these occasions. At one gathering to promote Anglo-American amity held in late April, Patton declared that "since it is the evident destiny of the British and Americans to rule the world," it was fitting that they get to know each other better. This remark was widely reported and had embarrassing implications for relations with other allies, especially the Soviet Union. Patton's indiscretion infuriated Eisenhower and Marshall, but again, they valued his generalship too highly to send him home. After making an abject apology to Eisenhower, he retained command of the Third Army, which was to land in Normandy after D Day.

The publicity generated by the Patton incident probably helped deceive the Germans into believing he commanded a mighty army group. In any event, they retained troops in Norway and at the Pas de Calais and wildly exaggerated the number of Allied divisions in Great Britain. Even after D Day, they were not sure whether the Normandy operation constituted the main thrust or whether it was a diversion for landings at Calais. Consequently, troops that might have been thrown into the battle for Normandy waited for an invasion that never came.

PREPARATIONS FOR BATTLE

The invasion of Normandy was by far the largest amphibious operation ever mounted. Although fewer troops were put ashore during the first landings than at Sicily, their job was to force a door through which tens of thousands more would pass. The Americans alone had more than 1.5 million soldiers stationed in England, along with the British and troops from several other nations. The invasion fleet numbered more than 5,000 ships and 4,000 landing craft, escorted by 600 warships. Some 2,500 bombers and 7,000 fighters and fighter bombers were committed, to provide overwhelming air superiority against the depleted Luftwaffe. The target was a 60-mile stretch of beach between Cherbourg and Le Havre.

OVERLORD was a unified operation both in command structure and in the composition of forces. General Montgomery, who played a key role in planning the invasion, served as Eisenhower's commander on the ground during the opening phase. The commanders of naval and air forces also were British, as was Eisenhower's deputy supreme commander, Air Chief Marshal Sir Arthur Tedder. Of the six divisions assigned to make the initial landings, three were American, two British, and one Canadian.

Remarkable ingenuity was shown in devising equipment for the operation. Two huge structures called Mulberries were built to be towed across the channel in sections, then joined to form artificial harbors. Pipelines were laid on the channel floor to provide fuel after the beachheads were secured. British General Sir Percy Hobart had developed a variety of specialized tanks. Collectively referred to as Hobart's "funnies," there were Crabs mounted with flails to make paths through minefields, flamethrowing Crocodiles, and a host of other adaptations including the DD, an amphibious tank that could propel itself to shore. Except for the latter, American commanders were unimpressed with the "funnies" and made far less use of them than did the British. This proved costly to American troops on the Normandy beaches.

The Germans had sixty divisions with which to defend the coasts of Europe, most of them understrength and not of first quality. Field Marshal Gerd von Rundstedt commanded the western forces, while Rommel commanded Army Group B, charged with coastal defense. They disagreed over strategy. Although inclined to believe the main Allied thrust would be at Calais, Rundstedt was pessimistic about preventing landings. Instead, he wanted to launch powerful counterattacks against the beachheads during the period of buildup. Rommel, fearing that Allied air power would smash any large-scale efforts to move men and tanks, thought the invasion had to be met at the beaches during the first hours. Hitler was inclined to agree with Rommel, but in the end, he split the difference. Significant forces, especially armor, were withheld from Rommel's operational command. This may have had a crucial impact on the outcome because Allied air operations were not as well coordinated during the first days after the invasion as they would become later.

In keeping with his philosophy of forward defense, Rommel energetically tried to shore up what German propaganda called the "western wall." There was no wall in the sense of a continuous line of fortifications. Rommel had bunkers and pillboxes constructed, of course, but he tried to supplement these with extensive minefields and an imaginative array of obstacles designed to wreck landing craft and airborne gliders. The most common of these, called "Rommel's asparagus," were steel beams to which mines often were attached, driven into beaches and meadows. He was unaware, of course, that Ultra had successfully located the disposition of most German divisions.

D DAY

Postponed in May, the invasion had been rescheduled for the period of June 5–7. Favorable moon and tide conditions would occur again two weeks later, then not for months. This generated enormous pressure to go ahead at the early date if at all possible. A two-week delay would be bad enough for logistical and psychological reasons, but it also would leave the Allies only one more chance before losing most of the summer. If bad weather forced yet another postponement, the Germans would gain additional months to strengthen their positions, and the time available for offensive operations before winter closed in would be drastically curtailed. Eisenhower could consult anyone he wished, but the decision was his to make.

The weather hardly could have been worse during the first days of June. Severe storms began to rage, which would have made landing operations impossible and eliminated the moonlight needed by the airborne units. By early morning on June 4, Eisenhower learned that, although the sea had calmed somewhat, air operations still would be impossible the following day. Against Montgomery's advice but with the support of others, Eisenhower ordered a standdown. That evening brought the welcome prediction that conditions would improve during the latter part of June 5 and continue through the next day. Eisenhower set the operation in motion. Early on June 5, when the invasion still could have been called off, he met with subordinates again. Informed

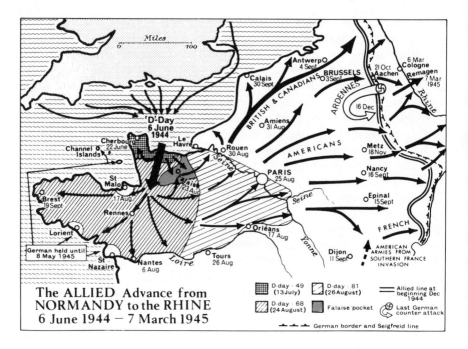

The ALLIED Advance from
NORMANDY to the RHINE
6 June 1944 — 7 March 1945

that the favorable forecast still stood but aware that disaster loomed if it were mistaken, Eisenhower made the decision: "Okay, we'll go." June 6 would be D Day.

The weather conditions that bedeviled Eisenhower actually benefited the Allies in ways they did not foresee. The Germans failed to detect a break in the weather because they lacked meteorological stations in the Atlantic. Believing an invasion impossible, they called off naval channel patrols and did not have army units on alert. Key commanders had left their posts, including Rommel, who was visiting his family and was unable to get back until late in the evening of June 6. These factors caused the initial German response to be sluggish and uncoordinated.

As the huge armada plowed toward France on the night of June 5, aircraft passed overhead carrying paratroopers or towing gliders. These airborne units were to seize exits from the beaches and prevent the Germans from reinforcing coastal defenses. Three divisions were employed to capture bridges and causeways in their respective sectors: the British 6th and the American 82d and 101st. Many of the airdrops, beginning shortly after midnight, went badly. Through navigational error or efforts to evade antiaircraft fire, transports scattered men miles away from their target areas. Glider pilots performed more reliably. Despite faulty drops and the difficulty of operating at night on unfamiliar terrain,

"Full victory—nothing else": Gen. Dwight D. Eisenhower gives the order of the Day to paratroopers in England, just before they board their airplanes to participate in the first assault in the invasion of the continent of Europe, June 6, 1944. (National Archives photo no. W&C 1040)

the airborne units took most of their objectives and sowed great confusion among the German defenders.

The main landings began shortly after dawn. On the Allied left, troops of the British Second Army, commanded by General Miles Dempsey, went ashore on beaches designated Sword, Juno, and Gold. They were to drive inland toward Caen, an important rail and highway center that Montgomery had boasted would be taken on the first day. The British salient would then serve to shield American units from German armored divisions that Ultra had revealed were available for counterattack.

The American First Army, under General Bradley, was assigned the beaches Omaha and Utah further down the coast. Bradley's primary task, after establishing his positions and getting reinforcements ashore, was to drive to his right across the Cotentin Peninsula, which jutted out into the Channel. His objective was the port of Cherbourg, through which far greater amounts of supplies and equipment could be shipped than the Mulberries could handle. Once the buildup was completed, major offensives would be launched against Paris and Germany.

Little went as planned. British landings went off relatively smoothly, but their drive on Caen soon bogged down. The Americans fared even

U.S. soldiers disembarking from a Coast Guard landing boat on the coast of France under heavy Nazi machine gun fire, June 6, 1944. (National Archives photo no. W&C 1041)

more poorly. At Utah, although currents swept landing craft away from designated areas, the troops going ashore encountered only light resistance and quickly established themselves. Omaha, on the other hand, was a near disaster that jeopardized the entire operation.

The cards had been stacked against the men going ashore at Omaha. Preliminary bombings had overshot targets, leaving the defenders unscathed. The beaches were fronted by steep cliffs from which the Germans had unobstructed fields of fire. To make matters worse, one of the better German infantry divisions occupied the area. But the Americans compounded their own difficulties. Men loaded on pitching landing craft much too far out arrived seasick and waterlogged. Amphibious tanks also were launched too early, with the result that most of them sank before reaching the shore. And failure to use Hobart's "funnies" proved costly when the Americans came up against obstacles, barbed wire, and land mines. By nightfall, the lodgment at Omaha was only a mile deep.

CONSOLIDATION

The Allies had gained a foothold on the coast of France, but the invasion still was in jeopardy. Omaha was the weak link. Its left flank lay 7 miles from the nearest British beachhead, and Utah was more than 10 miles further down the coast. Poor weather hampered the Allied ability to stop the movement of German armor by air strikes. In fact, if a panzer division had struck at Omaha during the first few days, it might have destroyed the beachhead. Then, with Utah so far away from the British sector, the Germans could have dealt with the two pockets separately. Fortunately, Rommel committed his panzers as they arrived to blocking the British around Caen. He did so because he believed the greatest threat was a breakout through that area into open country beyond. Three days after D Day, the Allies finally linked their beachheads, and the immediate danger was over.

While the British and Canadians continued to engage the German panzers and best infantry divisions, Bradley extended the depth of his beachheads and sent General J. Lawton ("Lightning Joe") Collins's VII Corps across and up the Cotentin Peninsula toward Cherbourg. VII Corps made disappointingly slow progress. Although few German units in this area were of high quality, they had the advantage afforded by terrain known as the *bocage*. Early farmers in this region had divided their plots by constructing earthenworks, some more than ten feet high. Over time, the growth of bushes and small trees made these hedgerows even more formidable obstacles and provided excellent defensive cover. American armor often had to stay on the roads, where it was most vulnerable to German antitank fire.

On June 19, several days before General Collins began his final assault on Cherbourg, violent storms struck the Normandy beaches. The Mulberry at Omaha was destroyed and the one at Gold badly damaged, resulting in a drastic curtailment of available supplies. Allied timetables were set back by weeks. Although occurring too late to affect the campaign against Cherbourg, the disaster prevented Bradley from moving south on schedule, and it forced Montgomery to scale back his operations. Allied planning was further disrupted when the capture of Cherbourg on June 27 revealed that the Germans had rendered the port unusable through demolition and scuttled ships. It would be almost three months before Cherbourg became fully operable.

The severity of the storms that began on June 19 underlines the significance of Eisenhower's decision to "go" earlier. Those very days, it will be remembered, were the last until late summer when moon and tide would be suitable for invasion. Eisenhower would have had no choice except to postpone again, thereby altering the course of OVERLORD in ways that can only be imagined.

British and Canadian soldiers finally occupied Caen on July 10, more than a month after Montgomery had predicted. For neither the first nor the last time, American military leaders (and some British, particularly

Air Marshal Tedder) attributed the delay to Montgomery's lack of boldness on the attack. Eisenhower, though unwilling to jeopardize Allied relations by sacking Montgomery as some wished, fumed at the Briton's failure to break out into open country.

Montgomery *was* cautious, and he tried to account for every contingency before acting. But he was a thorough professional with much more combat experience than the American and British officers who criticized him. His forces engaged four panzer divisions within days of the landings and a total of eight by the time Caen fell. Continued British and Canadian pressure forced Rommel to keep these divisions in the line, instead of withdrawing them for use as mobile reserves with possibly devastating effects.

Privately, Montgomery was contemptuous of Eisenhower and others who were forever talking of "breaking out" as though taking territory was an end in itself. A headlong advance in insufficient strength, even if it were possible, might be destroyed by a counterattack, at which the Germans excelled. In any event, expecting men worn out by weeks of bloody fighting to accomplish such a task struck Montgomery as absurd. Whatever the truth, the charge of excessive caution damaged Montgomery's standing at SHAEF and lessened his influence on future strategic planning.

Meanwhile, on July 3, III Corps and a division of VII had begun the delayed movement southward. Even after another corps joined the battle a few days later, little progress was made at the cost of high casualties. The bocage was ill suited for offensive operations, and for the first time, Americans began to confront panzer and elite infantry divisions. By July 18, Bradley's troops had established a line running from the coast at the base of the Cotentin Peninsula southeast to St. Lo, an objective that had taken far longer to reach than had been expected. At that point, the Americans paused to regroup and pour in fresh divisions in preparation for a major offensive, code-named COBRA, scheduled to begin on July 25.

SECRET WEAPONS AND SECRET PLOTS

Hitler had professed to subordinates that he welcomed a cross-channel invasion. German victory, in which he expressed confidence, would afford his country a breathing space of at least a year, probably more. During that time, secret weapons would become operational, and Germany could devote all its resources to stemming the Soviet tide in the east. To what degree he actually believed that this version of events was possible is not clear.

American howitzers shell German forces retreating near Carentan, France, July 11, 1944. (National Archives photo no. W&C 1047)

One week after D Day, the first German V-1s were launched against England. They were pilotless jet aircraft that flew at nearly 500 mph, carrying a one-ton warhead. Within two weeks, 2,000 had been launched, killing 1,600 people and wounding almost 5,000 more. The British quickly devised sophisticated techniques of combating the V-1s with antiaircraft fire. In September, the Germans began using V-2s, rockets capable of speeds in excess of 3,500 mph and therefore impervious to British defenses. The V-2s were formidable weapons.

By the end of the war, Germany had produced 32,000 V-1s and 6,000 V-2s. But they were too few and had come too late to have an appreciable impact on the outcome. Hitler had hoped to have them operational much sooner, but jurisdictional squabbles over control of the programs delayed progress, as did repeated bombing attacks on developmental and launching sites. Had the V weapons become available earlier, they might have inflicted catastrophic damage on British transportation and shipping facilities with great consequences for the invasion buildup.

The German use of jet aircraft also raises some imponderables. Development had begun even before the war, but neither Hitler nor Goering showed any early enthusiasm because they believed the war would be over before jets could become a factor. Even when Hitler ordered the ME 262 into production partway through the war, he ordered that it be converted into a fighter-bomber rather than a true fighter, as the Luftwaffe fighter command wanted. More maneuverable and capable of speeds better than 100 mph faster than the top operational Allied fighters, the ME 262 came into use only during the latter part of 1944. By that time, shortages of fuel and trained pilots, as well as the small number of ME 262s available, prevented the aircraft from making any difference. Had it been assigned a high priority at an early stage, it might have taken an unacceptable toll on Allied strategic bombers and played havoc on the Normandy beaches.

To the great benefit of the Allies—indeed, of humanity—Germany did not produce the greatest secret weapon of all, the atomic bomb. Nuclear fission had been discovered in Germany in 1938, and Allied leaders feared German scientists might win the race to construct these terrible weapons. In fact, as early as 1943, committees formed in the United States to study the subject recommended that, if and when atomic bombs became available to the Allies, they not be dropped on Germany. The planners speculated that that nation would retaliate if it already had them or might gain the necessary technical information to build them if one of the Allied bombs turned out to be a dud.

Germany never came that close. Although some German scientists later claimed that their own moral reservations retarded development, there were more important reasons. Hitler never authorized anything like the resources devoted to the Anglo-American program, German scientists for a long time pursued a method that led to a dead end, and Allied bombing and sabotage destroyed or damaged facilities and critical materials.

On July 20, while Allied armies paused to launch COBRA, an attempt was made to assassinate Hitler at his headquarters in East Prussia. Colonel Klaus von Stauffenberg placed a briefcase containing a time bomb, set to go off minutes after it had been primed, beneath a table at which Hitler was conferring with military subordinates. Stauffenberg left the room but remained on the grounds until the bomb went off. An officer sitting near the briefcase moved it out of his way so that it rested behind a heavy wooden slab supporting the table. This inadvertent act almost certainly saved Hitler's life: The explosion killed four men, but the table support shielded Hitler from its direct blast. He suffered a punctured eardrum, temporary paralysis of his right arm, and abrasions, but he remained alive.

Stauffenberg was part of a group that plotted to kill Hitler, led by the former head of the German General Staff, Ludwig Beck. Beck had long been convinced that killing Hitler was the only way to save Germany from total destruction. He had enlisted a number of generals and other army officers in the conspiracy, the most prominent of whom was Rommel. These men hoped to take power after Hitler's death and to end the war on the best terms they could get. Stauffenberg, as a courier for the German high command, enjoyed frequent access to Hitler. He had made several earlier attempts to kill the dictator but had been stymied by altered schedules or other reasons.

Stauffenberg, believing the blast had killed Hitler, took advantage of the confusion to drive to the nearest airfield. There, he took a plane to Berlin, where he was to lead a coup to seize control of the War Ministry and to signal fellow conspirators elsewhere that a revolt had begun. (Rommel, who had suffered severe wounds during a strafing attack several days earlier, was now out of the picture.) The plan degenerated into shambles with the revelation that Hitler still lived. When loyal SS troops broke into the ministry and apprehended the conspirators, some were given the opportunity to commit suicide. The rest, including Stauffenberg, were taken into the courtyard and shot.

Hitler reacted to the assassination attempt in several ways. Prone to look for "signs" that some turn of events would reverse his fortunes, he chose to interpret his survival as just such a sign. It was, he told Mussolini, whom he met later that day, "the pronouncement of Divine Providence." Against the real and suspected plotters, he visited savage retribution. After farcical trials designed to humiliate the accused, rather than to determine guilt, some 2,000 individuals were executed in barbaric fashion: They were hung from meathooks by piano wires. Hitler ordered films taken of the killings, some of which he viewed at his leisure. Rommel, because of his stature in Germany, was permitted to commit suicide to escape such a fate. His role was kept secret, and he was buried with full military honors.

Hitler's most significant reaction with regard to the course of the war was to assume almost complete control of combat operations. Always convinced of his military genius, he had never hesitated to assert himself in the conduct of campaigns and, at times, had been proven correct. Nevertheless, he could be influenced, particularly by those generals who were willing to stand up to him. Following the attempt on his life, however, he became virtually immune to advice from men he began to think of as cowards at best, traitors at worst. Within weeks, he ordered a disastrous offensive in Normandy that virtually decimated the best German units in France.

ALLIED VICTORY IN NORMANDY

After preliminary bombardment the day before, Operation COBRA began on July 25. On the American right, two corps of General Patton's newly activated Third Army burst west and south into Brittany against light opposition. In the center and on the left, the First Army, with General Courtney Hodges as commander-designate, encountered much heavier going as it moved southeast. Five days later, the British opened their own offensive to the south. The long-awaited breakout was under way.

Patton garnered a great deal of publicity for his dramatic dash into Brittany. Always a source of good copy, the flamboyant general did not disappoint. He was constantly on the move, exhorting his troops to go faster. At one point, where two roads joined into one, he acted as a traffic cop, signaling first one lane, then the other to move ahead. The speed of advance *was* remarkable for any army. Heartening photographs of passing American trucks being cheered by French villagers appeared soon after; the fact that most of the region already was in the hands of the French Resistance was overlooked. German forces had retreated into the fortified ports, some of which held out to the end of the war.

Despite fierce resistance along the main front, American forces made better progress than before for several reasons. The air support of ground operations became much more effective through experience, although confusion over targets at times resulted in Allied planes bombing their own men. Use of the "Rhino" tank, first suggested by an enlisted man, also made movement easier. The Rhinos had steel tusks welded to their fronts, enabling them to chew paths through hedgerows, which other tanks could then use. Ironically, most of the tusks were made out of Rommel's "asparagus." The most important American advantage, however, was the sheer weight of the numbers they could throw at German units ground down by weeks of incessant fighting.

On August 1, a planned change in the Allied command structure went into effect. In anticipation of Eisenhower's taking over at a later date, Montgomery now became "temporary" commander of Allied ground forces. His 21st Army Group lost its American components, which were reorganized into the 12th Army Group under Bradley, with the First Army going to Hodges. Because it appeared to constitute a repudiation of Montgomery, despite his subsequent promotion to field marshal, the changeover stirred resentment in Great Britain. Actually, the creation of an American army group merely reflected the fact that the United States was beginning to provide an ever-greater preponderance of Allied forces in Europe.

Such a reorganization in the midst of battle showed yet again the problems inherent in waging a coalition war, and it violated the sound military principle of unified command. Though Montgomery ostensibly retained tactical command, Bradley for all practical purposes became answerable only to Eisenhower. The latter, who had only recently arrived in France from England, necessarily had to afford both men wide latitude. This arrangement made proper coordination difficult, and within weeks, it led to a controversy that historians continue to fight.

Having cleared Brittany, Patton's divisions swept east in an effort to get behind German forces concentrated against Hodges's First Army and the British. Instead of retreating to avoid encirclement, Hitler believed he saw an opportunity to snatch victory from defeat. By driving west toward Avranches on the west coast of the Cotentin Peninsula, Hitler thought he could cut off Patton's spearheads and then turn north to get behind the Allied main forces. By now impervious to any dissent, Hitler personally drew up plans for a German counterattack, scheduled to begin August 6.

Hitler's scheme was the product of a mind that had lost touch with military realities. Allied forces had such overwhelming strength, including control of the air, that they could deny the Germans any chance of success. Bradley welcomed the attack and told a visitor to his headquarters that "we're about to destroy an entire hostile army." Indeed, the farther the Germans advanced during the first few days, the better the chance of killing or capturing them all became.

Bradley's prediction was accurate—almost. He and Montgomery planned to envelop advancing German forces as they embedded themselves deep within Allied lines. Patton was to push his XX Corps, commanded by General Wade Haislip, north toward the town of Argentan, there to be joined by the Anglo-Canadian forces striking south. By the time Haislip's advance units arrived outside Argentan on August 12, however, the British and Canadians had bogged down against stiff opposition 20 miles away. Patton thereupon requested Bradley's permission to continue northward to the town of Falaise to link up forces there. Bradley refused. It took eight more days before elements of the Canadian First Army closed the gap, by which time some 20,000 Germans had escaped.

Who was responsible? Americans at the time blamed Montgomery for not reaching his objective on time and saw the failure as another example of his excessive caution and lack of flexibility. Many historians since have echoed this charge. Montgomery's defenders, on the other hand, have argued that Bradley should have sought permission to move his units north to Falaise. Bradley himself took full responsibility for keeping the Americans at Argentan. He did not ask to go beyond the agreed-upon boundary because he was afraid that XX Corps, already committed to blocking several escape routes, would be stretched too thin and would be overrun when German units began plunging eastward. Whatever the case, Montgomery's stock sank even lower at SHAEF.

Controversy over the Falaise pocket should not obscure the magnitude of the Allied victory. The Germans lost more than 60,000 men, of which

50,000 were taken prisoner. They were able to take out with them only 24 tanks and some artillery. Those who entered the pocket after the battle were stunned by what they saw. Bodies of men and horses were strewn everywhere amidst burnt-out hulks of tanks and other vehicles. "It was literally possible," Eisenhower later wrote, "to walk for hundreds of yards at a time, stepping on nothing but dead and decaying flesh." Hitler's foolish counteroffensive had ended in the virtual destruction of German forces in Normandy.

The second Battle of France (the first having taken place in the summer of 1940) was all but over. Since D Day, the Germans had lost about 450,000 men, 1,500 tanks, 3,500 artillery pieces, and 20,000 vehicles. This was an enormous drain on German resources that were already being siphoned off for the eastern front. The Allies had suffered approximately 37,000 ground troops killed, 172,000 wounded. German forces remaining in the Pas de Calais region began retreating, as did those in southern France after ANVIL-DRAGOON began on August 15. Paris fell on August 25, and by the end of the month, the Allies had cleared almost all of France and were entering Belgium and Luxembourg.

MEN AND ARMS

Early historians of the war in Europe tended to focus on the performance of the top commanders. With only passing references to individual divisions or other units, they analyzed the relative merits of Montgomery, Bradley, or Rommel as though their troops were virtually interchangeable. More recently, emphasis has been placed on the attributes of men and equipment in battle. Such studies have concluded that the German soldier, on average, was far superior to his Allied counterparts of every nationality. The weapons he fought with, moreover, were in most categories better than those he faced.

Cultural or social factors that affect soldierly merit are difficult to weigh with precision. Certainly, the Germans were aided by a history of obedience to authority and a long military tradition. Some, especially those in SS divisions, were motivated by an almost fanatical devotion to Adolf Hitler. Perhaps most important, they were fighting to defend their homeland against what they were led to believe would amount to near total destruction. The unconditional surrender formula permitted German propaganda to portray defeat as meaning the end of Germany as a nation and as a people, despite repeated Allied denials that they intended any such thing.

American, British, and Canadian troops were inclined to be more independent and resistant to discipline than were the Germans. However desirable these characteristics may be in democratic societies, they do not lend themselves to military efficiency. Unlike their enemies, furthermore, Allied soldiers expected to return to secure homelands where they could resume their civilian lives when the war ended. This attitude inspired caution, rather than the sense of desperation that the Germans had. Men in divisions that had fought in Africa, Sicily, or Italy were apt to feel that they had done their share and that they should have been replaced by those in the rear who had never seen combat.

The American army had particular deficiencies. Its divisions were top-heavy in terms of the proportion of officers to men, and they contained a high percentage of noncombatants relative to frontline soldiers. Discipline and training were lax by British standards, let alone German ones. American army doctors were far more likely to designate men unfit for combat because of "battle fatigue," a condition the Germans scarcely recognized. And U.S. desertion rates were high—as many as 40,000 men deserted by war's end. Men left for the rear in the knowledge that if apprehended, they faced, at worst, a prison sentence; they might even be returned to their units with no punishment at all. Only one American soldier was executed for desertion in the entire war. By contrast, the Germans shot more than 1,000 men for this act, and several thousand more for "cowardice."

The infantry was the orphan of the American armed forces. Branches such as the air force had top priority in selection, and they skimmed off thousands of the most able men. The army tried to accommodate those qualified for assignments in specialties that promised to be more rewarding and less dangerous than serving as infantrymen. But such losses diminished the pool of capable leaders at the noncommissioned and junior officer level, the backbone of every army. And whereas Americans went directly from civilian life into officer training to become "ninety-day wonders," Germans had to spend six months in combat before becoming eligible for these ranks. The result was that, although individual American officers and men fought as skillfully and courageously as any German, ordinary American infantry units were markedly inferior.

Perhaps surprisingly for a nation proud of its technological know-how, American weapons often were not as good as those the Germans used. The American semiautomatic M-1 rifle was better than the bolt-action types used by other armies in Europe. But engagements often fought under conditions where there were few chances to take aim and shoot at specific targets, and pouring as much fire as possible into enemy positions was the goal. For this purpose, German machine guns, with firing rates almost double those of the Allies, were far more effective. German submachine guns also outperformed any of the various kinds used by the Americans and British, and there were more of them per unit.

Allied armor did not match up well. The basic American tank (which also made up two-thirds of the British armor) was the Sherman, a reliable, fast, and maneuverable vehicle. The Sherman was, however, underarmored and undergunned. It also had a pronounced tendency to catch fire when hit, affording survivors only a few seconds to bail out. Allied soldiers derisively referred to Sherman tanks as "Ronsons," after a popular cigarette lighter. Shermans could knock out German Tigers and Panthers only by hitting them in certain spots at relatively close range, yet they were extremely vulnerable to the high-velocity weapons used against them. And German tanks frequently bested much larger formations of American or British armor.

The list can be extended. The American hand-held antitank weapon was a 2.3-inch rocket launcher called the bazooka. Most often, its projectile simply bounced off German armor. The British spring-loaded PIAT was even worse. German *Panzerfausts*, on the other hand, were lethal rocket launchers that Allied soldiers picked up and used whenever possible. The German use of mortars was devastating, especially the multibarreled *Nebelwerfer*. Its projectiles fitted with sirens for psychological effect, the Nebelwerfer was one of the most feared weapons on the western front. And the multipurpose, high-velocity German 88 was the best artillery piece used in the war. In bleak humor, a standard song was revised by American soldiers to become "Those 88s Are Breaking Up That Old Gang of Mine."

Better troops and weapons meant that the Germans would win engagements fought on anything like equal terms. The solution for Allied commanders was to throw against them unstoppable concentrations of troops and tanks, supported by massive artillery fire. This they were increasingly able to do during the Normandy campaign for the Allies had far greater reservoirs of manpower and could draw on the enormous productive capacity of the United States. Aided by total mastery of the air and information supplied by Ultra, Allied forces simply overwhelmed and chewed up enemy units, no matter how hard they fought. The German nation was by no means defeated, however, and much bitter fighting lay ahead.

EISENHOWER TAKES THE REINS

On September 1, General Eisenhower assumed direct command of all Allied ground forces in France. Although his performance as supreme commander has been widely praised, his abilities as a strategist and as a commander of armies in the field have been the subject of debate for decades. A week before he took command in France, he had decided on a strategy that would determine the course of the war in western Europe. His commitment to what became known as the "broad front," as opposed to the "narrow front," approach has been criticized as resulting in a missed opportunity to defeat Germany by the end of 1944. Of course, it is always easier to cite the virtues of what should have been done, rather than what was done, and it must be remembered that Eisenhower still had to preside over a host of competing claims and interests.

Even before the Falaise pocket was secured, Montgomery had begun trying to persuade Eisenhower and others as to the proper course. He said that the 12th and 21st army groups should concentrate their forces in a drive north toward the major Belgian port of Antwerp, taking other channel ports and overrunning V-1 sites as they went along. When supplies and equipment began flowing through Antwerp and necessary air bases had been constructed, Montgomery wanted to head east toward the Ruhr Valley, the industrial heartland of Germany, then on to Berlin. This mighty push of forty divisions, he argued, would be invulnerable to counterattack and would knock Germany out of the war by the end of the year. Bradley initially favored Montgomery's plan but later backed away.

Eisenhower rejected Montgomery's proposal for a number of reasons, not least of which was the Briton himself. Montgomery's abrasive arrogance and his habit of talking to others as though they were slow-witted aides at times infuriated Eisenhower, who interrupted one lecture by saying, "Steady, Monty. You can't talk to me like that. I'm your boss." More important, Montgomery's penchant for predicting dazzling results that failed to materialize now came home to roost. His own reputation for methodical preparation before acting did not endear him to Americans who were enamored of rapid movement: Put simply, they did not wish to be harnessed next to a slow horse. Aside from purely military considerations, there is no question that Eisenhower was influenced by the desire to have American armies win their own victories as part of the Allied effort.

Eisenhower's later description of Montgomery's strategy as a "pencil thrust" was unfair, in view of the size of the proposed striking force. But Eisenhower viewed the situation differently. He wanted Montgomery's 21st Army Group to advance north to Antwerp, accompanied by only enough American divisions to provide flank support. The destruction of German units in Normandy had left the way clear in the center for Bradley to drive directly east to the Rhine and the Siegfried line, which lay just inside German territory. Meanwhile, Patton pleaded for the chance to unleash his Third Army to lead the way. The U.S. 6th Army

Group, advancing from Marseilles after ANVIL-DRAGOON, would take up position on the southern wing. Hammering away along this broad front, Eisenhower hoped, would so stretch depleted German forces that early breakthroughs would be inevitable.

Prospects for decisive offensives against Germany quickly dimmed. Montgomery took Antwerp by September 4, but the port did not become operational until November. Antwerp lies at the head of an estuary 60 miles inland from the English Channel. The Germans, strongly entrenched on both sides of the estuary and on land formations that divided it, proved difficult to dislodge. Montgomery's strength had been dissipated when forces were detached to take the minor channel ports and when preparations were made for an operational code-named MARKET-GARDEN. Lacking access to major port facilities like those at Antwerp, Patton's Third Army bogged down due to shortages of critical supplies, especially fuel.

MARKET-GARDEN

His single-thrust strategy rejected, Montgomery quickly devised a plan to achieve an early penetration of German defenses. He proposed an operation designed to pave the way for an offensive to the Rhine via Holland, north of Germany's "west wall." It was a complicated scheme, requiring the coordinated seizure of a series of bridges by airborne troops who would keep them intact until relief arrived overland. That the conservative Montgomery, who usually stressed simplicity and the elimination of variables, would support such a plan raises questions about his motives. Some believe he regarded MARKET-GARDEN as the last chance for British forces—and, by extension, himself—to play the lead part in defeating Germany before the sheer size of American forces dominated the entire campaign.

Why Eisenhower accepted the plan also can be questioned. He must have had doubts about entrusting such an audacious operation to a man unaccustomed to acting audaciously. Possibly he thought he owed Montgomery a debt after having rejected his narrow-front strategy. But Eisenhower always had been intrigued by the possibilities of airborne assaults, and he set great store by "bold" moves to achieve quick success. In any event, both men chose to emphasize the positive, and they ignored warning signs, such as Ultra reports that two panzer divisions mauled in combat were being refitted in the vicinity of Arnhem.

Airborne operations involved a unique blend of strengths and weaknesses. The combat units were composed of elite troops and officers who were highly trained and disciplined. They were extremely mobile in the sense that they could be flown anyplace suitable for parachute drops and glider landings. Getting them to designated target areas was

Parachutes open overhead as waves of paratroops land in Holland during operations by the 1st Allied Airborne Army, September 1944. (National Archives photo no. W&C 1066)

a chancy undertaking, however, as was shown on D Day. Once on the ground, they were relatively immobile except for whatever light vehicles could be brought in by glider. Finally, they lacked both armor and effective antitank weapons.

The success of MARKET-GARDEN, which began on September 17, depended on a combination of speed and coordination that was easier to plan than to carry out. Bad weather delayed some of the early drops and later prevented resupply. The American 101st Division took its objective on the first day, and the 82d, after a courageous river crossing on small boats, was in place a few days later. The British 1st Airborne Division at Arnhem ran into trouble from the start. Fear of antiaircraft fire caused the air transport commander to make drops up to 10 miles away from target areas. Then, when most of the glider-borne jeeps were destroyed on landing, the troops had to advance on foot as lightly armed infantry going against forewarned panzers. As if all this were not bad enough, on the first day, the Germans captured an American officer who had foolishly carried with him a copy of the battle plan.

MARKET-GARDEN still might have been salvaged had relief forces been able to move overland quickly enough. They made it to the American positions but bogged down under fire before they could reach the British at Arnhem. Finally, after nine days, what remained of the 1st Airborne fought its way out to safety. Of the 9,000 men at Arnhem, only 2,000 escaped. Some 6,000 were captured, many of them wounded, and the rest were killed. That the operation nearly worked in spite of foul-ups and bad luck was due solely to the magnificent performance of the airborne divisions, especially the British 1st at Arnhem—"the bridge too far."

The failure to break through German defenses in the north dashed Allied hopes of ending the war in 1944. American commanders, especially Patton, grumbled that they could have achieved decisive results had they not been denied resources allocated to Montgomery. U.S. forces had advanced and pierced the Siegfried line at Aachen, but they were still miles from the Rhine. Just south of Aachen, divisions of General Collins's VII Corps were stopped cold in the Hurtgen Forest, touching off the longest and bloodiest battle on the western front. "The death factory," as Americans called Hurtgen, would cost nearly 30,000 U.S. casualties before it was over. Meanwhile, Adolf Hitler was planning an offensive that he hoped would dramatically alter the course of the war.

SELECTED BIBLIOGRAPHY

Blumenson, Martin. *Breakout and Pursuit* (Washington, D.C.: Office of the Chief of Military History, Department of the Army, 1961).
———. *The Duel for France, 1944* (Boston: Houghton Mifflin, 1963).
Eisenhower, David. *Eisenhower: At War, 1943–1945* (New York: Random House, 1986).
Eisenhower, Dwight D. *Crusade in Europe* (Garden City, N.Y.: Doubleday, 1948).
Essame, Hubert. *Patton: The Commander* (New York: Scribner, 1974).
Farago, Ladislas. *Patton: Ordeal and Triumph* (New York: Dell, 1970).
Frost, John. *A Drop Too Many* (London: Cassell, 1982).
Gavin, James M. *On to Berlin: Battles of an Airborne Commander, 1943–1946* (New York: Viking, 1978).
Hamilton, Nigel. *Monty: Final Years of the Field Marshal, 1944–1976* (New York: McGraw-Hill, 1986).
Keegan, John. *Six Armies in Normandy from D-Day to the Liberation of Paris, June 6th–August 25th, 1944* (New York: Viking, 1982).
Lamb, Richard. *Montgomery in Europe, 1943–1945: Success or Failure?* (London: Buchan & Enright, 1983).
Lucas, James, and James Barker. *The Battle of Normandy: The Falaise Gap* (New York: Holmes & Meier, 1978).
MacDonald, Charles B. *Mighty Endeavor: The American War in Europe* (New York: William Morrow, 1986).
MacPherson, Malcolm. *Time Bomb: Fermi, Heisenberg, and the Race for the Atomic Bomb* (New York: Dutton, 1986).

Montgomery, Field Marshal Viscount. *Memoirs of Field Marshal Montgomery: Normandy to the Baltic* (London: Hutchinson, 1958).

Morgan, Frederick. *Overture to Overlord* (New York: Doubleday, 1950).

Ryan, Cornelius. *The Longest Day* (New York: Fawcett, 1960).

———. *A Bridge Too Far* (New York: Simon & Schuster, 1974).

van Creveld, Martin. *Fighting Power, German and U.S. Army Performance, 1939–1945* (Westport, Conn.: Greenwood, 1982).

Warlimont, Walter. *Inside Hitler's Headquarters* (London: Weidenfield & Nicolson, 1965).

Weigley, Russell F. *Eisenhower's Lieutenants: The Campaigns of France and Germany, 1944–1945* (Bloomington: Indiana University Press, 1981).

14
Closing the Vise (1945)

By December 1944, the German army had taken a terrible pounding on both fronts. The Luftwaffe had been reduced to impotence, and Allied bombers ranged freely over German skies against little or no opposition. In spite of all this, Germany's military and civilian morale had remained intact, and arms production in some categories actually had risen. But even German resilience had limits. Barring some dramatic reversal of fortunes, the Allies were bound to prevail by the sheer weight of their numbers. Hitler sought to provide such a reversal through bold military strategy. When that failed, he could only go on hoping for some miracle, while Germany was being crushed between the jaws of a massive vise.

THE ARDENNES OFFENSIVE

In mid-September, just as Allied forces were about to launch MARKET-GARDEN, Hitler informed his astonished staff that he intended to mount his own offensive. Advancing through the Ardennes forest as they had in 1940, German forces would, he said, puncture Allied lines and drive toward Antwerp. The thrust would divide Allied armies, isolating Montgomery's British and Canadian troops in the north. The threatened destruction of this command might at least force revision of the unconditional surrender formula, Hitler hoped, and at best it would destroy the Anglo-American coalition he regarded as extremely fragile. This, in turn, would enable Germany to devote its full energies to repelling the Soviets on the eastern front. It was a repetition of his August counteroffensive in Normandy on a larger scale.

To command the German push, Hitler brought Rundstedt out of forced retirement to become commander in chief in the west and installed

Field Marshal Walter Model as commander of Army Group B. Model, a blunt-spoken, opinionated officer who was widely disliked by his peers, had performed ably on the eastern front and enjoyed as much trust as Hitler was still willing to bestow upon any of his generals. Twenty-four of Germany's best divisions were organized into three armies, two of them panzers. Most of the troops, tanks, and other equipment had been diverted from the eastern front, as were supporting artillery and rocket-launching units. To ensure secrecy, the Germans avoided all radio communication about the operation, relying instead on secure telephone lines and couriers. They also spread false information indicating that they were deploying most of their strength against expected Allied offensives in other sectors.

The operation was scheduled to begin on December 16. Anglo-American strength was concentrated to the north and south of the Ardennes, leaving only four infantry divisions with one armored division in reserve from General Troy Middleton's VIII Corps to cover an 80-mile front. This was far in excess of what even crack divisions could be expected to defend; those forces in the Ardennes were composed mostly of inexperienced troops recently put into the line and others sent to recover from combat exhaustion. The Germans also counted on overcast skies and the fog and mists that usually shrouded the region during that time of year, both to avoid detection and to nullify Allied air strength.

To preserve secrecy, Rundstedt and Model were not told of Hitler's intentions until October. Both men were shocked at the scope of the operation, believing it far too ambitious to succeed against the strength arrayed against them. Rundstedt endorsed a proposal drawn up by Model for a more modest envelopment around Aachen, to be followed by an advance upon Antwerp if the first stage succeeded quickly enough. The latter phase clearly was a sop to Hitler, who would have none of it. The larger plan was to be carried out, he informed them, and was "not to be altered."

The failure of the Allies to detect what was about to be thrown against them engendered criticism then and to this day. Despite Hitler's precautions, there had been indications of what was in the offing, including an Ultra intercept of a message to Tokyo from the Japanese ambassador in Berlin, informing his superiors of an impending German offensive. Probably the most important reason why separate bits of information were not pieced together was the Allied commanders' belief that the enemy had taken such a beating in France that it was incapable of offensive operations. On the day before the operation began, Montgomery asked Eisenhower's permission to "hop over" to England for a visit, and the supreme commander himself had planned a champagne party for December 16 to celebrate his acquisition of a fifth star and an aide's marriage.

At 5:30 in the morning of December 16, German artillery began raining shells down on the unsuspecting Americans. Then, German units began moving forward, the main thrust headed by the SS panzer divisions that Hitler insisted lead the way as a rebuke to the regular army for its involvement in the assassination plot. Resistance was mixed. Some American units broke and fled under the onslaught; others remained in place and fought doggedly until they had to give way. Middleton committed the reserves he had available, but it soon became apparent that these were insufficient to cope with an assault of such size.

Because of the wooded, hilly terrain, the battle was fought for the possession of roads, junctions, and bridges. Good communications between widely separated commands were essential. To facilitate the German advance, a special force of more than 3,000 men who spoke "American English" was assembled under Colonel Otto Skorzeny, who earlier had masterminded the daring raid to rescue Mussolini. These soldiers, dressed in American uniforms, infiltrated defensive lines to seize bridges and crossroads, misdirect American units, and destroy telephone lines and message centers. They spread a great deal of confusion during the first few days. Once word got out about what was happening, however, Americans began asking all strangers questions about popular sports and entertainment figures. Those who did not know who "Joltin' Joe" was or who played Rhett Butler were taken prisoner or shot on the spot.

Word of the offensive began arriving at Eisenhower's headquarters that afternoon, but information was incomplete due to faulty communications, caused in part by Skorzeny's men. General Bradley, who had arrived to discuss another matter, believed the operation was a feint, but Eisenhower sensed it was something bigger. He had Bradley begin directing units from other commands to move against the German thrust. When, as anticipated, Patton argued against detaching his 10th Armored Division to strengthen Middleton's southern flank, Eisenhower overruled him. Even the supreme commander, however, had underestimated the threat.

By the second day of the offensive, December 17, the Germans had reached some objectives and fallen short of others. They then ran into a major obstacle at the crossroads town of St. Vith in the northern part of their salient. The 7th Armored Division, detached from General Hodges's First Army, had arrived to shore up defenses that had survived the first assaults. Together, these units held St. Vith against repeated attacks, forcing the Germans to detour north and south around it. Battlegroup Pieper, a powerful armored force named after its commander,

A Nazi soldier, heavily armed, carries ammunition boxes forward with a companion in territory taken by their counteroffensive in this scene from captured German film, Belgium, December 1944. (National Archives photo no. W&C 1070)

took the only available east-west route north of St. Vith. It was a poor road for tanks, and Pieper eventually ran out of fuel and bogged down after unsuccessful efforts to break out. The Americans had to evacuate St. Vith several days later but not before they had blunted the northern wing of the German drive.

Battlegroup Pieper achieved notoriety for perpetrating one of the worst atrocities on the western front. An artillery observation battery attached to 7th Armored had been ordered to St. Vith with the division.

Composed of about 150 lightly armed men in a convoy of trucks, the battery ran into Pieper's forces just outside the town of Malmedy. After a brief, hopelessly one-sided encounter, the survivors gave up. Approximately 130 men were gathered in a field, guarded by two tanks. The tanks proceeded to machine-gun the huddled men, after which German soldiers walked among them firing at any signs of movement. Fewer than 50 men survived by playing dead. Pieper himself had left before the shooting began, and whether he ordered it was never determined.

Bastogne, about 20 miles southwest of St. Vith, stood at the junction of two east-west roads that the Germans needed to sustain their rapid advance. The town lay undefended except for the remnants of General Middleton's headquarters and men who had retreated from the original front. The 101st Airborne, still recovering from MARKET-GARDEN, and a combat group of the 10th Armored were hurried into place. They arrived during the night of December 18, just in time to meet the German onslaught the next morning. Three panzer divisions and one infantry division mounted repeated attacks, only to be repulsed by the determined garrison.

On December 21, an event occurred that has become a legend in American history. By then, the Germans had the town surrounded, and German armor could have resumed its advance on roads west of the city. But Bastogne remained a chokepoint for the resupply of ammunition and fuel, without which the panzers eventually would stall. Lacking heavy artillery that might have devastated defensive positions, the German commander resorted to bluff. He sent word to the besieged Americans that they must surrender or be wiped out. General Anthony C. McAuliffe, commander of the garrison, sent a reply consisting of one word: "Nuts!" The officer who delivered the message to the Germans gave a rough translation and added that if the attacks continued, "We will kill every goddam German that tries to break into the city." The impudent simplicity of "Nuts!" greatly appealed to American soldiers and civilians when they learned of it.

Heroic resistance at St. Vith, Bastogne, and other points had thrown the Germans badly off schedule, but still they were advancing deep within Allied lines. Eisenhower and Bradley ordered counterattacks from Hodges's First Army in the north and from Patton's Third Army in the south. Patton's ability to cover long distances in the shortest possible time never showed to greater advantage. The German offensive reached its high-water mark on December 25, by which time it had forced a bulge into Allied lines some 60 miles deep and 40 miles wide. On the next day, Patton's advance units relieved Bastogne, and skies already had cleared sufficiently for the Allies to begin mounting air attacks.

Chow is served to American infantrymen of the 347th Infantry Regiment on their way to La Roche, Belgium, January 13, 1945. (National Archives photo no. W&C 1075)

Though the Germans gave up ground reluctantly, the bulge was reduced during the next few weeks and eliminated by the end of January.

The Ardennes offensive, or the Battle of the Bulge as Americans called it, probably never would have reached Antwerp as Hitler intended. Even if it had, the corridor would have been vulnerable to counterattack and massive air strikes. In any event, the Anglo-American coalition was nowhere near as shaky as Hitler willed himself to believe. Had it not been for the stout resistance at places such as St. Vith and Bastogne, however, the operation would have set the Western Allies back for months, at a severe cost to morale. As it was, the Anglo-American advance was delayed approximately six weeks, but the Germans paid far more dearly. They suffered about twice the number of casualties— 120,000 to the Allied total of 60,000—and had lost large numbers of precious tanks and other equipment. Equally important, the commitment of two panzer armies in the west denied Germany vitally needed mobile reserves to meet the Soviet winter offensive that began in mid-January.

The victory snatched from defeat ended on a dismal note. During the German drive, Bradley's 12th Army Group had been split, rendering the general unable to communicate directly with his forces north of the bulge. For this reason alone, Eisenhower, over Bradley's heated objections, placed these American units under Montgomery's temporary command. No great leadership was required to direct the American forces to do what everyone knew had to be done. Indeed, American generals chafed under what they regarded as Montgomery's everlasting caution, and at times, they acted on their own initiative. At a press conference on January 7, when German defeat was assured but fighting continued, Montgomery gave a version of the battle that can only be described as bizarre.

After a few perfunctory remarks about the American role in halting the offensive, Montgomery went on to describe it as a triumph made possible only by his own generalship and by the Anglo-Canadian troops of the 21st Army Group. Frequently using the word "I," he described it something like this: Alone among Allied generals he had seen immediately what had to be done and had taken the necessary defensive steps to ensure that the offensive could not succeed. Still, American forces had been split, and Eisenhower had to relinquish command of his American troops to Montgomery in order to avoid disaster. He then managed to turn the tide by adeptly committing his 21st Army Group at the proper time.

Americans—and not a few British—were outraged by Montgomery's performance. The field marshal had taken the proper measures to block the Germans from reaching Antwerp—no one faulted him on that. But by failing to mention the communications problem, he made it appear as though Eisenhower had made the command change because no American general was capable of handling the job. His insinuation that the 21st Army Group had rescued the Americans also had no basis in fact. Just a few British divisions actually fought in the battle and then only after the Germans had begun retreating. Montgomery had attempted to appropriate what was almost exclusively an American achievement.

Eisenhower, who had suffered the insufferable Montgomery long enough, could take no more. With Air Marshal Tedder's enthusiastic agreement, a message was prepared for the Combined Chiefs of Staff stating that unless Montgomery was relieved, Eisenhower and his staff would resign. Montgomery's astute chief of staff, General Francis ("Freddie") de Guingand, defused the crisis. Forewarned of what was being done at SHAEF, he immediately flew there and persuaded Eisenhower to hold off sending the message. He returned to 21st Army Group headquarters to impress upon Montgomery how close he was to being sacked. Montgomery at first scoffed at the very idea, but he caved in when de Guingand pointed out that Churchill and others might be pleased to replace him with Alexander, whom they had preferred for the job in the first place. Montgomery finally sent a message to Eisenhower proclaiming his loyalty, signing it, "Your most devoted subordinate."

Eisenhower relented. His personal dislike of Montgomery had grown, but he believed the field marshal's military strengths compensated for his weaknesses, and he had no wish to precipitate an uproar in Great Britain by humiliating an authentic national hero. Churchill made amends for Montgomery's behavior and set the record straight by telling the House of Commons that the Ardennes campaign was "the greatest American battle of the war and will, I believe, be regarded as an ever-famous American victory."

THE SOVIET WINTER OFFENSIVE

By the end of 1944, Soviet armies were positioned along a 600-mile front running from the Baltic Sea in the north to the southern boundary of Bulgaria. Their forces overall were approximately twice as large as those Germany had deployed to stop them. Field Marshal Heinz Guderian, chief of the General Staff, urged Hitler to reinforce German armies facing the Soviets by transferring divisions from Norway, Italy, and elsewhere. He also wanted to reduce the length of the front by withdrawing from exposed positions on both wings. Hitler refused. He always had opposed withdrawals regardless of reasons, and he did not wish to lose access to the strategic raw materials that Germany needed in the long run. He remained deaf to Guderian's assertion that unless the Soviets were stopped during the next few months, there would *be* no long run.

Hitler had sought to break apart the Anglo-American coalition with his Ardennes offensive. When that failed, he concocted a new scenario to explain how Germany could avert disaster. Soviet advances into the heart of Europe, he claimed, would so alarm anti-Communists in Britain and the United States that these nations would make some sort of compromise with Germany to provide a bulwark against the Bolshevik menace. There *was* concern within these two nations about Soviet expansion, but that they would modify the unconditional surrender formula at this late date was pure fantasy.

Originally scheduled for January 20, the Soviet winter offensive was opened by Stalin eight days earlier in response to Anglo-American requests to relieve pressure on the western front. The operation came too late to have any effect on the Ardennes campaign, where the tide had already turned and Allied forces were rapidly eliminating the bulge. Indeed, Hitler's diversion of two panzer armies to the Ardennes stripped German defenders in the east of the mobile reserves needed to meet the new Soviet onslaught.

Although attacks were launched all along the front, the main thrust took place in Poland. Three Soviet army groups plunged forward after massive artillery barrages. In the north, Marshal K. K. Rokossovski's 2nd Belorussian Army Group smashed German defenses along the Narew River and headed northwest toward Danzig. In the center, Marshal G. K. Zhukov's 1st Belorussian Army Group crossed the Vistula River and encircled Warsaw, which fell on January 17. Zhukov then headed directly west toward Berlin. Marshal I. S. Konev's 1st Ukranian Army Group in the south initially fanned out, then began moving northwest to the German border.

German resistance was quickly overwhelmed. The Soviets had massive superiority in men, tanks, guns, and aircraft. Aside from the forces Hitler had diverted to the Ardennes, he had further stripped German defenses in Poland of divisions that he sent south in a futile effort to defend Hungary. Gaining an average of more than 30 miles a day, the Soviets had reached the Oder River (and beyond it in the south) by February 2. Their most forward position lay only 30 miles from Berlin. Aside from its military implications, the offensive placed Stalin in an enviable position when he met with Roosevelt and Churchill at Yalta in the Crimea on February 4.

The spectacular success of the Soviet offensive across Poland and into Germany has caused speculation as to why Stalin did not push on to Berlin, which Guderian believed could be taken in a few days. Some scholars have suggested that Stalin's innate cautiousness was the reason. Soviet advances had created a huge salient with its tip on the Oder. Stalin may have overestimated German strength north of the salient and feared that it would be pinched off by a German counteroffensive. Guderian did launch such an attack in mid-February, but the forces at his disposal were too puny to stand a chance.

An intriguing but unprovable view is that Stalin deliberately refrained from driving on Berlin because he did not wish to alarm his Western allies. Always suspicious of their motives, he may have shared with Hitler the idea that they might make some accommodation with Germany if the Soviets pushed too far into central Europe while they were still west of the Rhine. Roosevelt's remark to Stalin at Yalta that American forces would not remain for long in Europe after the war ended may have convinced the Soviet dictator that time was on his side. Another reason to avoid provocation was Stalin's wish to ensure Anglo-American cooperation in getting reparations from postwar Germany, as well as American loans, to help rebuild Russia's shattered economy. In any event, except for small operations to clear out pockets of resistance and to straighten lines, Soviet armies held at the Oder until April.

THE REMAGEN BRIDGE AND
THE DECISION TO HALT AT THE ELBE

Even after the crisis brewed up by Montgomery's disruptive press conference, the British hoped Eisenhower would permit the American First and Ninth armies to remain under Montgomery for a massive drive to Berlin. American commanders protested mightily against being subordinated to the British, particularly to Montgomery, whom they hated and held in low esteem for his inability to move rapidly. Eisenhower compromised. He opted for a double thrust: Simpson's Ninth Army would coordinate with Montgomery's forces in the north, while the remainder of Bradley's 12th Army Group would launch operations independently in the center. General Jacob Devers's 6th Army Group in the south also would begin offensives.

Montgomery began his advance on February 8. His Anglo-Canadian armies met stiff resistance from the Germans fighting to defend the industrial Ruhr Valley, which lay to their rear across the Rhine. Despite massive artillery and aerial support, Montgomery's divisions gained ground slowly, in part due to swollen rivers and muddy roads. By the time they reached the Rhine, the Germans facing them had crossed the river and blown the bridges. Simpson, on Montgomery's right flank along the west bank of the Roer River, was to move northeastward to catch the Germans in a pincer movement, but his kickoff was delayed for two weeks when the Germans manipulated dams to produce a constant state of flooding. Simpson's advance units hooked up with Montgomery's on March 3, and a week later, all German resistance west of the Rhine ceased in that sector.

In the center, Hodges's First Army and Patton's Third had easier going against defenses that were less formidable than those the Germans had stationed in the north. American forces had reached the Rhine in several places by early March, only to find that the Germans had destroyed all the bridges—all except one. At the town of Remagen, through an incredible blend of error and plain bad luck on the part of the Germans, an advance unit of Hodges's First Army found a railroad bridge still intact. After some initial hesitation, orders were given to cross the span. At first tentatively, then with growing confidence, Americans began pouring across to form a bridgehead on the eastern side. As word flashed upward, Bradley recognized the significance of the prize and ordered the bridgehead secured at all costs. He, in turn, informed Eisenhower, who also was overjoyed.

The Germans understood the magnitude of what had happened, as well. In addition to fierce counterattacks, they sent some of their new jet fighter-bombers to destroy the bridge and tried to hit it with V-2s.

All failed. The bridge eventually was destroyed by artillery fire but not before American engineers had thrown up a number of crossings. Within weeks, there were more than sixty bridges across the Rhine, five of them capable of handling trains. The Remagen area now became a gateway through which American divisions from both north and south poured to form a battering ram poised to strike deeply into Germany.

The fortuitous capture of the Remagen bridge caused Eisenhower to shift the focus of Allied strategy from Montgomery's command to Bradley's. Montgomery was directed to strike north into Holland and northeast across upper Germany into Denmark. Simpson's Ninth Army, on Montgomery's right flank, was returned to Bradley and ordered to envelop the Ruhr from the north while Hodges's First Army swung behind it from the south. Patton was to move his Third Army due east across the middle of Germany, then send part of his command south to Czechoslovakia. Devers's 6th Army Group was to occupy southern Germany.

Montgomery, of course, was infuriated at being denied the opportunity to push on toward Berlin. But Churchill was less concerned about the field marshal's vanity than he was about Eisenhower's decision that Berlin no longer was an objective for any of the SHAEF forces, which would go no farther than the Elbe River. Churchill, who had become increasingly suspicious of Stalin's intentions since the Yalta Conference, wanted to "shake hands" with the Soviets as far to the east as possible. He sought the prestige of having taken Berlin and Prague, capital of Czechoslovakia, to counter Soviet claims that they alone had defeated Hitler. And if the wartime alliance broke down, as he feared it might, he wished to keep as much territory and population as possible in Western hands.

Eisenhower, with Marshall's support, argued that his mission was to end the war as quickly as possible. Many of the units in Europe were earmarked for transfer to the Pacific to fight against Japan. He considered Berlin a political target, rather than a military one, and a diversion from his main task. However, if Roosevelt and the prime minister directed him to move against Berlin, Eisenhower said, he would do so without complaint. But FDR did not countermand the supreme commander's decision.

Whether Eisenhower could have taken Berlin before the Soviets is moot. When Simpson and Hodges encircled the Germans in what became known as the "Ruhr pocket," the area east of the pocket became virtually an open corridor. Advance elements of Simpson's Ninth Army reached the river by April 11 and established a beachhead on its eastern bank two days later. After the war, Simpson and others claimed that he could have covered the remaining 50 miles to Berlin and taken the city before the Russians got there. Perhaps that is true. But most of Simpson's command, as well as his supplies, lay well to his rear. The Germans certainly would have sent mobile reserves to meet his thrust and, if a protracted battle developed, he might have run out of fuel and ammunition. Just as certainly, the Soviets would have jumped off earlier than they had planned, raising the possibility of accidental clashes between the converging forces.

In his memoirs, Eisenhower defended his refusal to even compete in a race on two grounds. Occupation zones for Germany, including Berlin, had been drawn up by a tripartite commission months earlier and had been confirmed at Yalta. Why, he asked, should he incur unnecessary casualties in taking the city—Bradley estimated them at 100,000—when occupying troops subsequently would move back into predesignated sectors anyway? Second, he had reason to believe the Germans were preparing to stage a last-ditch stand in the Bavarian and Austrian Alps to the south. In this "practically impenetrable" region, according to one intelligence report, a vast maze of underground fortifications and weapons factories called the National Redoubt had been constructed to sustain resistance indefinitely. Delay in reaching the area would permit evergreater numbers of German units to occupy the complex. The National Redoubt proved to be nonexistent, but Eisenhower had no way of knowing it at the time. Intelligence (including Ultra, we now know) was not conclusive, but it indicated a possibility that Eisenhower could not ignore.

The supreme commander's decision has been criticized as an example of American naiveté in not recognizing, as Churchill and Stalin did, that political and military objectives are inseparable. The opposite is true. What Eisenhower did not emphasize in his memoirs, because U.S.-Soviet relations had become extremely hostile by the time he wrote them, was that his reluctance to challenge the Russians over Berlin stemmed at least as much from political considerations as anything else. Eisenhower had given a great deal of thought to the postwar world and had concluded that Anglo-American-Soviet collaboration would be necessary to create a lasting peace. He shared some of Churchill's apprehensions about Stalin's motives, but he believed that provocative acts would dash all hopes of accommodation. Eisenhower may have been wrong, but he was by no means the simple soldier some have made him out to be.

THE DEATH OF HITLER AND VICTORY IN EUROPE

At the beginning of April, Stalin had summoned marshals Zhukov and Konev to the Kremlin and asked which of them would take the city. Both, of course, claimed they would gain the prize. Whether Stalin thought pitting one rival against the other would spur them on or whether he wished to prevent the popular Zhukov's emergence as the "conqueror of Berlin" whose prestige might challenge his own is unclear. In any event, he purposely left operational jurisdiction vague. Zhukov, who had at his disposal much larger forces located directly east of the city, had the advantage over Konev, who was attacking from the south, but at least he would have to share the honor.

On April 16, preceded by the most massive artillery barrage of the war, the Soviets mounted their long-awaited assault. Desperate German resistance held up the advance briefly, then was steamrollered by masses of Soviet tanks and men. Zhukov pushed around the northern flank of Berlin, and Konev sealed off the southern perimeter. The envelopment was completed on April 25, denying any chance that German relief columns could fight their way to the beleaguered city. That same day, other units of Konev's army group reached the Elbe south of Berlin, where they met American patrols at Torgau. Soldiers of both nations happily embraced one another, and language difficulties were surmounted by frequent toasts from bottles of "liberated" wine and cognac.

During this period, the Western Allies advanced on all fronts. More than 300,000 Germans surrendered in the Ruhr pocket, Montgomery began seizing the ports of northern Germany, and Patton had crossed all the way to the border of Czechoslovakia. At long last, German discipline and morale had shattered as disorganized and leaderless German units surrendered without fighting. Soldiers and civilians began welcoming Anglo-American forces from which they sought protection against Soviet troops advancing from the east. The Russians, it quickly became known, acted as barbarically in the areas they occupied as the Germans had during BARBAROSSA.

At the beginning of the year, Hitler had moved from his command post in East Prussia to a bunker under the Reich Chancellery in Berlin. By the war's final weeks, the fuhrer had disintegrated into a trembling physical wreck whose condition was worsened by the injections and pills prescribed for him by his personal doctor, a quack named Theodore Morrell. If one definition of insanity is the inability to distinguish between reality and fantasy, Hitler by this time also was quite mad. From his bunker, he issued a stream of orders and directives that bore no relevance to the actual military situation. He alternated between moods of deep despair and maniacal highs, during which he raved about some miracle or other that would deliver Germany from defeat. His ever-loyal propaganda minister, Goebbels, encouraged him in these delusions, greeting news of President Roosevelt's death on April 12 as

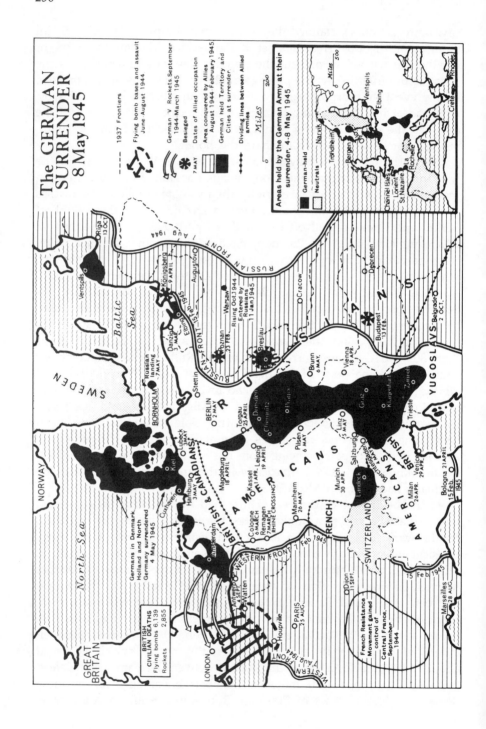

The GERMAN
SURRENDER
8 May 1945

Happy 2nd Lt. William Robertson and Lt. Alexander Sylvashko, Russian Army, shown in front of a sign ("East meets West") symbolizing the historic meeting of the Russian and American armies, near Torgau, Germany, April 25, 1945. (National Archives photo no. W&C 1096)

"the turning point for us" because it was "written in the stars" that fortunes would change during the second half of April.

Impotent with regard to the military situation, Hitler remained a dangerous figure. He concluded that the German people had proved unworthy of him and his noble dreams for them. Having so failed, it was better that they cease to exist as an organized society. He ordered Defense Minister Albert Speer to destroy whatever remained of German industry, transportation, and communications facilities to prevent them from falling into Allied hands. That such action would further desolate an already shattered nation did not concern him. Speer proved unwilling to carry out Hitler's demented wishes, thereby sparing the German people further misery.

During the last days of April, with Russian soldiers advancing block by block closer to his bunker and the city being pounded to rubble by artillery fire, Hitler realized the end had come. He felt betrayed by almost everyone. He denounced as traitors Goering, who had offered to take command of the reich after Berlin's encirclement, and Himmler, who actually had begun surrender negotiations with the Allies. Only the faithful Eva Braun and the entire Goebbels family had remained loyal. On April 28, after turning over leadership to Admiral Karl Doenitz, Hitler composed his final testament to the German people and to the world. It was a rambling screed of denunciations, above all against the evils of "international Jewry." A few minutes after midnight, he married Eva.

Shortly after midday on April 30, Hitler and Eva retired to a room where he shot himself and his new wife took poison. Aides carried their bodies aboveground and set fire to them in an effort to prevent the Russians from obtaining Hitler's recognizable corpse and displaying it. Some of those remaining in the bunker committed suicide; others tried to make their way through advancing Soviet lines afoot. Goebbels poisoned his wife and children, then took some poison himself. Three days later, resistance in Berlin ceased, and Russian soldiers raised the Soviet flag over the ruins of the chancellery. The Thousand Year Reich had lasted fewer than thirteen years.

Sporadic fighting continued for a few days more on various fronts, largely because German communications had broken down. Admiral Doenitz made several attempts to cut a deal for the German military by offering to surrender all forces to the Western Allies only. Eisenhower refused his offer and similar ones made by other German commanders. By this time, a mass exodus of German soldiers and civilians was taking place across the Elbe to escape the dreaded Russians. Eisenhower had issued a directive prohibiting such movement, but little effort was made to enforce it. Doenitz finally accepted unconditional surrender. Early on the morning of May 7, Field Marshal Alfred Jodl, chief of the German General Staff, appeared at SHAEF headquarters in Rheims to sign the surrender documents. In attendance were high-ranking officers representing the United States, Great Britain, France, and the Soviet Union.

Eisenhower, whose detestation of the Germans had grown even more venomous after he had visited a liberated concentration camp, refused to attend the signing. He waited in another room until it was over, then had Jodl ushered into his presence. Eisenhower spoke briefly and without the courtesies usually observed between general officers. First, he asked the field marshal whether he understood what he had signed. When Jodl replied that he did, Eisenhower informed him that he was to be held fully responsible for carrying out the agreed-upon terms and that he should make himself available to the Soviets at their pleasure. Jodl was then dismissed.

The Russians were not to be denied their due. Stalin made it clear that he did not recognize the legality of what appeared to be a separate peace with the Western Allies, and he recalled the officer who had signed the document to Moscow for "harsh" punishment. He insisted that the agreements be formally ratified in Berlin under Soviet auspices in order to properly acknowledge the terrible sacrifices made by the Soviet people. This was done in an impressive ceremony the next day, May 8. The war in Europe was officially over.

There was a curious anticlimax. Stalin had requested his allies to refrain from announcing the surrender publicly until May 9 for some German forces in the east had not yet surrendered. This was impossible to do because American and British military radio stations had begun openly broadcasting the capitulation in order to persuade German soldiers everywhere to lay down their arms. The result was that, as huge demonstrations erupted in the capitals and other cities of Western Allied nations, Moscow remained silent. Then, when word began leaking out during the early morning hours of May 10, Moscovites began streaming into the streets without official sanction. They formed huge crowds in front of the British and American embassies, despite police efforts to disperse them, and lustily cheered diplomats who appeared at windows and balconies. That evening, the Soviet government marked the occasion with a 30-salvo salute from 1,000 guns located around the city.

THE AIR WAR

Germany's continued resistance on both fronts through the spring of 1945 called into question the commitment Great Britain and the United States had made to strategic bombing throughout the war. Air force generals and their civilian allies had predicted that, at best, Germany would be pounded into submission by bombing alone. At the very least, they contended, it would so weaken the enemy's ability to wage war that if ground operations became necessary, they would amount to a walk-through. Such claims grew more hollow with each passing month. What has stirred debate ever since is whether the results of the strategic bombing even justified its costs or instead amounted to a colossal error.

German bombing raids against British cities during the Great War had caused little damage and few casualties. They nonetheless fired the imaginations of air power enthusiasts during the following years. Modern war was total war, such advocates pointed out, which meant that factors such as industrial production, transportation, and civilian morale were as important as the numbers of divisions a nation could muster. Indeed, those divisions could not function without the supplies and equipment necessary to sustain them. Destroy the heart of a nation's war-making capacity, champions of strategic bombing argued, and its military arms would wither.

Prospects of sending clouds of bombers to devastate civilian production and population centers struck some people as barbaric. Not so, replied the proponents of air power. Pointing to the more than four years of bloody slaughter recently concluded, they defended their proposals as being more humane in the long run. Sufficiently powerful bombing attacks would cause so much destruction and disruption that frenzied civilian populations would force their governments to sue for peace in a matter of weeks, thereby saving lives.

Though not without critics, the doctrine of strategic bombing gained the most support in Great Britain and, to a lesser extent, the United States. Although peacetime budgetary limitations retarded development, both nations had prototypes of four-engine heavy bombers by the late 1930s. Germany took a different path. The Luftwaffe was designed, above all, to support ground operations. To this end, emphasis was placed on dive-bombers, light and medium conventional bombers, and fighters. Germany built no heavy bombers throughout the war.

The implementation of strategic bombing by the British came about slowly. When the war broke out, top priority was given to the production of fighters for defense against German attacks. Bomber Command possessed fewer aircraft than did Germany, and some types were clearly obsolete. Raids against German cities at first were carefully avoided for fear of provoking retaliation, but such restrictions were lifted when German planes inadvertently dropped bombs on London during the Battle of Britain. Churchill ordered strikes against Berlin, which, in turn, provoked Hitler into directing his bombers to hit London and other cities. There were no rules after that.

Despite the poor results of early raids, the British government embarked upon a massive program of building bombers in the following months. Churchill pushed the effort against considerable internal opposition. Suppressing his own reservations about the utility of strategic bombing, he argued that it provided Great Britain with the only means of waging an offensive war against Germany: British morale, if nothing else, demanded such an effort. RAF generals, their allies in government, and the press cooperated in portraying the air war as a potentially decisive weapon against the Nazis.

Practical considerations dictated the way Great Britain waged its air campaign. RAF generals had claimed that bombers flying in proper formation could defend themselves against fighters. However, they were never able to do so even after the new four-engined Stirlings and Halifaxes began appearing in 1941 and the superior Lancasters came out in 1942. Spitfires and Hurricanes, having been designed as interceptors, lacked sufficient range to serve as escorts all the way to Germany. Unable to sustain the losses that daylight operations entailed, the British shifted almost entirely to nighttime attacks in late 1941.

Raids conducted at night proved grossly inaccurate. Even after new equipment and techniques improved performance, bombers were fortunate to drop their payloads within an area of several miles, let alone hit specific facilities. Although the fiction was maintained that German industry and transportation constituted primary targets, some of which were struck as a matter of course, the real goal of area bombing was to break the will of the German people by devastating population centers. Mixtures of incendiaries and high explosives were used to create massive fires that swept through city blocks. Some Britons protested in vain against this strategy of terror, but most were disinclined to feel great sympathy for an enemy who had, after all, started the war and freely bombed British cities.

U.S. Army Air Forces generals disagreed with the British. They remained wedded to the idea of daylight precision bombing as the best means of destroying Germany's ability to wage war. They believed they could avoid losses such as the British had suffered because American heavy bombers were superior. B-17 Flying Fortresses and, to a lesser extent, B-24 Liberators flew higher and faster and were better armored than the British heavies. Carrying a host of .50-caliber machine guns that could fire in all directions, the bombers were considered capable of defending themselves in formation without fighter protection. Such characteristics had been achieved at the cost of smaller bomb loads, but Americans were confident that superior accuracy provided by the Norden bombsight would more than compensate.

The U.S. Army Eighth Air Force began assembling in Great Britain during the spring of 1942 and mounted its first raids in August. By the end of the year, it had flown nearly thirty operations. Early results seemed to bear out predictions. Losses were low, and gunners reported an astounding number of kills against German fighters. But the optimism was unwarranted. Raids had been conducted against lightly defended targets, such as marshaling yards in France, Belgium, and the Netherlands—all close enough for the British to provide fighter escorts. In addition, inexperienced crews had wildly exaggerated the numbers of enemy aircraft they shot down, and events would show that American bombers were not self-defending against heavy fighter attack. Imprecise bombing, discounted at the time as due to inexperience, remained a problem. The Norden bombsight, so accurate when tested under optimum conditions, produced no miracles under combat conditions in German skies that frequently were overcast.

The air war against Germany entered its maximum phase in 1943. At Casablanca in January, the Combined Chiefs of Staff directed the RAF and USAAF to form the Combined Bomber Offensive; its goal was the "progressive destruction and dislocation of the German military, industrial and economic system, and the undermining of the morale of the German people." Emphasis on this program derived in great part from the desire to placate the Soviets for having put off the cross-channel invasion for another year. It was touted as the "third front" in compensation for the failure to establish a second front.

Later christened Operation POINTBLANK, the stepped-up air offensive provided British and American airmen the opportunity to make good on their boasts that they could bring Germany to its knees without an invasion. Both services had accumulated large fleets of bombers over the preceding months, and by the spring of 1943, they began mounting raids in ever-increasing numbers. Nothing changed with regard to the division of labor, whatever the Combined Chiefs of Staff intended. American bombers struck at submarine bases, air force production facilities, ball-bearing factories, and the like. And Bomber Command's Air Marshal Arthur Harris interpreted that part of the directive referring to "the morale of the German people" as a green light to continue nighttime terror bombing of German cities.

Operation POINTBLANK unquestionably visited great devastation on Germany. The problem was that, at any given time, there was no way of accurately gauging its cumulative effect. Facilities that appeared destroyed in aerial photographs might be repaired and functioning again in days or weeks. German morale did not crack as the bombing went on, but who knew when it might? Lacking hard evidence to go on and loath to admit that such an enormous commitment of men and resources might have been wasted, Allied leaders had little choice but to hope the airmen's rosy predictions would come true. Meanwhile, the bombing campaign served as a British-American pledge of good faith to the Soviets.

The air war over Germany exacted a heavy price in Allied planes and men. Although more formidable than the British heavies, B-17s and B-24s suffered appalling losses against German targets that were heavily defended by fighters and antiaircraft guns. In raids against ball-bearing factories at Schweinfort in August and October of 1943, for instance, the USAAF lost 60 of 375 bombers the first time and 60 of 290 the second. Similarly, the effort to cripple German fighter production in late 1943 and early 1944 probably cost more in bomber strength than it was worth. Nor did the British escape unscathed as German night fighters equipped with radar became increasingly effective.

Strategic operations were reduced between the spring and fall of 1944 so the bombers could provide tactical support for OVERLORD, but thereafter, they resumed on an ever-larger scale. They were aided immeasurably by several developments. Advancing Allied armies progressively weakened German defenses as they overran early-warning radar installations and forward air bases. Even more important, the introduction of the P-51 Mustang at last provided the bombers with a

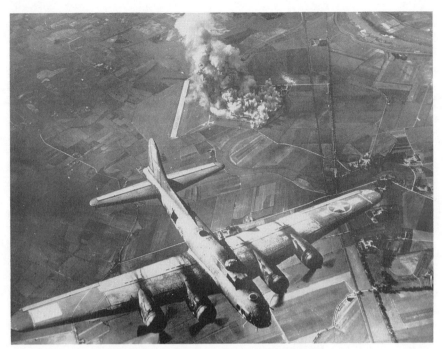

"The first big raid by the 8th Air Force was on a Focke Wulf plant at Marienburg. Coming back, the Germans were up in full force and we lost at least 80 ships—800 men, many of them pals" (1943). (National Archives photo no. W&C 1087)

truly effective fighter escort. Previously, P-47 Thunderbolts and P-38 Lightnings equipped with auxiliary wing tanks had helped a little. Neither aircraft was able to accompany the heavies to targets deep within Germany, however; consequently, enemy fighters could wait until these planes had to turn back before attacking. But Mustangs not only had the range, they were far superior to any conventional German fighter. Just as German air raids were meant to lure RAF fighters to their destruction during the Battle of Britain, the U.S. strikes were deliberately staged against heavily defended targets in order to annihilate the Luftwaffe.

A change in strategy also made the raids more effective during the final months of the war. Whereas bombers previously had been sent against a wide range of targets, now they concentrated on two: synthetic oil refineries and transportation. This was so successful that planes and tanks coming off production lines sat idle for lack of fuel, and the movement of goods within Germany eventually came almost to a standstill.

As the number of such facilities diminished, the USAAF began using its surplus capacity to join Bomber Command in destroying cities under the guise of "blind bombing of transportation centers." The most notorious of these occurred in mid-February 1945 against Dresden, a city of little industrial importance that was crammed with refugees who had fled before Russian armies. First, the British attacked at night, using incendiaries to create enormous firestorms that fed upon themselves. Then, while the Germans were struggling to extinguish the still-raging fires, American bombers hit the next day and the next. When it was over, almost the entire city had been gutted, with approximately 35,000 killed and at least as many more wounded. Churchill had initiated this campaign because he wanted to demonstrate a willingness to facilitate Soviet advances and, not incidentally, to impress Stalin with Anglo-American air power.

The contribution of strategic bombing to the Allied war effort has been endlessly debated. One fact stands out: Use of area bombing to shatter civilian morale was an abject failure. Despite an estimated cost of 400,000 dead and as many wounded, the German people supported the war effort until the very end. Whether such slaughter could have been morally justified even if it had shortened the war significantly is a matter of opinion. Air Marshal Arthur Harris later became a convenient scapegoat, but ultimate responsibility for Bomber Command's actions and for USAAF's complicity rested with the top levels of government.

As to the cost-effectiveness of the air war on Germany's economy, too many variables obtained to permit an accurate judgment. On the one side, there were the vast Allied expenditures of materials, productive capacity, and manpower. Would the war effort have been better served by emphasizing the construction of fighters and such crucial items as landing craft instead? Would the airmen, who constituted an elite group among the services, have contributed more as officers and NCOs in combat units? Weighing the impact on Germany similarly involves too many unknowns. Production statistics, usually cited to minimize the effects of strategic bombing, tell only part of the story. Fighters assigned to protect cities were unavailable for duty on the various fronts, for example, as were the men and equipment deployed in antiaircraft units.

Among those who have studied the subject, there is near consensus that strategic bombing at most shortened the war by one or two months, at the cost of 40,000 aircraft and 160,000 men. The campaign *might* have achieved what the air generals predicted but for their own errors of judgment. Had they recognized and admitted early on that bombers were not self-defending and insisted that the development of long-range fighters be given top priority, they could have carried the war to Germany, in daylight, well before they actually did. Then, if they had concentrated on oil and transportation facilities from the outset, instead of alternating targets and wasting effort on nearly useless area bombing, they might have caused the German war machine to collapse much sooner than it did. Hindsight, as usual, provides enlightenment.

SELECTED BIBLIOGRAPHY

Ambrose, Stephen E. *Eisenhower and Berlin, 1945: The Decision to Halt at the Elbe* (New York: Norton, 1967).

Beck, Earl R. *Under the Bombs: The German Home Front* (Lexington: University Press of Kentucky, 1986).

Chuikov, Vasili I. *The Fall of Berlin* (New York: Holt, Rinehart and Winston, 1967).

Copp, DeWitt. *Forged in Fire: Strategy and Decisions in the Air War over Europe, 1940–1945* (Garden City, N.Y.: Doubleday, 1982).

Craven, Wesley Frank, and James Lea Cate (eds.). *Army Air Forces in World War II*, 7 vols. (Chicago: University of Chicago Press, 1948–1966).

Elstrob, Peter. *The Last Offensive: The Full Story of the Battle of the Ardennes* (New York: Macmillan, 1971).

Hastings, Max. *Bomber Command* (New York: Dial, 1979).

Hechler, Ken. *Bridge at Remagen* (New York: Ballantine, 1957).

MacDonald, Charles Brown. *A Time for Trumpets: The Untold Story of the Battle of the Bulge* (New York: William Morrow, 1985).

Overy, R. J. *The Air War: 1939–1945* (New York: Stein & Day, 1980).

Pogue, Forrest C. *Command Decisions: The Decision to Halt at the Elbe* (Washington, D.C.: Center of Military History, U.S. Army, 1990).

Ryan, Cornelius. *The Last Battle* (New York: Simon & Schuster, 1966).

Schaffer, Ronald. *Wings of Judgment: American Bombing in World War II* (New York: Oxford University Press, 1985).

Sherry, Michael S. *The Rise of American Air Power: The Creation of Armageddon* (New Haven, Conn.: Yale University Press, 1987).

Speer, Albert. *Inside the Third Reich* (New York: Macmillan, 1970).

Toland, John. *The Last 100 Days* (New York: Random House, 1966).

Trevor-Roper, Hugh R. *The Last Days of Hitler* (New York: Collier Books, 1962).

Webster, Sir Charles, and Noble Franklin. *The Strategic Air Offensive Against Germany*, 3 vols. (London: Her Majesty's Stationery Office, 1961).

Whiting, Charles. *Battle of the Ruhr Pocket* (London: Ballantine, 1970).

15
Across the Pacific
(1943–1944)

The war against Japan was the most complicated military endeavor in history. Waged across vast expanses of ocean on land, in the air, and at sea, the conflict rendered most traditional strategic and tactical doctrines obsolete. Proper coordination of all these elements would have been difficult even if the United States had been able to devote its entire energies and assets to the struggle. As it was, conflicting views on the priorities assigned to Europe and Asia resulted in ongoing struggles over the commitment of both men and resources. The army, with the notable exception of General MacArthur, consistently stressed the primacy of the European theater. The navy, relegated to support functions in the Atlantic, just as consistently emphasized the war against Japan. Finally, the interrelatedness of naval, air, and ground operations caused intense rivalries between the services, often resulting in command structures that verged on the bizarre.

Such hindrances might have proven critical had the war in Asia been waged on anything resembling equal terms. This was not the case. As the conflict wore on, American productivity and technological advances resulted in a mismatch. By early 1943, the United States began employing faster, more powerful fighters, such as the P-38 Lightning, the F6F Hellcat, and the F4U Corsair. In the months that followed, the navy began receiving fast aircraft carriers and battleships in numbers the Japanese could not hope to duplicate. The introduction of the proximity fuse—a radio device that caused shells to explode if they passed even close to the target—provided surface vessels with far greater protection against air attack. The list could be extended. And the ability to decrypt enemy messages continued to give American commanders a valuable edge. The war lasted as long as it did primarily because the United States had to dislodge the enemy from defensive positions piecemeal, rather than being able to engage him in massive battles where American advantages would have been decisive.

CARTWHEEL

The seizure of Guadalcanal and the Papuan peninsula, both completed in January 1943, marked the opening phase of a campaign to attack the powerful Japanese naval and air base at Rabaul, on the northeastern tip of New Britain. General MacArthur at first proposed a direct assault that would have required far more men and resources than the Joint Chiefs of Staff were willing to allocate. After a great deal of wrangling between the army and navy, the chiefs finally authorized a more modest campaign, later code-named CARTWHEEL, in March. MacArthur, in overall command of the operation, was to proceed up the eastern coast of New Guinea to a point parallel with New Britain, then move across the Vitiaz Strait to the island's western end. Admiral Halsey was to advance up the Solomon Islands chain to Bougainville, which lay to the southeast of Rabaul. It was from these two positions that the final assault on the Japanese base was to be launched. Probably to everyone's surprise, the feisty Halsey and the arrogant MacArthur worked well together through the months that followed.

Although CARTWHEEL did not get under way until June, several significant events took place during the months before. In late February, the Japanese sent eight troop transports, guarded by eight destroyers, to reinforce garrisons on New Guinea. They were attacked several times on March 2 by B-17s, which left two of the transports sinking. The next day, as the range closed, MacArthur's air force commander, General George C. Kenney, sent a force of medium bombers and fighters against the convoy. Using low-level bombing and strafing tactics they had long been practicing, the attacking pilots sank all the remaining transports and four destroyers.

The Battle of Bismarck Sea, as it came to be known, was important for two reasons. Previously, land-based bombers operating at high altitudes had proved relatively inefficient against moving ships. Kenney's innovative tactics changed all that, and they were widely used for the rest of the war. The Japanese also were impressed. To avoid any more such disasters, they began supplying their troops on New Guinea by submarine, air transport, and a trickle of barges. Shortages of everything resulted during the remainder of the campaign.

In April, Admiral Yamamoto launched a series of air strikes against Allied shipping and landing fields. Although these raids actually achieved very little, inexperienced pilots—rapidly becoming the norm in Japanese squadrons—reported fantastic results. Yamamoto, convinced the air of-

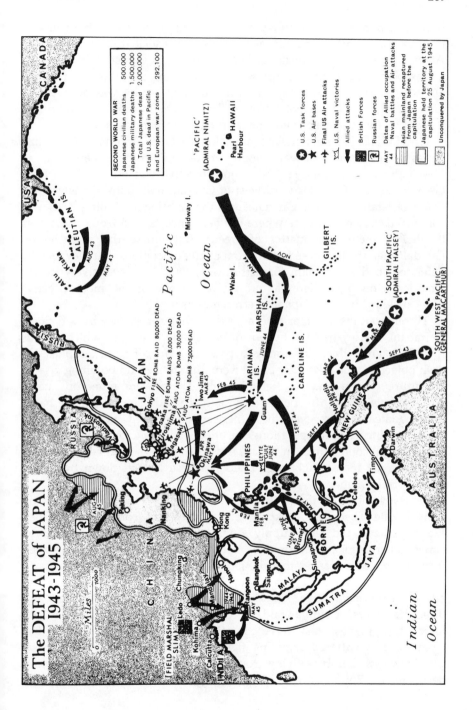

fensive had been successful, planned a visit to southern Bougainville to congratulate his airmen. Radio reports of his visit were decrypted by American intelligence officers at Pearl, and a trap was set. On April 18, as his plane and fighter escort were approaching the island, a flight of eighteen P-38s was waiting for him. The bomber he was aboard was an easy target, and it went down in flames. The loss of Yamamoto was a blow to the Japanese high command and to national morale.

CARTWHEEL began in late June. MacArthur's American-Australian forces began a series of leapfrogging operations up the eastern coast of New Guinea, and Halsey's first major objective was the island of New Georgia, about 200 miles northwest of Guadalcanal. Both offensives met fierce resistance. As on Guadalcanal, the fighting in both places was conducted in dense jungles where the heat, insects, and tropical diseases debilitated men in a matter of weeks. But unlike the situation on Guadalcanal, the Japanese fought from fortified positions that they usually defended to the last man. Flamethrowers, first used extensively by the Americans on New Georgia, proved to be one of the most effective ways of knocking out Japanese strongpoints.

Throughout the summer and fall, MacArthur and Halsey moved closer to Rabaul. Halsey had the benefit of being able to choose which islands to assault and which to simply bypass and cut off from supplies. As each objective was taken, air bases were built to step up bombing attacks on future targets and on Rabaul itself. There were numerous naval engagements during this period, just as there had been during the battle for Guadalcanal. However, the American navy fared much better this time. Training in night operations, the effective use of radar, and improved torpedoes all contributed. In the air, American pilots scored very favorable ratios against increasingly outmoded Japanese aircraft flown by inadequately trained men.

On November 1, the Third Marine Division was put ashore on Bougainville. That night, a Japanese task force sent from Rabaul to shell the beachhead and sink supply ships in the harbor was repulsed by American cruisers and destroyers. A few days later, when Halsey learned from decrypted messages that the Japanese were amassing a larger naval force at Rabaul to send against Bougainville, he ordered a daring carrier attack on the naval base. American planes damaged three cruisers and three destroyers. A similar raid five days later caused more damage and forced the Japanese task force to retire from Rabaul for repairs. The Japanese also suffered crippling fighter losses in defending the base. Within weeks, bombers flying from airfields built within the American perimeter on Bougainville were pounding Rabaul.

U.S. troops go over the side of a Coast Guard manned combat transport to enter the landing barges at Empress Augusta Bay, Bougainville, as the invasion gets under way, November 1943. (National Archives photo no. W&C 1164)

MacArthur's soldiers and marines landed on the western end of New Britain in late December, capturing yet another airfield from which to strike at the once great naval base. By this time, it had become clear that there no longer was any need to seize Rabaul, which, for all practical purposes, had been neutralized. After mid-February 1944, the Japanese lost the ability to send up more than a token number of fighters against the relentless bombing raids. Although a few more islands in the area were seized and mopping-up operations continued, CARTWHEEL came to an end. Instead of Rabaul, the new objective became the Philippines, where the Americans had suffered such a humiliating defeat at the beginning of the war.

ISLAND HOPPING

Even before CARTWHEEL entered its final stages, the focus of American offensive operations shifted to the central Pacific. The objective was to seize a succession of island chains stretching across the ocean, thereby obtaining air bases within bombing range of the Japanese home islands and, finally, staging areas for an invasion. The navy brass originally had approved the New Guinea-Solomon Islands operations as a means of neutralizing Japan's offensive capabilities, but they regarded the central Pacific as the surest path to victory. The rapidly growing numbers of carriers and battleships could be used to best advantage there, and prospects of luring Japan into decisive naval battles made it all the more attractive.

Advancing through the more than 1,000 islands making up these chains offered some advantages. Only a few actually had to be assaulted. And by taking those on which airfields were located or could be built, the Americans could use air power to interdict the flow of supplies to others occupied by the Japanese, leaving them to "wither on the vine." This forced the Japanese to disperse their forces over a number of likely targets.

Drawbacks existed, as well. There were only so many likely targets, which the Japanese had fortified with great skill and hard labor. Some of their strongpoints, constructed of reinforced concrete, sandbags, and logs, were capable of withstanding even direct hits by shellfire or bombs. Worse yet, most of these atolls consisted of small islands clustered around lagoons where the only beaches existed. This enabled the Japanese to concentrate their defenses and firepower in one direction against attackers who had no choice except to plow on in.

The first objective was the Gilbert Islands, running about 2,000 miles southwest of Pearl Harbor. Specific targets were Tarawa in the chain's center and Makin at its northwestern end, both consisting of several coral islets. The newly created Fifth Fleet, commanded by Admiral Raymond A. Spruance, carried out the operations. Tarawa was by far the stronger of the two outposts. There were about 5,000 Japanese troops on the atoll, most of them concentrated on the island of Betio, where the airfield was located. They possessed all kinds of weapons, including several 8-inch guns captured in earlier campaigns. By contrast, intelligence estimated there were only about 500 troops on Makin, some 200 fewer than the actual number.

Shortly after midnight on November 20, a powerful force of three battleships, three heavy cruisers, five escort carriers, and twenty-one destroyers stood offshore of Tarawa. They were accompanied by seventeen cargo and troop ships. The assault would be carried out by the Second Marine Division. At dawn, the battleships, cruisers, and destroyers began hurling tons of shells at the atoll in a long bombardment that was lifted only to allow air strikes from the nearby carriers. American planners hoped such an unprecedented pounding would destroy most of the fortifications and so stun the survivors as to render them unable to oppose the landings. The barrage was timed to end only a few minutes before the first landing craft began hitting the beaches in order to maximize the effects of the shelling.

Little went according to plan. Some strongholds were pulverized, and communications between Japanese units were destroyed, but many blockhouses and pillboxes remained operable. The first salvos fired by the flagship *Maryland* knocked out its own communications center, rendering the task force commander incapable of signaling other ships. This breakdown would not have been critical had the landing craft reached the beaches according to schedule. When it became clear that they were running behind time, however, the commander was unable to restart the bombardment or call in additional air strikes. The result was that the Japanese gained a breathing space to recover before the first troops reached shore.

The tides, unpredictable during that time of year, caused even greater problems. The atoll was surrounded by coral reefs that conventional landing craft could not pass over during low tide, which is what the Americans encountered. The first waves of marines rode in on amphibious tractors (LTVs) designed to cross just such reefs. Buffeted by high winds, choppy seas, and strong currents, the LTVs were exposed to fire much longer than anticipated as they struggled to reach land. Many were sunk or blown apart, and hundreds of marines were killed or wounded.

The men who followed had it worse. Because there were not enough LTVs to go around, succeeding waves had to debark from regular landing craft and wade across the reefs for distances up to almost 1,000 yards. Slowed by water that was waist high and above, the marines were easy targets. Those killed outright were fortunate; many of the wounded were drowned by the weight of their packs and equipment. One battalion that had to wade in suffered 70 percent casualties in its first wave and even higher losses in succeeding ones. The marines nonetheless established a thin beachhead at the cost of 1,500 casualties out of a total of 5,000 men. They were fortunate that the Japanese were unable to launch a counterattack that night because their communications had been destroyed by the preliminary bombardment.

The battle for Tarawa lasted for three more days. Because there were so few LTVs left, reserves sent in on D Day +1 also had to wade ashore under heavy fire. Air strikes were helpful, but the marines still had to clear out most fortified positions with flamethrowers, tanks, and hand-thrown explosives. The Japanese, as usual, fought almost to the last man. On the night of November 22, they mounted a suicidal charge that broke apart against marine lines. By the next morning, only small pockets of resistance remained on Betio, which the marines quickly eliminated. The island was declared secure by 1:30 that afternoon.

The assault against Makin to the northwest brought a different kind of tragedy. An army regimental combat team encountered only light resistance, but its troops were mostly inexperienced National Guardsmen who were baffled, blocked, and sometimes panicked by Japanese snipers, infiltrators, and small patrols. The soldiers soon learned how to deal with these tactics, but the operation took four days when it should have been ended in two. The delay was costly. On the last day, an escort carrier that remained offshore to provide support while the fighting continued was sunk with heavy losses by a Japanese submarine.

Reports on the slaughter at Tarawa shocked the American public. The marines had suffered 3,000 casualties on an atoll that was only a speck if it appeared at all on maps. Widely published photographs of beaches littered with the often shattered bodies of young Americans provided a glimpse of what actually happened in combat, as opposed to what people were used to seeing in propagandistic war films. Such photos also destroyed any illusions that the war in the Pacific could be won cheaply.

The battle also provided some bitter lessons for military planners as they prepared for operations on the next chain of islands, the Marshalls. They worked to improve every phase of future campaigns, from communications (particularly fire control) to directing traffic on the beaches. More effective equipment, such as armored, cannon-firing LTVs, was devised. Above all, Tarawa taught them that they had underestimated the resilience of the Japanese and the ability of their fortifications to survive naval and air attacks. Operations henceforth would be mounted on a far larger scale and only after a much longer period of preliminary sea and air bombardment.

Planning for operations in the Marshall Islands had begun even before Tarawa and Makin were secured. Admiral Nimitz decided that the main target should be the huge atoll of Kwajalein, located in the chain's center. He overruled subordinates who argued that Kwajalein was within striking distance of numerous Japanese air bases that would subject occupying forces to constant bombing raids. To cancel such a threat, Nimitz ordered air strikes against the Marshalls from Tarawa and Makin as soon as their fields became operational. The carrier arm of the Fifth Fleet, Task Force 58 under command of Admiral Mark A. Mitscher, entered the campaign in late January 1944. Now boasting twelve fast carriers divided into four groups, the task force not only inflicted severe bombing damage on installations throughout the islands but eliminated Japanese air strength as a factor in the assault against Kwajalein.

Tarawa had provided harsh but fruitful training for operations in the Marshalls. In addition to the massive land- and carrier-based air strikes against Kwajalein, battleships, cruisers, and destroyers stood offshore for three days hurling thousands of tons of shells against its battered defenders. Timing and coordination were vastly improved in all areas. Bombardments moved inland only minutes before the first waves reached shore, and the landings themselves proceeded much more smoothly than before. The results were impressive. Although Japanese defenses were only slightly less formidable than on Tarawa, the entire atoll was secured by the late afternoon on February 4. The Japanese lost more than 7,000 men, while the Americans suffered fewer than 400 dead and 1,500 wounded.

The comparative ease with which Kwajalein was taken caused American commanders to revise their plans. Eniwitok, at the northwestern end of the Marshalls, had been scheduled for invasion in May. Because of its location, the Japanese were not strongly entrenched there, but they were certain to build up defenses now that Kwajalein had fallen. The assault date was moved up to February 17 to deny them time to do so. Attack forces were to consist of two reserve regiments that had not been committed at Kwajalein, supplemented by units that had suffered the least in the operation.

There was potential danger. Fewer than 700 miles west of Eniwitok lay the mighty Japanese naval base at Truk, one of the atolls in the Caroline chain. Truk was the headquarters and advance base for the Combined Fleet, and it contained submarine facilities and, most important for the Eniwitok operation, air bases capable of handling up to 400 planes. The configuration of islands and coral reefs at Truk provided protected anchorage against surface attack. The job of neutralizing Truk was given to Mitscher's Task Force 58, in what was to be the first assault on a major naval base carried out exclusively by carrier-based aircraft.

On February 4, the day Kwajalein fell, photo reconnaissance revealed that elements of the Combined Fleet, including two giant battleships, were moored at Truk. Mitscher therefore hoped not only to protect the Eniwitok operation but to catch the big ships in harbor. Unfortunately, the American scout planes had been detected by the Japanese, who realized that Truk was now within easy bombing range of Kwajalein.

They prudently sent the battleships to safer waters in the Philippines before Task Force 58 could reach the base.

Denied the chance to get at Japanese battleships, Mitscher's attack nonetheless succeeded brilliantly. Over a period of two days, February 17 and 18, Task Force 58 launched thirty strikes, every one of them more powerful then either of the two Japanese waves that had struck Pearl Harbor. Fighters were sent in first to clear the air of Japanese interceptors and to bomb and strafe the landing fields. Once the Japanese were stripped of air defenses, flights of fighters, bombers, and torpedo planes went after ships at anchor. A few vessels managed to clear the harbor, only to be sunk by battleships and cruisers waiting outside. Truk was a shambles after it was all over and never again served as a base for the Combined Fleet—all at the cost of thirty American aircraft and a slightly damaged carrier.

While Mitscher's airmen were battering Truk, American forces went ashore at Eniwitok after heavy pounding by aircraft and warships, in a smaller version of the battle for Kwajalein. Japanese troops who survived the preliminary bombardments fought courageously, but they stood no chance against the firepower and numbers thrown against them. Their entire garrison of nearly 3,000 men was wiped out. As at Kwajalein, American casualties were relatively light: 184 men killed, another 540 wounded.

The rapid advance across the Pacific had exceeded all expectations, rendering previous timetables obsolete. Planning now began for an early assault against the Mariana Islands, 1,000 miles northwest of Eniwitok. The primary targets were the large islands of Saipan, Tinian, and Guam. Their capture would provide naval bases to help cut enemy supply lines to the South Pacific and airfields from which Japan's home islands could be bombed by the new B-29 Superfortresses.

Several months were needed for preparations. Military offensives move in the manner of inchworms: First, the head advances; then, it fastens its grip while the tail catches up. Men have to be rested, replacements trained, equipment overhauled, and new supply lines established. The problem was magnified for Nimitz's operations because he had to compete for resources with both the European theater and MacArthur's command to the south.

American successes also had caused the Japanese to revise their thinking. Carrier and aircraft losses, coupled with the increasing devastation of their merchant marine by U.S. submarines, had led to the obvious conclusion that they could not successfully defend their far-flung empire. Instead, they would create an "absolute national defense sphere" of much smaller proportions that would be held at all costs. This shrunken perimeter would conserve shipping and permit a greater

His face grimey with coral dust, this Marine returns to a Coast Guard assault transport after two days and nights of hell on the beach of Eniwitok in the Marshall Islands, February 1944. (National Archives photo no. W&C 1198)

concentration of their armed forces. They would continue to resist American advances in places such as the Solomons and the Marshalls but only to gain time to replace losses and fortify the inner ring. That is why they did not commit major naval forces to defend Tarawa or Kwajalein. The Marianas, however, lay within the "absolute national defense sphere."

In June, more than 500 American ships, carrying 127,000 men, left staging areas at Guadalcanal and Pearl Harbor. They rendezvoused in midocean and made way for the Marianas. Admiral Spruance was in overall command of what was the largest amphibious operation thus far attempted against the Japanese. The first assault began on June 15 against Saipan, only 1,200 miles from Tokyo. The landings were preceded by four days of air strikes and naval bombardment, and ships of all kinds remained offshore to provide fire support for the ground troops. Although there were more Japanese on Saipan than intelligence had estimated, their fortifications were incomplete. This was partly because the American attack had come much earlier than the Japanese had expected and partly because U.S. submarines had sunk a large number of ships trying to deliver equipment and building materials.

Saipan combined the worst characteristics of New Guinea and the Solomons with those of the central Pacific atolls. Measuring six miles long by four miles wide, it contained some open areas but also had jungles, swamps, and steep mountains honeycombed with caves. Men had to cope with oppressive heat, malaria, and other jungle diseases, as well as an exotic mixture of reptiles and insects. The island also was surrounded by coral reefs that could tear the bottoms out of unwary landing craft.

The commander of ground operations was marine General Holland M. ("Howlin' Mad") Smith, who had at his disposal two marine divisions for the first assaults and an army division in reserve. The Japanese garrison consisted of 32,000 men, dispersed to defend several possible landing sites. Smith's plan was to have troop-carrying amphtracs preceded by armored ones carrying cannon and machine guns (LTVAs). The offensive punch provided by the LTVAs, he hoped, would suppress defensive fire enough to permit the troop carriers to establish deep beachheads on the first thrust. Results were poor. Accurate Japanese artillery fire destroyed many of the LTVAs, and the unarmored regular amphtracs made such vulnerable targets that marines preferred to bail out of them and advance on foot. Beachheads were secured with heavy casualties, and it took a week to extend them, bring reserve units ashore, and prepare to go on the offensive.

The drive across Saipan was a bloody affair, punctuated by frequent Japanese night attacks. It also gave rise to a heated dispute between the army and navy. The advancing line consisted of the Second and Fourth Marine divisions on the wings with the 27th Army Division in the middle. After a late start originally, the 27th gained ground much more slowly than the marines on either side, exposing their flanks to Japanese counterattack. After repeatedly warning the division commander to speed up his advance, Smith, with Spruance's approval, sacked him. Army officers were outraged that a marine general and an admiral would

The first Marines to hit the Saipan beach in the Marianas invasion take cover behind a sand dune while waiting for the following three waves of Marines to come in, June 1944. (National Archives photo no. W&C 1175)

relieve an army officer from command. The controversy made the press and caused great bitterness between the services.

Gradually, the Japanese were pushed back into the far corner of the island. On the night of July 6, they staged the largest banzai attack of the war as thousands of screaming men charged in a sector occupied by the 27th. It was a massacre. Although the attackers broke through the lines in some area, they had no hope of victory; when daylight came, weary American soldiers counted more than 4,000 Japanese bodies. It was the end of organized resistance on the island, although some isolated pockets had to be cleared. Saipan cost the United States 3,400 killed and 13,000 wounded, and almost the entire Japanese garrison of 32,000 perished.

Veterans of other campaigns had seen Japanese troops kill themselves rather than be taken prisoner, but they were not prepared for what happened on Saipan. Thousands of Japanese civilians lived there, many of whom had stayed within the defensive perimeter as it shrank to the northern tip of the island. As the end drew near, they, too, began committing suicide before the horrified eyes of the Americans, who could do nothing to stop them. Some used guns or hand grenades; others threw themselves off cliffs or waded into the sea. Parents killed children who were too young to know what was happening. Perhaps as many as 9,000 civilians died this way.

Four days after the initial landings on Saipan, the last great aircraft carrier battle of the war began. On June 16, an American submarine reported sighting a Japanese battle fleet heading for Saipan. Commanded by Vice Admiral Ozawa Jisaburo, the force consisted of five heavy and four light carriers, five battleships, thirteen cruisers, and twenty-eight destroyers. Opposing it was Admiral Mitscher's Task Force 58. Divided into four carrier groups and one of battleships, Task Force 58 counted seven heavy and eight light carriers, seven battleships, twenty-one cruisers, and sixty-nine destroyers. Unlike the situation at Midway, American pilots were now better trained than their Japanese counterparts and flew superior, if shorter-range, aircraft.

Mitscher would have liked to close on the Japanese as quickly as possible, but he was overruled by Admiral Spruance, who accompanied the battle fleet in his flagship, the heavy cruiser *Indianapolis*. Spruance ordered Mitscher to keep his ships in a position to guard operations at Saipan. This enabled the Japanese to locate the Americans before being spotted themselves and to launch their first strikes on the morning of July 9, while they were still beyond the range of American planes. It did them little good. Radar detection permitted American fighters to intercept the incoming planes more than 50 miles short of the carriers. In the resulting air battles, American pilots shot down more than three hundred Japanese aircraft, while losing only thirty of their own. Officially designated as the Battle of the Philippine Sea, it became known informally as "the Great Marianas turkey shoot." To make matters worse for the Japanese, they lost two of their heavy carriers that day to submarine attack.

American scout planes did not locate the Japanese force until late afternoon of the next day. Strikes were ordered even though the distance was at the far end of fighting range and only a few hours of daylight remained. Reaching the Japanese force just before dark, the attackers sank one carrier, damaged two more, and sent some tankers to the bottom. To help them find their way home, Mitscher ordered ships in the force to maintain full illumination even though this increased the chance of being spotted by enemy submarines. Some of the aircraft ran out of fuel before reaching the carriers, and some crashed on landing. The operation cost about fifty men.

Admiral Spruance has been criticized for ordering Task Force 58 to provide cover for Saipan, instead of intercepting the Japanese as Mitscher wanted to do. Some of Mitscher's commanders grumbled that they had been denied the opportunity to sink all or nearly all the Japanese carriers. Still, the battle all but destroyed Japanese naval air strength. Japan lost more than four hundred planes and about as many fliers, both of which were growing increasingly irreplaceable. The Japanese fleet steamed away from the waters near Saipan with only thirty-five serviceable aircraft.

Guam, which had been seized by Japanese troops only days after Pearl Harbor, was invaded on July 21. Thousands of shells, bombs, and rockets had rained down on the island to help soften defenses. The Third Marine Division, First Provisional Marine Brigade, and the 77th Army Division participated in the assault. This time, relations between the services ran smoothly as the combined forces encountered fierce resistance moving inland against the Japanese garrison of about 19,000 men. On the night of July 26, the Japanese launched all-out banzai attacks against American lines. As on Saipan, they broke through in some places but had no hope of ultimate success. After expending so much blood in these suicide charges, the Japanese had little left with which to oppose the Americans, although mopping-up operations continued until August 10. The United States suffered about 8,000 casualties; the Japanese were annihilated. (Guam offered American troops an unexpected bonus: The Japanese had used the island as a supply depot for alcoholic beverages in that part of the Pacific, and American soldiers and marines were delighted to capture thousands of cases of whiskey, sake, and beer as war booty.)

The third large island of the Marianas group, Tinian, had fallen a week earlier. After feinting an attack near Tinian Town, where the Japanese expected the assaults because of suitable beaches, the Americans landed at the other end of the island. The Japanese mounted several frontal assaults the next day, but they were hurled back with heavy losses. After that, the dwindling number of defenders retreated to the southern tip of the island, where the inevitable suicides began. Only a few prisoners were taken.

The capture of the Marianas not only pierced Japan's inner ring of defense but secured for the United States air bases within range of the home islands. Coming on the heels of Japanese setbacks against the British in Burma and the start of the first B-29 raids from China, the Marianas campaign had great repercussions in Tokyo. On July 18, General Togo Hideki had been forced to resign as premier, and a new cabinet was formed. Some of the more thoughtful Japanese politicians knew the war was lost and hoped to find some way out of it, but the military still exercised such power that these sentiments could not be expressed openly.

BACK TO THE PHILIPPINES

During the spring and summer of 1944, with the once great Japanese base at Rabaul neutralized, General MacArthur continued his advance northward along the coast of New Guinea, while seizing offshore islands for air bases. To the dismay of the Australians, MacArthur used their troops to slog up the coast as American forces engaged in more spectacular amphibious operations to leapfrog behind Japanese strongpoints. He was aided immeasurably in these assaults by code decryptions that revealed the Japanese troop dispositions.

One of the bloodiest of the island battles—and one that was nearly disastrous—took place at Biak, several hundred miles north of New Guinea. The Allies had captured or built landing sites as they advanced, but soft ground conditions typically made them unsuitable for heavy bomber operations. Biak's airfields, on the other hand, were adequate. An invasion by elements of the 41st Army Division was scheduled for May 27. But intelligence in this instance had underestimated the strength of Japanese defenses. There were actually more then 11,000 troops on Biak, including a crack infantry regiment, and most of the men, as well as their artillery and supplies, were located in labyrinthean caves along steep cliffs looking down on the airfield.

The Japanese commander at Biak made no effort to repulse the landings. Instead, he permitted American troops to come ashore and advance on the largest airfield before catching them in an ambush. Firing all sorts of weapons from their caves and forward fortifications, the Japanese pinned down the attackers and inflicted heavy casualties. One American battalion had to be evacuated at night by amphtracs, and even after reinforcements arrived, it took a week to capture the principal airfield. Frustrated by his inability to make better progress in the face of constant exhortations from above, the American commander asked to be relieved, and he was.

What the Americans did not know was that the Japanese had decided to defend the island by sending in a powerful task force, built around the giant battleships *Yamato* and *Musashi*. The task force would provide reinforcements and use its heavy guns to blast American troops on the ground and supply ships offshore. At the same time, only a few U.S. cruisers and destroyers were deployed off Biak as a shield. Fortunately for the Americans there, the Japanese canceled the sortie when the first air strikes from Task Force 58 were launched against the Marianas. *Yamato, Musashi,* and the other ships were ordered to rendezvous with the rest of the Combined Fleet in the Philippine Sea. Otherwise, they might have smashed the entire operation at Biak, which eliminated the last Japanese stronghold toward the end of August.

In late July, President Roosevelt had traveled to Pearl Harbor to confer with his Pacific theater commanders, General MacArthur and Admiral Nimitz. Few doubted that he was motivated, in large part, by political considerations. Having just received the nomination for an unprecedented fourth term, he clearly wished to emphasize his role as an active commander in chief of American forces advancing on all fronts. A well-photographed meeting with MacArthur had particular advantage. The colorful "hero" of Bataan and Corregidor had so carefully managed all publicity emanating from his headquarters that it gave the impression that he was winning the war against Japan almost singlehandedly. MacArthur was furious at having his popularity exploited by FDR, whom he detested, but he hoped to benefit from the meeting, as well.

The main topic of the president's talks with MacArthur and Nimitz involved future operations against Japan. There were three sites from which the final assault could be mounted: the southern coast of China, Formosa, or the Philippines. China was eliminated as a possibility because recent Japanese advances had overrun air bases there and because the Chinese Nationalist government was unreliable. Which of the other two should be the first objective?

Nimitz, who had the strong support of Navy Chief of Staff Ernest J. King, argued in behalf of Formosa. He favored seizing some bases in the Philippines but thought an invasion of the entire group would take too long and be an unnecessary expenditure of men and resources. MacArthur spoke eloquently in behalf of giving the Philippines priority. He defended such a strategy on military grounds but emphasized, above all, the moral issue involved. The United States had a special obligation to the Filipino people, he said, and failure to liberate them and the American prisoners of war there as quickly as possible would be perceived by all Asian peoples as a dishonorable act. He later claimed that, at one point when they were alone together, he told FDR directly that bypassing the Philippines would so anger the American people that it would affect the election in November. Whether he actually did so cannot be corroborated, but Roosevelt, in any event, sided with him.

The debate did not end at Pearl Harbor, but FDR's support and several later developments clinched MacArthur's case. The entire affair provides another illustration of how often during the war strategic decisions were affected by other than purely military considerations. There can be little room for doubt that MacArthur's plea on behalf of the Filipino people was heartfelt. There is equally little room for doubt that he was motivated by his own personal stake in the matter ("I shall return") and the fact that the invasion of and operations from the Philippines would fall under his jurisdiction. Navy commanders, on the other hand, had vested interests in a strategy that would thrust their service to the forefront.

In September, Roosevelt and Churchill, together with their chiefs of staff, met in Quebec to discuss a number of subjects relating to the war in Europe and in the Pacific. An agreement that MacArthur would invade Mindanao in the southern Philippines that November was scrapped upon receipt of a message from Admiral Halsey via Nimitz. Halsey stated that carrier-based raids had revealed that Japanese air power in the Philippines was far less formidable than previously supposed. He therefore recommended that Mindanao be bypassed in favor of an assault on Leyte in the central Philippines. When MacArthur's headquarters confirmed that assessment, the Joint Chiefs of Staff authorized him to proceed against Leyte in October. Actually, the Japanese were reserving available aircraft to defend against an invasion, and MacArthur's intelligence staff knew that Halsey had underestimated their strength.

Before moving against the Philippines, the United States undertook a series of carrier raids against them and other islands and seized one chain for its air base. Japanese efforts to repel the raids further reduced their fighter strength, especially the carrier-based planes. By now, air battles were so uneven that one Japanese admiral likened them to throwing eggs against a stone wall. The invasion of the Palaus by the First Marine Division was much more costly. The main island, Peleliu, was a coral atoll of steep cliffs pocked with hundreds of caves. The Japanese had converted the caves into fortresses that were virtually impervious to bombs or shellfire, and defenders had to be burned or blasted out at close quarters. Although the airfield was secured relatively quickly, the fighting went on for months, at the cost of more than 6,000 American casualties.

The invasion of Leyte began on the morning of October 20, 1944. It was carried out along four separate beachheads, where more than 160,000 men would be landed. The Japanese put up only light resistance because they planned to conserve their strength for counterattacks later on. By early afternoon, although there still was sniper fire, General MacArthur went ashore. Because the landing craft drew too much water to make it all the way in, he and his party had to wade through the last yards. Photographs and movies of this historic occasion were shown widely throughout the United States. MacArthur then made a radio broadcast, beginning with the words: "People of the Philippines, I have returned!" Modesty was not one of his stronger characteristics.

Both army and navy commanders had believed that the Japanese would forgo a strong response to the invasion of Leyte in order to conserve resources for defending Luzon to the north. They were mistaken. In addition to the 20,000 troops already on the island, the Japanese began sending reinforcements from Luzon. They also determined that they would try to smash the entire operation by all-out naval attack.

Gen. Douglas MacArthur wades ashore during initial landings at Leyte, the Philippines, October 1944. (National Archives photo no. W&C 1207)

The Battle of Leyte Gulf began on October 23 and lasted for two days in a series of engagements too complicated to be discussed in detail here. Put briefly, the Japanese hoped to use their last four aircraft carriers—now with only a few planes on each—to lure the American carriers away from the Leyte beachheads. Then, two task forces of battleships and cruisers, one moving through the San Bernardino Strait in the north and the other through Surigao Strait to the south, would converge offshore to sink supply shipping and to bombard American depots and troop concentrations on the ground. The plan almost worked.

There were two American fleets in the area, Admiral Halsey's Third and Admiral Thomas C. Kinkaid's Seventh. Halsey's command was simply Spruance's former Fifth Fleet renamed, with Mitscher's fast carrier group now called Task Force 38. When the Japanese carriers were sighted, Halsey took the bait. By nature aggressive and undoubtedly influenced by criticism of Spruance's caution in the Battle of the Philippine Sea, Halsey ordered his entire fleet to pursue the enemy carriers steaming far to the north of the beachheads. Because of an ambiguous message that Halsey sent about his intentions, Kincaid thought he had left a task force behind to guard the San Bernardino Strait, thereby permitting the Seventh Fleet to concentrate on the Surigao Strait. There was no such covering force.

As the Japanese southern force neared Surigao Strait, most of the Seventh Fleet was waiting for them. Under direct command of Rear Admiral Jesse B. Oldendorf, there were six battleships (five of them survivors of Pearl Harbor), eight cruisers, destroyers, and patrol torpedo (PT) boats. PT boats stationed along the approaches to the strait sighted the enemy first and launched runs that proved to be ineffectual. Now alerted, destroyers that were ranged along both sides of the strait began torpedo attacks when the Japanese entered. They sank one battleship, damaged another, and sent four enemy destroyers to the bottom. U.S. battleships and cruisers, which had been steaming back and forth across the entrance, opened fire as soon as the remaining Japanese ships came within range. Only one Japanese cruiser and a destroyer managed to escape the way they had come, and the cruiser later was sunk by air attack.

The more powerful Japanese central force, commanded by Admiral Kurita Takeo, was composed of five battleships (two of them supers), twelve cruisers, and destroyers. It had lost two cruisers to submarine attacks on the first day and had retreated on October 24 after repeated attacks by planes from Halsey's carriers sank one superbattleship and damaged other ships. By the time Kurita changed course and started toward San Bernardino again, Halsey had taken off in pursuit of the enemy carriers. The Japanese were astounded when they steamed through the strait unopposed. They headed toward the American beachheads on the eastern coast of Leyte.

The only American ships offshore were a few destroyers and three groups of escort carriers. The latter were nothing more than merchant ships with flight decks on them. Intended primarily for antisubmarine duty, they were also used to provide air support for ground operations. Slow, unarmored, and practically unarmed, they were unsuited for any kind of surface engagements, let alone one against the powerful fleet bearing down on them. The commander of the first escort carrier group to spot the oncoming Japanese sensibly ordered his ships to flee, while sending planes and the destroyers to disrupt pursuit. Incredibly, the Japanese misidentified these small ships as fleet carriers and followed after them.

The ensuing battle between such unequal forces ended almost miraculously. Through a combination of good luck in the form of rain squalls that provided cover and the intrepid action of American destroyers and airmen, Kurita became confused and dispirited. Wildly exaggerating the strength he already faced and afraid that more American forces might appear at any time, he gave orders to retreat back through the San Bernardino Strait. A handful of baby carriers and destroyers had prevented the Japanese armada from ravaging the entire landing operation.

Meanwhile, despite pleas for help from the beleaguered ships facing Kurita, Halsey had continued in pursuit of the toothless Japanese carriers and sank all of them before turning back. In just three days, the Japanese had lost four carriers, three battleships, ten cruisers, and eleven destroyers. The United States had lost the large carrier *Princeton* to a single bomb hit that set off fires and explosions, and a number of smaller ships. The Battle of Leyte Gulf, the largest naval engagement in history, broke the spine of Japanese fleet strength.

On the last day of the battle, Japan had employed a new weapon that did not affect the outcome but had ominous implications for the future. This was the kamikazi, which, roughly translated, means "divine wind" and referred to a fortuitous typhoon that had prevented a Chinese invasion force from reaching Japan centuries earlier. Kamikazis were suicide units whose pilots would fly their bomb-laden aircraft directly into American ships, preferably aircraft carriers or troop transports. Kamikazis had a number of advantages: Little training was required, obsolete planes could be used, and they had to be blown out of the air to be stopped. Large-scale use of these squadrons against future landing operations, especially the anticipated invasion of Japan proper, was a dismal prospect. And their existence reinforced the American assumption that the Japanese were a fanatical race against whom the use of any means of destruction was justified.

American ground operations were no longer threatened by naval attack after the Battle of Leyte Gulf. The Japanese continued to send reinforcements from Luzon, however, via convoys to the port of Ormac on the west coast. Until beefed up by carrier-based planes in November, American air power was relatively ineffectual in stopping these convoys or in providing support for troops because monsoons rendered most airfields unusable. Ormoc, through which flowed most of the Japanese reinforcements and supplies, was the key to the Leyte campaign. Excessive caution on the part of the American ground commander delayed the advance on the city, giving the Japanese time to dig in along nearby heights. After much bloody fighting and several Japanese counterattacks, American troops finally took Ormoc by amphibious assault on December 10. Effective resistance ended within a few weeks, although some Japanese held out in the mountains for months.

Victory on Leyte had taken longer to achieve than MacArthur and other commanders had expected, and the invasion of Luzon, originally scheduled for December 20, was postponed to early January. But Japanese efforts to defend Leyte had cost them most of what remained of the Combined Fleet, and the troops expended there would not be available to fight on Luzon. Even before Leyte was secured, American forces had taken Mindoro, a smaller island just south of Luzon, to obtain forward

Signpost at a crossroads in Tacloban on Leyte reflects the GI's keen sense of humor and an equally sharp yearning for home, ca. 1944–1945. (National Archives photo no. W&C 1213)

air bases. Landings were virtually unopposed, although the invasion fleet had taken a battering from land-based kamikazis. By the end of 1944, therefore, the United States was poised for the final campaign in the Philippines, where they had suffered such a disastrous defeat in 1942.

SELECTED BIBLIOGRAPHY

Belote, James, and William Belote. *Titans of the Seas: The Development and Operations of American Carrier Forces During World War II* (New York: Harper & Row, 1975).

Buell, Thomas B. *The Quiet Warrior: A Biography of Admiral Raymond A. Spruance* (Boston: Little, Brown, 1974).

Cannon, M. Hamlin. *Leyte: The Return to the Philippines* (Washington, D.C.: Office of the Chief of Military History, Department of the Army, 1954).

Crowl, Philip A. *Campaign in the Marianas* (Washington, D.C.: Office of the Chief of Military History, Department of the Army, 1960).

Dexter, David. *The New Guinea Offensives* (Canberra: Australian War Memorial, 1961).

Dull, Paul. *A Battle History of the Imperial Japanese Navy* (Annapolis, Md.: U.S. Naval Institute, 1978).

Falk, Stanley W. *Decision at Leyte* (New York: Norton, 1966).

Halsey, William F., and Joseph Bryan. *Admiral Halsey's Story* (New York: Whittlesey House, 1947).

Hayes, Grace P. *The Joint Chiefs of Staff and the War Against Japan* (Annapolis, Md.: U.S. Naval Institute, 1982).

Hoffman, Carl W. *Saipan: The Beginning of the End* (Washington, D.C.: U.S. Marine Corps, 1950).

Hoyt, Edwin Palmer. *The Battle of Leyte Gulf: The Death Knell of the Japanese Fleet* (New York: Weybright & Talley, 1972).

Isley, Jeter A., and Philip A. Crowl. *The U.S. Marines and Amphibious War* (Princeton, N.J.: Princeton University Press, 1951).

McMillan, George. *The Old Breed: A History of the First Marine Division in World War II* (Washington, D.C.: Infantry Journal Press, 1949).

Miller, John. *Cartwheel: The Reduction of Rabaul* (Washington, D.C.: Office of the Chief of Military History, Department of the Army, 1959).

Reynolds, Clark G. *The Fast Carriers: The Forging of an Air Navy* (New York: McGraw-Hill, 1968).

Sherrod, Robert. *Tarawa: The Story of a Battle* (New York: Duell, Sloan and Pearce, 1954).

Walker, Alan S. *The Islands Campaign* (Canberra: Australian War Memorial, 1957).

Y'Blood, William T. *Red Sun Setting: The Battle of the Philippine Sea* (Annapolis, Md.: U.S. Naval Institute, 1980).

16
Japan Subdued (1945)

During the early months of 1945, the United States acquired the last bases deemed necessary for the invasion of Japan. By this time, U.S. submarines had virtually driven Japan's merchant marine from the seas, and B-29s were pounding its cities to rubble. Yet, the Japanese showed no signs of crumbling. They resisted American assaults as ferociously as they ever had and began inflicting even greater casualties by sending ever-larger waves of kamikazis against landing operations. Some Japanese officials began casting about for ways to end the conflict, but their freedom of action was limited by hard-liners who were determined to fight to the finish. American policymakers, aware that atomic bombs *might* be available by late summer, meanwhile had to proceed as though an invasion of the Japanese home islands would be necessary to end the war.

CONQUEST OF THE PHILIPPINES

On January 8, 1945, a massive armada of 1,000 ships moved into the Lingayen Gulf on the west coast of Luzon. Warships preceding them had taken a beating from land-based kamikazis, which came in low to escape radar detection. But such attacks diminished as the Japanese ran out of planes. Landings, which began on the morning of January 9, were virtually unopposed. They were carried out by General Walter Krueger's Sixth Army, with I Corps on the left and XIV Corps on the right. By nightfall, more than 50,000 men had gone ashore, and within the next few days, another 125,000 had landed along a 20-mile beachhead.

MacArthur, in overall command of the operation, went ashore on the first day. Apparently enamored of the publicity he had garnered at Leyte, he again waded in the last yards, though this time by choice. "The

decisive battle for the liberation of the Philippines and the control of
the Southwest Pacific is at hand," ran his first communiqué; "General
MacArthur is in personal command at the front and landed with his
assault troops." Actually, the general retired to his ship a few hours
later, where he remained for several days. When he did return to land,
however, he toured the various fronts extensively, at times under haz-
ardous conditions.

Japanese defenses on Luzon were commanded by General Yamashita
Tomoyuki, who had masterminded the campaign in Malaya at the
beginning of the war. Although many of his best troops had been sent
to Leyte over his protests, he still had about 275,000 men to defend
the island. As the shoreline could not be defended against massive naval
and air bombardment, Yamashita made no attempt to contest the landings.
He divided his forces into three parts. The *Shobo* group, the largest,
occupied the mountainous country of north Luzon. The *Kembu* group
was sent to shield the Clark air bases in the southwest, and the *Shimbu*
group took up positions east of Manila.

The mission of I Corps was to attack and seal off Yamashita's northern
Shobo group, thereby protecting the left flank of XIV Corps as it drove
south toward Manila and Clark Field. Although the Japanese fought
stubbornly to defend the air bases, they had made no preparations to
defend the city. When this became clear, MacArthur began badgering
Krueger to move ahead as quickly as possible. Krueger hesitated because
he feared his flanks were not yet secure and possibly because he suspected
MacArthur was influenced by personal, rather than military, considerations. MacArthur simply went around him, personally urging several
division commanders to create special battle groups and send them
racing for the city. One of these forces reached the outskirts of Manila
on February 3, whereupon MacArthur issued a communiqué announcing
the city's imminent liberation.

Yamashita had not intended to defend Manila. It lacked strategic value
and lay on an open plain unsuitable for defense. To avoid unnecessary
bloodshed, he had withdrawn occupation troops to the east. Against
Yamashita's wishes, the city's naval commander independently decided
to resist. Naval and marine personnel, together with a few army battalions
stranded there, were pressed into service. The unanticipated battle for
Manila, fought virtually block by block, resulted in heavy casualties
and great devastation. During its course, Japanese defenders ran amuck
among the civilian population, killing as many as 100,000 noncombatants.
Finally, on March 3, Manila was secured.

MacArthur's Luzon campaign has been highly praised by his admirers
and faulted by his critics. Some operations, a few involving combined
amphibious and airborne assaults, were well conceived and executed,

and he was adept at keeping the Japanese off balance. But other aspects appear less admirable. I Corps in the north slugged away at Yamashita's main force in a series of bloody battles reminiscent of the long Allied struggle up the boot of Italy. Indeed, the Shobo group held out to the end of the war. Instead of using the Eighth Army, commanded by General Robert Eichelberger, to help subdue Japanese forces in the north, MacArthur gave it the more dashing task of invading the southern islands, without authorization from the Joint Chiefs of Staff. Whether he acted out of the wish to become the "great liberator" or whether he was genuinely motivated by humanitarian concerns is open to conjecture. Probably it was a combination of both.

The recapture of the Philippines marked the end of large-scale operations in the southwest Pacific theater. Although the Japanese continued to fight in various parts of the archipelago, the repair and enlargement of Clark Field and restoration of harbor facilities at Manila Bay were well under way by April. The struggle for Luzon had been costly for the United States and catastrophic for the Japanese. More than 8,000 Americans had been killed; Japan lost nearly 200,000 men.

IWO JIMA

While the battle for Luzon still raged, U.S. forces assaulted Iwo Jima, a tiny island halfway between the Marianas and Japan. In Japanese hands, Iwo Jima provided airfields for attacks against the Marianas and against B-29s en route to their targets. Even when the bombers made time- and fuel-consuming detours, radar installations on the island enabled the Japanese to signal Tokyo of their approach. In American hands, the air bases could be used to provide long-range fighter escorts for the B-29s and emergency landing sites for those crippled in combat or by mechanical problems. Fully aware of the island's importance, the Japanese had constructed sophisticated fortifications all over the island and had garrisoned it with 20,000 of their best troops.

American commanders knew Iwo Jima would be well defended, but they underestimated what they would come up against. Beginning on February 16, the island was subjected to three days of intense naval and aerial bombardment. It was not enough. The marines had asked for ten days of fire support, but they were turned down on the grounds that naval forces were needed for carrier raids against the Japanese home islands. Originally, these raids were directed against airfields to prevent kamikazi attacks on the Iwo Jima operation, but the carriers stayed on to begin hitting Japanese factories. The latter mission appears to have been decided on primarily for political reasons. Put simply, the U.S. Army Air Forces were getting credit for "bringing the war home" to the Japanese, and the navy wanted a piece of the action. Some marines died unnecessarily as a result.

Iwo Jima, less than 5 miles long, is shaped like a pork chop. At its southern tip lies Mt. Suribachi, which had been converted into a fortress bristling with guns of all kinds. Running in a northeasterly direction, the island remains relatively narrow for about a quarter of its length, then widens to a depth of 2 miles across its "meaty" portion. The only suitable beaches were on the southeastern shore, directly under the guns of Suribachi. Landings were to be carried out by the Fourth and Fifth Marine divisions, with the Third Marines kept in reserve.

The first assault waves began heading for the beaches on the morning of February 19. Defensive fire at first was light, but it increased steadily as the morning wore on. The Fifth Marines, on the left, quickly drove across the narrow shank of the island, while the Fourth drove inland against the island's southernmost airfield. The beaches and the waters just offshore, however, became a slaughterhouse as the Japanese poured massive fire down on approaching landing craft and the men already ashore. Although 30,000 marines had landed by dusk, they had taken an appalling 2,000 casualties. The Japanese launched no night attacks but instead continued to ravage the beaches. Iwo Jima became hell in a very small place.

The next morning, the 28th Infantry Regiment of the Fifth Marines began assaulting Mt. Suribachi as other units continued punching inland. It took the marines three days of savage fighting to scrabble up the steep slopes of Suribachi. At last, on February 24, a group of men raised a tiny flag on its peak. Marines below cheered, and ships offshore sounded their horns, bells, and whistles. A few hours later, when a larger flag was put up, a civilian photographer was there to take what became one of the most famous pictures of the war. Unaccountably, a myth later developed that the event was "staged" solely for publicity purposes.

The Third Marines landed on the day Suribachi was captured, and all three divisions began moving north against the Japanese main lines. A campaign some hoped would be over in a few days lasted more than a month as the Japanese, fighting from mazes of concealed fortifications, contested every inch of ground. By the time it ended, only 200 survived out of the garrison of 20,000; the marines lost nearly 7,000 men killed and another 20,000 wounded. Naval construction battalions, known as the Seabees, had begun repairing the airfields as soon as they were overrun, and the first crippled B-29 landed weeks before the fighting was over. Well over 2,000 emergency landings had been made on Iwo Jima by the time the war ended.

Observer who spotted a machine gun nest finds its location on a map so he can send the information to artillery or mortars to wipe out the position, Iwo Jima, February 1945. (National Archives photo no. W&C 1218)

OKINAWA

Okinawa, the largest island of the Ryukyu chain, is only 350 miles from the southernmost Japanese home island of Kyushu. Part of the Japanese empire since the nineteenth century, it is nearly 70 miles long and varies in width from 2 to 18 miles. With two spacious harbors and plenty of level ground for airfields, it was intended to serve as the major staging area for the invasion of Japan.

The northern two-thirds of Okinawa is relatively open country; therefore, Japanese defenses were concentrated in the mountainous southern region. Commanded by General Ushijima Mitsuru, the Japanese troops had constructed three strong defensive lines across the island. Ushijima had decided not to contest the landings on the beaches but to wait behind his fortifications. If kamikazis operating from Japan could smash the support fleet offshore, he hoped to chew up and destroy the ground forces left stranded.

In late March, an enormous flotilla of nearly 1,200 ships, protected by most of the Fifth Fleet, converged on the island. After preliminary bombardment, landings began on April 1. They were carried out by the newly created Tenth Army, a mixed force of veteran army and marine

Flag raising on Iwo Jima, February 23, 1945. (National Archives photo no. W&C 1221)

divisions commanded by General Simon B. Buckner. By nightfall, more than 50,000 troops were ashore and 100,000 more would follow in the next few days. There was little fighting at first, leading some to hope the Japanese were giving in.

Prior to the landings, Admiral Mitscher's Task Force 38 had conducted carrier attacks on fields in the home islands to disrupt Japanese air operations against Okinawa. Four U.S. flattops had been badly damaged in the process, a sobering example of how effective kamikazis could be. By April 6, the Japanese had recovered sufficiently to send nearly 700 aircraft against Okinawa, half of them kamikazis. They struck the ships offshore in swarms, causing considerable damage to a number of

The *Bunker Hill*, after being hit by two kamikazes in thirty seconds on May 11, 1945, off Kyushu. Dead: 372; wounded: 264. (National Archives photo no. W&C 980)

vessels and sinking two precious ammunition ships. During the following weeks, the Japanese mounted ten massive attacks and countless smaller ones against the support ships and installations on the island. The U.S. Navy lost about 5,000 men killed and an equal number wounded.

The Japanese also sent what amounted to a kamikazi naval expedition against Okinawa. On the day of the first large-scale air raid, the superbattleship *Yamato*, accompanied by a cruiser and eight destroyers, emerged from Japanese home waters. Carrying only enough fuel to get there, *Yamato's* mission was to attack the ships offshore, then plunge onto the beach where it would become a giant steel fortress boasting, among other weaponry, huge 18-inch guns. However, the battleship and its escort never had a chance of reaching their destination. Spotted immediately by U.S. submarines, *Yamato* was attacked by hundreds of bombers and torpedo planes from Mitscher's carriers. The mighty ship was torn apart by repeated hits, and it sank with a great loss of life. Only four destroyers got away.

Meanwhile, on Okinawa, American forces began running up against the first Japanese line of defense along the Kakazu Ridge. There, they slowed down, then came to a halt against fierce opposition. In mid-April, the Japanese launched several counterattacks, which in turn failed to dislodge the Americans. On April 18, General Buckner renewed the offensive, but it, too, bogged down. Instead of a walkover, Okinawa was turning into a bloody stalemate. And the kamikazis continued to take a terrible toll of American ships supporting the operation.

Relations between the services, which had started out well, began turning sour. The navy and marines grew impatient with Buckner's methodical approach and began urging him to mount an amphibious assault behind enemy lines. Buckner refused, citing such things as the loss of the ammunition ships that, he claimed, precluded supplying two separate operations. At one point, Admiral Nimitz, appalled at the rate of ships being sunk, visited Okinawa to warn Buckner that he must speed up the advance or be replaced.

Nimitz also clashed with the U.S. Army Air Forces. The B-29s, now commanded by General Curtis LeMay, had been ordered to switch their attacks from cities to landing fields in order to hamper Japanese air operations against Okinawa. When Nimitz requested that the heavy bombers continue this mission, LeMay protested that his planes should be permitted to resume bombing industrial targets. Nimitz bucked the argument back to Admiral King in Washington, who resolved the issue in Nimitz's favor by threatening to take his ships out of Okinawan waters and let the army fend for itself.

The battle for Okinawa went on. In late April, American troops broke through the Kakazu complex, only to have the Japanese retreat a few miles to a previously prepared line anchored at the town of Shuri. The Shuri line held out for a month before being broken, with both sides taking heavy casualties. The final act began on June 17 when American units, spearheaded by flamethrowing tanks, overran Japanese positions on the southern tip of the island. On June 22, the island at last was declared secure, although pockets of resistance held out for weeks.

Okinawa had been a costly venture. Almost the entire Japanese garrison of more than 100,000 men had been killed, including an unknown number sealed up in caves and tunnels. There were also about 80,000 Okinawan civilian casualties. American ground forces suffered nearly 8,000 dead and more than 30,000 wounded, in addition to the 10,000 navy casualties. Such stubborn dedication to a losing cause had dismaying implications for the future, indicating as it did that the Japanese fighting spirit had remained undiminished. The Japanese troops could be expected to defend their home islands with at least equal ferocity, and thousands of kamikazis operating at short ranges would be even more devastating than at Okinawa.

STRANGULATION AT SEA AND FROM THE AIR

The Japanese Empire often was likened to a gigantic octopus, with its head in the home islands and its tentacles coiling around areas seized by conquest. Successive campaigns had chopped off many of the tentacles but only at great cost. Striking at the body of the beast, however, might destroy its ability to continue struggling. As a densely populated island nation lacking virtually all the natural resources required to sustain its economy, Japan was particularly vulnerable to such a strategy. Submarines and B-29s would be the instruments used.

American submariners initially regarded enemy warships as their main targets. Such vessels continued to be looked upon as prizes—there was more satisfaction in sinking a battleship than a freighter, after all—and submarines eventually counted four aircraft carriers among their kills. They also performed invaluable service as pickets, frequently relaying vitally needed information about Japanese fleet movements. But their role in strangling Japanese supply lines probably had the most profound effect on the course of the war.

Japan's merchant marine quickly became strained after the war began because of the need to supply its newly acquired possessions scattered across the western Pacific. U.S. submarines at first were unable to exploit the situation for a number of reasons: There were not enough boats, training methods were inadequate, and their torpedoes were defective. These drawbacks eventually were remedied, although some took an unconscionable length of time. Reliable torpedoes, for instance, did not become available in quantities until September 1943.

The submarine offensive began achieving truly awesome results in 1944. More and better boats, improved tactics such as operating in "wolf packs," and reliable torpedoes combined to produce the devastation. Advances across the Pacific also provided forward bases from which U.S. submarines could intercept Japanese convoys based on information provided by message decrypts. More tonnage was sunk in 1944 than had been accounted for since the war began. Between January and June

Standing in the grassy sod bordering row upon row of white crosses in an American
cemetery, two Coast Guardsmen pay silent homage to the memory of a fellow Coast
Guardsman who lost his life in action in the Ryukyu Islands, ca. 1945. (National Archives
photo no. W&C 1352)

of that year, oil imports were cut in half, and they continued to diminish. By spring 1945, there were so few targets available on the high seas that submarines began serving other purposes, such as rescuing the survivors of ditched aircraft. The air force helped to cut alternative supply lines by dropping mines at various chokepoints in inland waters.

The air campaign against Japan also began inauspiciously. Flying from distant fields in China, B-29s began hitting the home islands and other targets during the summer of 1944 with disappointing results. Even when operations were shifted from China to the Marianas, permitting much larger numbers of planes to be used, the B-29s achieved little in comparison with the resources employed. And the cost in planes was high. Many were lost to Japanese fighters and antiaircraft fire, and B-29s were also plagued at first by an unusual number of mechanical problems.

Larger, faster, and capable of carrying a heavier bomb load than the B-17s, B-29s had been designed for high-level precision bombing. As in Europe, such bombing proved less than precise in combat. The skies over Japan presented unique difficulties. Impenetrable clouds often obscured targets, and varying wind currents at different altitudes rendered even the most sophisticated bombsights virtually useless. In January 1945, General LeMay, who had performed impressively in Europe, was named to command the B-29s in hopes of improving their effectiveness. However, he failed to alter the situation significantly, despite instituting a number of reforms, such as altering formation patterns.

Air force generals and their supporters had predicted enormous dividends from strategic bombing. Earlier, some had boasted that it would bring Germany to its knees without the need for invasion. Such claims proved groundless, and now their credibility was in jeopardy again. Thousands of soldiers, sailors, and marines had died fighting for barren islands to provide bases for air operations against Japan. Their sacrifices would have been in vain if the bombers could produce no better results than they had so far, and the future of strategic bombing would be called into question.

Frustrated by the skimpy effects produced by conventional methods, LeMay decided to "throw away the book," as he put it. Instead of high-altitude, daylight bombing, he opted for low-level nighttime attacks using incendiaries, rather than high explosives. Most Japanese structures were made of wood and other highly inflammable materials. Recently developed incendiaries, containing a devilish concoction of jellied gasoline called napalm, would be used. As Japanese night fighters were few and ineffective, LeMay even had his bombers stripped of weapons and gunners to permit heavier payloads.

On the night of March 9, more than 300 B-29s firebombed the Shitimachi section of Tokyo. Results were horrifyingly effective as the entire area turned into a raging inferno, with brisk winds feeding flames that reached hundreds of feet in the air. Inhabitants were burned to death, asphyxiated, or boiled like lobsters when they sought sanctuary in pools or water tanks. Japanese firefighting techniques, primitive at best, were useless against such a holocaust. By the time it was over, 16 square miles of the most densely populated city in the world had been set aflame. As many as 100,000 Japanese died, many more were wounded, and 1 million were rendered homeless.

LeMay's innovation gave a new meaning to strategic bombing. Even more devastating than the saturation attacks against German cities such as Dresden, subsequent raids literally burned Japanese urban centers to the ground. Priority was given to those with greater concentrations of industry, but when they were destroyed, planners simply worked down the list. Americans who had long since accepted the bombing of German cities as a legitimate act of war had little difficulty adjusting to the new level of destruction being visited upon the Japanese. They had started the war, after all, and deserved what they got. Japan's industrial output was being diminished, which lessened the military's capacity to resist Allied advances. Finally, if the punishment inflicted on Japan caused it to surrender before an invasion was necessary, the American lives that would be saved would make it all worthwhile. War creates its own morality.

JAPAN SEEKS PEACE WITHOUT DEFEAT

Japan's cause grew increasingly hopeless during the first six months of 1945. That nation's loss of the Philippines and Okinawa had placed the United States in a position to invade the home islands. Meanwhile, the naval blockade was strangling Japan's industry, and its cities were being incinerated by bombing raids. In April, the Soviet Union ominously served notice to Tokyo that it would not renew the nonaggression pact. And Hitler's defeat one month later meant that the Allies could devote all of their considerable resources to winning the Pacific war.

A faction within the Japanese government had been searching for a means to end the conflict since 1944. In April 1945, Baron Suzuki Kantaro, a retired admiral, was appointed premier with the understanding that he would try to end the war in a manner consistent with honor. There was the rub. Japanese hard-liners, especially in the army, steadfastly refused to admit the war was lost. All along, they had predicted that American resolve was so fragile that a major Japanese victory would cause Washington to accept a negotiated peace, rather than insist on unconditional surrender. Even after Okinawa fell, the generals did not soften. Now, they claimed to welcome an invasion of the home islands for it was there that the crushing blow would be administered to the enemy by a determined army, backed by the entire civilian population. The military still exercised such influence that Suzuki had to conceal his intentions by professing to be committed to achieving victory.

Suzuki and his like-minded foreign minister, Togo Shigenori, concocted a scheme designed to spare Japan the consequences of defeat. With the approval of Emperor Hirohito, they attempted to enlist the Soviet Union as an intermediary. If offered sufficient inducements, they hoped, Stalin might gain a negotiated peace for the Japanese that would avoid the humiliation of surrender. The concessions they were prepared to make included relinquishing control of several strategic islands and a dominant position in Manchuria, most of which had been obtained from Russia after the Russo-Japanese war of 1904–1905. To swing the deal, they proposed sending Prince Konoye to meet with top Soviet leaders in Moscow.

The Suzuki-Togo initiative was as unrealistic as the hard-liners' vision of averting disaster by winning a decisive battle for the homeland. In early July, when the Japanese ambassador in Moscow was advised to tell the Soviets that Japan had no intention of trying to retain territories seized by conquest, he reacted with disbelief. He ridiculed the notion of offering to give up areas "we have already lost" and warned against approaching the Soviets "with pretty little phrases devoid of all connection with reality." He offered a piece of simple advice: If the government sought peace "we should inquire what the peace conditions will be."

The ambassador was correct in believing that the United States would refuse to stop the war in place, even if Moscow had been inclined to make such a proposal. President Roosevelt had announced the doctrine of unconditional surrender in 1943 and had shown no signs of retreating from it by the time of his death in April 1945. That the new president, Harry S. Truman, would repudiate the established policy of his predecessor was out of the question. What none of the Japanese officials knew was that their offer to the Soviet Union was worthless. Roosevelt already had agreed to make the same concessions to the Soviets in return for Stalin's pledge to join the war against Japan approximately three months after V-E Day. And whereas the United States was in a position to deliver, Japan most assuredly was not.

The Japanese cable traffic between Moscow and Tokyo was being monitored in the United States, and some writers have therefore criticized American leaders for not trying to follow up Japanese peace feelers in order to end the war sooner. It is more accurate to say that one of the reasons they did not do so was precisely *because* they were reading the decrypted messages. Suzuki and Togo were trying to cut a deal that would enable Japan to survive intact after almost four years of a bloody war that it had started. An American overture to modify unconditional surrender at that point would have encouraged the Japanese to hold out for a better deal.

THE ATOMIC BOMB AND THE POTSDAM DECLARATION

In mid-July, Allied leaders met at Potsdam, a suburb of Berlin. Although the conference was devoted primarily to European affairs, Truman, Churchill (replaced halfway through by Clement Attlee as a result of British elections), and Stalin discussed prosecution of the war against Japan. The Soviet leader renewed his pledge to join the conflict, although now with some reservations as to timing. Truman later secured British approval of what became known as the Potsdam Declaration, an ultimatum to the Japanese calling upon them to surrender immediately or face "prompt and utter destruction." The president wrote in his diary that he was "sure they will not do that [surrender], but we will have given them the chance." China was invited to sign, though the Soviet Union was not because it was then still at peace with Japan. The document was issued on July 26.

On July 16, only hours before the conference began, Truman had received word that an atomic device had been successfully tested at a remote desert site in New Mexico. Subsequent reports indicated that the size of the explosion far exceeded estimates. A few days before issuing the Potsdam Declaration, Truman learned that the first atomic bomb would be ready in two weeks. He thereupon issued orders to drop it as soon after August 3 as weather permitted. He told Secretary of War Stimson that these orders would stand unless he, the president, determined that Japan's reply to the Potsdam Declaration was acceptable.

Truman and his advisers realized that the Japanese willingness to surrender might hinge on whether they could retain their emperor, the living embodiment of their national polity. Accordingly, the Potsdam Declaration was kept vague on that issue. The emperor was nowhere mentioned specifically in the document, and its final point called for unconditional surrender "of all Japanese armed forces," rather than of the nation. The vagueness was deliberate: If there were to be any deviation from unconditional surrender, it must not appear as a sign of eroded American will but as a generous gesture to a defeated enemy.

Japanese leaders began to discuss how to answer the declaration the day after it was released. Suzuki and Togo proposed stalling. They wished for time to seek clarification of the ultimatum and to step up efforts to secure Soviet mediation. The hard-liners, still claiming to welcome an invasion, insisted on outright rejection. Suzuki and Togo prevailed, or so it seemed, in gaining agreement to make no reply at all.

In making his case for delay, Suzuki had argued that the proper response to the Potsdam Declaration was to *mokusatsu* it, by which he meant withholding comment at the time. Unfortunately, the word has harsher connotations, among them "to kill with silent contempt." When an account of the meeting was leaked to the press, "mokusatsu" was used in its most belligerent sense. The hard-liners apparently prevented Suzuki from trying to clarify the issue because it would appear to constitute a face-losing retreat. Truman, lacking knowledge of what actually had gone on in the meeting, had no choice but to regard the Japanese response as a flat rejection of the Potsdam Declaration.

HIROSHIMA AND NAGASAKI

Initially, U.S. leaders feared that Germany, where nuclear fission had been discovered in 1938, would be the first nation to construct atomic bombs and use them. But early in the war, the United States had launched a massive program to construct such weapons. And by 1943, committees formed to study the subject recommended that Japan, rather than Germany, should be the target if the United States developed and decided to use an atomic weapon. They reasoned that if Hitler already possessed these weapons, he would retaliate, or a dud might be recovered and provide German scientists with the necessary information to construct their own. The Japanese were considered a much safer bet because it was correctly assumed that they had no viable program of their own.

In April 1945, a new committee of scientists and top government officials was formed to advise the president on atomic matters. There was no real debate over *whether* to use the bomb when it became available; the question was *how*. Three options were considered: staging a demonstration in an uninhabited area, to which Japanese representatives would be invited; bombing a city in Japan, but only after giving a warning so that it could be evacuated; and bombing without warning.

The first option was rejected because a dud would make the U.S. threat appear ridiculous, and even an impressive explosion would fail to sway the Japanese military. The second option also had drawbacks: A dud would be just as embarrassing, and the Japanese might move American prisoners of war into the designated area or try to destroy the mission in flight. The committee's unanimous recommendation was that "the bomb should be used against Japan as soon as possible, that it be used on a war plant surrounded by workers' homes, and that it be used without prior warning."

In June, Truman had approved the Joint Chiefs of Staff's unanimous recommendation for the invasion of Japan. It was to proceed in two phases: OLYMPIC provided for landings on the southern island of Kyushu on November 1, and, assuming success, CORONET entailed landings on the main island of Honshu on March 1, 1946. He later wrote that military advisers had predicted the United States might sustain as many as a million casualties before Japan was defeated. A few recent writers have challenged that figure as too high, but there is no question that Truman thought casualties would be heavy. He told the joint chiefs that he hoped to avoid another Okinawa "from one end of Japan to the other," and at Potsdam, he complained to Churchill "of the terrible responsibilities that rested upon him in regard to the unlimited effusion of American blood." The Japanese, after all, had more than 2 million regular troops and 10,000 kamikazis to defend the home islands. The use of atomic bombs, he hoped, would render an invasion unnecessary.

Truman has been faulted for dropping the bombs when all he had to do was await Japan's collapse, which he must have known was imminent. The source most often cited to "prove" this allegation is the Strategic Bombing Survey, conducted after the war, that stated that "Japan would have surrendered even if the atomic bombs had not been dropped, even if Russia had not entered the war, and even if no invasion had been planned or contemplated." But to criticize him on the basis of a document that did not exist at the time he made his decision is to misuse history. Even if it did exist, its conclusion rested on the assumption that conventional bombing raids would continue for months. Such operations would have inflicted far greater casualties on Japan than did the atomic bombs.

Truman had to proceed on a worst-case basis, and there was reason for him to do so. Air force generals had predicted that bombing alone would defeat the Germans, yet the struggle had continued until Hitler's death in his bunker. Why expect anything less from the Japanese? The bloodbath at Okinawa appeared to be a preview of coming attractions, and Truman naturally shrank from repeating that dreadful experience "from one end of Japan to the other." And Tokyo's response to the Potsdam Declaration made it appear that that was precisely what was in store.

Another charge against Truman is that he did not signal the Japanese that they might be permitted to retain the emperor in some capacity. Had that been done, it is alleged, the moderates might have prevailed in securing agreement to a conditional surrender. But the wording of the Potsdam Declaration *was* the signal, calling only for the unconditional surrender of the armed forces, rather than of the nation. When the

Japanese merely stepped up efforts to secure Soviet help, instead of making overtures to the United States for a favorable interpretation of the declaration with regard to the emperor, Truman could only conclude that the hard-liners were still in control. An American initiative on the matter would have strengthened the hard-liners argument that U.S. resolve was weakening and that even better terms could be gotten by holding out.

A few hours after midnight on August 6, three B-29s took off from Tinian in the Marianas. One of the planes, *Enola Gay*, piloted by Colonel Paul W. Tibbets, carried an atomic bomb referred to as "Little Boy." The two other aircraft contained cameras and various kinds of scientific equipment. As part of the 509th Composite Group, a top-secret unit specially formed for the task, the crews had practiced dropping simulated atomic bombs for months. Hiroshima had been designated the primary target, but the mission was to proceed to an alternate site if cloud cover was too heavy. Shortly before 8:00 A.M., word was received that the skies over Hiroshima were clear. At 8:05, the bombardier took over control of the plane for its run, and "Little Boy" was dropped ten minutes later.

Set to detonate by a barometric pressure device, the bomb exploded 2,000 feet above the city in a blinding flash quickly followed by an enormous shock wave. A fireball hotter than the sun incinerated hundreds of square blocks, killing tens of thousands of people. Colonel Tibbets later remembered thinking that below the mushroom cloud that was billowing up, the area resembled a gigantic boiling tar pot: "It was black and boiling underneath with a steam haze on top of it." Nearly 100,000 people died instantly, thousands more from burns and radiation poisoning over the next few weeks, and still more thousands would die prematurely in the following years from long-term radiation effects.

A few hours after the raid, the White House issued a release stating that an atomic bomb had been used against the Japanese and that "if they do not now accept our terms, they can expect a rain of ruin from the air, the like of which has never been seen on this earth." When no response was forthcoming from Tokyo, another B-29 named *Bock's Car* took off from Tinian on August 9. It carried "Fat Man," a bomb made of plutonium instead of the uranium that had been used in "Little Boy." Kokura was the primary target, but heavy clouds over the city resulted in a switch to Nagasaki. "Fat Man," dropped at 11:00 A.M., caused fewer casualties than its predecessor because it was set to explode on impact and the effect was contained by hilly terrain. Still, more than 35,000 Japanese perished. The atomic age had begun with a vengeance.

A dense column of smoke rises more than 60,000 feet into the air over the Japanese port of Nagasaki, the result of the second atomic bomb ever used in warfare, which was dropped on the industrial center on August 8, 1945, from a U.S. B-29 Superfortress. (National Archives photo no. W&C 1242)

JAPAN SURRENDERS

Reports of Hiroshima's destruction reached Tokyo within an hour, but they provided few details. At dawn the next morning, word was received that "the whole city of Hiroshima was destroyed by a single bomb." A cabinet meeting was held later that day. Moderates hoped the catastrophe would swing support toward accepting the Potsdam Declaration, with the qualification that the emperor be retained. Some thought the military might be more inclined to bow to superior technology without having to admit defeat on the battlefield. They were mistaken. The hard-liners professed to doubt that the bomb was atomic and claimed that, even if it were, adverse world opinion would prevent the United States from dropping another. They insisted on conditions involving the method of surrender, terms of occupation, and treatment of war criminals that the moderates knew would be unacceptable. The meeting adjourned without agreement.

The Supreme Council for the Direction of the War met two days later. By this time, the Soviets had declared war on Japan and were advancing rapidly against depleted Japanese forces in Manchuria. While the meeting was in session, word arrived that another bomb had been dropped on Nagasaki. The militarists still refused to bend and went on claiming that a decisive battle for the homeland would force the Allies to negotiate. When that session failed to break the deadlock, moderates arranged for an imperial conference with the emperor later in the day. Following his personal plea for peace, a decision was reached to accept the Potsdam Declaration, with the proviso that it "does not comprise any demand which prejudices the prerogatives of His Majesty as a Sovereign Ruler."

Japan's response, broadcast by radio, stirred debate in Washington. When he learned of it early in the morning of August 10, President Truman summoned his closest advisers to the White House. Secretary of War Stimson, supported by Admiral William D. Leahy, favored accepting the proposal to avoid chaos in Japan and to facilitate an orderly surrender. Japanese troops in the field, they argued, would lay down their arms only under direct order of the emperor.

Secretary of State James F. Byrnes led the argument for rejection. Although those familiar with the Japanese political system knew the emperor's role was limited, American propaganda during the war had lumped Hirohito with Hitler and Mussolini as the leaders of the Axis powers. Why should he escape punishment? Furthermore, Byrnes pointed out, accepting anything short of unconditional surrender would appear to be a betrayal of Roosevelt's legacy and might result in the "crucifixion of the president."

The meeting ended in compromise. Byrnes drafted a reply that agreed to the retention of the emperor but demanded that his authority "shall be subject to the Supreme Commander of the Allied Powers," a post to which General MacArthur soon would be named. In his draft message, Byrnes restated a provision of the Potsdam Declaration stipulating that the "ultimate" form of government would be decided "by the freely expressed will of the Japanese people." This placed the Allies in the position of dictating terms, and it was intended to deflect criticism that the system responsible for the war was being left in place. After securing the approval of Great Britain, China, and the Soviet Union, Truman had the message conveyed to Tokyo.

The compromise offer met furious resistance in Japan. The hard-liners pronounced it totally unacceptable and continued their litany of preserving honor by a last, great battle on the shores of Japan. Even Premier Suzuki balked. But Foreign Minister Togo, expressing his own apprehensions, pleaded that it was the best they could hope to get. Only the emperor's second personal intervention broke the stalemate. Shortly after 4:00 Washington time on the afternoon of August 14, American time, Truman learned of Japan's capitulation through an intercepted cable to neutral Switzerland. A Swiss official formally presented the Japanese reply.

There has been much debate over the role of atomic bombs in causing Japan's surrender. Some have minimized it, emphasizing instead the battlefield defeats, naval blockade, conventional bombing, and Soviet entry. All of these factors would have defeated Japan eventually, of course, but the bombing of Hiroshima and Nagasaki caused the war to end when it did, not weeks or months later. When informed that a new type of bomb had destroyed Hiroshima, Hirohito replied that "we must put an end to the war as speedily as possible so that this tragedy will not be repeated." His influence in the end proved decisive. But admiration for his conduct must be tempered by the fact that he did not use his influence to prevent Japan from embarking on war in the first place.

A few Japanese diehards, mostly junior officers, refused to abide by the verdict. Learning that the emperor was scheduled to record a surrender speech that would be broadcast the next day, they embarked on a rampage to find and destroy the recording and to assassinate those officials who had so betrayed Japanese honor. The uprising was quickly put down, and the record was played as scheduled at noon on August 15. Millions of awed Japanese listened to the sacred voice they had never heard before call upon them to accept their fate. Avoiding words such as "defeat" or "surrender," Hirohito told them that, because the "war situation has developed not necessarily to our advantage . . . the unendurable must be endured." Although some acts of defiance took place, the Japanese people and military forces obeyed their emperor.

V-J Day in New York City, August 15, 1945. Crowds gather in Times Square to celebrate the surrender of Japan. (National Archives photo no. W&C 1359)

Word of Japan's surrender touched off delirious celebrations in those Allied nations engaged in the Pacific war. Huge crowds swarmed into Times Square in New York, and similar demonstrations took place across the nation. People cheered and sang for those who would be coming home and wept for those who would not. Perhaps no one felt greater joy than the servicemen who were scheduled to take part in the final assault against Japan. Young men already training in the Philippines and on Okinawa and the thousands more slated for transfer from the European theaters to the Pacific rejoiced at their deliverance from the threat of death or maiming.

The formal surrender ceremony took place in Tokyo Bay on the morning of September 2. U.S. and Allied warships filled the harbor. One by one, Allied delegations came aboard the battleship *Missouri* until the quarterdeck was crowded with men wearing a bewildering variety of uniforms. The ship's crew had swarmed all over the superstructure to witness the historic event. Finally, the Japanese came aboard—military officers in full uniform but without swords, civilian officials in top hats, cutaway coats, and striped trousers. Shortly after 9:00 A.M., General MacArthur appeared on deck, flanked by admirals Nimitz and Halsey.

Spectators and photographers pick vantage spots on the deck of the *Missouri* in Tokyo Bay to witness the formal Japanese surrender proceedings, September 2, 1945. (National Archives photo no. W&C 1361)

Striding to the microphones, MacArthur began reading from a single sheet of paper.

The theme of his brief address was reconciliation. This was a time to put aside past hatreds, he said, in order to cooperate in fulfilling a higher duty toward humanity. "It is my earnest hope, and indeed the hope of all mankind," he stated, "that from this solemn occasion a better world shall emerge out of the blood and carnage of the past—

a world dedicated to the dignity of man and the fulfillment of his most cherished wish for freedom, tolerance and justice."

When he finished, he signaled the Japanese to approach the mess table on which the surrender documents lay. After a few moments of confusion about where to sign, they finished and were followed by representatives of nine Allied powers, including Admiral Nimitz for the United States. MacArthur, as supreme commander, was the last to sign. Using five pens to complete the task, he handed one to the emaciated General Wainwright, only recently liberated by the Russians from a Japanese prison camp in Manchuria. Then MacArthur rose from the table to announce that "these proceedings are now closed."

As the Japanese were being piped off ship and representatives of the Allied nations began congratulating one another, the first waves of nearly 2,000 American planes appeared overhead. But MacArthur was not yet finished. He returned to the microphones to broadcast a message to the American people, beginning, "Today the guns are silent." After reviewing the tragedy of war and emphasizing the need to build a peaceful world, he closed with a tribute to those who had served: "And so, my fellow countrymen, today I report to you that your sons and daughters have served you well and faithfully. . . . They are homeward bound—take care of them."

SELECTED BIBLIOGRAPHY

Belote, James, and William Belote. *Typhoon of Steel: The Battle for Okinawa* (New York: Harper & Row, 1970).

Berger, Carl. *B–29: The Superfortress* (New York: Ballantine, 1970).

Bernstein, Barton J. *The Atomic Bomb: The Critical Issues* (Boston: Little, Brown, 1976).

Blair, Clay, Jr. *Silent Victory: The U.S. Submarine War Against Japan* (Philadelphia, Pa.: J. B. Lippincott, 1975).

Brooks, Lester. *Behind Japan's Surrender: The Secret Struggle That Ended an Empire* (New York: McGraw-Hill, 1968).

Bundy, McGeorge. *Danger and Survival: Choices About the Bomb in the First Fifty Years* (New York: Random House, 1988).

Butow, Robert J.C. *Japan's Decision to Surrender* (Stanford, Calif.: Stanford University Press, 1954).

Feis, Herbert. *The Atom Bomb and the End of World War II* (Princeton, N.J.: Princeton University Press, 1966).

Herken, Gregg. *The Winning Weapon: The Atomic Bomb in the Cold War, 1945–1950* (New York: Knopf, 1980).

———. *Counsels of War* (New York: Knopf, 1985).

Holmes, W. J. *Undersea Victory: The Influence of Submarine Operations in the Pacific* (Garden City, N.Y.: Doubleday, 1966).

Jones, Vincent C. *Manhattan: The Army and the Atomic Bomb* (Washington, D.C.: Center of Military History, United States Army, 1986).

Leahy, William D. *I Was There* (New York: Whittlesey House, 1950).

Maddox, Robert James. *From War to Cold War: The Education of Harry S. Truman* (Boulder, Colo.: Westview, 1988).

Mee, Charles L., Jr. *Meeting at Potsdam* (New York: M. Evans, 1975).

Newcomb, Richard F. *Iwo Jima* (New York: Holt, Rinehart and Winston, 1965).

Rhodes, Richard. *The Making of the Atomic Bomb* (New York: Simon & Schuster, 1987).

Shaw, Henry I., Jr. *Victory and Occupation* (Washington, D.C.: U.S. Marine Corps, 1968).

Sherwin, Martin. *A World Destroyed: The Atomic Bomb and the Grand Alliance* (New York: Knopf, 1975).

Sigal, Leon V. *Fighting to a Finish: The Politics of War Termination in the United States and Japan, 1945* (Ithaca, N.Y.: Cornell University Press, 1988).

Smith, Robert Ross. *Triumph in the Philippines* (Washington, D.C.: Department of the Army, 1963).

United States Strategic Bombing Survey. *Japan's Struggle to End the War* (Washington, D.C.: Government Printing Office, 1946).

17
Wartime Diplomacy

World War II had begun less than twenty-one years after what President Woodrow Wilson had called "the war to end all wars" came to a close with the armistice of November 1918. Seeds of the later conflict had been planted by the kind of settlement Allied statesmen had formulated at the Versailles conference and by the failure of the League of Nations to halt aggression in the intervening years. The enormous sacrifices of the present war could only be justified if they resulted in lasting peace, rather than just another lull before fighting began again. The question was whether the wartime coalition would last. If it did, the chances of another large-scale confrontation would be small, if it did not, a constant threat to humanity would prevail.

THE SOVIET CONNECTION

The Grand Alliance—the United States, Great Britain, and the Soviet Union—was a strange partnership because the two Western nations had little in common with the Soviet Union beyond the need to defeat their mutual enemies. Coalitions usually unravel when the common threat is ended, and this one was inherently less stable than most. The United States and Great Britain had opposed the Communists after they had seized power in Russia in 1917, and relations in the following years had been characterized by suspicion and hostility. This was especially true after the Soviets signed the nonaggression pact with Hitler, participated in the destruction of Poland, and invaded Finland in 1939. Despite past quarrels and hugely different political and economic systems, President Roosevelt considered it his most important diplomatic task to convince Stalin of Anglo-American goodwill and to persuade him that Soviet interests would best be served by ongoing collaboration.

Roosevelt revealed his desire to secure the Soviets' trust in numerous ways. He insisted that they be given top priority with regard to lend-lease supplies, and he constantly prodded subordinates to meet Soviet demands. He did so because of the burden they bore against Nazi Germany, but he also wanted to impress them with American earnestness. His unfortunate promise to Foreign Minister Molotov in the spring of 1942 that a second front would be opened later that year constituted another example. The failure to redeem his pledge damaged his cause, but the intent was there. His statement of the unconditional surrender formula was partly intended to compensate for his failure to establish a second front by assuring Stalin that his Western partners would not negotiate separately with Hitler. Finally, the deferential way he treated Stalin in cabled messages and in personal meetings was calculated to forge a close personal relationship in which FDR set great store.

Roosevelt shared President Wilson's enthusiasm for a world organization but not his reliance upon collective security. Disillusioned by the failure of the League of Nations, FDR had become convinced that only the large nations possessed the ability to take prompt and effective action against aggression. The world body he envisioned would be open to all, but decisions involving steps such as a blockade or the resort to arms would be reserved for a council made up of the United States, Great Britain, the Soviet Union, and China (which he hoped would overcome its weakness). These "four policemen," to use his phrase, would enforce peace throughout the world. The success of what would become known as the United Nations depended upon full Soviet cooperation.

THE TEHERAN CONFERENCE

Stalin had declined to attend the Casablanca Conference on the grounds that he was needed at home to manage the war effort. Roosevelt finally had a chance to meet him at the Teheran Conference, which began in late November 1943. Sure of his own persuasiveness, the president believed he could convince Stalin of America's sincerity. FDR's much-vaunted charm does not translate well in printed accounts; it consisted largely of jokes and quips, often at Churchill's expense. Stalin's responses led him to believe he had succeeded, and he later told an aide that the more he teased the prime minister, the more Stalin warmed up, until at last he "broke into a deep, heavy guffaw. . . . The ice was broken and we talked like men and brothers." That Roosevelt succeeded in doing anything other than encouraging Stalin to exploit Anglo-American differences is unlikely.

Aside from the decision to launch the much-delayed cross-channel invasion by the spring of 1944, most of the discussions at Teheran were exploratory. They did, however, permit all parties to state their positions on issues that would have to be negotiated into firm agreements later. Roosevelt also took the opportunity to informally convey to Stalin his ideas about a United Nations. Although the talks were cordial for the most part, they revealed some differences that would emerge to undermine solidarity within the Grand Alliance.

With regard to Europe, questions of policy toward Germany and Poland dominated the conversations. All three leaders agreed that nazism and militarism would have to be uprooted and that Germany must be made to pay for the destruction it caused. In addition, all favored some sort of dismemberment to keep Germany weak, but they differed over how radically this should be carried out.

Poland caused more controversy. Stalin made it clear that he intended to insist upon a Soviet-Polish boundary roughly corresponding to what the USSR had seized in 1939 and that Poland be compensated with territory taken from Germany. He made it equally clear that he wanted a "friendly" Polish regime on the Soviet border, rather than the London-based Polish government in exile, which six months earlier had accused the Soviets of murdering nearly 5,000 Polish officers taken prisoner in 1939 (the allegation was true). Although Churchill agreed on the matter of territorial compensation, he supported the London Poles as the legitimate government. Roosevelt said little during the sessions but privately informed Stalin that he sympathized with Soviet desires. He also said he could not be a party to any agreement because he did not wish to offend voters of Polish descent prior to the elections in 1944.

Asian matters were discussed briefly. As the prospect of acquiring atomic bombs was only a possibility at that time, Roosevelt had to assume that many months of fighting lay ahead and that an invasion of Japan would be necessary. He therefore wanted the Soviets to engage Japanese troops in Manchuria and North China so they could not be used to oppose landings in the home islands. Stalin repeated a promise that he had made a few weeks earlier to Secretary of State Cordell Hull in Moscow: The USSR would enter the war against Japan two or three months after the defeat of Germany. When he said he expected compensation for such assistance, FDR proposed special rights in Manchuria and the acquisition of several strategic islands then held by Japan. The president understandably regarded saving American lives as his highest priority, but he later would be criticized for bartering with Russia over privileges in Manchuria without consulting the Chinese government.

FDR's performance at Teheran symbolized his approach throughout the war. Determined that differences should not be permitted to impede military operations, he was reluctant to deal with potentially divisive issues. He had a tendency to stall in such situations, always hoping a solution would turn up. But in this case, he had another reason. He

Conference of the Big Three at Yalta, where *(left to right)* Winston S. Churchill, President Franklin D. Roosevelt, and Josef Stalin make final plans for the defeat of Germany, February 1945. (British Information Services photo no. BNAM 235/LA)

believed that public support for an active role in postwar affairs, including membership in the United Nations, might easily dissipate if the United States became involved in open disputes with the Soviet Union. He apparently did not consider that a stronger public reaction might result when divisions no longer could be disguised by statements of solidarity.

YALTA

The most important Allied conference of World War II took place on February 4–11, 1945, at Yalta, a Soviet resort area on the Black Sea. With the end of the European war in view, the time for exploratory talks such as those that had taken place at Teheran was over. Decisions had to be made about such matters as the treatment of Germany and policies toward Poland and other nations liberated from Nazi control. The broad outlines of a United Nations organization had been drawn at a conference the previous summer, but several important matters still pended. And President Roosevelt wanted very badly to formalize Stalin's promise to enter the Pacific war after Germany's defeat.

Of the three leaders who met at Yalta, Stalin is the most difficult to analyze. What did he mean when he said he wanted "friendly" nations on the Soviet border? Would it be enough that they not be hostile, or did he intend all along to dominate them, as eventually happened? What did he really think about the United Nations? Lacking access to Soviet archives, historians can only speculate about his attitudes toward these and other matters. In shorthand notes taken at the conference, he came across as well informed, economical with his words, and, above all, moderate. Although unyielding on certain issues, he seemed ready to accept compromise for the sake of Allied unity on others.

Churchill was the most learned of the three and by far the most eloquent. At times, he got carried away with his own words, however, and, to the dismay of subordinates, he strayed from positions previously agreed upon within the British delegation. In any case, he played from a weak hand. Great Britain by this time had become a junior partner in the Anglo-American relationship, and it alone could have little influence. Painful though it must have been to him, Churchill understood that he depended on American support in any disputes with the Soviets.

Roosevelt's performance does not compare favorably with that of the others. He had neither Churchill's gift for language nor Stalin's command of facts. Frequently, he substituted vague generalities for reasoned argument. One must recognize that FDR's position was not as strong as it might appear looking back. Soviet armies were already in Poland and other East European countries, and a failure to reach agreements about these areas would eliminate any restraints on Soviet behavior. Soviet participation in the war against Japan, Roosevelt believed, might shorten the war by months and save tens of thousands of American lives. He also feared that open disputes at the conference might cause the American people and Congress to reject the United Nations and retreat into isolationism, thereby losing the chance to construct a lasting peace.

Almost every account of the Yalta Conference includes an evaluation of Roosevelt's health. Pictures show a haggard, at times slack-jawed man (subordinates claimed this was due to sinus problems) who was obviously in poor health. Some have claimed his condition had deteriorated to the point that he was unable to negotiate effectively. Others have denied this, saying he was at all times mentally alert. The issue probably has been exaggerated. Had he been in better health, he might have pressed some points more vigorously, but it is doubtful that different wording in the agreements would have significantly altered the subsequent course of events.

Discord first arose over the question of how Germany should be treated. No one showed any enthusiasm for dismemberment by this time, so it was agreed to "in principle" and shelved. The matter of reparations proved more troublesome. Stalin proposed that $20 billion worth of equipment and goods be extracted from Germany, with half going to the Soviet Union because of the destruction it had suffered. Part of this would be taken in the form of factory removal as soon as Germany was occupied, and the rest would come from current production over a ten-year period. Churchill objected that the figure was too high. It would impoverish Germany, he said, and retard European economic recovery. Roosevelt opposed setting any amounts; he suggested waiting until the Allies got into Germany so that economic experts could analyze its capacity to pay.

A compromise was reached, or so Roosevelt thought. In response to the plea that the Soviets needed at least an approximate figure as a guide for their own reconstruction plans, he agreed that the amount of $20 billion could be used "as a basis for discussion" by a reparations commission that would set the final sum after on-site inspections. As long at the Germans were afforded a minimum standard of living, he said, he had no objection to using all surplus production for reparations. But Churchill refused to sign the agreement, arguing that the mention of a figure might later be construed as a commitment to that amount. Events would prove him correct.

More time was spent discussing Poland than any other issue. There were two concerns: Poland's boundaries and its postwar government. All agreed that the Soviet-Polish border should run approximately along what was known as the Curzon line, drawn at the Versailles Peace Conference after World War I. The Curzon line lay about 150 miles west of what had been the Soviet-Polish border before World War II began. FDR and Churchill were prepared to compensate Poland by awarding it German territory up to the Oder River, which is what Stalin had proposed at Teheran. Now, however, the Soviets insisted that the border be drawn at the Oder-Western Neisse, giving Poland an additional 8,100 square miles of German lands. When Roosevelt and Churchill refused to agree, the dispute was papered over by substituting, in place of a specific boundary, the statement that Poland would receive "substantial accessions."

Who would govern Poland caused more dispute. As Soviet armies moved into Poland, Moscow had installed a puppet government in the city of Lublin, known as the National Committee of Liberation. Although Stalin claimed the Lublin group enjoyed popular support, FDR and Churchill knew its power rested upon Red Army bayonets. Meanwhile, relations between the USSR and the Polish government in exile had grown worse since Teheran. On July 31, 1944, as Soviet armies reached the Vistula River a few miles away from Warsaw, groups loyal to the exile government launched an uprising against the Nazis. Instead of advancing on the city, Soviet troops stood in place for two months while the insurrection was crushed. Stalin, who referred to the Polish rebels as "criminals," even refused to permit U.S. and British planes to land behind Soviet lines after dropping their supplies.

Realizing that Stalin would not accept the London-based government, Roosevelt and Churchill proposed that a broad coalition be established to administer Poland until free elections could be held. Stalin and Molotov disagreed. The Lublin group should be recognized as the legitimate provisional government, they argued, because it was functioning effectively and fully represented the Polish people. At most, they said, it might be "enlarged" by the addition of an unspecified number of representatives from Poland and from abroad.

With reluctance, Roosevelt and Churchill accepted a compromise providing that the Lublin Committee be "reorganized on a broader democratic basis" and that it hold "free and democratic elections as soon as possible." When an adviser complained that the agreement could be "stretched all the way from Yalta to Washington," Roosevelt replied, "I know Bill—I know it. But it's the best I can do for Poland at the time." If Stalin wished to continue the wartime coalition, FDR hoped he would admit enough non-Communists of stature into the provisional government to permit the semblance of an independent Poland.

Even more vague was Roosevelt's proposal for what became known as the Declaration on Liberated Europe. It called on the three leaders to commit their governments to assisting "the peoples liberated from the domination of Nazi Germany and the peoples of the former Axis satellite states of Europe to solve by democratic means their pressing and political problems." This was to be accomplished through relief programs and free elections. Poland would be the first test of the declaration, Roosevelt said, and he wanted elections there to be as "pure" as Caesar's wife. "They said that about her," Stalin replied, "but in fact she had her sins." The document, accepted with little debate, would become a source of friction even before the war ended.

With regard to the United Nations, Roosevelt had long since abandoned the "four policemen" phrase because it was objectionable to the smaller powers. A large-power conference at Dumbarton Oaks, an estate on the outskirts of Washington, D. C., had produced a proposed charter in the early autumn of 1944. The executive authority of the UN would be lodged in the Security Council, consisting of the Big Five (France had been added) as permanent members and seven other seats occupied on a rotating basis. The General Assembly, composed of all nations deemed eligible, would have little substantive power and would function largely as an arena for debate.

Two major questions about the UN had to be settled at Yalta. The Soviets insisted that unanimity had to exist among the Big Five even before an issue could be brought to the Security Council, thereby giving each permanent member an absolute veto. Roosevelt and Churchill agreed that permanent members should have a veto on enforcement measures involving their own security but believed that an affirmative vote by seven members ought to be sufficient for discussion. As U.S. Secretary of State Edward R. Stettinius (who had replaced the ailing Cordell Hull) put it, the American people would insist that "there be provision for a fair hearing for all members of the organization, large and small." Stalin and Molotov also asked that at least two "independent" Soviet republics be awarded membership in the General Assembly, in addition to the USSR.

Stalin eventually accepted the Anglo-American position that the veto should be limited to issues requiring enforcement. In return, FDR agreed to support the Soviet request for additional seats in the assembly but with great misgivings. He feared it might undermine American public and congressional support for the UN if the USSR had three votes (everyone understood the republics were ruled by Moscow) to only one for the United States. He tried to cover himself by obtaining written pledges from Churchill and Stalin that they would support an additional two votes for the United States. He was right to be concerned for an embarrassing, though brief, furor arose in the United States when the story was leaked to the press a month later. In any event, the founding conference of the UN was scheduled to begin in San Francisco on April 25.

The last major accord signed at Yalta involved the Far East. Roosevelt still sought Soviet help against the Japanese because there was no guarantee that atomic bombs could be made operational in time to render an invasion unnecessary. As at Teheran, he was prepared to offer concessions, such as island possessions taken from Japan and special rights in Manchuria. He tried to preserve the Chinese government's position in Manchuria by recommending that the railroads and port cities in question be jointly administered, rather than leased to the Soviet Union as Stalin proposed. An ambiguous agreement was reached that referred to China's "full sovereignty" over Manchuria but also to Soviet "preeminent interests" there. The incompatibility of these phrases would emerge in the following months.

The Far Eastern agreement, together with the one over Poland, later came under scathing criticisms. Some charged that Roosevelt "sold out" China because he was influenced by pro-Communist advisers. Of course, the saving of American lives was uppermost in his mind, but at the time, he thought he had done the best he could for China, as well.

Had no settlement been reached, the Soviet Union would have been free to bide its time until Japan was on the verge of collapse and then move into Manchuria with no restraints at all. And Stalin had agreed to support the fragile Nationalist regime as the legitimate government of China.

Reparations excepted, Stalin played from a strong hand at Yalta. The defeat of Germany was not far off, and Soviet troops already were in eastern and parts of central Europe. A failure to compromise on those areas would have had the effect of abandoning them completely. As no one in a position of responsibility even suggested military intervention against the Soviets, Western leaders were reduced to making appeals for "fair play." FDR and, to a lesser extent, Churchill regarded the UN as crucial to world stability. No one knew at what point Stalin would refuse to participate if his stipulations were not accepted. And he held virtually all the cards on the matter of the terms under which the USSR would enter the war against Japan.

Stalin enjoyed yet another advantage. Roosevelt and Churchill constantly had to weigh decisions on the scales of public opinion. FDR was particularly vulnerable because he believed that active U.S. participation in the postwar world would be undermined if open disputes with the Soviet Union developed. What constraints Stalin worked under are unclear, but he did not have to worry about a critical press, an opposition party, and the need to obtain a two-thirds majority to get treaties through the Senate. In view of these circumstances, FDR and his advisers had reason to be gratified with what had been accomplished. "We really believed in our hearts," one of them later recalled, "that this was the dawn of a new day we had all been praying for."

AFTER YALTA

The honeymoon did not last. On March 1, Roosevelt reported on the Yalta Conference before a joint session of Congress. He obviously was in poor health: He read his speech while sitting, his hands shook, and his speech at times was slurred. After discussing in general terms the agreements that were made, omitting the Far Eastern accord, he concluded by saying he was confident the American people and Congress "will accept the results of this Conference as the beginnings of a permanent structure of peace."

Only a few days after he spoke, the Anglo-American-Soviet commission, meeting in Moscow to form the Polish provisional government, bogged down over which Poles would be invited to participate. Roosevelt and Churchill had hoped Stalin would permit representatives of major non-Communist parties to participate in the provisional government prior to the free elections. But the Soviet representative on the commission, Foreign Minister Molotov, soon made it clear that he would agree to name only those who were Communist or pro-Communist. Otherwise, he said, "we might find a fascist in our midst." Roosevelt and Churchill, who feared the Grand Alliance might break apart if the Polish question were not resolved, grew more alarmed as the deadlock continued through March. Reports from inside Poland indicated that the Communists, aided by the Red Army and secret police, were closing rival newspapers, breaking up organizations, and arresting individuals in large numbers. FDR and Churchill became convinced that the stalemate in Moscow had less to do with interpretations of the Yalta accord than with sealing off Poland until the Communists had eliminated all potential opposition.

Roosevelt at first rejected Churchill's pleas to confront Stalin directly as a means of breaking the deadlock. The president hoped Stalin would come around, and he was afraid of causing a rupture over a situation he was powerless to alter. Finally, in late March, FDR decided to "bring the matter to a head." In a blunt message, he warned Stalin that the United States could not accept "a thinly disguised continuance" of the Communist regime in Poland and that unless the matter were resolved "fairly and speedily," the future of Allied unity was in danger. A few days later, referring both to the Polish question and to Soviet allegations that the Western powers were negotiating a separate peace on the Italian front, FDR cabled Churchill that the military situation very shortly "will permit us to become 'tougher' than has heretofore appeared advantageous to the war effort." How much further he would have gone is unknown. On April 12, while sitting for a portrait at his retreat in Warm Springs, Georgia, Roosevelt complained of a "terrific headache" and collapsed. A few hours later he was dead.

Replacing the man who had led the United States through the two great traumas of depression and world war would have been difficult for anyone. Harry S. Truman struck many as being "too small" for the job. Although his early reputation was tarnished by connections with a corrupt political machine in his native state of Missouri, Truman had compiled a solid but unspectacular career in the Senate. During the war, he had received some national recognition as head of a committee charged with investigating profiteering in defense industries. FDR had agreed to his nomination for the vice presidency only because the two front-runners were unacceptable to various factions within the Democratic party. Since taking office, Truman had seen Roosevelt only on a few ceremonial occasions, and he was excluded from the president's inner circles. Unimpressive in appearance and demeanor, Truman utterly lacked the commanding presence of the charismatic Roosevelt.

Although he expressed a sense of inadequacy several times during his first few days in office, Truman soon began asserting himself. One of his first decisions was that the founding conference of the UN, scheduled to open in San Francisco on April 25, would not be postponed because of Roosevelt's death. To familiarize himself with foreign policy matters, particularly those involving the Soviet Union, the new president had countless meetings with advisers, and he immersed himself in recent exchanges of cable messages. He told others that he intended to carry out all the agreements FDR had made "to the letter."

Truman had his first personal encounter with the Soviets less than two weeks after taking office. Stalin had sent Foreign Minister Molotov to Washington to pay his respects to the fallen Roosevelt (and, undoubtedly, to size up Truman) en route to San Francisco for the UN conference. Molotov was authorized to continue negotiations over the stalled Polish issue with Secretary of State Stettinius and British Foreign Minister Anthony Eden, who also was in town. After several days of fruitless wrangling, during which Molotov insisted that only those Poles acceptable to the Communist regime could be invited to participate in the provisional government provided for at Yalta, Truman's patience wore thin. On April 23, he met with Molotov personally in an effort to break the deadlock. When the foreign minister proved unyielding, Truman, in undiplomatic language, accused the Soviets of failing to carry out the Yalta accord on Poland.

In his memoirs, Truman wrote that, at the end of his lecture, an astonished Molotov burst out, "I have never been talked to like that in my life." To which, Truman said he replied, "Carry out your agreements and you won't get talked to like that." Some writers have seized upon this alleged exchange to show that Truman was intent on reversing FDR's policy of getting along with the Soviets. Actually, notes taken at the meeting reveal no such exchange, and the interpreter present denied it took place. More important, the American proposals that Truman handed Molotov in no way stiffened the American position inherited from Roosevelt.

The dispute continued at San Francisco when Molotov insisted that the Communist regime in Poland be seated as a UN member. The American delegation, headed by Stettinius, opposed this move on the grounds that the existing regime did not fully represent the Polish people. The Soviets, in turn, disputed the seating of Argentina because of its Fascist government and its failure to join the war. This placed the United States in an awkward situation: At Yalta, FDR had promised Stalin that he would support additional seats for two Soviet "republics." Latin American nations, seeking the admittance of Argentina, linked the two issues, making their votes on additional Soviet seats contingent upon

U.S. support for Argentina. Truman, who personally opposed admitting Argentina, reluctantly agreed in order to redeem FDR's pledge to Stalin. These clashes, together with renewed differences over the veto power of permanent members, dampened hopes that the wartime alliance would continue within the United Nations.

Truman nevertheless remained hopeful that problems with the Soviet Union could be worked out. Several advisers had convinced him that two factions existed in Moscow: moderates headed by Stalin and hard-liners represented by Molotov. Their conduct at various conferences appeared to support this view. Molotov frequently took inflexible positions on issues, only to have Stalin intercede at some point and suggest splitting the difference. Rather than factionalism, this probably represented a variation on the "good cop, bad cop" technique used by law enforcement agencies. Alternating verbal or physical abuse by one interrogator with soothing treatment by the other, police have found that suspects often make admissions to the "good cop" out of gratitude or out of fear of what the other might do. Similarly, after crude harangues by Molotov, American officials tended to welcome Stalin's proposals as gestures of good faith that should be reciprocated.

His belief that a split existed in the Kremlin led Truman to conclude that the best way to smooth differences was to deal directly with Stalin. In late May, he sent former Roosevelt confidant Harry Hopkins to Moscow for personal talks. Though ravaged by illness that would kill him within months, Hopkins was chosen because he had served as Roosevelt's personal emissary to Stalin, and Truman wanted to assure the Soviet leader that FDR's policies would be continued. His instructions to Hopkins are revealing. He told him to make clear to Stalin that what happened in Eastern Europe "made no difference to U.S. interests" except as it affected world peace. With regard to Poland, Truman said, he would be satisfied if Stalin permitted elections as free as those that American political bosses would allow "in their respective bailiwicks." In short, the president wanted Stalin to know that he would accept virtually any settlement in Poland, provided it *appeared* to conform with the Yalta accord.

Only a week before Truman asked Stalin to receive Hopkins, an incident involving lend-lease placed a further strain on U.S.-Soviet relations. Lend-lease materials were, by law, to be distributed solely for the purpose of waging war against the Axis powers. Immediately following Germany's surrender, Truman signed a directive reducing lend-lease shipments, limiting them to those intended for use in fighting Japan. Subordinate officials interpreted the directive so zealously that they issued instructions to reroute ships destined for the Soviet Union and to off-load those still in port. Although Truman had these instructions rescinded as soon as he learned of them, everyone realized that the Soviets would interpret the blunder as a crude attempt to apply economic blackmail.

As expected, Stalin launched into a bitter tirade against the lend-lease curtailment in his first meeting with Hopkins. Referring to it as a "scornful act," he said that if it was intended to "soften up" the Soviets, it was mistaken and would have "the exact opposite effect." Only after Hopkins gave repeated assurances that the lend-lease reduction was not intended as a "pressure weapon" did Stalin pronounce himself "fully satisfied" that the American was telling the truth. Whether he actually believed it is unknown.

Hopkins's talks with Stalin appeared to justify the view that it was better to negotiate directly with him, rather than through the stubborn Molotov. The two men agreed upon a list of individuals who would be invited to participate in the provisional government of Poland, some of whom the foreign minister previously had said were unacceptable. When conversation turned to the Far East, Stalin repeated his promise to join the war against Japan, though stipulating that agreement must first be reached with the Chinese over Soviet rights in Manchuria as specified in the Yalta accord. He went on to say that he endorsed the policy of unconditional surrender toward Japan and approved the U.S. policy of backing Chiang Kai-Shek's government in China. Chiang, he said, "was the best of the lot."

The idea that Stalin spoke for those in the Soviet government who were most friendly to the United States appeared to be further validated during his last meeting with Hopkins on June 6. A few days before, the Soviet delegation at the UN conference in San Francisco had caused a furor by rejecting the American position on the veto power, which U.S. officials thought had been settled at Yalta. Secretary of State Stettinius had cabled Hopkins, asking him to appeal to Stalin in an effort to prevent the conference from falling apart. When Hopkins raised the issue, Molotov insisted that the Soviet interpretation "rested squarely" on the Yalta agreement. Stalin overruled the foreign minister, after a short discussion between them, saying that he thought the matter was insignificant and that he accepted the American view. The crisis was over.

Truman also had instructed Hopkins to invite Stalin to a Big Three summit conference in mid-July. Some writers have placed great importance on the date because the first test of an atomic device was scheduled to take place during these days. Truman wanted to wait, the story goes, because a successful test would permit him to become "tougher" at the bargaining table. Among other things, Soviet help against the Japanese no longer would be necessary. Actually, Truman tried to resolve as many issues as he could *before* the conference began. He accepted the Hopkins-Stalin agreement concerning the Polish provisional government, for example, and officially recognized the regime in early July. And he intended to seek Stalin's reaffirmation of the Soviet intention to join the war, regardless of how the atomic test came out.

THE POTSDAM CONFERENCE

The last summit conference of the war, code-named TERMINAL, began July 17 in Potsdam on the outskirts of Berlin. Truman arrived at the "little White House," former home of a German publisher in nearby Bablesburg, on July 15. The following morning, he was visited by Churchill, and the day after by Stalin. His reactions to the two men are revealing. Churchill, Truman noted in his diary, "gave me a lot of hooey about how great my country is and how he loved Roosevelt and how he loved me, etc. etc." He thought they would get along, Truman wrote, unless the Briton tried "to give me too much soft soap." He was more favorably impressed by Stalin, who "looked me in the eye when he spoke." "I can deal with Stalin," he concluded, "he is honest—but smart as hell."

On the evening before the first formal session, Secretary of War Stimson conveyed to the president word from the United States that the first atomic test had succeeded beyond expectations. Truman did not, as he later claimed, regard the atomic bomb as just another weapon. "We have discovered the most terrible bomb in the history of the world," he wrote in his diary; "it may be the first destruction prophesied in the Euphrates Valley era, after Noah and his fabulous ark." Although naturally pleased by the prospect of ending the war against Japan more quickly, Truman's order of priorities was little changed by the news. As Secretary of State Byrnes later pointed out, there was no guarantee that a bomb "would of certainty explode when dropped from a plane." Besides, only two such weapons would be available in the near future, and it could not be known whether Japan would surrender even if they did work.

Most of the discussions at Potsdam involved differing interpretations of the Yalta accords. The issue of reparations from Germany is a case in point. At Yalta, FDR and Stalin had agreed to use the Soviet request for $20 billion as a "basis for discussion" in subsequent negotiations. Just as Churchill had predicted, the Soviets had since begun claiming that the figure represented a commitment rather than a target to be sought. All along, American officials had assumed that on-site inspections of the German economy should precede the setting of reparations figures. Without such analyses, they argued, reparations might be pegged so much higher than Germany's capacity to pay that they might produce starvation. The issue was complicated by the fact that the Soviets were carting away everything they could lay their hands on under the guise of "war booty," which would not count as reparations. When protracted negotiations failed to make headway, Secretary of State Byrnes began proposing a scheme whereby each occupying power would extract what it chose from its zone. As most German manufacturing was located in the west, industrial goods would be traded for agricultural products from the Russian area. Molotov indicated that the Soviets had no objection to this plan "in principle."

The western boundary of Poland had a direct bearing on the reparations issue. At Yalta, Churchill and Roosevelt had supported a Polish-German boundary at the Oder River but had rejected Stalin's proposal to set the border at the Oder-Western Neisse, which would have ceded to Poland an additional 8,100 square miles. Shortly before Potsdam, word had been received that the Soviets were unilaterally turning over lands as far as the Oder-Western Neisse to Poland and that this territory would provide no reparations. All this would reduce the German economic base and further burden it with the need to provide for millions of evicted people "bringing their mouths with them," as Churchill put it.

Conditions in Eastern Europe also produced disagreement. Although the United States and Great Britain had recognized the Polish provisional government, they refused to recognize the regimes imposed by the Soviets in Romania, Bulgaria, and Hungary on the grounds that they did not conform to the Declaration on Liberated Europe. "When these countries were established on a proper basis," Truman declared, "the United States would recognize them and not before." Anglo-American complaints that their representatives were being subjected to so many restrictions in these nations that they could not even find out what was going on were dismissed by Stalin as "all fairy tales."

After a morning session on July 25, Churchill, Foreign Minister Eden, and Labour leader Clement Attlee, who was a member of the delegation, left for London to await the results of Britain's national elections. To the surprise of Truman, Byrnes, and likely Stalin, Labour won. Three days later, Attlee returned as the new prime minister, with Ernest Bevin as foreign minister. Anyone who thought the Labour government would prove more accommodating to the Soviet Union was mistaken. Bevin's first words upon landing were, "I will not have Britain barged about." Truman and Byrnes, who were more inclined to compromise than the British, began negotiating with the Soviets privately.

On July 30, Byrnes offered Molotov three proposals that, he stressed, the United States regarded as a package—the acceptance of any one depended on the acceptance of all. First, he put forward his plan to have each power take reparations from its own zone in Germany, this time citing specific percentages of industrial goods that would be made available to the Soviets in return for agricultural products. He then stated that the United States was prepared to accept Polish administration of German territories east of the Oder-Western Neisse pending a final peace settlement. Finally, he proposed that recognition of the Soviet-sponsored regimes in Eastern Europe should be referred to the foreign ministers for settlement after elections were held in these nations. The key point here is that Byrnes and Truman already had made it clear that the United States no longer insisted on participating in such elections but would be content to send observers.

On the next morning, July 31, Byrnes met again with Molotov to discuss the American proposals. He told the foreign minister that the United States had gone as far as it could to satisfy Soviet demands. Unless the package was accepted in its entirety, he said, "the President and I would leave for the United States the next day." At a plenary session that afternoon, Byrnes formally submitted the American "package." Stalin grumbled a bit about tying the issues together, but his only specific criticism was that the percentages of industrial equipment that Russia was slated to receive from the western zones was too low. Over British objections that the percentages already were "liberal," Truman and Byrnes promptly accepted the higher figures that Molotov suggested, and the deal was done.

With regard to the Far East, Stalin repeated his pledge to join the war against Japan. Soviet armies would be ready about August 15, he said, but would not move until Sino-Soviet negotiations over Manchuria were completed. This hedge did not disturb Truman because he knew that the atomic bombs would be ready before August 15, and the scheduled invasion of Japan was still months away. The president was rankled, however, by Molotov's proposal that the United States and its allies formally request Soviet entry. After nearly four years of fighting, he did not wish to be placed in the position of pleading for what was expected to be a brief contribution. He sidestepped the issue by having Byrnes suggest that the Soviets base their declaration of war on sections of the UN Charter.

One aspect of Truman's behavior at Potsdam remains unclear. Midway through the conference, at the end of a session, the president walked over to Stalin, who was standing with the Soviet interpreter. With deliberate casualness, he told the Soviet leader that the United States had developed a "weapon" or "bomb" (it is unclear which word he used, let alone how it came out in translation) of unusual destructive force; he did not say it was atomic. With equal casualness, Stalin replied that he hoped it would be used to good effect against the Japanese. Truman thereupon left.

Because Truman previously had agreed with advisers and with Churchill that he should inform the Soviets about the atomic bombs, his failure to be specific has been criticized as a deliberate effort to mislead Stalin into thinking he was referring only to some powerful conventional weapon. A more likely explanation is that Truman fully expected Stalin to ask about the weapon—a perfectly natural reaction—and was prepared to answer in a general way. When the Soviet leader showed no interest, however, Truman must have been pleased because it meant there would be no embarrassing requests to be brought into partnership, which he was not prepared to grant. Truman probably thought Stalin knew the truth, anyway. Secretary of War Stimson had told FDR that Soviet spies most likely had penetrated the American atomic program, and it is improbable that he failed to so inform Truman.

Records of the Potsdam Conference belie the notion that Truman either grew "tougher" after learning of the atomic test or no longer sought Soviet help against Japan. Quite the opposite was true. He accepted Molotov's proposals on reparations percentages, over British objection. He agreed to a Polish-German boundary farther west than FDR had been willing to concede at Yalta. (The part about waiting for the final peace settlement was a fig leaf: No one believed the Soviets later would permit the disputed area to be given back to the Germans.) Although he refused to recognize existing East European governments, his request merely to have observers present at subsequent elections signaled that he would go along with Polish-style arrangements without being sticky about compliance with the Declaration on Liberated Europe. And he had not changed his mind about Soviet entry into the Pacific war. "I've gotten what I came for," he wrote his wife from Potsdam; "Stalin goes to war with no strings on it. . . . I'll say that we'll end the war a year sooner now and think of the kids that won't be killed."

Secretary of State Byrnes later referred to the Potsdam Conference as "the success that failed." By that, he meant that the agreements reached there were sound enough, provided both sides had carried them out in good faith. At the time, Truman had reason to be pleased with what had been done, although his confidence in being able to "deal" with Stalin had been somewhat shaken. Several times during the conference, he had put forward a pet scheme of his to internationalize certain European waterways to reduce national rivalries. Stalin not only refused to discuss the plan but objected even to mentioning in the official report that Truman had brought it up. On the last day, the president made a final appeal: "Marshal Stalin, I have accepted a number of compromises during this conference to conform with your views, and I make a personal request now that you yield on this point." Without waiting for a translation, Stalin burst out, "Nyet," then in English, "No, I say no!" Flushing in anger, Truman turned to his aides and said, "I cannot understand that man."

Events moved quickly after the conference ended. The atomic bomb was dropped on Hiroshima while Truman was still at sea, and Japan made its first peace overture shortly after he arrived in Washington. The behavior of the Soviets during these days was troublesome. Their declaration of war against Japan on August 8 obviously constituted an effort to get in on the kill because Stalin had said their forces would not be ready until later. This was understandable, but their delay in endorsing the proposed Allied reply to Japan's offer made it appear that they were trying to prolong the war. Every day the fighting continued, they were seizing more territory in Manchuria and strengthening their claim to assume a part in administering Japan, which Truman was determined to prevent.

The president remained optimistic in spite of these aggravations. Before and during Potsdam, he had referred to Stalin as a "horse trader." When selling, a horse trader first demands an absurdly high price without expecting it to be met. He then appears "reasonable" as he lowers the figure during subsequent negotiations, but he still hopes to get more than the horse is worth. Truman said as much of Stalin at Potsdam when an adviser expressed alarm at how much the Soviet leader was asking for. He replied that a good deal of what the Soviets were claiming was "bluff" and went on to explain what he thought their "real claims were confined to." He maintained that attitude at war's end. Well after Japan's surrender, he told an American official that "it was inevitable that we should have real difficulties but we should not take them too seriously." They could be resolved "amicably if we gave ourselves enough time." Unfortunately for humanity, his prediction proved untrue.

SELECTED BIBLIOGRAPHY

Andersen, Terry H. *The United States, Great Britain, and the Cold War, 1944–1947* (Columbia: University of Missouri Press, 1981).

Bennett, Edward M. *Franklin D. Roosevelt and the Search for Victory: American-Soviet Relations, 1939–1945* (Wilmington, Del.: Scholarly Resources, 1990).

Buhite, Russell D. *Soviet-American Relations in Asia, 1945–1954* (Norman: University of Oklahoma Press, 1981).

_____ . *Decisions at Yalta: An Appraisal of Summit Diplomacy* (Wilmington, Del.: Scholarly Resources, 1986).

Churchill, Winston S. *Triumph and Tragedy* (Boston: Houghton Mifflin, 1953).

Cochran, Burt. *Harry Truman and the Crisis Presidency* (New York: Funk & Wagnalls, 1973).

Davis, Lynn Etheridge. *The Cold War Begins: Soviet-American Conflict over Eastern Europe* (Princeton, N.J.: Princeton University Press, 1974).

Donovan, Robert J. *Conflict and Crisis: The Presidency of Harry S. Truman, 1945–1948* (New York: Norton, 1977).

Feis, Herbert, *Churchill-Roosevelt-Stalin: The War They Waged and the Peace They Sought* (Princeton, N.J.: Princeton University Press, 1957).

––––––. *From Trust to Terror: The Onset of the Cold War, 1945–1950* (New York: Norton, 1970).

Ferrell, Robert H. *Off the Record: The Private Papers of Harry S. Truman* (New York: Harper, 1980).

––––––. *Harry S. Truman and the American Presidency* (Boston: Little, Brown, 1983).

Gaddis, John Lewis. *The United States and the Origins of the Cold War, 1941–1947* (New York: Columbia University Press, 1972).

––––––. *The Long Peace: Inquiries into the History of the Cold War* (New York: Oxford University Press, 1987).

Gallicchio, Mark. *The Cold War Begins in Asia: American East Asian Policy and the Fall of the Japanese Empire* (New York: Columbia University Press, 1988).

Gormly, James L. *From Potsdam to the Cold War: Big Three Diplomacy, 1945–1947* (Wilmington, Del.: Scholarly Resources, 1990).

Harbutt, Fraser J. *The Iron Curtain: Churchill, America and the Origins of the Cold War* (New York: Oxford University Press, 1986).

Herken, Gregg. *The Winning Weapon: The Atomic Bomb and the Cold War, 1945–1950* (New York: Knopf, 1980).

Herring, George. *Aid to Russia, 1941–1946* (New York: Columbia University Press, 1973).

Hodgson, Godfrey. *The Colonel: The Life and Wars of Henry Stimson, 1867–1950* (New York: Knopf, 1991).

Irye, Akira. *The Cold War in Asia* (Englewood Cliffs, N.J.: Prentice-Hall, 1974).

Kuniholm, Bruce R. *The Origins of the Cold War in the Near East: Great Power Conflict and Diplomacy in Iran, Turkey, and Greece* (Princeton, N.J.: Princeton University Press, 1980).

Larson, Deborah Welch. *Origins of Containment: A Psychological Explanation* (Princeton, N.J.: Princeton University Press, 1985).

Lukacs, John. *1945: Year Zero* (Garden City, N.Y.: Doubleday, 1978).

Lundestad, Geir. *The American Non-Policy Towards Eastern Europe: Universality in an Area Not of Essential Interest to the United States* (Oslo: Universitetsforlaget, 1975).

Maddox, Robert James. *The New Left and the Origins of the Cold War* (Princeton, N.J.: Princeton University Press, 1974).

––––––. *From War to Cold War: The Education of Harry S. Truman* (Boulder, Colo.: Westview, 1988).

Mastny, Vojtech. *Russia's Road to the Cold War: Diplomacy, Warfare, and the Politics of Communism, 1941–1945* (New York: Columbia University Press, 1979).

McCagg, William O. *Stalin Embattled, 1943–1948* (Detroit, Mich.: Wayne State University Press, 1978).

Messer, Robert L. *The End of an Alliance: James F. Byrnes, Roosevelt, Truman, and the Origins of the Cold War* (Chapel Hill: University of North Carolina Press, 1982).

Rose, Lisle A. *After Yalta* (New York: Charles Scribner's Sons, 1973).

————. *Dubious Victory: The United States and the End of World War II* (Kent, Ohio: Kent State University Press, 1973).

Sainsbury, Keith. *The Turning Point: Roosevelt, Stalin, Churchill and Chiang Kai-Shek, 1943: The Moscow, Cairo, and Teheran Conferences* (New York: Oxford University Press, 1985).

Smith, Gaddis. *American Diplomacy During the Second World War, 1941–1945* (New York: Knopf, 1985).

Thomas, Hugh. *Armed Truce: The Beginnings of the Cold War* (New York: Atheneum, 1987).

Ulam, Adam. *The Rivals: America and Russia Since World War II* (New York: Viking, 1971).

Wheeler-Bennett, John, and Anthony Nichols. *The Semblance of Peace: The Political Settlement After the Second World War* (London: Macmillan, 1972).

Yergin, Daniel. *Shattered Peace: The Origins of the Cold War and the National Security State* (Boston: Houghton Mifflin, 1977).

Epilogue

The costs of World War II were even more staggering than those of the Great War twenty-five years earlier. Estimates of deaths, both military and civilian, run as high as 55 million. Several more times that many were wounded, and another 30 million were rendered homeless. The long-range effects on the physical and mental health of the survivors are beyond estimation. Germany and Japan lay prostrate, their surviving leaders tried as war criminals, but disputes between the victorious nations doomed the postwar collaboration that men like Franklin D. Roosevelt had so ardently sought. Some parts of the world, such as Europe and Korea, were divided into hostile camps by what became known as the Cold War. In Asia and Africa, long-simmering nationalist sentiment erupted against colonial control and exploitation. Despite the wish of most Americans to tend their own gardens, the United States began playing a larger role in world affairs than ever before.

President Truman's hope that differences with the Soviet Union could be "worked out amicably if we gave ourselves enough time" was not realized. Time worked against amicable settlements. There was ongoing friction in Eastern Europe, and Soviet behavior in Manchuria and in Iran alarmed American officials. Having recognized China's "full sovereignty" in Manchuria, the Soviets proceeded to loot its industrial and mining equipment and to impede Chinese Nationalist efforts to regain control. In Iran, Stalin reneged on a wartime agreement to withdraw his troops within six months after the end of hostilities. Instead, he began reinforcing them.

These events took place against a domestic background that increasingly limited Truman's freedom of action. Complaints against the economic repercussions of reconversion—strikes, inflation, shortages—and against the pace of demobilizing the armed forces made the administration wary of taking unpopular stands on foreign policy issues. The Congress, which had grudgingly knuckled under to the executive branch's domination of foreign policy during the war, began flexing its muscles. And most public opinion polls taken between V-E Day and the end of 1945 showed a growing distrust of the Soviet Union.

Over all these issues loomed the atomic monster. Only a few weeks after V-J Day, retiring Secretary of War Henry L. Stimson urged Truman to share with the Soviet Union basic research data about atomic energy (not the technology to construct a bomb) as a means of avoiding a disastrous arms race. Truman at first told subordinates he agreed with Stimson's proposal and signaled his intentions in several speeches in October and November. And despite repeated denials that he intended to give away "the secret of the bomb," Truman encountered shrill resistance to giving *anything* to a power that more and more people were defining as the enemy. A compromise plan, submitted through the United Nations, ultimately foundered on American insistence that safeguards, such as on-site inspections, be built into any program for sharing information. The Soviet Union denounced these safeguards as representing an attempt to retain nuclear monopoly and called upon the United States to destroy all atomic weapons and weapons-building facilities.

The failure to reach agreement led to the arms race Stimson had predicted, which, in time, produced weapons that made those dropped on Hiroshima and Nagasaki seem puny. Some have regarded this failure as one of those "lost opportunities" of history. This is doubtful. Although the arms race ultimately took on a life of its own, it was the *result* of mutual hostility and suspicion, rather than the cause. No American president could have gained acceptance for a program without means of verification. From Stalin's standpoint, even if the United States ostensibly destroyed its arsenal and facilities, how could he be sure that atomic bombs were not stored in some remote, underground cave? Even if they were not, the fact that the United States *knew* how to build bombs would afford it an inestimable advantage in the event of protracted war with the Soviet Union at some later date. The atomic genie, once out of the bottle, could not be placed back in.

American relations with the Soviet Union, already antagonistic by the end of 1945, entered a new phase in 1947. A Communist-led insurrection (wrongly believed to be directed by Moscow) against the royalist government in Greece and threatening Soviet moves against Turkey appeared to indicate that Stalin meant to dominate the entire Mediterranean region and perhaps even beyond. When the British informed Washington that they could no longer afford to aid Greece and Turkey, President Truman went before a joint session of Congress on March 12 to ask for an appropriation of $400 million for military and economic aid to the two nations. "I believe," he said, "that it must be the policy of the United States to support free peoples who are resisting attempted subjugation by armed minorities or by outside pressures." This Truman Doctrine, as it came to be known, placed the United States in the role of the world's policeman, guarding against Communist aggression or subversion.

Greece and Turkey were not the only trouble spots in Europe. Many nations, some of which had suffered enormous physical damage during the war, were in dire economic straits. Industrial recovery had been slow to nonexistent, and bad weather had destroyed crops and caused coal shortages. Europe, Winston Churchill lamented, was a "rubble heap, a charnel house, a breeding ground of pestilence and hate." Failure by the United States to alleviate the situation would prolong human misery, undermine the governments of Italy and France that were already threatened by disciplined Communist minorities, and retard the growth of foreign trade in which the United States had a direct stake.

In June 1947, Secretary of State George C. Marshall provided the American response in a commencement speech at Harvard. What would become known as the European Recovery Program—or, more popularly, the Marshall Plan—called for a massive American commitment to the recovery of Europe. The proposal was notable in two respects. First, instead of inviting the various nations to submit individual requests, it called on them to take the initiative by preparing a joint program to which the United States would contribute. Second, it did not preclude participation by the Soviet Union and its allies.

Prodded by British Foreign Minister Ernest Bevin, the foreign ministers of Great Britain, France, and the Soviet Union met in Paris in late June. After several days of fruitless wrangling, Soviet representative V. M. Molotov left without agreement. The British and French proceeded to call a conference of European nations to draw up the proposals Marshall had requested. Several Soviet-dominated governments initially took part, but their delegates were recalled on orders from Moscow. This boycott probably saved the Marshall Plan because sentiment in Congress made it improbable that appropriations would be forthcoming for an assistance program that would benefit Communist nations.

Between April 1948 and June 1952, when the Marshall Plan ended, the United States provided nearly $13.5 billion worth of aid. Although some groups fared better than others, the results were impressive. European productivity rose dramatically in the following years, and by 1952, it was 200 percent higher than in 1938. The Soviets predictably savaged the Marshall Plan as a tool of American imperialism and announced their own Molotov Program, which was a charade.

Also in 1947, an anonymous article appeared in the journal *Foreign Affairs* that outlined what came to be known as the doctrine of "containment." Put briefly, its thesis was that traditional Russian insecurities, combined with Marxist dogma, had made the Soviet Union an inherently expansionist state. Using every means available—including subversion and economic, political, or military pressure—the USSR would seek to extend its domination whenever and wherever possible, short of risking all-out war. The United States and its allies should block such efforts, the article stated, through the patient and relentless application of whatever countermeasures were necessary. If this prescription were followed long enough, the article predicted, the Soviet empire would either crumble or mellow from within because of its own internal contradictions.

The revelation that the author of the article was Russian expert George F. Kennan, then head of the State Department's Policy Planning Staff, caused it to be regarded as an authoritative statement of President Truman's Cold War policy. And it was, although Kennan himself later would criticize what he regarded as an undue emphasis upon military responses. Truman's successor, Dwight D. Eisenhower, denounced "containment" as a negative concept and offered "liberation" in its stead. But no one actually was liberated, and containment formed the basis of American foreign policy for decades. Recent developments in the Soviet Union and in Eastern Europe make Kennan's analysis and recommendations appear prescient.

Events beginning in 1948 escalated the Cold War to yet another level. The Soviets ousted a merely compliant regime in Czechoslovakia, replacing it with an utterly subservient one. They also cut off land routes to the western zones of Berlin, which lay deep in eastern Germany. Unwilling to either abandon Berlin or go to war, Truman mounted a year-long airlift that sustained the western zones until Stalin relented. In 1949, the Soviets detonated their first atomic device, and civil war in China culminated in the expulsion of Nationalist forces to Taiwan, accomplished by Communists who were widely believed to be directed from Moscow. That year, the United States joined the North Atlantic Treaty Organization (NATO), a military alliance aimed at Russia that provided that an attack on one member would be regarded as an attack on all.

On June 25, 1950, Soviet-trained and -equipped North Korean armies smashed southward across the 38th parallel, a boundary established at the end of World War II. Truman and his advisers, probably incorrectly, interpreted the invasion as a Soviet military challenge carried out by proxies. The need to "contain" this thrust seemed obvious. A generation of men steeped in the "lesson" of Munich believed that a failure to halt aggression would only encourage further aggression by Stalin, just as it had encouraged Hitler. Only five years after V-J Day, the United States found itself at war again.

The Korean War demonstrated the failure of the United Nations to become the truly international body its supporters had hoped for. From its founding conference in April 1945, the UN had been all but paralyzed by Cold War hostilities between coalitions dominated by the two superpowers. American domination of the UN Security Council was offset by the Soviets' frequent use of their veto power to block unwelcome policies. The United States was able to enlist the UN in the "police action" against North Korea only because the Soviets at the time were boycotting the organization over its failure to seat the People's Republic as the legitimate government of China. Although other nations contributed in varying degrees, the Korean War remained largely an American enterprise.

The United States and its allies had slain the dragons during World War II, and the U.S. had emerged unscathed as the world's foremost power. Yet, in the space of a few years, American goals had been frustrated in Europe and Asia, the Soviets had acquired nuclear capability, and American boys were dying in a far-off place. What had gone wrong? Some individuals provided answers. Dangerous as the Soviet Union and its allies were, they said, the real threat came from disloyal Americans who permeated the government and other institutions. China had been "lost" because traitors in the State Department had undermined Chiang Kai-Shek, for instance, and spies in the atomic program had enabled the Soviets to acquire the bomb years earlier than they would have on their own. Further setbacks could be expected, they warned, unless such elements were purged from the system.

The phenomenon that came to be known as "McCarthyism"—though Senator Joseph R. McCarthy of Wisconsin was merely its foremost practitioner—had been building for years. In 1948, future president Richard M. Nixon first achieved national attention as a young congressman pursuing the case of Alger Hiss, a former government official accused of being a Soviet spy. But the frustrations of the Korean War fueled what can only be described as a national hysteria. Allegation piled upon allegation. That Roosevelt had "sold out" Poland and China at Yalta and that the Truman administration still harbored those who had advised him were but a few of the charges made. No individual or organization was immune. George Marshall was accused of being a dedicated Communist agent, and the Girl Scouts of America were branded subversive. Communists did hold positions of some influence in various areas, but they posed nothing like the apocalyptic threat that red-baiters claimed.

The Korean War and McCarthyism combined to undo previous restraints. Military budgets soared to astronomical levels and remained there long after the fighting ended. More and more, the Cold War was defined as a kind of zero-sum game in which every square mile of territory around the globe had to be contested lest it "fall" to international communism. This perception frequently led the United States to violate its own stated ideals. It not only allied itself with some of the most brutal, corrupt regimes in the world but also supported efforts by some of its European allies to reimpose control over former colonies—most notably, the French in Indochina—all in the name of anticommunism.

The high fervor of the 1950s eventually waned, and events such as the split between the People's Republic of China and the Soviet Union undercut the notion of a monolithic Communist bloc. Both President Eisenhower, during the latter years of his tenure, and his successors sought to "regularize" relations with the Soviet Union in order to minimize the chances of an all-out conflict. But the arms race continued despite limitation agreements, and both superpowers jockeyed for advantage in various parts of the world. The latter process often included arming client nations or supporting one side against another in a civil conflict. There were grave consequences. The Cuban missile crisis of 1962, for example, brought the world close to nuclear Armageddon, and America's deepening commitment to the Vietnam War ultimately brought down the presidency of Lyndon B. Johnson and nearly tore the society apart.

Until a few years ago, it could be said that we lived in a world largely created by World War II. Europe, including Germany, still lay divided along boundaries established by Soviet occupation. The war, as John Lukacs put it in 1945: Year Zero, marked "the end of European predominance in the history and in the political geography of the world." Colonial peoples everywhere were emboldened to seek their own destinies. Japan emerged from the ashes of its burnt-out cities to prosper beyond the wildest dreams of its former leaders. And eight years of devastating war on the Chinese mainland profoundly influenced the subsequent course of events there.

Recent developments in Eastern Europe and in the Soviet Union have brought an end to the Cold War. Communism—so feared by some in the West, so stoutly defended by others—has proven utterly bankrupt as a means of organizing society. The collapse of Communist regimes in Eastern Europe, Germany's reunification, and the profound changes that are taking place within the Soviet Union herald a new era in international relations, the precise outlines of which are not yet clear. Certainly, it will not bring an end to conflict, as war in the Persian Gulf showed. Perhaps, at long last, the United Nations may come to play the part its architects intended.

About the Book
and Author

World War II was a colossal military struggle that helped shape the world in which we live today. The division of Germany and Korea, the long subjugation of Eastern Europe, and the decline of European imperialism are all consequences of the war. The United States and the Soviet Union fought in the conflict as allies yet emerged from it as hostile rivals, superpowers locked in a dangerous nuclear arms race with the potential to end civilization as we know it. Truly our era can be said to owe much of its nature to the course and the outcome of World War II.

This single-volume history of World War II explores the war's causes, its conduct, and its enduring consequences. Total war involves more than the clash of armed forces: Great changes are wrought on the societies of victor and vanquished alike. This book therefore treats the home fronts as well as the battle fronts, with particular emphasis on the United States. Mobilization, propaganda, the role of women and blacks in the labor force and armed services, and the internment of Japanese-Americans are just a few of the subjects included. Unlike conventional military histories, *The United States and World War II* goes beyond the field of combat to present the era in its broader context. Based on the most up-to-date scholarship, this volume is written for the general reader and for use in courses on World War II and on recent American history.

Robert James Maddox is professor of American history at Pennsylvania State University, where he teaches courses on World War II.

Index